Critical Race Studies Across Disciplines

Critical Race Studies Across Disciplines

Resisting Racism through Scholactivism

Edited by
Jonathan Chism, Stacie Craft DeFreitas,
Vida Robertson, and David Ryden

LEXINGTON BOOKS
Lanham • Boulder • New York • London

Published by Lexington Books
An imprint of The Rowman & Littlefield Publishing Group, Inc.
4501 Forbes Boulevard, Suite 200, Lanham, Maryland 20706
www.rowman.com

6 Tinworth Street, London SE11 5AL, United Kingdom

British Library Cataloguing in Publication Information Available

Library of Congress Cataloging-in-Publication Data

Names: Chism, Jonathan, editor. | DeFreitas, Stacie Craft, editor. | Robertson, Vida, editor.
Title: Critical race studies across disciplines : resisting racism through scholactivism / edited by Jonathan Chism, Stacie Craft DeFreitas, Vida Robertson, and David Ryden.
Description: Lanham : Lexington Books, 2021. | Includes bibliographical references and index.
Identifiers: LCCN 2021003102 (print) | LCCN 2021003103 (ebook) | ISBN 9781793635884 (cloth) | ISBN 9781793635891 (ebook)
Subjects: LCSH: Race relations—Research. | Racism—Study and teaching. | Ethnicity—Study and teaching. | Race discrimination—United States. | African Americans—United States.
Classification: LCC HT1523 .C75 2021 (print) | LCC HT1523 (ebook) | DDC 305.80071—dc23
LC record available at https://lccn.loc.gov/2021003102
LC ebook record available at https://lccn.loc.gov/2021003103

♾™ The paper used in this publication meets the minimum requirements of American National Standard for Information Sciences—Permanence of Paper for Printed Library Materials, ANSI/NISO Z39.48-1992.

Contents

List of Figures and Tables

FIGURES

TABLES

Foreword

Early in my career as a scholar of African American literature, I fell in love with the study of narratives of enslavement and its legacy. Some people have responded to this declaration with questions of why would I study work that focuses on pain, degradation, and suffering. However, that is not my focus. My response has always been that narratives of enslavement convey struggle, but they also represent triumphant survival in the face of seemingly insurmountable opposition. Through this literature, we learn the meaning of humanity and freedom more profoundly than any other literary or artistic form. With Frederick Douglass' 1845 proclamation, "You have seen how a man was made a slave; you shall see how a slave was made a man," twenty-first century readers understand that dehumanization is a process that is reversible and that the struggle for freedom is essential to humanity.[1] Harriet Jacobs' Linda Brent may have pled, "Pity me, and pardon me, O virtuous reader," but she shamed her nineteenth-century readers with their ignorance and inspired empathy in the next breath, charging,

> You never knew what it is to be a slave; to be entirely unprotected by law or custom; to have the laws reduce you to the condition of chattel, entirely subject to the will of another. You never exhausted your ingenuity in avoiding the snares, and eluding the power of a hated tyrant; you never shuddered at the sound of his footsteps, and trembled within hearing of his voice.[2]

The eloquence and rhetorical mastery of each of these writers, formerly enslaved without benefit of formal education, demonstrates their intellectual and creative gifts that the degradation of slavery could not destroy.

This history of American slavery is riddled with horrors; horrors that were only slightly diminished with emancipation. Yet in the midst of this adversity,

African Americans created the most vibrant culture the world has ever known. Through writing, music, painting, sculpture, dance, performance, foodways, praise, and worship, Black Americans resisted oppression, created theory and praxis, expressed themselves, represented the world, and impacted others. In 1827, the editors of *Freedom's Journal*, the first African American newspaper, declared, "We wish to plead our own cause. Too long have others spoken for us." This declaration resounds throughout African America. It reverberates in James Baldwin's "Notes of a Native Son" as he recounts the tragedy of his father's life and concludes, "Thou knowest this man's fall; but thou knowest not his wrassling."[3] It is only by knowing the "wrassling," the struggle, can we understand Ralph Ellison's *Invisible Man* as he deconstructs his grandfather's riddle and contemplates why we should affirm the principle of freedom and equality.

Certainly struggles for freedom and equality are not solely the purview of African Americans. And Black experience is not solely defined by struggle. Nevertheless, the legacy of slavery is a reality and is compounded by other subjugated categories of difference such as gender, sexual orientation, socioeconomics, ability, and age that circumscribe lives. Thus, survival is not a given. As the self-proclaimed Black woman warrior poet, Audre Lorde acknowledges, "to survive in the mouth of this dragon we call america, we have had to learn this first and most vital lesson—that we were never meant to survive. Not as human beings."[4] Make no mistake by underrating survival. It is essential to freedom and social justice. Lorde explains that "survival is not an academic skill. It is learning how to stand alone, unpopular and sometimes reviled, and how to make common cause with those others identified as outside the structures in order to define and seek a world in which we can all flourish."[5] Lorde's assertion is evocative of the character Eva Peace in Toni Morrison's novel *Sula*. For Eva, struggling for her children's survival is her expression of love. This love is not soft and cuddly. This love is strong and rugged; forged in struggle, tempered by toil. According to Lorde, survival prepares one to work with others in greater love for humanity. The editors of this volume make common cause in an effort to work toward social justice. Indeed, this effort is an act of love focused on the existence, persistence, and resistance of African Americans over the course of 400 years.

These works inform our understanding of Black experience in America and how to understand our present moment. The current acts of racial violence, police brutality, and killing, when the rule of law is disregarded and violated, our survival is still under threat. Thus, this volume is not just an exercise. By looking back and reflecting on 400 years of Black experience and survival, we are committing speech acts crucial to achieving freedom, justice, and equality. For as the Sankofa sign symbolizes, we can only go forward if we know where we have been.

DoVeanna S. Fulton
Norfolk, VA 2020

NOTES

1. Frederick Douglass, *Narrative of the Life of Frederick Douglass, An American Slave, Written by Himself* (New York, Penguin Books, 1986, orig. 1845), 107.
2. Harriet Jacobs, *Incidents in the Life of a Slave Girl, Written by Herself*, Ed. Jean Fagan Yellin (Cambridge, Harvard University Press, 1987, orig. 1861), 55.
3. James Baldwin, "Notes of a Native Son," *Notes of a Native Son* (New York, The Dial Press, 1963), 96, Accessed from: https://masshumanities.org/files/programs/LitMed/readings/Baldwin_James_Notes_of_a_Native_Son.pdf. Accessed December 12, 2020.
4. Audre Lorde, *Sister Outsider* (Freedom, CA, The Crossing Press Feminist Series, 1984), 42.
5. Ibid., 112.

BIBLIOGRAPHY

Baldwin, James. "Notes of a Native Son," *Notes of a Native Son*. New York, The Dial Press, 1963. Accessed from: https://masshumanities.org/files/programs/LitMed/readings/Baldwin_James_Notes_of_a_Native_Son.pdf. Accessed December 12, 2020.

Douglass, Frederick. *Narrative of the Life of Frederick Douglass, An American Slave, Written by Himself*. 1845. New York, Penguin Books, 1986.

Jacobs, Harriet. *Incidents in the Life of a Slave Girl, Written by Herself*. (1861). Ed. Jean Fagan Yellin. Cambridge, Harvard University Press, 1987.

Lorde, Audre. *Sister Outsider*. Freedom, CA, The Crossing Press Feminist Series, 1984.

Morrison, Toni. *Sula*. New York, Plume, 1982.

Acknowledgments

The initial foundation for this edited volume began as a result of the Reflecting Black Research Symposium held at the University of Houston-Downtown (UHD), in Texas on October 24, 2019. The purpose of the symposium was to commemorate the 400th year anniversary of 1619, the date that marks the arrival of the first documented Africans to British North America. We observed 1619 by highlighting the achievements of African Americans and by advancing critical interdisciplinary discourse about race, racism, and intersecting oppressions among established and emerging scholars in African American Studies. In the spirit of Sankofa—an African term derived from the Akan tribe in Ghana which means "go back and fetch it"—the Symposium invited scholars to look backward and to reflect on the experiences and voices of Black Americans to facilitate movement towards the future. We appreciate all of the individuals across a variety of academic institutions in the United States who presented at the symposium, including graduate student contributors whose chapters are included in this volume as well as students not included. We appreciate Dr. Alexander Byrd (our keynote speaker), and Dr. Sonia Lee, Dr. Rachael Quinn, Mr. Charles Savage, and Ms. Nicola Springer for delivering special presentations to our faculty and student body. We thank the various symposium sponsors including College of Humanities and Social Sciences, College of Sciences and Technology, College of Public Service, Department of History, Humanities, and Languages, Department of Social Sciences, Department of English, Center for Latino Studies, Cultural Enrichment Center, Office of Research and Sponsored Programs, Title IX, Equity, and Diversity, Division of Academic Affairs and Student Support, and the Provost Office. We also appreciate members of the planning committee—Dr. Heather Goltz, Ms. Crystal Guillory, Dr. Erin Patten, and Ms. Shandra Robertson, and the numerous volunteers (Ms. Ashley Foyle,

Ms. Joselin Esobar, Cherilyn Pearson, and Myisha Williams) who aided in executing this symposium. Without the symposium, we would not have been able to develop the ties and relationships upon which this book is based.

In addition to the symposium, this volume centers on our interdisciplinary and collaborative work as fellows for the Center for Critical Race Studies (CCRS) at the University of Houston-Downtown. We express special gratitude to CCRS for fostering a space for scholars interested in critical race thought to work together. In this regard, we acknowledge Dr. DoVeanna S. Fulton, who served as the Dean of the College of Humanities and Social Sciences at UHD and as the founder of CCRS. We appreciate her vision and leadership over the years and her administrative support to our scholactivism. Besides the CCRS editors who worked directly on this project through serving as editors, we would like to acknowledge CCRS fellows, including Dr. Kristin J. Anderson, Dr. Sucheta Choudhuri, Dr. Chuck Jackson, Dr. Creshema R. Murray, Professor Daniel Peña, Dr. Douglas teDuits, and Dr. Antoinette Wilson. We would also like to thank Dr. Felicia Harris who serves as a CCRS fellow and assistant director to CCRS, in addition to contributing a chapter to this text. The CCRS fellows are important interlocutors in critical race studies at UHD and coconspirators in our work to advance social justice.

Introduction

Jonathan Chism

> As we conceive it, Critical Race Theory embraces a movement of left scholars, most of them scholars of color, situated in law schools, whose work challenges the ways in which race and racial power are constructed and represented in American legal culture and, more generally, in American society as a whole.[1]

This quotation from leading scholars of critical race theory (CRT) indicates the centrality of legal studies to the formation of CRT. This quote, however, begs the question: Is CRT today only "situated in law schools"? Respecting CRT's foundation in the legal academy, *Critical Race Studies Across Disciplines* contends that critical race thought now extends beyond schools of law and informs the ethical commitments of scholars affiliated with various interdisciplinary programs, departments, and centers seeking to grapple with race, racism, oppression, and their impact on society. This volume includes essays from scholars who directly and indirectly incorporate critical race thought through their commitment to scholar-activism or *scholactivism*, working to utilize analytical tools from their respective disciplines to understand and actively oppose racism and various forms of oppression. Additionally, in line with CRT's emphasis on counterstorytelling, the scholactivists in this volume aspire to challenge racism through conveying the stories and counternarratives of African Americans. Acknowledging the long history of racism endured by Indigenous, Latinx, Asian, Jewish, and Muslim Americans, the essays focus on the Black experience and posit that anti-Black racism undergirds systems of White supremacy that affect all.[2] The enslavement of African Americans, "America's original sin," was the cornerstone in the foundation of American capitalistic society.[3]

Despite the abolitionist movement, the Civil War, the First Reconstruction, and the Civil Rights Movement, anti-Black racism has persisted and is apparent in contemporary American life. Following the election of Barack Obama, the first Black and the forty-fourth president of the United States in 2008, many Americans were eager to declare that the United States had entered a "postracial" period. Ward Connerly, a former Regent at the University of California, expressed that Obama's election signaled the end of racism and destroyed the contention that "American society is institutionally racist, that the good ol' boys are the only ones that can succeed."[4] Obama's election prompted Abigail Thernstrom, a conservative commentator and former vice chair of the U.S. Commission on Civil Rights, to question whether civil rights laws such as the Voting Rights Act were still needed, as millions were able to successfully cast their ballot for Obama. Further, Obama's election to his second term in 2013 ostensibly influenced the Supreme Court's *Shelby County v. Holder* ruling, which declared by a 5–4 vote that section 4 of the Voting Rights Act was out-of-date and unnecessary because voter suppression based on race was no longer taking place. Section 4 originally aimed to address tactics used by mostly southern states to deny or suppress Blacks' voting rights during the era of Jim Crow. Striking down section 4, however, has allowed and enabled voter suppression to return. Many southern states eagerly purged voter rolls, enacted strict voter ID laws, cut back early voting times, and limited the number of poll places in minority communities. Contemporary voter disenfranchisement disproves the argument that voter suppression is a mere relic of the Jim Crow era.

The emergence of the Birther and Tea Party Movements also challenges the contention that America has entered a postracial epoch. Spearheaded by conservative media personalities such as Lou Dobbs, Rush Limbaugh, and Donald Trump, birthers attempted to delegitimize Obama's presidency through insisting that he was not born in the United States and was hence ineligible to be president according to the U.S. Constitution. Birthers claimed that Obama's birth certificate, which indicated he was born in Hawaii, was fraudulent. Many birthers joined the Tea Party Movement, which formed during Obama's first term largely in protest of the advancement of the Troubled Asset Relief Program (TARP), whose purpose was to bring stability to credit markets and alleviate the recession. The Tea Party also formed in protest to the passage of the Patient Protection and Affordable Care Act, more popularly known as Obamacare, whose aim was to expand access to healthcare, especially for persons with preexisting conditions. These initiatives influenced members of the Tea Party to portray Obama as a leftist, Black radical who was intent on transforming America into a socialist government.[5] Echoing the Islamophobia of the post-9/11 period, Tea Party sympathizers also alleged that Obama was a Muslim and hence posed a threat to the Christian foundations of American society. Many conservatives accepted these myths and debunked claims regarding Obama's birth and religion. Furthermore, instead of being an insubstantial bloc of conservatives, the Tea Party gained significant traction in the Republican Party. A poll conducted by the *New York Times* and *CBS News* in 2010 found that 32 percent of Republicans believed Obama was not born in the United States. Furthermore, a survey conducted by *Time* found that 46 percent of Republicans believed Obama was a Muslim.[6] Political scientist Gary Jacobson suggests that these "misconceptions" regarding Obama's birth and religion stemmed from "motivated reasoning," which he defined as Republicans' desire to "get a certain preferred outcome, regardless of correctness."[7] That is to say, some Republican voters ostensibly accepted outlandish and preposterous claims about Obama because they were deeply committed to their political agenda and intent on preventing America from becoming socialist. This argument, however, ignores the blackness in America's living room or the sheer presence of African Americans in the White House that ostensibly troubled many Tea Party sympathizers. Certainly, many birthers would avow to be colorblind. Yet, the evolution of the Birther Movement ties to Obama's race. Political scientist Joseph Lowndes suggests that it is hard to fathom that "an American president of Irish or Australian parentage being challenged on birthright grounds."[8] He asserts that "a Constitutional challenge to legitimacy couldn't gain traction without underlying racial appeals."[9] He supports this claim by citing data from the Cooperative Congressional Election Study conducted before and after the 2012 presidential election in coordination with the Arthur Levitt Public Affairs Center at Hamilton College. The survey results indicated persisting racial divisions following Obama's first term and found a strong correlation between birtherism and "high levels of racial resentments."[10]

Michelle Alexander's groundbreaking work *The New Jim Crow: Mass Incarceration in the Age of Colorblindness* (2010) also provocatively challenges the myth that Obama's presidency ushered in a postracial, colorblind period.[11] According to Alexander, the escalating numbers of Black and Brown persons entangled in the criminal justice system as a result of the aggressive War on Drugs, which targeted poor minority drug dealers and users, was additional evidence of persisting systemic racism. The War on Drugs, which started during the presidency of Richard Nixon and persisted throughout the administrations of multiple Republican and Democratic presidents, influenced mass incarceration, a pervasive, nefarious, and contemporary racial caste system that stripped numerous minorities of their basic civil liberties, including their right to vote and freedom to seek gainful employment after completing their prison terms. According to Alexander, "More African American men are in prison or jail, on probation or parole than were enslaved in 1850, before the Civil War began."[12]

The emergence of the Black Lives Matters (BLM) during Barack Obama's administration further dispels the myth of postracialism. Three Black, queer women, Alicia Garza, Patrice Cullors, and Opal Tometi, created the social media hashtag #BlackLivesMatter following George Zimmerman's acquittal of manslaughter charges in the death of Trayvon Martin. During the highly publicized trial, Florida prosecutors argued that Zimmerman, a neighborhood watch coordinator, racially profiled Martin who was wearing a hoodie sweatshirt, inappropriately confronted him, and ultimately murdered the unarmed teenager who was merely walking home after visiting a convenience store. Prosecutors provided the transcript of Zimmerman's 9/11 call and noted that the operator told Zimmerman not to pursue Martin. However, Zimmerman remarked, "F– – king punks . . . they always get away."[13] Zimmerman's defense attorneys convinced a jury that Zimmerman shot Martin in self-defense. Martin's death and Zimmerman's acquittal inspired a new generation of activists to agitate and organize for racial justice in new ways, especially to use social media platforms such as Twitter and Facebook as "organizing tool[s] . . . to amplify anti-Black racism across the country, in all the ways it showed up."[14]

BLM activists throughout the United States have continued to protest the ongoing numbers of Blacks who have died as a result of state-sanctioned violence, including, but not limited to, Michael Brown, Tamir Rice, Eric Garner, Janisha Fonville, Alton Sterling, Sandra Bland, Freddie Gray, Botham Jean, Aura Rosser, Stephon Clark, Philando Castille, and Atatiana Jefferson. As of 2020, a year marked by the COVID-19 pandemic, Blacks have continued to lose their lives as a result of police violence. On March 13, 2020, three undercover Louisville police officers executed a botched drug-warrant and forcefully entered the home of Breonna Taylor, a twenty-six-year-old Black emergency medical technician, and fatally shot her, as her boyfriend exchanged fire with the unknown intruders. On May 25, 2020, Minneapolis police officers arrested George Floyd, a forty-six-year-old Black man, for allegedly using a counterfeit twenty-dollar bill at a store. As a result of videos recorded by eyewitnesses, the world witnessed a White police officer haughtily hold his knee on Floyd's neck for eight minutes and forty-six seconds and mercilessly suffocate him to death as Floyd pleaded that he could not breathe. Despite the Centers for Disease Control and Prevention's admonition to shelter in place and practice distancing amid the COVID-19 pandemic, thousands of individuals of multiple races throughout the United States and in other countries voiced their discontent with the unjust deaths of African Americans at the hands of police and courageously took to the streets to protest in support of Black Lives Matter.

Notwithstanding the global public outcry, top administrators in President Trump's administration, including Attorney General William Barr and National Security Advisor Robert O'Brien, denied the existence of systemic racism in policing and the broader legal system and hold that Blacks who are killed by police are a mere aberration and that the overall system is just.[15] Rather than acknowledging and addressing racism in America, Trump has castigated CRT as the problem, referring to it as "a cancer" and as "hateful Marxist doctrine" that "paints America as a wicked nation that seeks to divide everyone by race, rewrites American history and teaches people to be ashamed of themselves and [to] be ashamed of their country."[16] He issued an executive order banning the teaching of CRT to the U.S. military, government employees, contractors, and grantees. Many hoodwinked Americans who shared Trump's sentiments regarding CRT and colorblindness seemingly accepted President Trump's argument that he is the "least racist person in the world" despite his blatant racially derisive references to Haiti and African nations as "shithole countries," to Mexican immigrants as "rapists," and his designations of the coronavirus as the "Chinese Virus" or "Kung Flu."[17]

While strides have been made in the long struggle for racial justice in the United States, America has certainly not reached a postracial horizon. Undeterred by the Trump administration's misunderstanding of CRT and effort to undermine it, this volume centers on CRT and upholds its continued advancement. CRT provides an indubitably necessary theoretical framework and lexicon to raise awareness concerning contemporary manifestations of colorblind racism and to construct a more socially just and inclusive society.[18]

THE HISTORICAL CONTEXT OF CRT

The ideology of racial colorblindness predates the presidencies of Barack Obama and Donald Trump. Revisiting the social and political climate of 1970s and 1980s is necessary to understand the historical context that led to the establishment of CRT. The legal and legislative achievements of the Civil Rights era, including but not limited to the Supreme Court's landmark *Brown versus Board of Education* ruling (1954), the Civil Rights Act of 1964, the Voting Rights Act of 1965, and the Fair Housing Act of 1968, influenced many conservatives and traditional liberals to view American society as colorblind. They perceived that Martin Luther King's Dream that his children would live in society where they would "not be judged by the color of their skin but the content of their character" became a reality. The Civil Rights Movement essentially enabled America to become a colorblind meritocracy in which the social construct of race was inconsequential. Despite his reluctance due to his suspicion that King had ties to communism, in 1983 President Ronald Reagan signed a bill into law to establish a federal holiday to honor King. When signing the bill, Reagan expressed, "Dr. King had awakened something strong and true, a sense that true justice must be colorblind."[19]

Affirming colorblindness, the Reagan administration endeavored to reverse many of the reforms of President Lyndon B. Johnson's Great Society, including social welfare programs and affirmative action programs that they perceived to be granting unfair advantages to African Americans and other minority groups. Reagan appointed conservative judges to federal judiciaries who viewed the law as colorblind and did not consider the limited life options of members of underserved minority communities when rendering judgments in civil rights cases. For example, rulings of the Burger and Rehnquist courts did not protect minorities from experiencing discrimination in employment and housing or ensure that they receive equitable access to quality education in public schools and to professional opportunities afforded by affirmative action programs.[20]

Indeed, many Blacks as well as other racial and ethnic groups, including women, benefited from the Civil Rights Movement. The Voting Rights Act helped precipitate an increase in the numbers of Black elected officials. During the 1970s, the numbers of Blacks who entered the middle class and who held professional jobs as attorneys, physicians, teachers, and corporate executives slightly rose. Popular Black television sitcoms like *The Cosby Show* made Black success highly visible during the 1980s. The Huxtable family of seven lived a comfortable upper middle-class life in a brownstone in Brooklyn Heights, New York. Dr. Heathcliff Huxtable was an obstetrician, and his wife Clair was a lawyer.[21] Albeit some Blacks gained access to the middle class, the majority of Blacks were not comfortably living the American Dream. A significant wealth disparity remained between the masses of Blacks and Whites during the 1980s, as it still exists today. Historian Manning Marable notes that "the combined personal wealth held by all African Americans [in 1979] was $211 billion, which amounted to only 4 percent of the more than $5 trillion owned by [W]hite Americans."[22] Millions of Blacks throughout the country remained impoverished and lived in urban ghettoes; they had inadequate access to healthcare, higher unemployment rates, and suffered a lower life expectancy compared to Whites.[23] As the Black elite moved into suburbia and Black power advocacy demised as a result of COINTELPRO and internal conflicts within Black power organizations, the rate of homicide and violent crime rose in Black communities. White political and business leaders eagerly aspired to get tough on crime through increasing the presence of police officers in Black communities.[24] Federal law enforcement agencies' budgets increased 1,000 percent in the 1980s, while funding for drug prevention and treatment decreased 400 percent.[25] As crack and cocaine infiltrated urban communities in the 1980s, precipitating even higher levels of violence, police departments responded by arresting drug addicted Blacks and Latinos. The legal system stressed rehabilitation for middle-class White first-time drug abusers but punished low-level Black drug users. Blacks in the criminal justice system received longer sentences than Whites for the same crimes and "rarely were placed in meaningful rehabilitation programs before their release into society."[26]

Legal scholars such as Derek Bell, who served as an attorney for the NAACP Legal Defense Fund during the Civil Rights Movement, were deeply disappointed and disillusioned as they witnessed the gains of the Movement slowly erode during the 1970s and 1980s. The *Regents of University of California v. Bakke* Supreme Court ruling (1978) was particularly an indicator of the clock of racial justice turning backward.[27] The Supreme Court upheld affirmative action but voted that giving consideration to race in the process of admissions was unconstitutional and violated the Equal Protection Clause of the Constitution. After being twice rejected from being admitted into the University of California, Davis Medical School, Allan Bakke, a White male applicant, filed a suit against the university because he held that it was unfair for the institution to reserve sixteen seats exclusively for minority students in the medical school program. Bakke deemed affirmative action was "reverse racism" and that institutions of higher learning should give consideration to merit rather than race. To critical race theorists, the court's ruling reflected the prevailing "race-neutral, merit-based perspective" of the law held by leftist legal scholars who argued that law should be "objective, bounded and neutral."[28]

THE LEGAL BACKGROUND OF CRT

CRT traces its roots to Derrick Bell, a Black civil rights activist and constitutional law professor, and Alan Freeman, a White liberal scholar who during the 1970s helped establish Critical Legal Studies (CLS), a progressive legal movement committed to a leftist political orientation.[29] Both scholars challenged the foundations of conventional civil rights discourse in the legal academy. Bell questioned the dominant view that integration was the ideal means of civil rights reform. In "*Brown v. Board of Education* and the Interest Convergence Dilemma," he argued that integration focused primarily on meeting the "interests" of White liberals rather than those of Black youth who attended "racially isolated and inferior" schools decades after the *Brown v. Board of Education*. Bell's theory of interest convergence asserted that Whites only supported advancements in civil rights like more racially equitable schools when it clearly benefited their interests.[30] Many Whites strategically evaded forced integration through White flight or moving into exclusive suburban White neighborhoods and through changing the boundaries of school districts. In "Serving Two Masters," Bell argued that civil rights lawyers who pursued racial integration via "racial balancing and busing" respected the interests of Whites and failed to seek guidance from their Black clients and the Black community.[31]

In "Legitimizing Racial Discrimination through Antidiscrimination Law," Freeman analyzes Supreme Court cases centering on Antidiscrimination Law in schools and employment and argues that "most judges and lawyers adopt a 'perpetrator' rather than a 'victim' perspective, ignoring the actual status of [B]lack Americans."[32] Numerous judges and lawyers failed to recognize that underprivileged minorities are victims of racism and economic injustice because of the challenging social conditions, limited life options, and prodigious barriers influenced by their experience of discrimination in society. The prevailing *perpetuator perspective* viewed "racial discrimination not as conditions" but as the irresponsible behavior or "misguided conduct of particular actors."[33] Pinpointing how the perpetrator's perspective prevailed in the courts, Freeman ultimately demonstrated ways that legal doctrine substantiates racial power and injustice.

Besides being influenced by the publications of leftist law professors such as Bell and Freeman and others like Richard Delgado and Girardeau Spann, a student protest at Harvard Law School was central to the development of CRT. Bell was the first tenured professor of law at Harvard Law School. He taught several courses to Harvard law students that examined race and American law throughout the 1970s. After Bell accepted a position as Dean at the University of Oregon in 1980, many of his former students demanded that the administration replace him with a tenure-tracked minority scholar who specialized in race and constitutional law. Pressing the administration to desegregate the faculty that only had one tenured and one untenured faculty of color among more than seventy professors, the students aspired to seize the opportunity to push for affirmative action at Harvard. Crenshaw, who participated in the protest demonstrations as a Harvard law student, explains, "As students of the post-integration generation, many of us were close enough to an activist tradition to question certain institutional arrangements-specifically, the dearth of minority law professors and the relative complacency of those who were convinced that this problem lay outside the discourse of desegregation and antidiscrimination."[34] Dean James Vorenberg questioned the need for a course on "Constitutional Law and Minority Issues" and contended that the administration could not find a qualified scholar of color of Bell's stature and should not compromise its elite standards. Subsequently, the law students organized a series of protests, including rallies and a sit-in at the Dean's office.[35] The administration responded to the students by offering a three-week mini-course on civil rights litigation taught by Julius Chambers and Jack Greenberg. Law students were dissatisfied with this arrangement and boycotted the mini-course. They developed "The Alternative

Course," which strove to continue Bell's course on race and law drawing on select chapters from Bell's seminal book, *Race, Racism, and American Law*. The course became "the first institutionalized expression of Critical Race Theory."[36] Many of the guest presenters such as Charles Lawrence, Linda Greene, Neil Gotanda, and Richard Delgado would emerge as leading CRT scholars. The Harvard protest moved early pioneers in CRT to critically evaluate "colorblindness," "formal legal equality," and "integrationism."[37]

In addition to being intricately connected to the "Alternative course" at Harvard, CLS conferences during the mid-1980s were integral to the development of CRT. Kimberlé Crenshaw, Neil Gotanda, and Stephanie Philips organized a workshop at the University of Wisconsin-Madison Law School in 1989 whose purpose was to "synthesize a theory" that responded "to the realities of racial politics in America."[38] The organizers coined the term "Critical Race Theory" to clarify that their work "locates itself in intersection of critical theory and race, racism, and the law."[39] This event was instrumental in outlining the methodologies for CRT, which are (1) "to understand how a regime of [W]hite supremacy and its subordination of people of color have been created and maintained in America, and, in particular, to examine the relationship between that social structure and professed ideals such as 'the rule of law' and 'equal protection" and (2) to change the "vexed bond between law and racial power."[40] Critical race theorists, also known as race crits, contend that the law is not colorblind but is itself "a constitutive element of race." The law participates in the "construction of racial hierarchy and racist ideology" and the racial power of law "shapes and is shaped by 'race relations' across the social plane."[41] More generally, race crits insisted that colorblind approaches to racism will inevitably fail because racism is systemic and structural. Furthermore, race crits such as Crenshaw posited that intersectional analysis, defined as giving consideration to the intersecting nature of oppressions including but not limited to racism, sexism, and economic injustice, is necessary to pursue radical societal transformation.[42] CRT also stresses the use of storytelling and counternarratives to challenge prevailing narratives that uphold the unjust status quo. Race crits strive to convey the stories and views of ordinary people of color to enable Whites and those in power to deepen their understanding of race and Blacks' experience with marginalization. The objective of counternarratives is not to promote a situation where Blacks replace Whites within a caste system. On the contrary, counternarratives seek to dismantle oppressive hierarchical arrangements, to decenter the "grand narratives" of the hegemonic establishment, and awaken dominant groups to the ethical necessity of working to advance an equitable and inclusive society where all people can live in harmony.[43]

THE EXPANSION OF CRITICAL RACE STUDIES BEYOND SCHOOLS OF LAW

Though CRT foundationally consisted of leftist, legal scholars who study and seek to contest the representation of race and racial power in the context of American jurisprudence, the movement certainly did not form in a legal vacuum. On the contrary, legal scholars drew upon diverse philosophical traditions, including but not limited to Marxism, postmodernism, pragmatism, and cultural nationalism.[44] Race crits have engaged a wide array of thinkers ranging from Antonio Gramsci, Jacques Derrida, Frantz Fanon, W. E. B. Du Bois, Martin Luther King Jr., Malcolm X, Anna Julia Cooper, Maria Stewart, Angela Davis, Maya Angelou, Cesar Chavez, and others.[45] Though race crits have attended to the work of scholars and activists outside of the legal profession, CRT has largely been situated in law schools and race crits have focused on analyzing the bond between race and law.

However, the colorblindness prevalent in the legal academy has also existed in other schools and academic disciplines.[46] Racism is pervasive in American society and permeates various institutions, structures, and cultural modes of expression. For example, racism bonds with history, impacting the production of historical narratives and influencing whose stories are told and whose voices are muted or silenced.[47] Scholars from other disciplines outside of the legal academy, especially within the humanities and social sciences, are utilizing the tools of CRT to concertedly interrogate racism in society at large. For example, sociologists Joe Feagin and Eduardo Bonnila-Silva have published multiple editions of books that are heavily influenced by CRT, including, respectively, *The White Racial Frame: Centuries of Racial Framing and Counter-Framing* (2020) and *Racism without Racists: Color-Blind Racism and the Persistence of Racial Inequality in America* (2017). Political scientist Wibur Rich insists that a CRT perspective is needed in the field of political science "analogous to that of critical race theory in legal scholarship."[48] He argues that "both race crits and scholars of critical race politics can advance further by building on each other's work rather than pursuing parallel courses of theory building and research."[49] Similarly, Chandra L. Ford and Collins O. Airhihenbuwa have introduced CRT to the field of public health. They discuss ways that CRT has aided in examining racism and HIV testing among Blacks. They argue that the field of public health inadequately addresses the impact that "structural" and systemic racism have on the health of marginalized groups and the "production of knowledge about populations, health, and health disparities."[50] In the various introductions to this volume, we discuss how CRT is being directly and indirectly engaged by scholars across a variety of disciplines, including history, education, literary and cultural studies, psychology, and religious studies (see the Introductions to the various parts of this volume for more of this discussion).

When discussing the future of CRT, legal scholar Adrien King focused squarely on how CRT is and has been a vibrant force in the legal academy. She provided several examples of how CRT has grown and advanced. For example, she mentioned a CRT conference that was held at the University of Iowa College of Law in 2009 to commemorate the twentieth anniversary of CRT. The conference had nearly three hundred persons in attendance, and the conference papers were published in journals. She notes that similar conferences, such as the Race (In) Action? Conference, were held at Yale in 2016 and the Conference of Asian Pacific American Law Faculty was held at UC Davis in 2016.[51] Furthermore, the establishment of UCLA Law's Critical Race Studies Program and the Aoki Center for Critical Race and Nation Studies at UC Davis School of Law demonstrate the vibrancy of the CRT in the legal academy. Wing's discussion of the institutions that have incorporated CRT centers on law schools and scholarship produced by legal scholars. She does not mention how CRT is being taught to undergraduate students at various institutions or how various universities and colleges have established Critical Race and Ethnic Studies Programs and centers, including but not limited to the University of Denver, University of Vermont, Miami University, the University of Santa Cruz, and the University of Houston-Downtown. Her discussion of the future of CRT does not consider the wide range of scholars outside of the legal academy who are collaboratively drawing upon critical race thought to help students develop a more sophisticated understanding of racism and other oppressions and the work that they are doing to inspire students to enter careers whereby they might work to advance social justice, including careers as community activists, lawyers, and leaders of nonprofit organizations.

Critical Race Studies Across Disciplines parallels introductory and edited volumes written by Richard Delgado, Jean Stefancic, and Kimberlé Crenshaw, distinguished legal scholars and pioneers in CRT. *Critical Race Theory: An Introduction* underscores the pervasiveness of racism in history and society, including but not limited to U.S. legal institutions, prisons, healthcare, and schools. The authors discuss several contemporary manifestations of racism, including hatred toward people of Middle Eastern descent following the 2001 terrorist attacks, hostility toward immigrants, and homophobia. They acknowledge how CRT has advanced since its inception in the 1970s, including discussing the formation of subdisciplines such as the Latino-critical movement and queer-crit studies. They discuss how several law schools have professors that teach CRT courses. Limiting their discussion of "partial incorporation" of CRT in academic disciplines to only a few pages, they highlight the entrenchment and frequent use of the term *intersectionality* by scholars across multiple disciplines. Coined by CRT theorist Kimberlé Williams Crenshaw to explain the unique experience of Black women, intersectionality examines how a person may experience oppression based on overlapping components of their identity including their race, sex, class, and sexual orientation. Intersectionality has become part of the lexicon of race, feminist, Marxist, and queer scholars, among others, interested in advancing the interests of particular social groups. *Critical Race Studies Across Disciplines* renders more attention to various ways scholars in various academic schools and disciplines have incorporated tenets of CRT to enhance their understanding of contemporary manifestations of racism and to advocate for marginalized groups and communities.[52]

In a more expansive edited volume, *Critical Race Theory: The Cutting Edge,* Delgado and Stefancic include essays from a variety of prominent scholars in the field of CRT. The third edition spans 856 pages and consists of seventeen major sections that center on core themes in critical race studies such as critique of liberalism, storytelling, counterstorytelling, revisionist interpretations of history and civil rights progress, critical understanding of the social science underpinnings of race and racism, critical race feminism, critical White studies, and gay-lesbian queer issues. The editors define CRT as "a dynamic, eclectic, and growing movement in the law."[53] While the third edition does include a few contributions from scholars outside of the legal field such as anthropologist Kathryn Milun, philosopher Cornel West, and historian Manning Marable while also tracing how CRT has advanced in the realm of education, law professors and legal scholars authored the bulk of the selections, drawing on material previously published in law journals.[54] The book provides limited engagement of historians, sociologists, political scientists, and scholars from other fields who are engaging and drawing on CRT. Steinberg holds that there is minimal engagement "between critical race theory and the social sciences" and contends that race crits do not yield enough attention to "the issues and debates that are so central" to scholars working in the social sciences.[55]

Critical Race Studies Across Disciplines accentuates the important place that praxis has in CRT. Scholars across multiple disciplines affiliated with the Center for Critical Race Studies (CCRS) at the University of Houston-Downtown (UHD) serve as compilers and editors for the volume. The CCRS facilitates public discourse about race and racism as well as other forms of oppression to foster social justice within the academy and broader community. CCRS *scholactivists* work collectively to equip students to critically and actively challenge various forms of social oppression and to pursue social transformation. In line with the mission of our CCRS, in this volume, we argue that the ultimate aim of CRT is to facilitate social transformation. We posit that the commitment to working for justice is the glue that binds critical race studies scholars together across disciplines. Although knowledge production is the primary modus operandi of CRT, race crits reject the notion that scholarship can be "neutral" or purely "objective" and hold that scholarship is "inevitably political."[56] Race crits essentially produce knowledge for the sake of racial justice and equity. In line with this core commitment of CRT, this book elevates how scholar-activists or *scholactivists* across a variety of disciplines are incorporating the tools of CRT in their research, pedagogy, and service to strive to influence equity and social justice.

The term "scholactivism" is distinct from scholasticism, a system of philosophy employed by medieval scholars that integrated Aristotelian thought with a Christian lens and aimed to harmonize reason and traditional Christian doctrine.[57] Scholastics reinforced the established religious system and the social order of the time. In contrast, scholactivism traces back to the rise of revolutionary socialism in the early 1800s and to Karl Marx's Eleventh Thesis on Ludwig Fuerbach, which stresses that the task of philosophy is not merely to interpret the world but "to change it."[58] Rather than profiting from allying with the established "hegemonic order," the scholactivist aligns with Antonio Gramsci's organic intellectual tradition and stands in solidarity with the "subaltern classes" and supports "political institutions" and grassroots movements that aspire to liberate oppressed social groups.[59] Congruent with the commitments of pioneering race crits, scholactivists are scholars whose intellectual work is "counterhegemonic" to the liberal and conservative intellectual establishment.[60] Like race crits who are committed to storytelling and counterstorytelling so as to respect the voices, experiences, and perspectives of marginalized groups, scholactivists aim to challenge and deconstruct "master narratives" and yield more truthful and "accurate" narratives so as to "transform popular consciousness" and influence social transformation.[61]

Scholactivism can occur both directly and indirectly. *Direct scholactivism* refers to when a scholar joins a social justice movement and works alongside persons unaffiliated with academic institutions. As movement insiders and participant-observers, scholactivists may gain special access to activists who are working to challenge the status quo that may not be afforded to scholars unaffiliated with the social movement. Direct scholactivism enables scholars to produce knowledge and critically reflect on their participation in social movements, including but not limited to graduate theses, dissertations, peer-reviewed journal articles, and monographs.[62] Angela Davis, professor emeritus at the University of California, Santa Cruz, is a notable direct scholactivist. While serving as an assistant professor of philosophy at the University of California, Los Angeles, Davis joined the Communist Party and the Black Panther Party during the 1960s. In 1997, she helped establish Critical Resistance, an organization committed to demolishing the prison-industrial complex.[63] Her experience as an activist certainly informs her broad corpus of academic works such as *Women, Race, and Class* (1981), *Are Prisons Obsolete* (2003), *The Meaning of Freedom* (2012), and *Freedom Is a Constant Struggle* (2015).

It is possible to not directly engage in protest demonstrations, voter registration drives, or other forms of explicit political activity and be a scholactivist. *Indirect scholactivism* is producing knowledge that contributes to movements for social justice. Indirect scholactivists "are not political activists in a strict sense but their writing are a form of activity which may serve one side or the other in a social conflict."[64] For example, the novelist James Baldwin did not have to lead a protest march during the Civil Rights Movement like the Reverend Dr. Martin Luther King to impact the struggle for justice; his vast repertoire of antiracist books and novels, including but not limited to *Notes of a Native Son* (1955), *Nobody Knows My Name* (1961), *The Fire Next Time* (1963), and *No Name in the Street* (1972), has inspired contemporary activists and hence positions him as a scholactivist. Baldwin clearly voiced his disdain for racism and commitment to social justice through his writing. The same reasoning applies to contemporary scholars such as Eddie Glaude Jr., Ibram X. Kendi, Brittney Cooper, and many others, who strive to resist racism and other forms of oppression through their scholarship and activism.[65]

PLAN OF THE VOLUME

The present volume offers a vista onto the expansion of critical race studies across disciplines and schools. Contributions from emerging scholars in graduate programs, assistant, associate, and full professors, and academic administrators at minority-serving institutions and at predominantly White institutions demonstrate the expansion of CRT into liberal arts colleges and universities and schools of humanities and social sciences. The volume features essays centering on the Black experience, including the lived experiences of Black men, women, youth, gays, and lesbians. The editors acknowledge the scholarly critique of the "black-white" paradigm in CRT scholarship and the important work that scholars are doing to understand and oppose the oppression endured by Indigenous, Latinx, Asian, Jewish, and Muslim Americans as well as women, gays and lesbians, and disabled Americans.[66] Rather than offering a survey of all marginalized groups that are utilizing CRT, our aim is to highlight the adoption of CRT by scholars from diverse disciplines beyond the legal academy.

The volume consists of four parts: (1) African American History; (2) African Americans and Education; (3) African American Literary and Cultural Studies; and (4) African American Psychology and African American Religion. With the exception of the discipline of history, the parts are organized according to the degree that scholars in the respective disciplines directly engage CRT. We start with African American history because all academic disciplines and liberation struggles are grounded in history. Furthermore, race crits uphold revisionist interpretations of American history that accentuate the counterstories of marginalized and oppressed groups. We conclude with African American Psychology and Religion because CRT has only recently started to receive explicit attention among race scholars in these fields. In their respective introductions, the editors explain how seminal scholars in the fields of study in their respective sections have produced scholarship that intersects with CRT either directly or indirectly. The editors also briefly introduce the chapters included in their respective sections.

In contrast to the bulk of CRT scholarship, the editors and contributors to this volume have not been trained in law. Yet, they signal a commitment to CRT through their embrace of scholactivism. As *direct scholactivists*, some of the editors and contributors have actively worked with protest movements and activist organizations at their universities or in their communities. Most of the contributors are *indirect scholactivists* who are committed to working to advance justice and equity through presenting the voices and stories of those who have been marginalized. In line with the commitments of critical race theorists, the contributors present the counternarratives of enslaved Blacks who resisted animalization, of Black soldiers during the Civil War who deified stereotypes about Blacks' ability to courageously take up arms, and of Black teachers, students, writers, psychologists, and theologians who have opposed racism in their respective spheres. Though this volume does not include representation from every academic discipline intersecting with CRT, the volume illuminates ways that CRT is proliferating beyond law schools despite efforts to discount its relevance in our post-Civil Rights period and even the Trump administration's recent effort to discredit and undermine it. The antiracist scholactivists in this volume directly and indirectly uphold CRT through striving to dismantle logics that uphold colorblind and anti-Black racism and through seeking to fashion a society that is more equitable, just, and inclusive.

NOTES

1. Kimberlé Crenshaw et al., eds., *Critical Race Theory: The Key Writings that Formed the Movement* (New York: The New Press, 1996), xiii.

2. In order to be consistent throughout this text, we will use three distinct terms to refer to individuals with African ancestry. *African American* will be used for individuals who have roots in the United States going back to the time of slavery, whether

their ancestors were enslaved or not. *Black American* refers to those of African heritage who may originally trace their family lines to other areas such as Africa, the Caribbean, and South America, but currently are American citizens. The term *Black people* is all-encompassing and refers to any individual(s) of African ancestry. Furthermore, we consistently capitalize both Black and White throughout the volume when referring to members of both respective racial groups.

3. Jim Wallis, *America's Original Sin: Racism, White Privilege, and the Bridge to a New America* (Grand Rapids, MI: Brazos Press, 2017).

4. Kristen Clarke et al., "'Post-Racial' America? Not Yet: Why the Fight for Voting Rights Continues After the Election of President Barack Obama," accessed August 6, 2020, https://www.naacpldf.org/wp-content/uploads/Post-Racial-America-Not-Yet_Political_Participation.pdf; Robert King, "A New America? Not so Fast," *Indianapolis Star*, November 15, 2008, at A1.

5. Gary C. Jacobson, "The Republican Resurgence in 2010," *Political Science Quarterly*, 126, no. 1 (Spring 2011): 32, https://www.jstor.org/stable/23056913.

6. Ibid., 33–34.

7. Ibid.

8. Joseph Lowndes, "Barack Obama's Body: The Presidency, the Body Politic, and the Contest over American National Identity," *Polity*, 45, no. 4 (October 2013): 488–89, https://www.jstor.org/stable/24540317.

9. Ibid.

10. Ibid; Philip A. Klinkner, Nicholas Anastasi, Jack Cartwright, Matthew Creeden, Will Rusche, Jesse Stinebring, and Hashem Zikry, "The 2012 Election and the Sources of Partisan Polarization: A Survey of American Political Attitudes," The Arthur Levitt Public Affairs Center, Hamilton College, 2013.

11. Michelle Alexander, *The New Jim Crow: Mass Incarceration in the Age of Colorblindness* (New York: The New Press, 2010).

12. *HuffPost,* "Michelle Alexander, 'More Black Men in Prison Than Were Enslaved in 1850,'" October 13, 2011, https://www.huffpost.com/entry/michelle-alexander-more-black-men-in-prison-slaves-1850_n_1007368.

13. Barbara Ransby, *Making All Black Lives Matter: Reimagining Freedom in the Twenty-First Century* (Oakland, CA: University of California Press, 2018), 29.

14. "About BLM," Black Lives Matter, accessed August 6, 2020, https://blacklivesmatter.com/herstory/.

15. Devan Cole, "Top Trump Officials Claim there's No Systemic Racism in US Law Enforcement Agencies as Americans Flood Streets in Protest," *CNN Politics,* June 10, 2020, accessed August 10, 2020, https://www.cnn.com/2020/06/07/politics/systemic-racism-trump-administration-officials-barr-carson-wolf/index.html.

16. Jeffery Martin, "Donald Trump Says Critical Race Theory is 'Like a Cancer,'" *Newsweek,* September 24, 2020, accessed November 2, 2020, https://www.newsweek.com/donald-trump-says-critical-race-theory-like-cancer-1534192.

17. Ali Vitali, Kasie Hunt, and Frank Thorp V., "Trump Referred to Haiti and African Nations as 'shithole' Countries," *NBCNews*, January 11, 2018, https://www.nbcnews.com/politics/white-house/trump-referred-haiti-african-countries-shithole-nations-n836946; Lauren Frias, "Trump has a Penchant for Calling the Coronavirus

the 'Chinese Virus' or 'Kung Fu,'" *Insider*, July 11, 2020, https://www.insider.com/experts-trump-racist-names-for-coronavirus-distract-from-us-response-2020-7; Katie Reilly, "Here Are All the Times Donald Trump Insulted Mexico," *Time*, August 31, 2016, https://time.com/4473972/donald-trump-&/.

18. Sociologist Eduardo Bonilla-Silva distinguishes contemporary *colorblind racism* from the blatant racism of the Jim Crow era. He states, "much as Jim Crow racism served as the glue for defending a brutal and overt system of racial oppression in the pre-civil rights era, color-blind racism serves today as the ideological armor for a covert and institutionalism system in the post-civil rights era." Eduardo Bonilla-Silva, *Racism without Racists: Color-Blind Racism and the Persistence of Racial Inequality in America* (New York: Rowman and Littlefield, 2018), 3–4.

19. "Speech on the Creation of the Martin Luther King, Jr., National Holiday," University of Virginia Miller Center, accessed August 6, 2020, https://millercenter.org/the-presidency/presidential-speeches/november-2-1983-speech-creation-martin-luther-king-jr-national.

20. Wilbur C. Rich, "Toward a Critical Race Theory of Political Science: A New Synthesis for Understanding Race, Law, and Politics," in *African American Perspectives on Political Science,* ed. Wilbur C. Rich (Philadelphia: Temple University Press, 2007), 214.

21. Manning Marable, *Race, Reform, and Rebellion: The Second Reconstruction and Beyond in Black America, 1945–2006* (Jackson, MS: University Press of Mississippi, 2007), 146–49.

22. Ibid., 150.

23. Ibid., 151.

24. Ibid., 152.

25. Alexander, *The New Jim Crow,* 49.

26. Marable, *Race, Reform, and Rebellion,* 188–94.

27. Charles R. Lawrence, "Who are We and Why Are We Here? Doing Critical Race Theory in Hard Times," in *Crossroads, Directions, and a New Critical Race Theory*, ed. Francisco Valdes, Jerome McCristal Culp, and Angela P. Harris (Philadelphia: Temple University Press, 2002), xiv.

28. Anthony V. Alfieri, "Black and White," A Review of *Critical Race Theory: The Cutting Edge,* by Richard Delgado, ed. and *Critical Race Theory: The Key Writings That Formed the Movement* by Crenshaw et al., *California Law Review*, 85, no. 5 (October 1997): 1658; David Kennedy and William Fisher, eds., *The Canon of American Legal Thought* (Princeton, NJ: Princeton University Press, 2006), 889–90; Crenshaw et al., *Critical Race Theory: The Key Writings that Formed the Movement,* xviii.

29. Kimberlé Williams Crenshaw, "The First Decade: Critical Reflection, or 'A Foot in the Closing Door'," in Francisco Valdez et al., *Directions and a New Critical Race Theory* (Philadelphia: Temple University Press, 2002), 10–15; Alan Hunt, "The Theory of Critical Legal Studies," *Oxford Journal of Legal Studies*, 6, Issue 1 (Spring 1986): 1, https://doi.org/10.1093/ojls/6.1.1.

30. Derrick A. Bell Jr., "Brown V. Board of Education and the Interest Convergence Dilemma," *Harvard Law Review*, 93, no. 3 (January 1980): 518, 523;

Richard Delgado, “Crossroads and Blind Alleys: A Critical Examination of Recent Writing About Race,” A Review of *Crossroad, Directions, and a New Critical Race Theory* by Francisco Valdes, Jerome McCristal Culp, and Angela P. Harris and *Ethical Ambition: Living a Life of Meaning and Wroth* by Derrick Bell, *Texas Law Review*, 82 (2003): 124.

31. Crenshaw et al., *Critical Race Theory: The Key Writings that Formed the Movement,* xx.

32. Alan D. Freeman, “Legitimizing Racial Discrimination Through Antidiscrimination Law: A Critical Review of Supreme Court Doctrine,” *Minnesota Law Review*, 804 (1978): 1049; Richard Delgado and Jean Stefancic, “Critical Race Theory: An Annotated Bibliography,” *Virginia Law Review*, 79, no. 2 (March 1993): 488.

33. Crenshaw et al., *Critical Race Theory: The Key Writings that Formed the Movement,* 29.

34. Crenshaw, “The First Decade: Critical Reflections,” 10, 13.

35. Crenshaw et al., *Critical Race Theory: The Key Writings that Formed the Movement,* xx.

36. Ibid., xxi.

37. Ibid.

38. Ibid., xxvii; Crenshaw, “The First Decade: Critical Reflections,” 15.

39. Crenshaw et al., *Critical Race Theory: The Key Writings that Formed the Movement*, xxvii.

40. Ibid., xiii.

41. Ibid., xxv.

42. Francisco Valdes et al., *Crossroads, Directions, and a New Critical Race Theory* (Philadelphia: Temple University Press, 2002), 2.

43. Richard Delgado and Jean Stefancic, eds., *Critical Race Theory: An Introduction,* 3rd edition (New York: New York University Press, 2017), 45, 53; Richard Delgado, “Storytelling for Oppositionists and Others: A Plea for Narrative,” *Michigan Law Review*, 87 (1989): 2414. Although we do not discuss them here, Delgado and Stefancic list the following themes as central in CRT scholarship: (1) *Critique of liberalism;* (2) *Storytelling/counterstorytelling and “naming one’s own reality*”; (3) *Revisionist interpretations of American civil rights law and progress*; (4) *A greater understanding of the underpinnings of race and racism*; (5) *Structural determinism;* (6) *Race, sex, class, and their intersections*; (7) *essentialism and anti-essentialism*; (8) *Cultural nationalism/separatism;* (9) *Legal institutions, Critical pedagogy, and minorities in the bar*; and (10) *criticism and self-criticism, responses.* Delgado and Stefancic, “Critical Race Theory: An Annotated Bibliography,” 462–63.

44. Adrien K. Wing, ed., *Critical Race Feminism: A Reader* (New York: New York University Press, 1997), 30.

45. Delgado and Stefancic, eds., *Critical Race Theory: An Introduction*, 4–5; Richard Delgado and Jean Stefancic, eds., *Critical Race Theory: The Cutting Edge* (Philadelphia: Temple University Press, 2013), 2; Crenshaw et al., *Critical Race Theory: The Key Writings that Formed the Movement,* 357–60.

46. Kimberlé Williams Crenshaw et al., *Seeing Race Again: Countering Colorblindness across the Disciplines* (Oakland: University of California Press, 2019).

47. Michel-Rolp Trouillot, *Silencing the Past: Power and the Production of History* (Boston: Beacon Press, 2015).
48. Rich, "Toward a Critical Race Theory of Political Science," 213.
49. Ibid.
50. Chandra L. Ford and Collins O. Airhihenbuwa, "Critical Race Theory, Race Equity, and Public Health: Toward Antiracism Praxis," *American Journal of Public Health,* 100, no. 51 (2010): 530.
51. Adrien K. Wing, "Is There a Future for Critical Race Theory?," *Journal of Legal Education,* 66, no. 1 (Autumn 2016): 51.
52. Delgado and Stefancic, eds., *Critical Race Theory: An Introduction.*
53. Delgado and Stefancic, eds., *Critical Race Theory: The Cutting Edge,* 2.
54. Stephen Steinberg, A Review of *Critical Race Theory: The Cutting Edge, Journal of American Ethnic History,* 21, no. 1 (Fall 2001): 124–25, http://www.jstor.com/stable/27502784.
55. Ibid.
56. Crenshaw et al., *Critical Race Theory: The Key Writings that Formed the Movement,* xiii.
57. Joseph G. Ramsey, "Introducing Scholactivism: Reflections on Transforming Praxis in and Beyond the Classroom," *Workplace,* 30 (2018): 1; Babak Amini, "Scholactivism: A Roundtable Interview with Ricardo Antunes, Pietro Basso, Patrick Bond, Michael Löwy, José Paulo Netto, and Leo Panitch," *Workplace,* 30 (2018): 46.
58. Ramsey, "Introducing Scholactivism," 1.
59. Amini, "Scholactivism: A Roundtable Interview," 47, 51; Efadul Huq and Xavier Best, "Untangling the Scholactivist Web," *Workplace,* 30 (2018): 283.
60. Edward J. Carvalho, "The Activist-Scholar: A Responsibility 'To Confront and Dismantle' Interview with Ward Churchill," *Workplace*, 30 (2018): 39–40.
61. Ibid.
62. Amini, "Scholactivism: A Roundtable Interview," 55.
63. Carvalho, "The Activist-Scholar," 40.
64. Amini, "Scholactivism: A Roundtable Interview," 52, 55.
65. Eddie S. Glaude Jr., *Democracy in Black: How Race Still Enslaves the American Soul* (New York: Crown Publishing, 2016); Eddie S. Glaude Jr., *Begin Again: James Baldwin's America and Its Urgent Lessons for Our Own* (New York: Crown Publishing, 2020); Ibram X. Kendi, *Stamped From the Beginning: The Definitive History of Racist Ideas in America* (New York: Nation Books, 2016); Brittney C. Cooper, *Eloquent Rage: A Black Feminist Discovers Her Superpower* (New York: St. Martin's Press, 2018); Brittney C. Cooper, Susana M. Morris, and Robin M. Boylorn, eds., *The Crunk Feminist Collection* (New York: Feminist Press, 2017).
66. Alfieri, "Black and White," 1650.

BIBLIOGRAPHY

Alexander, Michelle. *The New Jim Crow: Mass Incarceration in the Age of Colorblindness.* New York: The New Press, 2010.

Alfieri, Anthony V. "Black and White," A Review of *Critical Race Theory: The Cutting Edge,* by Richard Delgado, ed. and *Critical Race Theory: The Key Writings That Formed the Movement* by Crenshaw et al., *California Law Review*, 85, no. 5 (October 1997): 1647–1686. http://www.jstor.com/stable/3481067.

Amini, Babak. "Scholactivism: A Roundtable Interview with Ricardo Antunes, Pietro Basso, Patrick Bond, Michael Löwy, José Paulo Netto, and Leo Panitch," *Workplace,* 30 (2018): 46–53. https://doi.org/10.14288/workplace.v0i30.186379.

Bell, Derrick A. "Brown V. Board of Education and the Interest Convergence Dilemma," *Harvard Law Review*, 93, no. 3 (January 1980): 518–533. http://www.jstor.org/stable/1340546.

Black Lives Matter. "About BLM." Accessed August 6, 2020, https://blacklivesmatter.com/herstory/.

Bonilla-Silva, Eduardo. *Racism without Racists: Color-Blind Racism and the Persistence of Racial Inequality in America.* New York: Rowman and Littlefield, 2018.

Carvalho, Edward J. "The Activist-Scholar: A Responsibility 'To Confront and Dismantle' Interview with Ward Churchill," *Workplace*, 30 (2018): 38–45. Retrieved from: http://www.worksanddays.net/W&D%202016-2017.html.

Clarke, Kristen. "'Post-Racial' America? Not Yet: Why the Fight for Voting Rights Continues After the Election of President Barack Obama." Accessed August 6, 2020, https://www.naacpldf.org/wp-content/uploads/Post-Racial-America-Not-Yet_Political_Participation.pdf.

Cole, Devan. "Top Trump Officials Claim there's No Systemic Racism in US Law Enforcement Agencies as Americans Flood Streets in Protest." *CNN Politics.* June 10, 2020. Accessed August 10, 2020, https://www.cnn.com/2020/06/07/politics/systemic-racism-trump-administration-officials-barr-carson-wolf/index.html.

Cooper, Brittney C. *Eloquent Rage: A Black Feminist Discovers Her Superpower.* New York: St. Martin's Press, 2018.

Cooper, Brittney C., Susana M. Morris, and Robin M. Boylorn, eds. *The Crunk Feminist Collection.* New York: Feminist Press, 2017.

Crenshaw, Kimberlé, Neil Gotanda, Gary Peller, and Kendall Thomas, eds. *Critical Race Theory: The Key Writings that Formed the Movement.* New York: The New Press, 1996.

Crenshaw, Kimberlé Williams, Luke Charles Harris, Daniel Martinez HoSang, and George Lipsitz, eds. *Seeing Race Again: Countering Colorblindness across the Disciplines*. Oakland: University of California Press, 2019.

Delgado, Richard. "Crossroads and Blind Alleys: A Critical Examination of Recent Writing About Race." A Review of *Crossroad, Directions, and a New Critical Race Theory* by Francisco Valdes, Jerome McCristal Culp, and Angela P. Harris" and *Ethical Ambition: Living a Life of Meaning and Wroth* by Derrick Bell, *Texas Law Review*, 82 (2003): 121–152. https://papers.ssrn.com/sol3/papers.cfm?abstract_id=1154775.

Delgado, Richard. "Storytelling for Oppositionists and Others: A Plea for Narrative," *Michigan Law Review*, 87 (1989): 2411–2441.

Delgado, Richard and Jean Stefancic. "Critical Race Theory: An Annotated Bibliography," *Virginia Law Review*, 79, no. 2 (March 1993): 461–516. http://www.jstor.com/stable/1073418.

Delgado, Richard and Jean Stefancic, eds. *Critical Race Theory: The Cutting Edge.* Philadelphia: Temple University Press, 2013.

Delgado, Richard and Jean Stefancic, eds. *Critical Race Theory: An Introduction*, 3rd edition. New York: New York University Press, 2017.

Ford, Chandra L. and Collins O. Airhihenbuwa. "Critical Race Theory, Race Equity, and Public Health: Toward Antiracism Praxis," *American Journal of Public Health*, 100, no. 51 (2010): 530–535. doi: 10.2105/AJPH.2009.171058.

Freeman, Alan D. "Legitimizing Racial Discrimination Through Antidiscrimination Law: A Critical Review of Supreme Court Doctrine," *Minnesota Law Review*, 804 (1978): 1049–1119. https://scholarship.law.umn.edu/mlr/804.

Frias, Lauren. "Trump has a Penchant for Calling the Coronavirus the 'Chinese Virus' or 'Kung Fu,'" *Insider*. July 11, 2020. https://www.insider.com/experts-trump-racist-names-for-coronavirus-distract-from-us-response-2020-7.

Glaude Jr., Eddie S. *Begin Again: James Baldwin's America and Its Urgent Lessons for Our Own.* New York: Crown Publishing, 2020.

Glaude Jr., Eddie S. *Democracy in Black: How Race Still Enslaves the American Soul.* New York: Crown Publishing, 2016.

HuffPost, "Michelle Alexander, "More Black Men in Prison Than Were Enslaved in 1850." October 13, 2011. Retrieved from https://www.huffpost.com/entry/michelle-alexander-more-black-men-in-prison-slaves-1850_n_1007368.

Hunt, Alan. "The Theory of Critical Legal Studies," *Oxford Journal of Legal Studies*, 6, Issue 1 (Spring 1986): 1–45. https://doi.org/10.1093/ojls/6.1.1.

Jacobson, Gary C. "The Republican Resurgence in 2010," *Political Science Quarterly*, 126, no. 1 (Spring 2011): 27–52. https://www.jstor.org/stable/23056913.

Kendi, Ibram X. *Stamped From the Beginning: The Definitive History of Racist Ideas in America.* New York: Nation Books, 2016.

Kennedy, David and William Fisher, eds. *The Canon of American Legal Thought.* Princeton, NJ: Princeton University Press, 2006.

King, Robert. "A New America? Not so Sast." *Indianapolis Star*, November 15, 2008, at A1.

Klinkner, Philip A., Nicholas Anastasi, Jack Cartwright, Matthew Creeden, Will Rusche, Jesse Stinebring, and Hashem Zikry. "The 2012 Election and the Sources of Partisan Polarization: A Survey of American Political Attitudes." The Arthur Levitt Public Affairs Center, Hamilton College, 2013.

Lawrence, Charles R. "Who are We and Why Are We Here? Doing Critical Race Theory in Hard Times," in *Crossroads, Directions, and a New Critical Race Theory*, ed. Francisco Valdes, Jerome McCristal Culp, and Angela P. Harris, Philadelphia: Temple University Press, 2002.

Lowndes, Joseph. "Barack Obama's Body: The Presidency, the Body Politic, and the Contest over American National Identity," *Polity*, 45, no. 4 (October 2013): 469–498. https://www.jstor.org/stable/24540317.

Marable, Manning. *Race, Reform, and Rebellion: The Second Reconstruction and Beyond in Black America, 1945-2006*. Jackson, MS: University Press of Mississippi, 2007.

Martin, Jeffery. "Donald Trump Says Critical Race Theory is 'Like a Cancer.'" *Newsweek*. September 24, 2020. Accessed November 2, 2020, https://www.newsweek.com/donald-trump-says-critical-race-theory-like-cancer-1534192.

Ramsey, Joseph G. "Introducing Scholactivism: Reflections on Transforming Praxis in and Beyond the Classroom," *Workplace*, 30 (2018): 1–37. https://doi.org/10.14288/workplace.v0i30.186377.

Ransby, Barbara. *Making All Black Lives Matter: Reimagining Freedom in the Twenty-First Century*. Oakland, CA: University of California Press, 2018.

Reilly, Katie. "Here Are All the Times Donald Trump Insulted Mexico." *Time*. August 31, 2016, https://time.com/4473972/donald-trump-&/.

Rich, Wilbur C. *African American Perspectives on Political Science*. Philadelphia: Temple University Press, 2007.

Steinberg, Stephen. A Review of *Critical Race Theory: The Cutting Edge*, *Journal of American Ethnic History*, Vol. 21, No. 1 (Fall 2001): 124–25. http://www.jstor.com/stable/27502784.

Trouillot, Michel-Rolp. *Silencing the Past: Power and the Production of History*. Boston: Beacon Press, 2015.

University of Virginia Miller Center. "Speech on the Creation of the Martin Luther King, Jr., National Holiday. Accessed August 6, 2020, https://millercenter.org/the-presidency/presidential-speeches/november-2-1983-speech-creation-martin-luther-king-jr-national.

Vitali, Ali, Kasie Hunt, and Frank Thorp V. "Trump Referred to Haiti and African Nations as 'shithole' countries." *NBCNews*. January 11, 2018. https://www.nbcnews.com/politics/white-house/trump-referred-haiti-african-countries-shithole-nations-n836946.

Wallis, Jim. *America's Original Sin: Racism, White Privilege, and the Bridge to a New America*. Grand Rapids, MI: Brazos Press, 2017.

Wing, Adrien K., ed. *Critical Race Feminism: A Reader*. New York: New York University Press, 1997.

Wing, Adrien K. "Is There a Future for Critical Race Theory?" *Journal of Legal Education*, 66, no. 1 (Autumn 2016): 44–54. http://www.jstor.com/stable/26402418.

Part I

AFRICAN AMERICAN HISTORY

Introduction

Intersections between Critical Race Studies and History

David Ryden

The same social and intellectual forces that gave rise to the emergence of Critical Race Studies at the end of the twentieth century have shaped the field of history. Historians, since at least the late 1960s, have trained the focus on the history of the marginalized and have eschewed the "top down" approach that had been a hallmark of traditional political, military, and international histories. The "New Left" historians who led this movement took on the study of laborers, women, and immigrants in hopes of giving voice to the voiceless.[1] Historical actors who had once been considered superfluous were now central to the historian's craft. This trajectory of the field in the 1970s and 1980s was further aided by the poststructuralist intellectual revolution, where scholars in a variety of fields were prepared to challenge prevailing assumptions and methods to understanding within their discipline. In the case of history, researchers not only relished the idea of challenging national narratives but also worked to unpack the origins, features, and purpose of the ideology held by their historical subjects.[2] Ultimately, historians found that the simple stories of unfolding *progress*—such as the rise of individual freedom and liberty—had obscured historical realities that everyday people faced. It is this shifting perspective, from that of the mighty toward that of the oppressed, where critical race theory (CRT) and the discipline of history have found significant overlap and have complemented one another.

The preoccupation with counternarratives pushed the field of history toward some of the same conclusions made by CRT scholars. In the case of the United States, historians have long grappled with the tragic irony that the "founding fathers"—Thomas Jefferson ("Father of the Declaration of Independence"); James Madison ("Father of the Constitution"); George Mason ("Father of the Bill of Rights"); and George Washington ("Father of the Country")—were not only enormously wealthy but also slaveholders.

This paradox of Virginian planters acting as architects of America's liberal democracy was resolved for many by Edmund S. Morgan, who held out the importance of Virginia's early slave code, which defined Blacks as outsiders and deemed them mere chattel (movable property). For Morgan, this legal structure ultimately shaped a society where poor Whites (formerly, indentured servants) would come to see their identity bound with elites and not their fellow Black laborers. Colonial law cultivated an enormous social chasm that kept enslaved people oppressed while giving elites the latitude to embrace a radical rhetoric of liberty and equality, knowing full well that these liberal gestures toward all Whites would not be upended by social revolution; the enslaved, at the bottom of society, were fully and absolutely, deemed outsiders, thanks to the legal code.[3] For early critical race theorists, such as Cheryl I. Harris, these early slave codes shaped the institutional and social trajectory of America's racial divide down to this very day. Early colonial statutes diminished the personhood of Blacks while bestowing on "whiteness . . . privilege and protection" that would continue to hold in law and culture, well after slavery.[4]

While the law has a central focus among CRT scholars, historians have also taken a keen interest in unpacking the economic and social origins of racialized thinking in the United States. This task, however, involves a wide range of scholarship that extends beyond America's borders. Researchers working within the field of Atlantic History have worked to understand the connection between the growth of the colonial plantation system along the western rim of the Atlantic basin shaped racialized thinking in far-flung places, including Brazil, the Caribbean, North America, and Europe. This approach has elevated the significance of the transatlantic attack on the slave trade and the reactionary defense of the plantation system based on notions of biological hierarchy. Starting in the second half of the 1700s, this defense of slavery was first taken up by West Indian sugar planters. However, by the 1830s, North American planters—who then challenged by both Black and White abolitionists—became the primary defenders of slavery. It would be these champions of the plantation in South who put forth a particularly racist defense of slavery to the rest of the United States. Their hateful, racist remarks, which both Black and White abolitionists challenged, spread throughout the United States through pamphlets, books, and speeches that claimed slaveholding to be a benign institution that benefited all involved.

Historians and critical race theorists are generally in agreement that race and racism are both socially constructed and have a material basis, such as the self-interest of planters. This collective research also tends to emphasize the agency of African Americans in their response to racism and structural inequality. Starting in the early 1970s, historians of slavery followed John Blassingame's lead by shifting their emphasis toward underscoring the myriad acts of resistance by the slave community. Enslaved people sometimes violently challenged their captivity, but more often, they embraced subtle tactics, such as sabotage, work stoppages, or even feigning incompetence.[5] Today, historians continue to point to the production and reproduction of African American culture as a significant challenge to White authority. This emphasis on communal strength, resilience, and resistance in the face of adversity has eclipsed the liberal tradition that had emphasized a steady, forward movement along the path of equality.

The three chapters in this section reflect the patterns of overlap between the work of historians and that of critical race theorists. In Rachael L. Pasierowska's "I Was Like a Petty Dog": The Animalization of Black Bodies," we find an example of the *Atlantic History* analytical approach to Brazilian, Cuban, and North American proslavery thought. Taking particular attention to literary and visual texts, Pasierowska shows us how dehumanized conditions were justified by equating enslaved people with animals. Her argument informs the CRT critique of liberal progress by emphasizing how the pseudoscientific lexicon found in these texts aided in the justification of the proslavery position. Pasierowska also reflects the CRT approach by her emphasis on storytelling, as she concludes her chapter by including the testimonials of former slaves, who, in an act of resistance to White domination, bore witness to their maltreatment they suffered.

In a similar fashion, Scott Stabler and Martin Hershock review the Black experience in the Union Army, during the Civil War, to show how formerly enslaved soldiers endeavored to secure liberty and ultimately combat racism, through their heroism. What the coauthors show us is that even in the free North, White Americans discounted the abilities and competencies of Black soldiers. Institutionally, this racism manifested itself in military policies that paid Black recruits less than their White counterparts and that initially excluded them from the combat theater. Ultimately, the Union Army increasingly relied upon African American regiments and Black soldiers gained the respect of their White comrades; with little hope of fair treatment if taken prisoner, Black soldiers tended to battle Confederates to the death and exhibited genuine heroism. By picking up the gun, former slaves demonstrated that the plantation was neither paternalistic nor benign. For White southerners, Black soldiers were *the* rebels, and the decision of former slaves to take up arms shattered the myth of planter paternalism, which had been at the center of southern ideology. While African Americans won the praise of their Union colleagues during the war, the coauthors tell us that the respect garnered by African American soldiers was ephemeral, and that subsequent generations of Blacks returned to military service in later conflicts, carrying the same hope that their sacrifice would undermine America's racial caste system.

The final chapter in this section, by Jesús Jesse Esparza, also follows the theme of the Black response to racism. His focus is on two Houston African American communities and their collective effort to preserve self-determination. Esparza covers a broad range of time, from c.1890 to the present, and shows how Booker T. Washington High School (originally "Colored High") became a centerpiece for Black empowerment in Houston. The chapter explicitly applies CRT and trains our attention on the voices of the community in order to "captur[e] the 'narratives of people of color' [that . . .] challenge existing historical frameworks that are often rooted in White supremacy and patriarchy." What Esparza reveals is how these African American collectives prevailed in providing educational uplift, by capitalizing on their own talents and ambitions to improve the lives of their children. Esparza indicates that this inward-looking resolve to fight social inequality is alive today, not just at Booker T. Washington High School but also in the community's response to new social challenges, such as gentrification.

It is important to recognize that these three essays show that the field of history both informs and is *informed by* CRT. This relationship between the two overlapping fields is not at all unusual; historians often reflect on whether their research is done in the aid of a theoretical framework—whether it is economics, sociology, or a critical theory—or if their research is indeed aided by theory. CRT, however, is more grounded in American history compared to other social science theories. Thus, it is important that the reader compare the historical analysis of different places and periods in order to detect the patterns of social and racial injustice underscored by CRT.

NOTES

1. It is important to keep in mind that the interest in African American history generally grew out of the civil rights movement. Robert L. Harris made the point that White Americans, at that time, "were anxious to know why black people, apparently passive before, were now demanding equality." It is interesting that he observed the tension between White historians and the emergence of the Black Consciousness Movement, which the establishment considered emotionalism. "Coming of Age: The Transformation of Afro-American Historiography," *Journal of Negro History* 67:2 (1982): 107, 109.

2. One of the better overviews is Kevin Passmore, "Poststructuralism and History," in *Writing History: Theory and Practice,* ed. Stefan Berger, Heiko Feldner, and Kevin Passmore (London: Bloomsbury Academic), 123–146.

3. Edmund S. Morgan, "Slavery and Freedom: The American Paradox," *Journal of American History* 59:1 (1972): 28–29.

4. Cheryl I. Harris, "Whiteness as Property," *Harvard Law Review* 106:8 (1993): 1713–1721.

5. John W. Blassingame, *The Slave Community: Plantation Life in the Antebellum South* (Oxford: Oxford University Press, 1972).

BIBLIOGRAPHY

Blassingame, John W. *The Slave Community: Plantation Life in the Antebellum South*. Oxford: Oxford University Press, 1972.

Harris, Cheryl I. "Whiteness as Property," *Harvard Law Review* 106, no.8 (1993): 1707–1791.

Harris, Robert L. "Coming of Age: The Transformation of Afro-American Historiography," *Journal of Negro History* 67, no. 2 (1982): 107–121.

Morgan, Edmund S. "Slavery and Freedom: The American Paradox," *Journal of American History* 59, no. 1 (1972): 5–29.

Passmore, Kevin. "Poststructuralism and History." In *Writing History: Theory and Practice*, edited by Stefan Berger, Heiko Feldner, and Kevin Passmore, 123–146. London: Bloomsbury Academic, 2010.

Chapter 1

"I Wuz Like a Petty Dog"

White Animalization of Enslaved Blacks

Rachael Pasierowska

In the early 1870s, less than two decades before Cuban slavery was abolished, the Italian author and loyalist Antonio Carlo Napoleone Gallenga visited the island of Cuba.[1] For several years prior to the voyage, the largest Spanish Caribbean possession had waged insurrection against the Spanish government. Considering foreign news too contradictory, Gallenga and his compatriots sought to determine the real story behind the insurrection.[2] Like many travelers over the course of the long nineteenth century, Gallenga's purpose was not necessarily to observe the lives of slaves. But reading between the pages of Gallenga's report, several references to slaves emerge. Thus, Gallenga described some plantation slaves as "fat and sleek and shiny like [B] lack slugs, and, at certain hours, noisily merry."[3] These narratives help readers to better understand how Whites viewed and treated slaves. All too often they also underline Whites' inherent racism toward Blacks.

This chapter uses a collection of sources from travel narratives, journals, and images from across the nineteenth century to explore how travelers described their encounters and experiences with slaves. These sources sit alongside slave accounts, for instance, in autobiographies and interviews with former slaves. Travelers drew insight into the lives of slaves by observing the sale and treatment of slaves, and the language used by Whites to describe the enslaved. They both implicitly and explicitly concluded how free society worked to construct an image of the enslaved as animal-like. Taken together in an Atlantic context, travelers, whether they went to Brazil, Cuba, or the U.S. South, all shared a similar discourse on race that was shaped by prevailing scientific thought in Europe at the time.[4] In addition to delineating White attitudes toward people of color, this chapter explores the extent to which slaves were aware of such racism.

USE OF ANIMAL IMAGERY AS A PROP TO SCIENTIFIC RACISM

Europeans in North America commenced importing Black Africans (first from the Caribbean and then directly from Africa) when it became harder and more costly to obtain White indentured servants from the metropole.[5] Additionally, Whites claimed that Africans had higher survival rates against tropical maladies.[6] Soon White settlers turned to Christianity as a means to categorize certain groups—notably Africans—who they regarded as "unsavory" or "uncivilized." By nature of such uncivilization, they were thought inferior. Alongside these scholarly developments, during the seventeenth and eighteenth centuries, Europeans became more fascinated with what they believed to be Africans' innate "savageness." In this light, the system of slavery became a mechanism by which Whites could help to salvage the Africans from sin *and* civilize Africans.[7] This context provided an earlier backdrop to Europeans' later scientific reasonings behind the mass enslavement of Africans.

Science as a field did not initially dislodge religious justifications. But over time, scholars gradually abandoned religious and moral defenses of race for more modern scientific arguments. A new school of scholars looked for alternative explanations to Africans' perceived "inferiority." In the mid-nineteenth century Charles Darwin posited that while God had created the world, he had not created each individual species, hence the theory of evolution.[8] Darwin argued that many "savage peoples" had mental capabilities and senses of morality that were no greater than animals. This is crucial for understanding the crux of this chapter. Darwin relied on earlier works that connected the different species and races.[9]

The general consensus among scientists up until the eve of the twentieth century was that man could better understand God's design through studying the natural world. Scholars such as Carl Linnaeus and the Comte de Buffon looked to God as Creator. They viewed man and animal together in one great "Great Chain of Being." For these thinkers, man headed the chain that continued through the species concluding with inanimate matter.[10] Over time scholars positioned Caucasians at the top—closest to God—followed by the other racial groups culminating with the sub-Saharan African. The next component in the link was the ape. In *De Generis Humani Varietate Nativa* Blumenbach and Sir Joseph Banks coined the term "Caucasian"—the most "attractive" of the races—and placed this class at the top of the scale of humankind.[11] This developing pseudoscientific racism provided a common set of prejudices among nineteenth-century European and North American travelers to American slave societies.

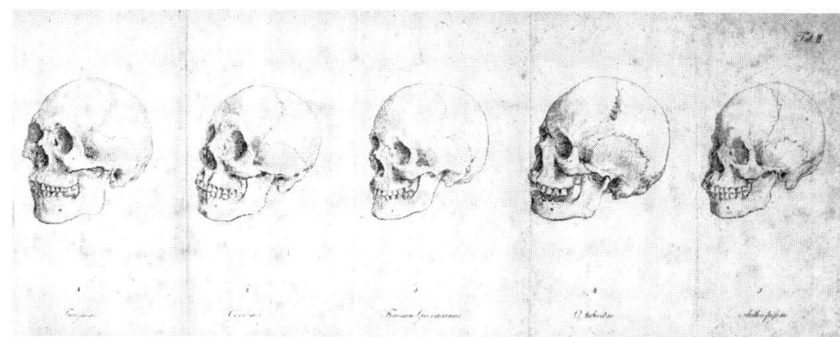

Figure 1.1 Skulls of the Five Main Denominations of Man. In Johann Friedrich Blumenbach & Sir Joseph Banks, *De Generis Humani Varietate Nativa* (Gottingae: Vandenhoek et Ruprecht, 1795). *Source*: Courtesy of the National Archives.

Encounters in the U.S. South

Such scholarly debates influenced travelers' narratives, such as Gallenga. Slaveholders also shared an awareness of such scholarship. Consequently, Whites' language—in verbal or written form—often foregrounds notions of scientific racism. Furthermore, this testifies to Whites' animalization of enslaved Blacks. We see this particularly in the U.S. South. One common antislavery argument that reached back to the eighteenth century was that White slaveholders treated their slaves as barbaric, beast-like, and soulless. Many Works Progress Administration interviewees recalled when Whites—both slaveholders *and* preachers—either failed to mention the souls of Blacks or simply referred to slaves as soulless. For Wes Brady of Marshall, Texas, the preaching during slavery times was "Hellish": there was "nary word 'bout having a soul to save."[12] Robert Burns from Agefield, Tennessee, told how White preachers said slaves had no souls. He continued that the preachers told slaves they "had no more souls than dogs, and dey couldn't go to heaven any more than could a dog."[13] Children also learned such lessons: Francis Fedric wrote in his autobiography how frequently his master pointed out horses, cows, sheep, and mules to the plantation slave children saying "you have no souls, you are just like those cattle, when you die there is an end of you; there is nothing more for you to think about than living."[14] The lesson concluded with the line "White people only have souls."

Reading ex-slaves' recollections in conjunction with religious and scientific debates concerning Africans, analogies between slave and animal stand out. White preachers and slaveholders' arguments about slaves' "soullessness" were central. Moreover, masters particularly aimed this language at young slaves.[15] Here, memories speak to the indelible print such sermons and lessons had on young brains that carried through into adulthood. Slaveholders most likely employed preachers to deliver these words to better shape the identity formation of their enslaved children to produce a more cooperative enslaved workforce. In conclusion, slaveholders both animalized and dehumanized slaves; some Whites going as far as decreeing slaves as soulless entities.

Encounters in Brazil

Descriptions of phenotypical appearances and characteristics offer insight into one way with which travelers to Brazil drew analogies between enslaved Blacks and animals. Writing of slaves in Rio de Janeiro, Charles Wilkes concluded that the "Creator" had been careless in sculpting the Black race for they were "badly formed, or clumsy." As to their character, Wilkes believed them to be "indolent, thoughtless, and licentious" who after work would lounge in the streets "enjoying themselves as mere animals, basking in the sun or sleeping in the shade."[16] Wilkes does not denigrate the intellectual capabilities of enslaved Blacks; rather, they never "aspired" to do more than was required of them: Blacks were not "dumb," but rather were "lazy" *like* animals. Wilkes' judgments conveniently gloss over the arduous work slaves undertook.

Foreigners saw the way African women carried infants on their backs as animal-like, and particularly apelike. Both anthropologists and historians have rightly linked this practice to its West and Central-African origins. While visiting Brazil, Maturin M. Ballou wrote how mothers went about their daily activities with infants secured to their backs with a shawl or "rebozo." For Ballou, Black infants were "always suggestive of monkeys."[17] A photograph from Bahia, North Brazil, demonstrates this style of conveyance. The fairness of the baby's skin and hair suggests that this was the child of a White slaveowner. While transporting infants in this way enabled enslaved women to better carry out their daily activities, for travelers such as Ballou, this practice indicated animal behaviorisms. Moreover, his assessment spoke to scientific understandings of the "chains of being": Africans occupied the bottom links of mankind followed by the ape.

Encounters in Cuba

Whites' analogies between enslaved Blacks and animals become more apparent when we look at Cuban slavery. Here, written and visual depictions illustrate how travelers were familiar with scientific scholarship from abroad. Thus, the Frenchman Jean J. Ampère wrote of Blacks' anatomies: "a bone in the negro's heel is nearly similar or not to the same bone in monkeys." He concluded by writing that "[W]hites shouldn't consider them as things when God created them as persons."[18] Ampère's citation falls into two separate parts: first was his strong grasp of contemporary scientific arguments regarding the physiognomy of Blacks as being more similar to apes than the White man. Second, Ampère refers to his personal experiences of travel, which suggests how travelers' preconceptions of slavery influenced their writings when they came into personal contact with slaves.

Artists also engaged with similar arguments of the epoch. A lithograph entitled "Iglesia y Plaza de Güines" by F. Mülhe speaks to the first part of Ampère's written depiction. The lithograph shows a large number of enslaved Blacks celebrating with music and dance in the "Guinea Square." Looking closely at the image shows how the artist sought to portray the Black faces as much more angular and apelike with noses and protruding jawbones. Furthermore, several men wave around or hold their arms and move their legs in a style reminiscent of animals and not humans: the unnatural angle of one man's hands is representative of paws rather than hands. Mülhe paints him as both "barbaric" and "savage." This is in sharp juxtaposition to a pair of White onlookers, who observe the scene and sport smart attire. Moreover, their faces and comportments appear much more refined and humanistic than the Black dancers and musicians. The lithograph illustrates an artist's attempts to animalize one race and humanize another race.

Such attention to slaves' phenotypes foregrounds how White travelers animalized their subjects. In another example, Geo. W. Carleton's caricature depicts a slave volante driver of the renowned carriages on the island of Cuba. The driver's hunched posture, in combination with his excessively oversized lips clenching a large cigarillo, makes him appear not so different from his mule. Even the saddle has so little differentiation in shading, making the upturned cantle appear much like a tail protruding from the rump of the driver. Finally, the driver's broad-brimmed sun hat draws parallels with the mule's ears. This makes the driver look slovenly and more animal-like and contrasts with other images from the same epoch that depict volante drivers with great prestige highlighting their smart attire and "correct" riding posture. Writers furthered such visual portrayals of the physiological similarities between Blacks and animals. Joseph J. Dimock penned the following during his travels: "The negroes are most of them pictures of ugliness, frightful to behold, of the true baboon class, projecting muzzle and retreating chin and forehead . . . their general appearance is very repulsive."[19] In images and written accounts, Whites animalized Blacks.

Across the Atlantic world, travelers tended to describe slaves with one voice. In Brazil and Cuba, written and visual sources illustrate enslaved Africans as animalistic in both appearance and comportment. In so doing, authors linked Blacks more closely with apes. Pictorial depictions deeply

STREETS OF HAVANA.—CALLE MERCADERES.

The first volante driver that our artist saw in Havana.

Figure 1.2 Streets of Havana—Calle Mercaderes. Geo. W. Carleton, *Our Artist in Cuba: Fifty Drawings on Wood* (New York: Carleton, 1865). *Source*: Courtesy of Cuban Heritage Collection, University of Miami Libraries, Coral Gables, Florida.

Figure 1.3 A Slave Sale. Printed in Henry Bibb, *Narrative of The Life and Adventures of Henry Bibb* (New York: Published by the author, 1849). *Source*: Courtesy of the National Archives.

underline such metaphorical representations showing how nineteenth-century artists and writers frequently conformed to post-Enlightenment scientific thoughts and scholarship. This is particularly apparent in travelers' portrayals of Black faces with accentuated jutting chins and lips. Furthermore, we see this with travelers' attention to how Black slaves moved, for instance, in dance or carrying children. When we contextualize these accounts and images with scientific documentation of the epoch, the metaphorical representations of Africans' animality come into sharper focus. In this light, the Brazilian and Cuban examples speak to the consecutive links between Africans and primates. Furthermore, this might have informed how slaveholders and White preachers referred to slaves in the U.S. South as similar to dogs and livestock; moreover, how by nature of this Blacks were ultimately "soulless."

USE OF ANIMAL IMAGERY TO CONVEY THE TREATMENT OF THE ENSLAVED

This section now looks at how Whites animalized and dehumanized Blacks through their treatment. Across the three slave societies, the following themes are apparent: corporal punishment, meal allocations, and slaveholders' language toward their slaves. Travelers' descriptions show how slaveholders did not hide their behaviors and words from outsiders. Rather, the sources underline slaveholders' apparent ease with their own actions. Moreover, the travel accounts show how foreign travelers also animalized enslaved Blacks. In this way, when travelers wrote about slaves for European audiences, they upheld beliefs of Blacks as animal-like.

Encounters in the U.S. South

Former slaves from the U.S. South looked back on their treatment under the institution of slavery as frequently being analogous to that of an animal. One former slave remembered how his master gave the animals better fare: "They gives the mules, ruffage and such, to chaw on all night. But they didn't give us nothing to chaw on."[20] As a consequence, slaves stole victuals. Shack Thomas from Florida recounted how slave masters frequently sold and traded enslaved persons just as though they were horses. Furthermore, Thomas went on to add that if a slaveowner had "a couple of old women who couldn't do much any more, and he'd swap 'em to the other man for a young 'un."[21] In this way, a master might boost his enslaved property through reproductive means. Here, slaveholders often allotted pregnant slaves higher food rations; however, this practice often underlined owners' concerns of boosting their capital revenues as though slaves were livestock. Frances Anne Kemble

observed precisely this in her diary as she wrote how slaves' lives were "for the most part those of mere animals, their increase is literally mere animal breeding."[22]

Slaveholders who "bred" their slaves in this way symbolized the animalization of slaves. Ex-slaves described masters who bred certain slaves to favor specific characteristics or traits in offspring or "stock." One ex-slave recalled how his owner only permitted the strong and healthy slave women to bear children. His master then bred these enslaved women "like livestock" to a male slave "who was kept for that purpose because of his strong phisique."[23] Slaveholders' conditioning and control of their slaves' sexual relations indicates how they treated enslaved peoples as analogous to animals with the primary motivation of increasing their capital. It is in this light that the term "Buck" for certain male slaves is noteworthy. In the U.S. South, the term "Buck" represented a White gender convention for a sexed Black male, which prevailed after the Civil War. Elizabeth Fox-Genovese wrote how a "Buck evoked a sexually active, perpetual adolescent" who threatened the pureness of White southern belles.[24] Lulu Wilson of Dallas, Texas, recalled how her master replaced her father with another slave—a "Buck"—because he failed to produce any more children. Concluding that Wilson's father was unable to reproduce anymore because he was "too old and wore out for breedin," the master forced Wilson's mother to "take with this here buck."[25] Wilson's use of the term "buck" in respect to breeding underlines Fox-Genovese's reference to the libidinous nature—in the eyes of nineteenth-century Whites—of the Black male. In concluding, Wilson made covert reference to the presumed carnal behavior of Black men. She stated how her mother then "took with my step-paw and they must of pleased the White folks what wanted niggers to breed like livestock, 'cause she birthed nineteen chillen."[26]

When Whites labeled male slaves as "Bucks," they also alluded to slaves' physical strength. Ex-slave W. L. Bost remembered how slave auctioneers would say something like "here is a big [B]lack buck Negro. He's stout as a mule."[27] Other former slaves spoke to interviewers of the term "buck and gag" that made reference to a specific form of punishment. Calvin Kennard from Louisiana, explained how "'Buck an' gag' means when de oberseer would hab a buck nigger or two to hold de one dat was to be whupped over a barrel or somet'in while he was bein' whipped."[28] In this light, the term "Buck" emphasized the physical strength of particular male slaves.

White slaveholders who referred to their slaves as "dogs" demonstrated their animalization and dehumanization of Blacks. Frenchman Ernest Duvergier de Hauranne concluded that slaves might "aspire to the happy lot of a favorite dog or docile horse that is petted by its master."[29] Former slaves frequently recollected how slaveholders treated their human property like dogs. As a child, Eli Davison encountered a female slave in chains. Her

"maser" had the enslaved woman "fastened to his saddle leading her just like you would a dog." At night, the slave's owner chained her "to the wagon wheel where she could get in the wagon and sleep."[30] This must have been a terribly uncomfortable experience in both a physical and emotional sense: first, the chains would have chafed and rubbed against the woman's neck causing blisters. Second, she would have most likely borne great shame at this treatment. In this instance, even the horse appeared to have more freedom: the master rode the horse with leather reins and *not* a metal chain. Years later, Davison remembered the woman as being similar to a dog. Yet, unlike a dog whose fidelity sets him apart from many animals, the enslaved woman was not to be trusted and thus followed in chains.

Some slaves resisted such treatment. John Finnely received just one whipping as a slave when he refused to swim into a pond to retrieve a duck. During hunting trips, Finnely's master used John as "de gun rest" and to "fetch an' carry de game" rather like a hunting hound. Finnely admitted that this was not "so bad" in itself; however, when his master shot a duck in the water and commanded his slave to swim and retrieve the game, Finnely desisted. He concluded that he "could never git used to bein' de wautah dog fo' ducks. Dat am de only whuppin' I's gits."[31] Finnely's apparent fear of deeper water and drowning—perhaps grounded in an inability to swim—prevented him from initially entering the pond. Thus, while Finnely submitted to the emotional degradation of acting as a hunt's dog on land, when commanded to do something frightening, Finnely first respected his fears in refusing to go into the pond. Only when lashed did Finnely overcame his fears. But although he might have had to repeat this action in future hunting trips, Finnely did not wholly succumb like an animal. His spirit remained unbroken and he stated how he "could never git used" to this treatment. Another former slave employed "doglike" behavior when he bit his mistress in response to her beating him for learning to read. Joseph Allen told an interviewer how "Ise bite'r like er dog, an hel' on wid me teeth to'er leg. Old Missus wuz lame fur a spell; I broke'r. I sez, 'I eat you up like a dog!'"[32] Allen's referral to a dog offers several possible interpretations. First, it speaks to the nature inherent in dogs. That while they can be docile and tame, they are nonetheless related to the wolf family and can turn very dangerous when hungry or protecting others. Second, Allen's reference to a "dog" is deeply symbolic in a slave society where owners employed dogs to hunt down runaway slaves. In drawing such an analogy Allen reversed the traditional places of mistress and slave.

Encounters in Brazil

In Brazil, slaveholders also animalized their slaves through their language and treatment. Travelers to plantations frequently drew connections between

slaveholders' treatment of slaves as not so dissimilar to and sometimes worse than that of an animal. When observing how slavery perpetually infantilized slaves, Alfred Wallace Russell wrote, "[c]hildhood is the animal part of man's existence, manhood the intellectual."[33] In this way, he spoke to the "animal-ness" of Brazilian slaves. Similarly, Maturin M. Ballou recounted a slaveholder's counsel for the treatment of slaves: "With plenty of food and sleep . . . they are as easily managed as any other domestic animals."[34] Both authors underlined the animalization of slaves. In imagery, the French artist Jean Baptiste Débret portrayed wealthy slave mistresses keeping enslaved children rather like small pet dogs. These children often spent their early years wholly removed from the slave plantations and their respective families. Living in the company of White owners, these children ate succulent delicacies until they reached the age of five or six years. Then, slaveholders cast out these little "pugs" to the slave quarters.[35] This cycle of animalization continued with another generation of slave infants. Other Whites described their slaves as goats. James W. Wells explained that "Bode, a male goat, is a slang term for a mulatto" similarly, "Cabra, a female goat, is a common name for any coloured individual."[36] In these ways, Whites labeled Blacks as animals on a daily basis. Moreover, terms such as "goats, dogs, mules, among others," all denote domesticated animals and suggest how slaveholders could employ slaves to serve their own personal needs. Perhaps this is why we see references to slaves as domestic animals in contrast to wild animals, which were neither tame nor controllable.

Whites further animalized Black bodies and personalities through corporal punishment. Slave owners and overseers could and *did* act with gross brutality. Here foreign visitors drew analogies between such actions as similar to the treatment of animals in their own home countries. During a voyage to Rio de Janeiro, Robert Elwes often saw slaves sporting "an iron collar round the neck, with three hooks sticking out in different directions, designed originally to prevent their running through the woods, just as refractory pigs in England are decorated with a wooden triangle."[37] Through such treatment, Brazilian slaveholders both animalized and dehumanized their slaves. Furthermore, when owners treated enslaved children as "dogs," slaveholders repeatedly underlined the belief that Blacks were like animals. Travelers were not oblivious to such treatment and came to understand the system of slavery as one that animalized and dehumanized Black Africans.

Encounters in Cuba

In Cuba, slaveholders also exhibited similar treatment and animalization of Black bodies. James W. Steele argued that slaveholders treated their chattel

worse in Cuba than in her North American counterpart. He observed how Whites treated slaves "worse than a mule." Steele concluded how slaves appeared "a mere human animal in common appreciation of those who own him . . . and without knowing a moment of peace."[38] Another traveler wrote of the enslaved how slaveholders employed great harshness in "breaking in" their slaves in a manner similar to how one "would break a horse or bullock." He concluded how "it assumed the slave to be a dumb animal, and so left him."[39] Julia Ward Howe in *A Trip to Cuba* wrote how Whites amused themselves with slave children. She remembered watching the elder slaves throwing little bits of "orange or chaimito" to the young children who would quickly "scramble like so many monkeys" to secure a portion of these sweet fruits.[40] These examples highlight how European travelers witnessed how slaveholders animalized slaves on a regular basis.

Whites' language toward slaves highlights a conscious decision to animalize Blacks. Furthermore, this was also highly insensitive to slaves *as* people. Slaves were likely aware of such language given that masters expected slaves to respond to such appellations. During a trip to Cuba, Joseph Judson Dimock spoke of encountering "bozales." Cubans employed this term to denote newly arrived Africans. It spoke of "the most filthy, ignorant and degraded of the human species. In fact [*sic*] they are animal in their natures and nothing else, and it seems almost an impossibility that such beings should possess a mind."[41] One translation of "bozal" means "novice," which fits Dimock's example as those slaves who had only recently arrived from Africa. But another translation defines "bozal" as "muzzle," an implement employed to prevent its wearer—namely dogs—from biting others. In this respect, "bozal" speaks of a deeper animalistic reference.

By means of concluding, the specific word choices to identify slaves reflected and reinforced White racism toward Blacks. Whites often employed the most dehumanizing lexicon when coming face-to-face with slaves. Moreover, European travelers *were aware* of such treatment and wrote about this in their journals. Looking at scientific arguments from the post-Enlightenment period such as the *great chain of being* theory is helpful when reading travel accounts. Furthermore, we have seen how the three slaveholding societies exercised similar treatment toward slaves. Sometimes slaveholders criticized Black males' supposedly "libidinous nature." In other examples, Whites argued that slaves possessed animalistic physique and strength or labeled certain slaves as "bozales," dogs, or goats. Taken together these examples all point to Whites' animalization of Blacks across the nineteenth-century Atlantic world. Finally, the enslaved were well aware of Whites' efforts to not simply construct slaves as the "other" but also to demean them and establish them as less than human.

USE OF ANIMAL IMAGERY TO CONVEY THE COMMODIFICATION OF THE ENSLAVED

Travelers expressed particular interest in witnessing slave sales, especially those visiting from countries or states where slavery did not exist. Abolitionist travelers and writers were wont to draw on both the brutality *and* inhumanity of the auction house. In their writings, they frequently noted the dehumanizing terms that described slaves in advertisements and auctions. Some travelers frequented slave "pens" or spaces that held enslaved men, women, and children before sale. Here, even the employment of the term "pen" underlines an animal connotation and brings to mind images of sheep and pig pens. This section draws together written sources, oral histories, and visual representations to show how the sale of slaves supported Whites' animalization of Black slaves.

Encounters in the U.S. South

When Whites auctioned, traded, and sold slaves, they frequently animalized enslaved persons. Across the U.S. south, in treating slaves like livestock, Whites separated—quite forcibly and often irreversibly—slave families. A former slave cited that "the [W]hite people . . . separated us like dogs." She went on to recount how this had so profound an impact on such individuals that many died from grief.[42] Another ex-slave, Samuel Hall wrote how traders specialized in purchasing enslaved children up until around eight years with the intention of later selling them. Traders fed and cared for these children "like pigs" and raised them "like what you would tell a dog to do." The traders sold the children before they reached adolescence.[43] The similarities between these children's lives and animals are paramount. Artists—both White and Black—portrayed similar visual representations. In Henry Bibb's narrative of his life in slavery, he wrote of the separation of mother and child. He paid special attention to note how the auctioneer ignored the mother's pleas, as he tore the child from the mother's breast.[44]

Slaveholders' language and behavior in the auction house also animalized slaves. As a small boy, George Womble recounted his personal experiences in a slave market. He recollected how a group of doctors examined his health and physique, concluding that Womble was "a thoroughbred boy," with good teeth, muscles, and eyes.[45] Another ex-slave Laura Stewart remembered how traders lined up slaves for sale like "horses or cows, and look in de mouf' at dey teef."[46] It is in this light that we might interpret the image "Dealers Inspecting a Negro at a Slave Auction in Virginia." While a White man lifts the lid of an enslaved man's eye to better inspect his physical health, the slave stands erect with a grotesque smile or grimace on his face. The artist

Figure 1.4 Henry Chamberlain, *Views and Costumes of the City and Neighborhood of Rio de Janeiro, Brazil* . . . (London, 1822). In "Slave Market, Rio de Janeiro, Brazil, 1819–1820," *Slavery Images: A Visual Record of the African Slave Trade and Slave Life in the Early African Diaspora*, accessed November 29, 2020. *Source*: http://slaveryimages.org/s/slaveryimages/item/1942.

depicts the slave's facial expression as resembling a monkey as both startled and obsequious. Across the U.S. south, slaveholders' actions underline the all too frequent animalization of Black slaves. This practice was not age-specific: indeed, slaveholders separated children from parents. Furthermore, this enforced animalization and dehumanization affected both male and female slaves. The sale of slaves deeply resonated with that of animals, as auctioneers and buyers inspected every part of slaves' bodies. The difference was that slaves could speak and were wholly cognizant.

Encounters in Brazil

Brazilian slave markets similarly underscore how such practices animalized and dehumanized slaves. While in Rio de Janeiro, the Frenchman Victor Jacquemont described the system of slavery as one that was lacking in "civilization." Jacquemont wrote of buildings heaving with newly arrived slaves who were "plagued with horrible diseases, heaped together, confused, and dumped like animals following their arrival."[47] In the lithograph "Boutique de la Rue du Val-longo," the artist Jean Baptiste Débret illustrated a storeroom filled with slaves awaiting sale following the crossing from Africa. In contrast with the traders who are neatly dressed, the slaves have nothing with which to clothe their bodies aside from a small wrapper. Like animals, the slaves' bodies remain clearly visible to onlookers.

Pictorial representation of slave markets and the activities within this theater further speak to Whites' animalization of slaves. In the image "Une vente d'esclaves," the painter François-Auguste Biard depicts a slave market also in Rio de Janeiro. Although she is not the center of the image, the lady with the White halo around her draws the viewer's eye immediately. A man counts and assesses the condition of her teeth as one would judge an animal's health before purchase. The artist crudely depicts the slaves' faces with jutting chins and bulging lips suggestive of an ape's phenotype. In contrast, the faces of the White men are much more detailed and display their features as more human. The artist created a juxtaposition in which the White faces appear more humanistic and the Black faces look more animalistic. In a color lithograph Henry Chamberlain also portrays a similar inspection. The viewer's eyes are drawn to the center of the scene in which two beautifully dressed White men stand either side of a slave. In contrast to the White men, the Black female slave is stripped to the waist and barefoot. Despite the misleading shorn head of the slave, her breasts show that this is a woman. The upheld hand of the White man hovers between checking her teeth or moving toward her breasts. When slaveholders shaved their slaves' heads—both male and female—they dehumanized them. This is especially true in Chamberlain's image that contrasts free and enslaved giving the impression of shorn sheep before market. Taken together, these images underline the various ways in which the environment of the slave market dehumanized *and* animalized slaves in the Atlantic world.

Encounters in Cuba

On a voyage to Cuba in the first half of the nineteenth century, Arthur Thomas Quiller-Couch depicted a slave market scene in the capital Havana. In the image, a male slave wears nothing but a loincloth and stands erect with his arms at his side and a blank countenance on his face. In contrast, the two White men—wearing coattails, riding boots, and broad-rimmed sun hats—scrutinize the enslaved man's physique while affecting a nonchalance pose. As with the images and written accounts from the U.S. south and Brazil, this sketch similarly illustrates how Whites dehumanized enslaved Blacks through bodily inspections. One of the White men uses a riding whip to force the slave's head up. The whip—the quintessential implement of castigation in New World slavery—reaffirms the man's status as an enslaved piece of property with a market value. But the riding crop also drips animalistic connotations speaking to notions of control: this object is symbolic of a rider's control over a horse. Taken together, the various components of this image underline animal imagery in a Cuban slave sale transaction.

When slaveholders sold slaves, they commodified them. But they *also* animalized them. Together the images and citations show how public marketplaces in conjunction with the more private spheres (holding cells, etc.), accentuated this animalization, in particular portraying slave as livestock. Before heading to markets, slave traders ushered slaves into pens or cells where they remained before sale. In such instances, travelers and former slaves described their treatment as analogous to that of a horse or livestock animal. Whites' scrutiny of slaves' various body parts spoke to this comparison. Like livestock, slave families were torn apart. Moreover, when taken together such experiences demonstrate parallels across the three slave societies in the dehumanization *and* animalization of enslaved persons. Both Whites and Blacks *were* cognizant of these processes, and this would ultimately shape slaves' attempts to craft a world in which they were *less* like an animal and *more* human.

CONCLUSION

When Antonio Carlo Napoleone Gallenga described slaves as being "fat and sleek and shiny like [B]lack slugs," he penned a written illustration of slaves that drew on the animal world. In so doing, Gallenga sought to convey an animalistic meaning to his readers. But his interpretation also perhaps attests to his personal views of Blacks in addition to any preexisting knowledge of scientific arguments from the nineteenth century. This scholarship argued that the Caucasian occupied a far superior position to the Black African, which was not so far removed from the ape. This chapter has sought to show the frequency with which White travelers drew analogies with the lives of slaves and animals. Looking to the three slave societies of America, Brazil, and Cuba, we see consistent examples throughout the nineteenth-century Atlantic world, which collectively broaden our overall understanding of slavery as an institution. Moreover, we have seen a variety of different experiences and perceptions from many historical actors such as artists, ex-slaves, slaveowners, and travelers. Through looking at themes such as owners' respective treatment of slaves—for example, sale, separation of slave families, heavy physical labor, and mealtimes—and owners' language toward their enslaved property, we see how the system of slavery often animalized and dehumanized those it held in bondage. Visual portrayals of the slave phenotype further underline an interpretation of slaves as similar to those of the animal kingdom. When travelers published such narratives, they played a role in molding perceptions of enslaved Blacks. For their own part, slaves in the U.S. South were not ignorant to such portrayals. In an environment that animalized *and* dehumanized Black Africans, slaves worked to carve an identity for themselves that was humanistic and *not* animalistic in nature. The subsequent chapters explore in greater detail how slaves from across the Atlantic world sought to make this a reality.

NOTES

1. The quotation included in the chapter title comes from the following source: "Born in Slavery: Slave Narratives from the Federal Writers' Project, 1936–1938," last modified March 23, 2001, http://memory.loc.gov/ammem/snhtml/snhome.html. Subsequent citations are referenced as follows: Ohio Narratives, Volume XII, 79.

2. Antonio Carlo Napoleone Gallenga, *The Pearl of the Antilles* (London: Chapman & Hall, 1873), 1.

3. Ibid., 99.

4. See for instance, Edward W. Said, *Orientalism*, Twenty-fifth anniversary edition. (New York: Vintage, 1994).

5. Initially, the Portuguese began the forced migration of Africans to the Americas in the first half of the sixteenth century. While the Portuguese and Spanish metropoles dominated the trans-Atlantic slave trade early on, soon English and French traders monopolized the trade. For a wonderful tool on visualizing the trans-Atlantic slave trade in quantitative format see the Slave Voyages database: https://www.slavevoyages.org/.

6. This was definitely true with respect to mosquito-borne diseases, such as malaria and yellow fever, although scholars today are beginning to question the full truthfulness to these schools of thought. See, for instance, Mariola Espinosa, "The Question of Racial Immunity to Yellow Fever in History and Historiography," *Social Science History*, Vol. 38 (3–4) (2014): 437–53.

7. This theory looked to the Old Testament story where Noah had fallen to a moment of drunkenness and was lying naked in his intoxication, when his youngest son Ham happened across him. Rather than preserving his father's dignity, Ham supposedly led his brothers to look upon the dishonorable scene. They, not wanting to be party to such a sight, brought with them a cloak with which to cover their father's nakedness. When Noah awoke, he is said to have placed a curse on the sons of Ham, stating that they would henceforth be servants and would so remain forevermore. Genesis, 9:20-27; Reverend Josiah Priest, *Bible Defence of Slavery; and Origin Fortunes, and History of the Negro Race* (Glasgow, KY: Rev. W. S. Brown, 1852). For secondary discussions about the Curse of Ham, see, for instance: Sylvester A. Johnson, *The Myth of Ham in Nineteenth-Century American Christianity: Race, Heathens* (New York: Palgrave MacMillan, 2004); Molly Oshatz, *Slavery and Sin: The Fight Against Slavery and the Rise of Liberal Protestantism* (Oxford: Oxford University Press, 2002); Chris L. de Wet, *The Unbound God: Slavery and the Formation of Early Christian Thought* (London: Routledge, 2018); Pius Onyemechi Adiele, *The Popes, the Catholic Church and the Transatlantic Enslavement of*

Black Africans 1418–1839 (Hindesheim: Georg Olms Verlag AG, 2017); Stephen R. Haynes, *Noah's Curse: The Biblical Justification of American Slavery* (Oxford: Oxford University Press, 2002).

8. "Evolutionists'" scholarship was in contrast to another school of "Catastrophists" that purported that God had repeatedly remade the world in a series of sudden events.

9. Nine seminal works include Johann Friedrich Blumenbach and Sir Joseph Banks, *De Generis Humani Varietate Nativa* (Gottingae: Vandenhoek et Ruprecht, 1795); Caroli Linnaei, *Systema Naturae per Regna Tria Naturae* (Holmiae: Impensis Direct, 1758); Jean-Baptiste Lamarck, *Philosophie Zoologique* (Paris: Dentu, 1809); Henri Marie Ducrotay de Blainville, *De l'organisation des Animaux, ou Principes d'Anatomie Compare* (Paris: Chez F. G. Levrault, 1822.).

10. Nancy Stepan, *The Idea of Race in Science: Great Britain, 1800–1960* (London: The Macmillan Press Ltd., 1982), 6.

11. The five races were the Caucasian (White), Mongolian (Yellow), Malayan (Brown), Negro (Black), and the American [Indian] (Red). See Blumenbach and Banks, *De Generis Humani Varietate Nativa*, 286, 289.

12. Texas Narratives, Volume II, 401.

13. Oklahoma Narratives, Volume XII, Supplement, Series 1, 80. For another example see Octavia V. Rogers Albert, *The House of Bondage, or, Charlotte Brooks and Other Slaves, Original and Life Like . . .* (New York: Hunt and Eaton, 1890), 22. See also Texas Narratives, Volume XVI, Part 3, 213.

14. Francis Fedric, *Slave Life in Virginia and Kentucky; or, Fifty Years of Slavery in the Southern States of America* (London: Wertheim, Macintosh and Hunt, 1863), 5.

15. Over half of the WPA interviewees were still under the age of ten when the institution of antebellum slavery came to an end.

16. Charles Wilkes, *Voyage round the World, Embracing the Principal Events of the Narrative of the United States Exploring Expedition* (Philadelphia: Geo. W. Gorton, 1849), 25.

17. Maturin M. Ballou, *Equatorial America Descriptive of a Visit to St. Thomas Martinique, Barbados, and the Principal Capitals of South America* (Boston: Houghton, Mifflin and Company, 1892), 110.

18. Jean Jacques Ampère, *Promenade en Amérique, États-Unis - Cuba – Mexique* (Paris: Michel Levy Frères, Libraires-Éditeurs, 1860), 146–47. Authors' translation.

19. Louis A. Pérez, *Impressions of Cuba in the Nineteenth Century: The Travel Diary of Joseph J. Dimock* (Lanham, MD: SR Books, 1998), 12.

20. Tennessee Narratives, Volume XV, 12.

21. Florida Narratives, Volume XVII, 337. A wide literature exists regarding the practice of slave "breeding" across the Atlantic world.

22. Frances Anne Kemble, *Journal of a Residence on a Georgian Plantation in 1838-1839* (New York: Harper & Brothers Publishers, 1863), 122.

23. Kansas, Kentucky, Maryland, Ohio, Virginia, and Tennessee Narratives, Volume 16, 72.

24. Elizabeth Fox-Genovese, *Within the Plantation Household: Black and White Women of the Old South* (Chapel Hill: The University of North Carolina Press, 1988), 291.

25. Norman R. Yetman, ed., *Voices from Slavery: 100 Authentic Slave Narratives* (Mineola, NY: Dover Publications, Inc., 2012), 322.

26. Ibid.

27. Ibid.

28. Texas Narratives, Volume 6, Supplement Series 2, Part 5, 2178.

29. Ernest Duvergier de Hauranne, *A Frenchman in Lincoln's America*, Vol. II (Chicago: R. R. Donnelley & Sons Company, n.d.), 464. See also Ohio Narratives, Volume XII, 79.

30. Texas Narratives, Volume 4, Supplement Series 2, 1100.

31. Alabama Narratives, Volume XVI, Part 2, 1344.

32. Indiana and Ohio Narratives, Volume 5, 3.

33. Alfred Russell Wallace, *A Narrative of Travels on the Amazon and Rio Negro: with an Account of the Native Tribes, and Observations on the Climate, Geology, and Natural History of the Amazon Valley* (London: Reeve and Co., 1853), 122.

34. Ballou, *Equatorial America Descriptive of a Visit to St. Thomas Martinique*, 278.

35. Jean Baptiste Débret, *Voyage Pittoresque et Historique au Brésil: Séjour d'un Artiste Français au Brésil. Tome III* (Paris: Firmin Didot Frères, 1834), 39.

36. James W. Wells, *Exploring and Travelling Three Thousand Miles through Brazil from Rio de Janeiro to Maranhão*, Vol. II (London: Sampson Low, Marston, Searle & Rivington, 1887), 16.

37. Robert Elwes, *A Sketcher's Tour Round the World* (London: n.d., 1854), 30.

38. James W. Steele, *Cuba Sketches* (New York: G. P. Putnam's Sons, 1881), 88.

39. Gallenga, *The Pearl of the Antilles*, 107.

40. Julia Ward Howe, *A Trip to Cuba* (New York: Negro Universities Press, n.d.), 76–77.

41. Pérez, *Impressions of Cuba in the Nineteenth Century*, 98.

42. Rogers Albert, *The House of Bondage*, 22.

43. Samuel Hall, *47 Years a Slave; A Brief Story of His Life Before and After Freedom Came to Him* (Washington: Journal Print, 1912), 37. See also an account by Jack Terriell in Texas Narratives, Supplement, Series 2, Volume 9, Part 8, 3774.

44. Henry Bibb, *Narrative of The Life and Adventures of Henry Bibb, an American Slave, Written by Himself with an Introduction by Lucius C. Matlack* (New York: Published by the author, 1849), 202. By positioning the enslaved woman in a half-kneeling stance, Bibb makes a symbolic reference to the English anti-slavery icon "Aren't I a man and a brother?"

45. Georgia Narratives, Volume IV, Part 4, 180.

46. Georgia Narratives, Volume 4, Supplement, Series 1, Part 2, 594. Basil Hall's autobiography makes numerous references to the sale of slaves as being analogous to that of selling horses and cattle. Basil Hall, *Forty Etchings from Sketches Made with the Camera Lucida* (Edinburgh: Cadell & Co., 1829), 205.

47. Text in the original reads: "bâtimens [*sic*] chargés de ces malheureux, couverts de maladies affreuses, entassés, confondus, parqûes comme des animaux à leur débarquement." Victor Jacquement, *Voyage dans L'Inde, par Victor Jacquemont, pendant les Années 1828 à 1832* (Paris: Firmin Didot Frères, 1841), 28.

BIBLIOGRAPHY

Ampère, Jean Jacques. *Promenade en Amérique, États-Unis—Cuba—Mexique*. Paris: Michel Levy Frères, Libraires-Éditeurs, 1860.

Ballou, Maturin M. *Equatorial America Descriptive of a Visit to St. Thomas Martinique, Barbados, and the Principal Capitals of South America*. Boston: Houghton, Mifflin and Company, 1892.

Bibb, Henry. *Narrative of The Life and Adventures of Henry Bibb, an American Slave, Written by Himself with an Introduction by Lucius C. Matlack*. New York: Published by the author, 1849.

Blainville, Ducrotay de and Henri Marie. *De l'Organisation des Animaux, ou Principes d'Anatomie Compare*. Paris: Chez F. G. Levrault, 1822.

Blumenbach, Johann Friedrich and Sir Joseph Banks, *De Generis Humani Varietate Nativa*. Gottingae: Vandenhoek et Ruprecht, 1795.

"Born in Slavery: Slave Narratives from the Federal Writers' Project, 1936–1938," last modified March 23, 2001, http://memory.loc.gov/ammem/snhtml/snhome.html.

De Wet, Chris L., *The Unbound God: Slavery and the Formation of Early Christian Thought*. London: Routledge, 2018.

Débret, Jean Baptiste, *Voyage Pittoresque et Historique au Brésil : Séjour d'un Artiste Français au Brésil. Tome III*. Paris: Firmin Didot Frères, 1834.

Duvergier de Hauranne, Ernest. *A Frenchman in Lincoln's America*. Volumr II. Chicago: R. R. Donnelley & Sons Company, n.d.

Elwes, Robert. *A Sketcher's Tour Round the World*. London: n.d., 1854.

Espinosa, Mariola. "The Question of Racial Immunity to Yellow Fever in History and Historiography." *Social Science History* 38 (3–4) (2014): 437–53.

Fedric, Francis. *Slave Life in Virginia and Kentucky; or, Fifty Years of Slavery in the Southern States of America*. London: Wertheim, Macintosh and Hunt, 1863.

Fox-Genovese, Elizabeth. *Within the Plantation Household: Black and White Women of the Old South*. Chapel Hill: The University of North Carolina Press, 1988.

Gallenga, Antonio Carlo Napoleone. *The Pearl of the Antilles*. London: Chapman & Hall, 1873.

Hall, Ball. *Forty Etchings from Sketches Made with the Camera Lucida*. Edinburgh: Cadell & Co., 1829.

Hall, Samuel. *47 Years a Slave; A Brief Story of His Life Before and After Freedom Came to Him*. Washington: Journal Print, 1912.

Haynes, Stephen R. *Noah's Curse: The Biblical Justification of American Slavery*. Oxford: Oxford University Press, 2002.

Jacquement, Victor. *Voyage dans L'Inde, par Victor Jacquemont, pendant les Années 1828 à 1832*. Paris: Firmin Didot Frères, 1841.

Johnson, Sylvester A. *The Myth of Ham in Nineteenth-Century American Christianity: Race, Heathens*. New York: Palgrave MacMillan, 2004.

Kemble, Frances Anne. *Journal of a Residence on a Georgian Plantation in 1838-1839*. New York: Harper & Brothers Publishers, 1863.

Lamarck, Jean-Baptiste. *Philosophie Zoologique*. Paris: Dentu, 1809.

Linnaei, Caroli. *Systema Naturae per Regna Tria Naturae*. Holmiae: Impensis Direct, 1758.

Onyemechi Adiele, Pius. *The Popes, the Catholic Church and the Transatlantic Enslavement of Black Africans 1418–1839*. Hindesheim: Georg Olms Verlag AG, 2017.

Oshatz, Molly. *Slavery and Sin: The Fight Against Slavery and the Rise of Liberal Protestantism* Oxford: Oxford University Press, 2002.

Pérez, Louis A. *Impressions of Cuba in the Nineteenth Century: The Travel Diary of Joseph J. Dimock*. Lanham, MD: SR Books, 1998.

Priest, Reverend Josiah. *Bible Defence of Slavery; and Origin Fortunes, and History of the Negro Race*. Glasgow, KY: Rev. W. S. Brown, 1852.

Rogers Albert, Octavia V. *The House of Bondage, or, Charlotte Brooks and Other Slaves, Original and Life Like, As They Appeared in Their Old Plantation and City Slave Life*. New York: Hunt and Eaton, 1890.

Russell Wallace, Alfred. *A Narrative of Travels on the Amazon and Rio Negro: with an Account of the Native Tribes, and Observations on the Climate, Geology, and Natural History of the Amazon Valley*. London: Reeve and Co., 1853.

Said, Edward W. *Orientalism*, Twenty-fifth anniversary edition. New York: Vintage, 1994.

Slave Voyages database: https://www.slavevoyages.org/.

Steele, James W. *Cuba Sketches*. New York: G. P. Putnam's Sons, 1881.

Stepan, Nancy. *The Idea of Race in Science: Great Britain, 1800–1960*. London: The Macmillan Press Ltd., 1982.

Ward Howe, Julia, *A Trip to Cuba*. New York: Negro Universities Press, n.d.

Wells, James W. *Exploring and Travelling Three Thousand Miles through Brazil from Rio de Janeiro to Maranhão*. Volume II. London: Sampson Low, Marston, Searle & Rivington, 1887.

Wilkes, Charles. *Voyage round the World, Embracing the Principal Events of the Narrative of the United States Exploring Expedition*. Philadelphia: Geo. W. Gorton, 1849.

Yetman, Norman R., ed. *Voices from Slavery: 100 Authentic Slave Narratives*. Mineola, NY: Dover Publications, Inc., 2012.

Chapter 2

Slave to Soldier

United States Colored Troops in the West During the Civil War

Scott L. Stabler and Martin J. Hershock

"Once you let the black man get upon his person the brass letters U.S.; let him get an eagle on his button, and a musket on his shoulder and bullets in his pocket and there is no power on the earth . . . which can deny that he has earned the right of citizenship in the United States," said Frederick Douglass in 1863.[1] President Abraham Lincoln agreed. In March of that year, he wrote, "The bare sight of fifty thousand armed, and drilled black soldiers standing on the banks of the Mississippi, would end the rebellion."[2] Black troops did not just wear the ornaments of a soldier or "stand" on the banks of the Mississippi River in 1863. On the contrary, as Douglass and Lincoln expected, they served in crucial roles and fought bravely to not only aid freedom for their own race but also to preserve the country that they too called home. Recalling a story that his father, a slave near Augusta, Georgia, told him about the coming of freedom, Eugene Valsey Smith related, "When the colored troops came in, they came in playing:

Don't you see the lightning
Don't you hear the thunder
It isn't the lightning
It isn't the thunder
But the buttons on the Negro uniform![3]

The song, the uniform, the weapon, the presence, the awareness, and the pride are represented clearly in this photo of Private Hubbard Pryor (pictured both before and after the war) that nicely captures the transition from slavery to soldier.

Figure 2.1 Hubbard Pryor before and after Enlistment in the 44th U.S. Colored Troops, April 7, 1864. Courtesy of Photographer T.B. Bishop, RG 94: Records of the Adjutant General's Office, Series: Letters Received, 1863–1888; National Archives and Records Administration, Washington, D.C. *Source*: [retrieved from the digital National Archives Catalog at https://catalog.archives.gov/id/849127 and https://catalog.archives.gov/id/849136; December 1, 2020].

Until the late twentieth century, most would not know that African Americans even fought during the Civil War. On October 16, 1905, a letter to the editor of the *New York Sun* expressed the belief that Black soldiers had *not* actively participated in the conflict, "Can it be proved that any of our colored soldiers killed any rebels? If so, where?"[4] Historians of the same era, most of them White men, held a predilection for White generals or for their White soldiers. Indeed, many would have agreed with White historian W. E. Woodward's 1928 claim that "The American negroes are the only people in the history of the world, so far as I know, that ever became free without any effort of their own."[5] More troubling, however, is the lingering spell that such thinking has cast over this narrative. Fortunately, contemporary scholars (beginning with African American historian Benjamin Quarles' 1953 *The Negro in the Civil War*) recognized the agency and salience Black troops provided in facilitating their own freedom. As James McPherson wrote in his 1965 work *The Negro's Civil War*, "Perhaps most importantly of all, the contribution of Negro soldiers helped the North win the war and convinced many Northern people that the Negro deserved to be treated as a man and an equal."[6] McPherson's assertion comports with the perspective of the Black soldiers themselves. While being interviewed at his home in Gary, Indiana, former slave and U.S. soldier John Eubanks offered the following assessment of the impact of Black soldiers on the outcome of the war: "Since Lee was a proud southerner and did not want the negro present when he surrendered, Grant probably for this reason as much as any other refused to accept Lee's sword."[7]

Subsequent scholars have validated the importance that Eubanks attributed to African American military service during the war. Still, in doing so, the vast majority focus on only a few incidents: the Battle of the Crater, Fort Pillow, or the assault on Fort Wagner carried out by the Fifty-Fourth Massachusetts U.S. Colored Troops (USCT) and featured in the movie *Glory*. Even in this movie, praised as a long overdue corrective to the popular narrative that ignores the service of Black troops in the war, the White Matthew Broderick, as Robert Gould Shaw, serves as the primary focus. Despite increased attention, little scholarship exists on Black soldiers in the Western Theatre where they were numerous, active, agents of change, as much if not more so than in the East. In one sense, the western Black troops have achieved a semblance of equality with their White peers as this theater has long been treated as less significant and consequential than the more famous, and, from the perspective of the prevailing Lost Cause ideology that has dominated the general historical narrative on the war, more heroic and successful eastern theater featuring generals Robert E. Lee and Stonewall Jackson. Black troops, like their peers in the East, largely fought peripherally in major battles, yet that does not make their contributions insignificant. Indeed, beyond the important martial actions taken on the battlefield by these troops, the existence of Black soldiers in the West, fighting for the freedom of themselves, their families, and their peers, primarily in the heart of the Southern Black Belt, stood as a direct affront to southern White claims about Black docility and terrifyingly brought to life Whites' worst fears—the ever-present threat posed by the large numbers of aggrieved Blacks in their midst. This mix of tangible gain by dint of arms and symbolic force derived from their mere existence as Black soldiers in the heart of the Confederacy, had profound consequences for southern White morale and turned the tide of war. This chapter focuses on the efforts of the USCT west of the Appalachian Mountains and east of the Mississippi River and their agency during America's bloodiest conflict.

Beyond any doubt, Black troops, though organized late in the war, played a crucial role. In so doing, they affirmed their own claim to equality and swayed northern popular opinion about their abilities. Roughly 15 percent of the Union Army at war's end consisted of African American soldiers. That amounts to 188,571 men in 178 regiments, which held only 33,000 recruits from the free states. That number was equivalent to 20 percent of the overall strength of Confederate forces. USCT men had a 20 percent death rate—3 percent higher than White soldiers—though they faced much less combat. In yet another case of racial disparity, disease ran rampant among Black troops taking 90 percent of the 37,000 African Americans that died. The 65th USCT regiment, which consisted of two thousand men, had more deaths than any other regiment in the Union Army and yet had zero battlefield losses. However, despite being disproportionately held back from combat, twenty-four African Americans still won the Medal of Honor. Most importantly, the USCT turned the conflict from one of union to one of emancipation. Many of these men also served in the Reconstruction army and became leaders in the postwar South. The Union Army ended the war in April 1865 at 15 percent Black and by November that number stood at 36 percent.[8]

The path to enlistment for Black men during the Civil War was a contested one. Though President Abraham Lincoln privately endorsed mustering Black troops early in the war, he feared White backlash especially in the tenuous border states of Maryland, Delaware, Kentucky, and Missouri. "To arm the negroes," he wrote, "would turn 50,000 bayonets from the loyal Border States against us that were for us."[9] Frederick Douglass, on the other hand, immediately recognized the significance of Black troops for the Union cause. In a May 1861 newspaper column, "How to End the War," Douglass wrote, "Let the slaves and free colored people be called into service, and formed into a liberating army, to march into the South and raise the banner of emancipation among the slaves."[10]

Lincoln's reticence to use Black soldiers, however, proved insufficient in thwarting those determined to tap into this ready source of military manpower. Faced with the reality of occupying and administering a hostile population deep within the Confederacy, and confronted with a flood of fugitive slaves flocking to his lines, General Benjamin Butler commander of Union forces in the recently captured city of New Orleans, on August 22, 1862, issued his General Orders 63, calling on the free colored militiamen of Louisiana to enroll as volunteers in the Union army. By limiting his call to free Blacks already organized into legally authorized militia units, Butler avoided the thorny issue of arming former slaves, though he still enlisted Black soldiers for military duty without formal federal authorization to do so.[11]

Not until January 1863, with the implementation of the Emancipation Proclamation, however, were Black troops officially accepted on an unrestricted basis, into the U.S. army. Lincoln defended his decision as a war measure. In issuing the Proclamation he confided, "I thought that whatever negroes can be got to do as soldiers, leaves just so much less for white soldiers to do, in saving the Union." He continued, "[I] believe the emancipation policy and the use of colored troops constitute the heaviest blow yet dealt to the rebellion."[12]

In May 1863 as recruitment began in earnest, the War Department created the Bureau of Colored Troops. White backlash followed quickly, especially from Democrats who tended to be more antiwar than Republicans. The Democratic *Detroit Free Press* published an article from an unnamed soldier the next month that portrays a common theme—fear. The White soldier wrote, "If they make negroes soldiers and place them on an equality with the white soldier, they must give him all the rights and privileges of a white soldier. Equal political privileges must soon lead to equal social privileges, and then the intelligent, well-educated negro, though black as night, will come to these people and demand their fair daughters, and take them too."[13] Many also feared Black troops would not fight. Captain Henry Romeyn of the Fourteenth USCT recalled that the arming of Blacks elicited remarks of intense dislike and distrust, such as "The nigger won't fight" and "No white private will ever take orders from a nigger Sergeant!"[14] In a caustic editorial titled "The Enrollment of the Negro Soldier—Utter Futility of the Idea," the *New York Herald* dismissed the idea of employing Black soldiers as "an absolute waste of time and money . . . it is worse than ridiculous to talk of arming ignorant negro slaves, who have neither inclination nor intelligence for so important a work."[15]

Others viewed the opportunity presented more optimistically. In response to the question, "What is your opinion of the possibility of arming the negro?" asked by the General Superintendent of Contrabands in the Department of Tennessee, in February 1863, the Superintendent of the Memphis region replied,

> Yes, arm him! It will do him worlds of good. He will know then he has rights, and dare maintain them—a grand step towards manhood. Arm him! For our country needs soldiers. These men will make good soldiers. Arm him!–for the rebels need enemies, & heaven knows the blacks have reason to be that . . . Arm him, & let the world see the black man on a vast scale returning good for evil, helping with blood and life the cause of the race which hated, oppressed & scorned him.[16]

Such voices were, in early 1863, however, a distinct minority.

Racial prejudice continued to stymie efforts to place Black soldiers on an equal footing with Whites.[17] They made less money ($7 rather than $16) to start. Congress rectified this, but not until June 1864.[18] The *New York Herald* propped up this view arguing that

> these people can be serviceably employed in a variety of ways—on the trenches, in creating fortifications, in ploughing up the fields for cultivation, and in ministering to the many wants of the advancing army. Let their services be employed

in any way; but to enroll them as soldiers is to demoralize the regular army and to increase the difficulties we would avoid.[19]

General William T. Sherman proscribed Black soldiers from his command and used them predominantly as common laborers. The commander even banned their recruitment stating, "I believe that negroes better serve the Army as teamsters, pioneers, and servants, and have no objection to the surplus, if any, being enlisted as soldiers, but I must have labor and a large quantity of it."[20]

Aside from pervasive racial discrimination, Black enlistees, most of whom, skeptics noted had spent their lives in servile subordination, also faced the belief that they would prove unreliable in battle. One Democratic speaker in October 1864 exemplified this skepticism asserting: "Now this business of Negro soldiers is one of the most contemptible and foolish in which the pre-eminently foolish administration has ever been engaged. Where have they done any good? Where have they stood under fire?"[21] Again, Sherman's views are illustrative of the point. In a letter to General-in-Chief Henry Halleck, Sherman plainspokenly wrote,

> I have had the question put to me often: "Is not a negro as good as a white man to stop a bullet?" Yes, and a sandbag is better; but can a negro do our skirmishing and picket duty? Can they improvise roads, bridges, sorties, flank movements, like the white man? I say no. Soldiers must and do many things without orders from their own sense, as in sentinels. Negroes are not equal to this.[22]

Time and expediency eventually worked to overcome such inhibitions, though progress came in fits and starts. Many of the newly freed men exhibited signs of abuse, both physical and emotional. While some bore scars from whips and lashes on their bodies, others who were unaccustomed to full rations, habitually consumed several days' worth of in a single sitting. Many men also required instruction and encouragement in acquiring desirable military attributes related to manly comportment and personal hygiene—this due to a lifetime of forced labor as slaves. Despite these initial hurdles, most recruits proved quick studies and within a short time overcame a number of unhealthy habits. With these changes also came a pride in their appearance in full regulation Union blue uniform.[23]

Transformation in attitudes toward Blacks in the army, however, came as some White soldiers concluded that a black body could stop a bullet as well as a white one. As a columnist for the *Milwaukee Sentinel* put it, "As soon as it becomes a matter of life and death, as indeed it has, men will not hesitate long between the question of black or white, and saving their bodies from being pierced with the bullet of a rebel."[24] The best example of transformation came from an Illinois private. In a March 1863 letter to his wife, Charles Willis of the Eighth Illinois, initially compared USCT troops to eight-year-olds. Only one month later though, he made an "honest confession." At that time, he wished to "put muskets in the hands of the latter." By June, he had come 180 degrees writing home that he was considering "applying for a position in a [Black] regiment myself." This change in Union soldiers' outlooks continued throughout the war as Black troops proved their mettle in battle.[25] Attitudes also changed when, in the same month as Willis's letter, the draft of Whites between twenty and forty-five commenced in earnest. While some Whites disdained African Americans for this military need for more soldiers (the war had now become a fight for emancipation), others saw an opportunity in the pool of Black men a way to help meet draft quotas. For this latter group, they viewed Blacks in arms a positive addition to the Union Army.[26]

Brigadier General Lorenzo Thomas arrived in the West in early 1863 and took charge of recruiting men for the USCT. On April 8, 1863, Thomas spoke at Lake Providence, Louisiana. There he implored White soldiers to support Lincoln's call to enlist Blacks and to welcome them into the army.[27]

> You know full well, for you have been over this country . . . that the rebels have sent into the field all their available fighting men—every man capable of bearing arms against us, and have kept their slaves at home to raise the means of subsistence for this army. In this way he can bring to bear against us all of the strength of the so-called Southern Confederacy, whilst we at the North can only send into the field a portion of our whites, being compelled to leave at home another portion to cultivate our fields and raise supplies . . . The administration has determined to take from these rebels that source of supply; to take their negroes and compel them to send back a portion of their whites . . . I am here this day, to say that I am authorized to raise as many regiments of blacks as can possibly be collected.[28]

Thomas's appeal drew an immediate response. "Within twenty-four hours," the *Milwaukee Daily Sentinel* reported, "there was over a hundred and fifty applications for commissions in the negro units." Additionally, it noted, "four negro regiments were organized, under the supervision of General Thomas, and . . . others will speedily be organized."[29] Three of Thomas's early regiments served at the Battle of Milliken's Bend. By war's end, Thomas had helped enroll 76,000 Black troops, nearly half of the 180,000 total that joined the USCT.[30]

Early on, officials of the Bureau of Colored Troops determined that only White officers of high caliber could lead Black troops. In a civil service-style policy shift, the United States Army made a conscious effort to match skill and leadership ability to job demands.[31] Advocating a greater degree of professionalism for commanders of Black troops than White, examination boards felt duty bound to produce the best White leaders possible to command Black troops.[32] A part of this determination connected to the fact that officers of "colored troops" faced additional challenges not presented to their counterparts in White units. This was because service within a Black unit could be life-threatening off the field as well as in battle because members of USCT units suffered greater animosity from their enemies than their White Union counterparts. For Black soldiers, capture meant re-enslavement or execution.[33] White officers leading these troops likewise faced possible execution upon capture. For instance, on December 20, 1864, soon after the Battle of Nashville, Captain Charles G. Penfield, of the 44th USCT, Lt. Fitch of the 12th USCT and Lt. Cooke of the 17th USCT were captured. These White officers were marched to Columbia, Tennessee, and shot. Left for dead, Fitch survived the assault and escaped to tell the tale.[34]

The importance of armed Black soldiers in the Western Theater cannot be overstated. Beyond their crucial martial contributions, the very existence of Black troops in the heart of the southern slave empire was of tremendous symbolic importance and sapped southern White morale. These troops also stood as a potent symbol of and call for further self-emancipation for the region's African American population. Lincoln was not wrong to situate his then fictitious Black army on the banks of the Mississippi River. It was in the West, after all, where cotton was truly king and where the largest concentrations of slaves could be found. In the states comprising the Western Theater lived nearly 2,000,000 persons of African descent, the overwhelming majority of them slaves. The bonded, in fact, represented just under 42 percent of the region's overall population. Watching the Union put arms into the hands of this population, and then witnessing their former slaves' eagerness to use these arms against their former masters was nothing short of nightmarish for the region's already skittish White population; this action undermined the White southern will to fight. As Confederate Major General Patrick R. Cleburne wrote after the fall of Vicksburg, "slavery, from being one of our chief sources of strength at the commencement of the war, has now become, in a military point of view, one of our chief sources of weakness."[35] More pointedly, Louisianan Sarah Wadley noted, "[I]t is terrible to think of . . . white men and freemen fighting with their slaves, and to be killed by such a hand, the very soul revolts from it."[36] The sight of armed Black soldiers, authorized and empowered to kill, like the two USCT pickets pictured here, certainly stirred angst among White Confederates.

In the West, African American soldiers took part in many engagements, more so, in fact, than their counterparts in the East. Their pluck and steadfast determination but more important still, their actions, directly freed others and

Figure 2.2 Picket Station of Colored Troops Near Dutch Gap, Virginia. Civil war photographs, 1861–1865. *Source*: Courtesy of Library of Congress, Prints and Photographs Division, LC-DIG-cwpb-01930. https://www.loc.gov/item/2018670817/.

furthered the cause of emancipation while also advancing the Union goals of gaining and retaining possession of western lands.

As mentioned, General Butler began recruiting African American soldiers as early as August 1862. It was not until nearly nine months later, however, as Union armies moved north along the Mississippi River from New Orleans and south from Memphis toward the Confederate stronghold of Vicksburg that they would see their first action, at Port Hudson, Louisiana.

The twenty siege guns and thirty-one field guns posted in parapets along Port Hudson's bluffs posed a major obstacle to Union shipping and the effort to support Ulysses S. Grant's operations at Vicksburg, thus Grant ordered General Nathaniel Banks to neutralize it. After initially moving inland to cut off the port's supply line, Banks turned his 13,000 troops, including the 1st and 3rd Louisiana USCT, toward Port Hudson. By May 22, Banks had the post surrounded. Combat came to the USCT four days later. With verve, the USCT made seven separate assaults on Confederate positions, each stalling at an 8 × 30 foot entrenchment fifty yards in front of the enemy guns. In only a few short hours, the 1,080 USCT on the field incurred 308 casualties.

The unsuccessful attack marked the first engagement of any significance between Black and White troops in the Civil War. The African American soldiers performed very well. One Union officer described the Black troops' valor, "When we made two separate charges each in the face of heavy fire whose destructive guns would have confuse [*sic*] and almost disorganized the bravest troops. But these men did not swerve, or show cowardice. I have been in several engagements, and I ever before beheld such coolness and daring. Their gallantry entitles them to special praise. And I already observe the sneers of others are being tempered into eulogy."[37] It was this May assault that began to establish the reputation of the USCT.[38]

Later that summer, as his grip tightened on Vicksburg, Grant focused his attention on protecting his army's perimeter on the Louisiana side of the Mississippi River. The Union held three key positions here that, if lost, would allow General John C. Pemberton, the Confederate commander at Vicksburg, to resupply, thus breaking Grant's siege of the city. The USCT manned, in significant numbers, two of these positions, Milliken's Bend and Lake Providence. On June 7, Confederate General Richard Taylor tried to dislodge the Yankees from the aforementioned locations. The Confederates failed in their endeavor. At both Milliken's Bend and Lake Providence, the USCT performed bravely.[39]

At Milliken's Bend, as the rebel forces bore down on the Federal position, they met a frightful volley from the Union line which led the Confederates to "waver [*sic*] and recoil, a number running in confusion to the rear," wrote Union General Elias S. Dennis in his official report.[40] The rebels, however, quickly regained their composure and rushed forward, cresting the defensive walls. As the Union center, held by the 160 men of the White 23rd Iowa, gave way many of the unit's officers fled to boats docked along the shore.[41] Braver officers rallied the retreating Iowans, however, and they were immediately joined by their Black compatriots who, according to the *New York Herald*, "came up with volley after volley delivered with good effect and rapidity" driving the rebels back with much loss of life.[42] The battle devolved into hand-to-hand combat with bayonets and rifle butts serving as the primary weapons. The Confederate commander reported, "[our] charge was resisted by the negro portion of the enemy's force with considerable obstinacy, while the white or true Yankee portion ran like whipped curs almost as soon as the charge was ordered."[43] Indeed, the *Chicago Tribune* reported in its June 18, 1863 edition, "It is said that the colored men paid off the enemy man for man, and perhaps, a little more, for their inhumanity."[44]

Despite the USCT's best efforts and heavy loses, the Union line melted until the federal gunboat *Choctaw* arrived on the scene and forced the advancing rebel troops to retreat. The Confederates suffered 185 casualties while inflicting 652 upon the Union (63 killed and 130 wounded in the 9th Louisiana, African Descent alone, making for a 60 percent casualty rate) with 266 of these missing, including many fleeing White officers.[45]

Another skirmish during the Vicksburg Campaign showed a different type of engagement. It came five miles north of Goodrich Landing, at a place known locally as Mound Plantation, where Colonel William H. Parsons' Confederate troopers encountered two companies of the 1st Arkansas Infantry African Descent. These units, part of the force just recently recruited and organized locally by General Lorenzo Thomas, had only arrived on the plantation two weeks prior and likely trooped off to their new assignment singing the marching song (sung to the tune of John Brown's Body) penned for the unit by their New York born abolitionist commander:

We have done with hoeing cotton, we have done with hoeing corn,
We are colored Yankee soldiers, now, as sure as you are born;
When the masters hear us yelling, they'll think its Gabriel's horn,
As we go marching on.[46]

Here they entrenched in a strong position atop an Indian mound. Confederate officers reported that the position "was of great strength, and would have cost us many lives and much precious time to have captured by assault."[47] The Black troops, however, faced far greater numbers and, in an act of cowardice, their White officers winnowed and surrendered to the Confederates on condition that they be treated as prisoners of war while their Black soldiers were to be treated unconditionally.[48]

Upon surrender, the 113 African American soldiers and the three White officers of the 1st Arkansas endured brutal treatment by their captors, especially when they were handed off to the 22nd Texas, one of the units that had fought at Milliken's Bend. As one private in the unit recounted, "twelve or fifteen" of the African American soldiers were killed before the POWs even reached the holding area designated for them.[49] A survivor of the ordeal, Lewis Bogan, recalled, being allowed to stop "to get something to eat and the alarm was given 'the Yankees are coming' & they started us along again and I was very tired & fell & Jim helped me up; when one of the rebel guards, a soldier, told Jim to let go of me & another . . . gave out just then & they shot him." Another Bogan, Charles, also vividly remembered, "I know we were threatened with hanging & killing every minute & we were pretty badly scared."[50] Writing shortly after the engagement, Confederate Major General

John G. Walker lamented, "I consider it an unfortunate circumstance that any armed negroes were captured."[51]

Nevertheless, Grant prevailed at Vicksburg. In the aftermath, the commander's attention shifted eastward to Chattanooga, where General William Rosecrans commanded the Union Army of the Cumberland. After a disastrous defeat in north Georgia on Chickamauga Creek in mid-September, Rosecrans found his legion under siege by Braxton Bragg's Confederate army. In October, Grant was ordered to Chattanooga to assume command. In preparation for his army's move in relief of Rosecrans, Grant relegated his USCT forces to support/logistical roles. Some USCT units would thus accompany him to Chattanooga while others were left behind to protect recent Union gains. All the while, new African American recruits from the region eagerly enlisted into newly created USCT regiments. Grant's stunning victory at Chattanooga in late November, 1863 and stalemate in the Eastern Theater, quickly led to his being named General-in-Chief of all Union armies on March 9, 1864. Before departing for Washington, Grant appointed his most trusted general, William Tecumseh Sherman, as commander of all Union forces in the Western Theater.

Though USCT men largely performed occupation duty, this did not alleviate risk as proven by the massacre at Fort Pillow. A small, poorly designed outpost forty miles north of Memphis on the Mississippi River, Fort Pillow became the target of Confederate Major General Nathan Bedford Forrest (a prewar slave trader who later went on to become the first Grand Wizard of the Ku Klux Klan after the war) and his troopers as part of a campaign of raids to capture men, supplies, and to destroy Union fortifications in March/April of 1864. After an unsuccessful assault on the Union fort at Paducah, Kentucky, Forrest turned his roughly 7,000 men south and set his sights on Fort Pillow. Just over 500 men defended the fort, slightly more than half of whom were members of the recently arrived 6th U.S. Colored Heavy Artillery. Throughout the day fighting raged between the fort's defenders and Forrest's men. At 3:00 p.m., a truce was called and Forrest demanded the surrender of the fort. In spite of being heavily outnumbered, the Union troops refused. The Confederates quickly renewed their assault and rapidly overwhelmed the fort. The ensuing bloodshed was unprecedented with Forrest's men engaging in the slaughter of the garrison, especially its African American soldiers, as they attempted surrender or as they lay wounded along the banks of the Mississippi.[52]

Black soldiers were wantonly killed at Fort Pillow. As one badly wounded White survivor later recalled, "many of the colored soldiers, seeing that no quarters were to be given, madly leaped into the river, while the rebels stood on the banks or part way up the bluff, and shot at the heads of their victims. From where I fell wounded, I could plainly see this firing and note the bullets striking the water around the black heads of the soldiers, until suddenly the muddy current became red and I saw another life sacrificed in the cause of the Union." After being dragged out of a building set alight by Forrest's men as they withdrew on, April 13, the wounded man "heard considerable firing near me on different parts of the field, and presently a rebel soldier walked past me, halted, and with a curse aimed his gun at a wounded colored soldier who lay with his head and shoulders resting against a stump, some ten or twelve yards away. The soldier begged for his life, but the next instant a bullet crashed through his brain. Another colored soldier was standing a few feet away. He had an ugly wound through his wrist, and on him the same rebel turned, reloaded his piece and aimed at his head; the wounded man, meanwhile, pled for his life, and exclaiming, "de Yankees made me fight, massa." The murderer's gun snapped, and, as coolly as an executioner at a hog killing . . . the wounded soldier joined his comrade in death."[53] Yet another witness, Acting Master's Mate Robert Critchell, whose vessel, the *Silver Cloud* was early on the scene and drove off Forrest's men, noted, "we then landed at the fort, and I was sent out with a burial party . . . I saw several colored soldiers of the Sixth United States Artillery, with their eyes punched out with bayonets; many of them were shot twice and bayonetted also. All those along the bank of the river were colored. The number of the colored near the river was about seventy."[54] All told, roughly 300 of the fort's 587 men, and almost all of its African American defenders (the mortality rate for White soldiers was 30 percent while the corresponding rate for their Black soldiers stood at 65 percent), lost their lives at Fort Pillow.[55]

Throughout the summer of 1864, USCT regiments fought alongside their White peers in a series of skirmishes and sharp engagements against Forrest's cavalry and associated Confederate troops. From June to November 1864, the USCT participated in several engagements in Mississippi in pursuit of Forrest, most notably at Brice's Crossroads (a Union defeat) on June 10 (where the 55th USCT and the 59th USCT valiantly fought to cover the Union retreat) and at Tupelo, Mississippi (a Union victory) on July 14–15 where the men of the 2nd U.S. Colored Artillery, the 61st USCT, and 68th USCT helped to repulse a series of uncoordinated Confederate attacks that inflicted heavy casualties upon their foes.[56]

As USCT troops fought to fend off Forrest and prevented a Confederate incursion into middle Tennessee, Sherman's army continued its drive toward Atlanta. In his rear were many USCT units tasked with logistical support work and with defending the western army's ever lengthening supply line. White USCT leadership in Tennessee worked tirelessly to gain recognition of the combat ability of Black troops and a front-linc position in the fight, despite their soldiers' inexperience in combat.[57] Though his men habitually performed guard and picket duty, hard manual labor, or foraged for supplies, Colonel

Thomas J. Morgan of the 14th USCT argued unstintingly for the opportunity for his men to prove themselves in battle.[58] In August 1864, Morgan's men did precisely that when they were called upon to assist the beleaguered Union blockhouse garrison at Dalton, Georgia, then surrounded by Confederate Lieutenant General Joseph Wheeler's cavalry which had been sent into Northern Georgia by Major General Joseph Johnston in a desperate attempt to sever Sherman's connection to Chattanooga. At Dalton, the regiment took part in the charge that drove Wheeler from the town. Colonel Morgan reported: "The conduct of the entire regiment was good. It was its first encounter, and it evinced soldierly qualities; the men were brave, and the officers cool."[59]

Shortly after the Dalton skirmish, Confederate defeat led to a change in strategy. Johnston was relieved of command of the rebel army defending Atlanta and John Bell Hood replaced him. Recognizing that the city could not be saved, and believing that a move in force to the north might draw Sherman back to Tennessee, Hood, on September 2, abandoned Atlanta and fell back to Alabama to implement new plans. In particular, he planned to cut off Union supplies by invading Tennessee and retaking Nashville. If successful, Hood could refresh and re-equip his weary troops, gain new recruits, and move north to join Robert E. Lee in an assault on Washington.[60]

As Hood's army snaked its way toward Nashville, he found elements of his force frequently engaged with Union troops (often including USCT troops). On October 13, advance units of Hood's army descended once again on Dalton. There they found 600 members of the 44th USCT, under the command of Colonel Lewis Johnson, guarding the town. Vowing not to take any prisoners if the Union lines were breached, Hood demanded the surrender of Dalton's defenders. Johnson, in spite of the Black soldiers' "greatest anxiety to fight," brokered a surrender, including paroles for himself and the 150 White soldiers in the town. The men of the 44th, however, suffered a cruel fate. As a recent Chattanooga *Times Free Press* notes, "Ragged rebel soldiers robbed the black soldiers of shoes, overcoats and hats, actions not taken with the White prisoners. The African American soldiers were put to work at tearing up railroad tracks. A black sergeant refused, and his guards killed him. Rebels executed five men for not keeping up with the march. Some Confederates attempted to rush and massacre the Black prisoners but guards intervened. A Confederate newspaper reported, 'If any of them [the Black soldiers] should live long enough they will be reduced to their normal condition [as slaves].' Eventually 250 members of the 44th found themselves back with their former masters. Some 350 of their comrades started rebuilding railroads in Mississippi in early December. By the end of the year, 125 of these men were still alive but in desperate circumstances. They subsisted on only one pint of corn meal per man per day and a small portion of fresh beef once or twice per week."[61]

Two weeks later, Hood, planning to cross the Tennessee River in force at Decatur, Alabama, found his army blocked by a Union force that included USCT units, among them were the men of the 14th USCT. On October 28, they charged and carried a Confederate battery spiking its guns and capturing fourteen prisoners. The overall Union commander, Major General R. S. Granger, noted, "The action of the colored troops under Colonel Morgan was everything that could be expected or desired of soldiers. They were cool, brave, and determined; and under the heaviest fire of the enemy exhibited no signs of confusion."[62] These encounters proved substantial enough for Black soldiers to gain an appreciation of their fighting abilities and agency.[63] Indeed, the USCT did so well that the White regiment serving with them, "swung their hats and gave three rousing cheers" when the Black troops passed, according to Morgan.[64]

This confidence proved crucial as USCT soldiers faced an even more formidable task in December of 1864 when they participated in the defense of Nashville. Although, Hood's army had suffered terrible losses (over 6,000 casualties) just two weeks prior at the Battle of Franklin, the general nevertheless remained undaunted.[65] Hood arrived at Nashville with approximately 21,000 men. Though greatly outnumbered, his men were seasoned and dedicated veterans who hoped that a successful strike would win the day.[66] Holding an iron-willed determination, Hood promised his men that they should eat their Christmas dinner in Nashville that year.[67]

As Union forces concentrated around Nashville in December 1864, USCT regiments were among the last infantry troops to arrive just prior to the battle. Two brigades of Black infantry soldiers took part in the Battle of Nashville. Colonel Charles R. Thompson commanded the First Brigade that included the 12th, 13th, 100th, and 110th USCT. Colonel Morgan directed the Second Brigade. Among his troops were the 14th, 17th, 18th, and 44th USCT.[68] All told, some 13,000 former slaves, now enrolled in the U.S. army and commanded by General George Thomas, stood ready to defend Nashville. Indeed, the ensuing struggle serves as the only major western battle where the USCT actively fought. And fight they did with Black units suffering the highest casualty rates of any Union units on the field.[69]

The battle took place over two days. The first day the USCT troops made a feint so that General Thomas could launch a massive assault on Hood's left. The USCT suffered heavy casualties. The next day, at 1 p.m., combined Union forces, White and Black, under Major General James Blair Steedman and Brigadier General T. J. Wood, engaged in an all-out frontal assault on Overton's Hill.[70] The storming proved lethal. Though enthusiastic, the men of the 18th USCT lost five color bearers during their repulse. Trailing them, the 13th USCT attacked the rebels, virtually alone. Cheering wildly, they carried the parapet and held on until Hood sent two brigades of reinforcements from his left. The 13th failed to obtain support.[71] Reports termed the encounter a great slaughter. Local sources later substantiated this bloodbath, remarking that it would have been possible to "walk across the slope of the hill stepping from one dead Yankee to another."[72]

The next assault proved the most successful of the USCT's campaign at Nashville. Following the first failed attempt at taking the hill, the Second Colored Brigade retired behind the First Colored Brigade in order to regroup. At 3 p.m., they mounted a final assault. During this effort, six thousand soldiers, under the cover of a barrage of Union artillery fire, charged Confederate forces. Swarming over the top of the hill, Union soldiers overwhelmed their foe, giving them little opportunity to retreat. The assault weakened the Confederate right, fitting perfectly into Thomas's plan.[73] As in day one of the battle, Thomas again cleared the Confederate left forcing an all-out retreat. The battle was a complete Union triumph.[74]

After the Union victory and turning back the Confederates, the USCT garnered praise. Writing in response to critics of his decision to enlist Black troops, Lincoln affirmed, "More than a year of trial now shows . . . no loss by it anywhere or anyhow."[75]

By war's end, roughly 15 percent of the U.S. army consisted of Black soldiers serving in one of 138 Black infantry regiments.[76] Over 200,000 African Americans men served in both the Union Army and Navy with a little over half coming from the eleven seceded states. Of these, 38,000 died, suffering a casualty rate of 23.8 percent.[77] Historian James McPherson states that "Without their help, the North could not have won the war as soon as it did, and perhaps could not have won at all."[78] Though much research remains to be done, the men of the USCT and their military contributions during the Civil War are gaining increased recognition, not only for helping to preserve the nation but also for winning a newfound self-respect, full citizenship, and eventual equality. "They will have to pay us wages, the wages of their sin," soldiers of the First Arkansas USCT reminded those they encountered as they caroled the regiment's "marching song." From southern town to southern town they sang, "They will have to bow their foreheads to their colored kith and kin. They will have to give us house-room, or the roof shall tumble in! As we go marching on."[79]

That many were now, due to the bravery of these soldiers and their active participation in the struggle to mend the tear that was rending the national fabric apart, open to giving these soldiers and the race that they had fought to free "house-room" cannot be denied. The presence of formerly enslaved people in Union lines and within the ranks of the Union army led to hundreds of thousands of exchanges between African Americans and White soldiers, and those interactions brought change. White soldiers, who overwhelmingly did not enlist to end slavery, began to see the nefarious traits of chattel slavery themselves while also seeing the humanity of these new camp dwellers, effecting soldiers' perspectives on slavery and the freedpeople. One Illinois soldier wrote to his family in the summer of 1863, "An honest confession is good for the soul . . . A year ago last January, I didn't like to hear anything of emancipation. Last fall accepted confiscation of rebels' Negroes quietly. In January took to emancipation readily, . . . and now am becoming so colorblind that I can't see why they will not make soldiers . . . I almost begin to think of applying for a position in a black regiment myself." Silas Shearer of the 23rd Iowa echoed his fellow Midwesterner:

> My principles have changed since I last saw you . . . When I was at home I was opposed to the medling [*sic*] of Slavery where it then Existed but since the Rebls [*sic*] got to such a pitch and it became us as a Military needsisity [*sic*] . . . to abolish Slavery and I say Amen to it and I believe the Best thing that has been done Since the War broke out is the Emancipation Proclimation [*sic*].[80]

One White Union captain wrote his wife, "A great many [whites] have the idea that the entire Negro race are vastly their inferiors—a few weeks of calm unprejudiced life here would disabuse them, I think—I have a more elevated opinion of their abilities than I ever had before."[81] A more direct correlation between such White soldier attitudes and African Americans, however, manifest in the vote for emancipation in Maryland—a Democratic and pro-slavery stronghold. In November 1864, Maryland voters ratified a new constitution that included the abolition of slavery, with White soldiers voting 2,633–263 to affirm emancipation. If the soldiers, informed by their newfound respect for their Black comrades in arms, had not voted, the emancipation referendum would not have passed.[82]

Winning the immediate battle, however, did not, as the opening of this chapter makes clear, result in an unassailable place for the soldiers of the USCT in the emerging history of the war. On the contrary, Redeemers and other proponents of the Lost Cause mythology immediately set to work to shunt this important story back into the shadows where it better aligned with deep-seated racial views and Jim Crow thinking. Among those leading this charge was Nathan Bedford Forrest, one of the former Confederate officers most familiar with the ability and elan of the USCT. When apprised of the formation of a new organization—the Ku Klux Klan—by one of his former peers, George Gordon, Forrest is alleged to have replied, "That's a good thing; that's a damn good thing. We can use it to keep the niggers in their place."[83] More than that, however, the Klan, Jim Crow, and the Lost Cause narrative, actively worked to whitewash the military history of the war and to marginalize the contributions and struggles of the USCT; contributions these soldiers continued to make during their service in the occupied South.

As Redeemer governments reoccupied southern state houses and the soldiers of the USCT were mustered out of service and the federal government turned its back on Reconstruction, the stories of their bravery and agency, like the rights and privileges they helped to win for their race, quickly receded from sight and from memory, not to re-emerge for nearly another century.

NOTES

1. Andrew Lang, *In the Wake of War: Military Occupation, Emancipation, and Civil War America* (Baton Rouge: Louisiana State University Press, 2017), 129.

2. Lincoln to Andrew Johnson, March 26, 1863 in Roy P. Basler, ed., *The Collected Works of Abraham Lincoln*, 9 vols. (New Brunswick: Rutgers University Press, 1953), 6: 150–51.

3. *Federal Writers' Project: Slave Narrative Project, Vol. 4, Georgia, Part 4, Telfair-Young with Combined Interviews of Others*, 1936, Manuscript/Mixed Material, https://www.loc.gov/item/mesn044/.

4. "A Union Veteran's Questions," *New York Sun*, October 16, 1905, 4.

5. W. E. Woodward, *Meet General Grant* (New York: Literary Guild of America, 1928), 372.

6. James M. McPherson, *The Negro's Civil War: How American Negroes Felt and Acted during the War for the Union*, 3rd ed. (New York: Vintage Books, 2003 [1965]), xi.

7. *Federal Writers' Project: Slave Narrative Project, Vol. 5, Indiana, Arnold-Woodson*, 1936, Manuscript/Mixed Material, https://www.loc.gov/item/mesn050/.

8. Aaron Sheehan Dean, *The Calculus of Violence: How Americans Fought the Civil War* (Cambridge, MA: Harvard University Press, 2018), 157; David Blight, *Race and Reunion: The Civil War in American Memory* (Cambridge, MA: Harvard University Press, 2002), 193–94; Lang, *In the Wake of War*, 149; Ira Berlin, Joseph P. Reidy, Leslie S. Rowland, eds., *Freedom's Soldiers: The Black Military Experience in the Civil War* (Cambridge: Cambridge University Press, 1998), 20, 38, 47, 158–62.

9. James A. Rawley, *Abraham Lincoln and a Nation Worth Fighting For* (Lincoln: University of Nebraska Press, 2003), 227.

10. Frederick Douglass, *Frederick Douglass on Slavery and the Civil War: Selections from His Writings* (Mineola, NY: Dover Publications, 2003), 43.

11. Dudley Taylor Cornish, *The Sable Arm: Black Troops in the Union Army, 1861–1865* (Lawrence: University of Kansas Press, 1987), 65–6, and 80.

12. Abraham Lincoln to Roscoe Conkling, August 26, 1863 in Basler, ed., *The Collected Works of Abraham Lincoln*, 6: 406–10.

13. *Detroit Free Press,* June 10, 1863.

14. Henry Romeyn, "The Colored Troops," July 14, 1887, *The National Tribune* (Washington, DC), 1. Reader's note: Due to a spelling error, Henry Romeyn's last name is sometimes spelled "Romyen" in early military records.

15. *New York Herald*, April 24, 1863.

16. Excerpts from Chaplain John Eaton, Jr., to Lt. Col. Jno. A. Rawlins, April 29, 1863, filed with O-328 1863, Letters Received, series 12, Adjutant General's Office, Record Group 94, National Archives, www.freedmen.umd.edu/Eaton.html.

17. Romeyn, "With Colored Troops in the Army of the Cumberland," in *War Papers, Being Papers Read Before the Commandery of the District of Columbia* (Wilmington, NC: Broadfoot Publishing Company, 1993), 49.

18. Berlin, *Freedom's Soldiers*, 29–30.

19. *New York Herald*, April 24, 1863.

20. Quoted in Anne J. Bailey, "The USCT in the Confederate Heartland, 1864," in *Black Soldiers in Blue: African American Troops in the Civil War Era*, John David Smith, ed. (Chapel Hill: The University of North Carolina Press, 2002), 229–30.

21. "Extracts from the Copperheads Speeches," October 1, 1864, *The Big Blue Union* (Marysville, Kansas). Copperheads were Northern Whites who opposed the war.

22. General William Tecumseh Sherman to General Henry Halleck, September 4, 1864, in *Sherman's Civil War: Selected Correspondence of William Sherman, 1860–1865*, Brooks D. Simpson and Jean V. Berlin, eds. (Chapel Hill: The University of North Carolina Press, 1999), 700.

23. Romeyn, "Colored Troops," *The National Tribune* (Washington, DC), 14 and 21 July 1887; Thomas J. Morgan, *Reminiscences of Service with Colored Troops in the Army of the Cumberland, 1863–65* (Rhode Island: Soldiers and Sailors Historical Society, 1885), 20.

24. *Milwaukee Sentinel,* April 23, 1863.

25. Randall M. Miller and Jon W. Zophy, "Unwelcome Allies: Billy Yank and the Black Soldier," *Phylon*, 39:3 (3rd Quarter, 1978): 236–38.

26. Berlin, *Freedom's Soldiers*, 11–12.

27. Ibid., 13; William Wells Brown, *The Negro in the American Rebellion: His Heroism and His Fidelity* (Boston: Lee and Shepard, 1867), 125–27.

28. *North American and United States Gazette* (Philadelphia), April 20, 1863. George Washington Williams, *A History of the Negro Troops in the War of the Rebellion* (Memphis, TN: General Books, 2009 [1887]), 75.

29. *Milwaukee Daily Sentinel*, April 23, 1863.

30. Richard Lowe, "Battle on the Levee: The Fight at Milliken's Bend," in *Black Soldiers in Blue*, 108.

31. John H. Taggart, *Free Military School, for Applicants for Commands of Colored Troops* (Philadelphia: King and Baird, Printers, 1863), 4.

32. Bobby L. Lovett, "The Negro's Civil War in Tennessee, 1861–1865," *The Journal of Negro History* 61:1 (January 1976): 39; Taggart, *Free Military School*, 3–4.

33. James Lee McDonough, *Nashville: The Western Confederacy's Final Gamble* (Knoxville: University of Tennessee Press, 2004), 36 and 159.

34. Colonel L. Johnson to Brig. Gen L. Thomas, February 2, 1865, *The War of Rebellion: A Compilation of the Official Records of the Union and Confederate Armies* (*OR*), 128 vols. (Washington, DC: Government Printing Office, 1880–1901), ser. ii, vol. viii, 171.

35. Patrick Cleburne, "Proposal to Arm Slaves," January 2, 1864, https://www.battlefields.org/learn/primary-sources/patrick-cleburnes-proposal-arm-slaves-0.

36. Quoted in Noah Andre Trudeau, *Like Men of War: Black Troops in the Civil War, 1862–1865* (Boston: Little, Brown, and Co., 1998), 59.

37. Benjamin Quarles, *The Negro in the Civil War* (Boston: Little, Brown and Co., 1953), 214–20; Hondon B. Hargrove, *Black Union Soldiers in the Civil War* (Jefferson, NC: McFarland and Co., Inc., 1988), 128–34; Quote in Berlin, *Freedom's Soldiers*, 95–96.

38. Hargrove, *Black Union Soldiers*, 138–39.

39. Michael B. Ballard, *Vicksburg: The Campaign that Opened Up the Mississippi* (Chapel Hill: University of North Carolina Press, 2004), 391.

40. *OR*, Series I, vol. 24, 447.

41. Edward Cole Bearss, *The Campaign for Vicksburg*, 3 vols. (Dayton: Morningside Press, 1986), 3: 1180.

42. *New York Herald*, June 19, 1863.

43. Henry E. McCulloch quoted in Bearss, *The Campaign for Vicksburg*, 3: 1181; Berlin, *Freedom's Soldiers*, 98.

44. *Chicago Tribune*, June 18, 1863.

45. James R. Arnold, *Grant Wins the War: Decision at Vicksburg* (New York: John Wiley and Songs, Inc.), 283–84.

46. Quoted in Trudeau, *Like Men of War*, 99.

47. *OR*, vol. 24, 465.

48. Trudeau, *Like Men of War*, 100.

49. Ibid., 101.

50. Ibid.

51. *OR*, vol. 24, 465.

52. Mack J. Leaming, "The Fort Pillow Massacre, 1864," The Gilder Lehrman Institute of American History, https://www.gilderlehrman.org/history-resources/spotlight-primary-source/fort-pillow-massacre-1864.

53. Leaming, "The Fort Pillow Massacre."

54. Robert S. Critchell, *Recollections of a Fire Insurance Man* (Chicago: McClurg & Co., 1909). Quote found at: https://deadconfederates.com/2014/04/13/what-they-saw-at-fort-pillow-2/.

55. Leaming, "The Fort Pillow Massacre, 1864."

56. For a narrative account of the overall contours of this campaign see Bearss, *Protecting Sherman's Lifeline: The Battles of Brice's Cross Roads and Tupelo 1864* (Washington, DC: Office of Publications, National Park Service, U.S. Department of the Interior, 1971). On USCT at Brice's Cross Roads see, Ibid., 18 and at Tupelo see, Bearss, *The Tupelo Campaign June 22–July 23, 1864: A Documented Narrative & Troop Movement Maps* (Washington, DC: Division of History, Office of Archeology and Historic Preservation, 1969), 88.

57. Stanley F. Horn, *The Decisive Battle of Nashville* (Baton Rouge: Louisiana State University Press, 1954), 20.

58. Thomas J. Morgan, "Corbin's War Record," *St. Paul Globe* (Minnesota), March 25, 1900; Joseph T. Wilson, *The Black Phalanx: African American Soldiers in*

the War of Independence, The War of 1812, and the Civil War (New York: Da Capo Press, 1994), 297; Bailey, "The USCT in the Confederate Heartland," 233.

59. "14th U. S. Colored Infantry Regiment," Tennessee in the Civil War, https://tngenweb.org/civilwar/14th-u-s-colored-infantry-regiment/.

60. Ross Massey, "The Battle of Nashville," Battle of Nashville Preservation Society, Inc., http://www.bonps.org/the-battle/.

61. Caroline Wood Newhall, "'Under the Lash': Black Prisoners of War," Virginia Center for Civil War Studies Lecture, September 15, 2020, https://www.youtube.com/watch?v=y5pZQysm4_8; Phil Gast, "Honoring 44th U.S. Colored Troops: From slaves to Union warriors," October 4, 2010 in Civil War Picket blog, http://civil-war-picket.blogspot.com/2010/10/44th-usct-from-slaves-to-warriors.html.

62. Quote found at "14th U. S. Colored Infantry Regiment," November 27, 2016, Tennessee & the Civil War, https://tngenweb.org/civilwar/14th-u-s-colored-infantry-regiment/; Robert Scott Davis, "Story of an African-American Civil War Regiment," *Chattanooga Times Free Press*, April 21, 2013.

63. Berlin et al., *The Black Military Experience*, 520.

64. Morgan, *Reminiscences*, 28–38.

65. Ibid.

66. Patrick Brennan, "Last Stand in the Heartland: The Fight for Nashville, December 1864," *North and South* 8:3 (May 2005), 26; Williams, *A History of the Negro Troops*, 283.

67. Leverett M. Kelley, "Battle of Nashville," in *War Papers, Being Papers Read Before the Commandery of the District of Columbia*, 31.

68. Hargrove, *Black Union Soldiers*, 192.

69. Ibid., 176–77; Smith, *Black Soldiers in Blue*, xviii.

70. Morgan, *Reminiscences*, 46.

71. Report of Lieutenant General Stephen D. Lee, C. S. Army, commanding Army Corps, of operations November 2–December 17, 1861, *OR*, ser. 1, vol. 45, pt. 1: 689, 698, 705; Berlin, *Freedom's Soldiers*, 560–62; Christopher J. Einolf, *George Thomas: Virginian for the Union* (Norman: University of Oklahoma Press, 2007), 5, 277–78; Henry V. Freeman, "A Colored Brigade in the Campaign and Battle of Nashville," *Military Essays and Recollections: Papers Read Before the Commandery of the State of Illinois, Military Order of the Loyal Legion of the United States* (1891), 416–18.

72. Massey, "The Battle of Nashville."

73. Report of Colonel John A. Hottenstein, "Thirteenth U.S. Colored Troops, of operations November 30, 1864–January 15, 1865," *OR*, ser. 1, v. 45 (Part I), 548–49; Report of Major General George H. Thomas, U.S. Army, Commanding Department of the Cumberland, "Battle of Nashville," January 20, 1865, in http://www.civilwarhome.com/thomasnash.htm; John Walker, "Blood on the Snow," *Military Heritage* 8:5 (2007), 44.

74. Hottenstein, "Thirteenth U.S. Colored Troops," 548–9; Report of General Thomas, "Battle of Nashville," January 20, 1865; Walker, "Blood on the Snow," 44.

75. President Abraham Lincoln to Albert G. Hodges, April 4, 1864, Abraham Lincoln Online, http://showcase.netins.net/web/creative/lincoln/speeches/hodges.htm.

76. Paul D. Renard, "Reuben Delavan Mussey: Unheralded Architect of the Civil War's U.S. Colored Troops," *Military Collector and Historian* (2006), 181.

77. Walker, "Blood on the Snow," 41; Williams, *A History of the Negro Troops*, 85.

78. Quoted in Howard Zinn, *A People's History of the United States* (New York: Harper Collins, 2003 [1980]), 194.

79. Quoted in Trudeau, *Like Men of War*, 102.

80. Illinois volunteer Charles Wills to his sister, June 26, 1863 in Louis P. Masur, "From Liberty is Slow Fruit," *American Scholar*, Autumn 2012, http://theamericanscholar.org/liberty-is-a-slow-fruit/#.U-LxkFZQVTc.

81. Quote taken from Steve Mintz, "Blacks in Blue," Gilder Lehrman Institute of American History, http://www.gilderlehrman.org/history-by-era/american-civil-war/resources/blacks-blue.

82. Matthew Page Andrews, *History of Maryland: Province and State* (New York: Doubleday, 1929), 450–60.

83. Jack Hurst, *Nathan Bedford Forrest: A Biography* (New York: Alfred A. Knopf Inc., 1993), 284.

BIBLIOGRAPHY

"14th U. S. Colored Infantry Regiment." Tennessee in the Civil War. https://tngenweb.org/civilwar/14th-u-s-colored-infantry-regiment/.

Abraham Lincoln Online. http://showcase.netins.net/web/creative/lincoln/speeches/hodges.htm.

Adjutant General's Office. Letters Received. series 12. Record Group 94. National Archives.

African American Civil War Memorial. National Park Service. https://www.nps.gov/afam/index.htm.

American Battlefield Trust. https://www.battlefields.org/.

Arnold, James R. *Grant Wins the War: Decision at Vicksburg*. New York: John Wiley and Songs, Inc., 1997.

Ballard, Michael B. *Vicksburg: The Campaign that Opened Up the Mississippi*. Chapel Hill: University of North Carolina Press, 2004.

Barnickel, Linda. *Milliken's Bend: A Civil War Battle in History and Memory*. Baton Rouge: Louisiana State University Press, 2013.

Basler, Roy P., ed. *The Collected Works of Abraham Lincoln*. 9 vols. New Brunswick: Rutgers University Press, 1953.

Bearss, Edwin C. *Protecting Sherman's Lifeline: The Battles of Brice's Cross Roads and Tupelo 1864*. Washington, DC: Office of Publications, National Park Service, U.S. Department of the Interior, 1971.

———. *The Tupelo Campaign June 22–July 23, 1864: A Documented Narrative & Troop Movement Maps*. Washington, DC: Division of History, Office of Archeology and Historic Preservation, 1969.

———. *The Vicksburg Campaign: Unvexed for the Sea.* 3 vols. Columbus: Morningside Books, 1986.

Berlin, Ira, Joseph P. Reidy, and Leslie S. Rowland, eds. *The Black Military Experience*, Series II, *Freedom: A Documentary History of Emancipation, 1861–1867*. Cambridge: Cambridge University Press, 1982.

———. *Freedom's Soldiers: The Black Military Experience in the Civil War.* Cambridge: Cambridge University Press, 1998.

Blight, David. *Race and Reunion: The Civil War in American Memory.* Cambridge, MA: Harvard University Press, 2002.

Bobrick, Benson. *Master of War: The Life of George H. Thomas.* New York: Simon and Schuster, 2006.

Brennan, Patrick. "'Last Stand in the Heartland': The Fight for Nashville, December 1864." 8:3 *North and South* (May 2005): 26–46.

Brown, William Wells. *The Negro in the American Rebellion: His Heroism and His Fidelity.* Boston: Lee and Shepard, 1867.

Chicago Tribune, June 18, 1863.

Cleburne, Patrick. "Proposal to Arm Slaves." January 2, 1864. American Battlefield Trust. https://www.battlefields.org/learn/primary-sources/patrick-cleburnes-proposal-arm-slaves-0.

Cornish, Dudley Taylor. *The Sable Arm: Black Troops in the Union Army, 1861–1865.* Lawrence: University of Kansas Press, 1987.

Critchell, Robert S. *Recollections of a Fire Insurance Man.* Chicago: McClurg & Co., 1909. https://deadconfederates.com/2014/04/13/what-they-saw-at-fort-pillow-2/.

Davis, Robert Scott. "Story of an African-American Civil War Regiment." *Chattanooga Times Free Press*, April 21, 2013.

Dean, Aaron Sheehan. *The Calculus of Violence: How Americans Fought the Civil War.* Cambridge, MA: Harvard University Press, 2018.

Detroit Free Press, June 10, 1863.

Douglass. Frederick. *Frederick Douglass on Slavery and the Civil War: Selections from His Writings.* Mineola, NY: Dover Publications, 2003.

———. *Letter to the Colored People of the United States.* Washington, DC: Daniel A.P. Murray Collection, 1872.

Einolf, Christopher J. *George Thomas: Virginian for the Union.* Norman: University of Oklahoma Press, 2007.

"Extracts from the Copperheads Speeches," October 1, 1864, *The Big Blue Union* (Marysville, Kansas).

Federal Writers' Project: Slave Narrative Project. Vol. 4–5. 1936. Manuscript/Mixed Material. Library of Congress.

Freeman, Henry V. "A Colored Brigade in the Campaign and Battle of Nashville." *Military Essays and Recollections: Papers Read Before the Commandery of the State of Illinois, Military Order of the Loyal Legion of the United States* (1891).

Gast, Phil. "Honoring 44th U.S. Colored Troops: From Slaves to Union Warriors." October 4, 2010. Civil War Picket blog. http://civil-war-picket.blogspot.com/2010/10/44th-usct-from-slaves-to-warriors.html.

Hargrove, Hondon B. *Black Union Soldiers in the Civil War*. Jefferson: McFarland and Co., Inc., 1988.

Horn, Stanley F. *The Decisive Battle of Nashville.* Baton Rouge: Louisiana State University Press, 1954.

Lang, Andrew. *In the Wake of War: Military Occupation, Emancipation, and Civil War America.* Baton Rouge: Louisiana State University Press, 2017.

Leaming, Mack J. "The Fort Pillow Massacre, 1864." The Gilder Lehrman Institute of American History. https://www.gilderlehrman.org/history-resources/spotlight-primary-source/fort-pillow-massacre-1864.

Lovett, Bobby L. "The Negro's Civil War in Tennessee, 1861–1865." *The Journal of Negro History* 61:1 (January 1976): 36–50.

Lowe, Richard. *Walker's Texas Division C.S.A.: Greyhounds of the Trans-Mississippi.* Baton Rouge: Louisiana State University Press, 2004.

Massey, Ross. "The Battle of Nashville." Battle of Nashville Preservation Society, Inc. http://www.bonps.org/the-battle/.

McDonough, James Lee. *Nashville: The Western Confederacy's Final Gamble.* Knoxville: University of Tennessee Press, 2004.

McPherson, James M. *The Negro's Civil War: How American Negroes Felt and Acted during the War for the Union.* 3rd ed. New York: Vintage Books, 2003 [1965].

Miller, Randall M. and Jon W. Zophy. "Unwelcome Allies: Billy Yank and the Black Soldier." 39:3 *Phylon* (3rd Quarter, 1978): 234–40.

Milwaukee Sentinel, April 23, 1863.

Morgan, Thomas J. "Corbin's War Record." *St. Paul Globe* (Minnesota), March 25, 1900.

———. *Reminiscences of Service with Colored Troops in the Army of the Cumberland, 1863–65.* Rhode Island: Soldiers and Sailors Historical Society, 1885.

New York Herald, April 24, 1863.

Newhall, Caroline Wood. "'Under the Lash': Black Prisoners of War." Virginia Center for Civil War Studies Lecture. September 15, 2020. https://www.youtube.com/watch?v=y5pZQysm4_8.

North American and United States Gazette (Philadelphia), April 20, 1863.

Quarles, Benjamin. *The Negro in the Civil War.* Boston: Little Brown and Co., 1953.

Rawley, James A. *Abraham Lincoln and a Nation Worth Fighting For.* Lincoln: University of Nebraska Press, 2003.

Renard, Paul D. "Reuben Delavan Mussey: Unheralded architect of the Civil War's U.S. Colored Troops." *Military Collector and Historian* (2006).

Romeyn, "Colored Troops," *The National Tribune* (Washington, DC), July 14 and July 21, 1887.

Simon, John Y., ed. *The Papers of U.S. Grant.* Vols.1 through 20. Carbondale: University of Southern Illinois Press, 1995.

Simpson, Brooks D. and Jean V. Berlin, eds. *Sherman's Civil War: Selected Correspondence of William T. Sherman, 1860–1865.* Chapel Hill: University of North Carolina Press, 1999.

Smith, John David, ed. *Black Soldiers in Blue: African American Troops in the Civil War Era*. Chapel Hill: The University of North Carolina Press, 2002.

Taggart, John H. *Free Military School, for Applicants for Commands of Colored Troops*. Philadelphia: King and Baird Printers, 1863.

Trudeau, Noah Andre. *Like Men of War: Black Troops in the Civil War, 1862–1865*. Boston: Little, Brown, 1998.

"A Union Veteran's Questions." *New York Sun*, October 16, 1905.

Walker, John. "Blood on the Snow." *Military Heritage* 8:5 (2007). https://warfarehistorynetwork.com/2015/09/06/blood-on-the-snow-the-battle-of-nashville/.

War Papers, Being Papers Read Before the Commandery of the District of Columbia. Wilmington, NC: Broadfoot Publishing Company, 1993.

The War of Rebellion: A Compilation of the Official Records of the Union and Confederate Armies. 128 vols. Washington, DC: Government Printing Office, 1880–1901.

Williams, George Washington. *A History of the Negro Troops in the War of the Rebellion*. Memphis, TN: General Books, 2009 [1887].

Wilson, Joseph T. *The Black Phalanx: African American Soldiers in the War of Independence, The War of 1812, and the Civil War*. New York: Da Capo Press, 1994.

Woodward, W.E. *Meet General Grant*. New York: Literary Guild of America, 1928.

Zinn, Howard. *A People's History of the United States*. New York: Harper Collins, 2003 [1980].

Chapter 3

Fighting on Two Fronts

Black Educational Self-Determination and Community Preservation in Houston, Texas

Jesús Jesse Esparza

Black school-aged students have a long history of suffering from systemic oppression in American schools. They experienced high dropout rates, were tracked into vocational and industrial classrooms, were subjected to curriculum devoid of their history, and were confronted with hostile teachers and administrators. Further, they were segregated and arbitrarily suspended or expelled. Additionally, White school officials viewed them as intellectually inferior, unhygienic, and apathetic toward education. Moreover, their buildings, schools, and classrooms suffered from inadequate space and funding, and students lacked proper supplies.[1] Consequently, schools for African Americans were as unequal as they were oppressive. In Houston, however, there would be an exception. In 1892, the city saw the first high school establishment for African Americans, Colored High, later renamed Booker T. Washington. Located in the oldest Black neighborhood in Houston, this school maintained a dogged sense of educational self-determination that strove to provide students a safe and rigorous learning environment, devoid of the systemic oppression experienced by most African American students, especially at the height of Jim Crow America.

African Americans were also victims of an entrenched system of segregation. Life in Houston reflected the southern apartheid tradition that was widespread throughout Texas. Whites in Texas rebuilt a legalized system of racial difference at the end of Reconstruction when in 1876 the state's constitution was modified so that public schools separated Black and White schoolchildren. The legislature would be initially satisfied with school segregation but would soon join the rest of the South and parts of the North to pass a raft of Jim Crow laws that would endeavor to keep the races separated in private and public life. For example, in 1891, Texas required that railroad cars be assigned either Black or White. In 1903, the City of Houston went even further to segregate all streetcars, as well as public facilities (1907), parks (1922), and other forms of ground transportation (1924). Segregation would become the law of the land, and Houston's facilities, such as its schools, would become a laboratory for exploring how to implement these laws best.[2]

Within a harsh and absolute segregation milieu, however, Blacks in and around Houston were also able to establish and maintain two autonomous and, presently, historic African American neighborhoods: Freedman's Town in the Fourth Ward and Independence Heights. While both communities have received designations as historical areas, most of the period homes and buildings have been abandoned, razed, or replaced. Presently, these neighborhoods are going the same direction seen in many American cities, where new townhomes, lofts, and businesses are part of a gentrification process that ignores the history and the needs of the longstanding community.[3]

Therefore, this chapter endeavors to recover a small component of a rich history that is quickly slipping away and, in doing so, serves as a form of protest to the tide of economic and social structures that are erasing the physical dimension of an African American community. It provides a brief history of the first high school for Blacks in Houston and an account of the two African American communities that nourished it. African Americans in the Fourth Ward and Independence Heights, today, find themselves fighting on two fronts; for educational self-determination and historic preservation to confront the systemic forms of oppression in America's schools and the White supremacy manifested through neighborhood gentrification. Although these two neighborhoods provided space for the high school to survive and thrive, external forces have penetrated both communities, compromising their sense of autonomy and jeopardizing, by extension, their educational self-determination as well. This essay employs one of the analytical tools of Critical Race Theorists known as "whiteness as property." In this case, the gentrification of historic African American neighborhoods has perpetuated the notion of the right of White possession over Black spaces and properties. This constructed right by Whites has, in other contexts, justified the displacement, uprooting, and transplanting of indigenous peoples from the very same space. As Payne Hiraldo puts it in "The Role of Critical Race Theory in Higher Education," the idea that only Whites have the right of possession "perpetuate[s] . . . White supremacy because only White individuals can benefit from it."[4]

In Jim Crow Texas, African Americans in Houston had no other choice than to be self-reliant and turn inwards to build a strong community. It is important to recognize that in building the state's first Black incorporated township and first Black neighborhood in Houston, that the community considered a well-run high school as fundamental to their collective success.

The school trained African American teenagers while serving as a hub for both communities. Ultimately, the school built a sense of educational self-determination and entrenched community autonomy, thereby providing an institutional base in which Black educators, activists, entrepreneurs, and preservationists could combat racial discrimination and provide for their long-term sustainability community.

Using empirical data and oral histories, this essay positions the story of Booker T. Washington High School, the Fourth Ward, and Independence Heights within the context of racism and classism. The school's founding was a constructive reaction to a White supremacist educational system. Over its long history, it has served to help voice community concerns about the rapid gentrification and the severe manifestations of wealth inequality in the neighborhoods. To demonstrate the importance of the Booker T. Washington High School, this essay relies heavily on records produced, preserved, and promoted by African Americans and, in doing so, situates them as a historical authority. The intent is to provide a narrative that accurately reflects the experiences of African Americans. As Richard Delgado and Jean Stefancic explain, a central tenet of Critical Race Theory (CRT) requires a re-examination of historical records that challenge existing interpretations and replacing them with accounts more accurately representative of the community under investigation.[5] The use of oral histories of African Americans, in particular, aligns itself squarely with another tenet of CRT; counter-storytelling, which consists of capturing the "narratives of people of color" to challenge existing historical frameworks that are often rooted in White supremacy and patriarchy.

Similarly, personal collections from community members help set the record straight; that is, they help create a narrative that accurately depicts the Black experience.[6] In terms of the collections related to Booker T. Washington High School, for example, they not only provide a snapshot of the intellectual accomplishments of African Americans in early Houston, but they also illustrate the intense educational pursuits among those typically believed to be unworthy of an equitable educational experience. Here again, therefore, this essay aims to reposition those personal collections as the historical authority.

A TRAGIC LEARNING EXPERIENCE

In "Brown v. Board of Education and the Interest-Convergence Dilemma," Derrick Bell Jr., a leading critical race theorist, maintains that "most Black children [still] attend public schools that are racially isolated and inferior."[7] During the second half of the twentieth century, primarily because of poverty,

African Americans were more likely than Whites to have shorter school years. In a real sense, this pattern continued one that had been set in the early twentieth century, when most Black families clustered in rural areas and on farms. Thus, the seasonal demands associated with agriculture forced families to make the tough decision to remove their children from school to assist with the harvest. At times, students in rural communities received no more than six months of schooling per year. This pernicious pattern would continue for decades so that even at midcentury, Black students averaged only 147 days per school term versus White students that averaged 172 days. Black students also suffered from a curriculum that prepared them for labor by emphasizing technical, mechanical, and agricultural education rather than schooling that would prepare them for university study. María C. Ledesma and Dolores Calderón underscore in their "Critical Race Theory in Education" that this was deliberately done "to privilege the rich and underserve the poor."[8]

Further, Black school-aged students had a minimal range of course selections offered to them and were often subjected to a curriculum that "alienate[d] students of color."[9] Subsequently, Black students had high illiteracy rates.[10]

African American students and their schools also suffered from insufficient funds. The financing of Black schools is "inherently racist," and many of the existing policies regarding school funds stem from "White supremacist ideologies," which impacts "communities of color in disparate ways."[11] In 1910, for example, school districts in Texas spent, on average, about $10 on White school-aged students, but nearly half of that on Black students. While there may have been some closing of the gap into the twentieth century, state funding for White schools continued to outstrip those designated for African Americans. In 1929, Texas spent $40 a year on the African American students and almost $50 a year on White students. The state also spent one-third less on schools for African Americans than for White ones. But perhaps most telling, nearly 40 percent of the Black schools were without textbooks. Poorer funding also meant that Black educators received substandard wages. For example, in the early 1900s, Black teachers earned $46 a month compared to $62 a month to their White counterparts. As the years progressed and salaries increased, pay rates for Black teachers, nevertheless, remained less than White educators. In 1929, Black educators averaged about $92 a month versus White educators, who received $121 a month. In the 1930s, they average $581 annually compared to White educators, who made $950 a year.[12]

African Americans also suffered from inadequate and substandard buildings that often deteriorated quickly. Schools built for Black communities lacked libraries, laboratories, and playgrounds, and many still relied on outhouses. Further, space was at a premium, and students found themselves placed into overcrowded classrooms.[13]

All these factors provided African American students with an inequitable educational experience. The inequality gap, in turn, engendered a higher failure and dropout rate. This pattern in performance was by design and done deliberately: segregationists believed educated Blacks would be better equipped to challenge and undermine the economic, social, and political order.[14] Others "feared [a] loss of control over their public schools" if Black educators and administrators were brought in to work with a growing African American student population.[15] Whatever they believed, the result was the same; an inferior educational experience for African Americans. While Whites pushed to ensure separate and unequal education throughout much of the country, there were individual exceptions to the rule.

Booker T. Washington High School proved unique in that its students' success proved remarkable within the context of widespread segregation. Situated in the oldest Black neighborhood in Houston, the Fourth Ward, the community worked hard to provide students a safe learning environment filled with academic rigor. Teachers ensured that students would not only graduate but would also enroll in colleges and universities. Paradoxically, this school used segregation as a tool to deliberately insulate itself from the problems of typically oppressed Black school-aged children. While racial segregation certainly disadvantaged African Americans in "too numerous and obvious" ways, in Houston, at least for those attending Booker T. Washington High School, it also resulted in a strong sense of educational self-determination among parents, teachers, and administrators.[16] In turn, this self-determination cultivated a culture that refused to adopt the Black intellectual inferiority myth and eschewed students' tracking into remedial or vocational classes. The community took pains to support, encourage, and expect student success and college advancement.[17]

BOOKER T. WASHINGTON HIGH: MORE THAN JUST A SCHOOL

Founded in the early years of the Jim Crow South, Booker T. Washington High School was designed to be academically enriching, inclusive of parents, and culturally sensitive to the community it served. From inception, while inequitably funded, the high school became a model Black school in that it provided a "real educational effectiveness" experience.[18] For example, the school educated students labeled "high-risk" and found creative ways to deal with a dropout problem. Moreover, with help from parents, Booker T. Washington became more than just a school. It became a hub of academic rigor, cultural enrichment, and upward socioeconomic mobility. This was the benefit of insulating itself in an autonomous and self-sufficient community;

the school had the freedom to implement innovative approaches in and out of the classroom and truly impact students, their families, and the community by using an academically rigorous, culturally sensitive, and holistic approach. And in doing so, as Bell explains, school leaders were able to capitalize on the "cultural strengths of the Black community to overcome the many barriers to educational achievement."[19]

In 1865, former slaves created a community for themselves called Freedman's Town in the Fourth Ward, which before long became a thriving, self-sufficient area and the center of Black life in Houston. Having become filled with church houses, schools, businesses, sports teams, and civic and political organizations, this community quickly grew into the city's most active and autonomous African American neighborhood. The area was home, for example, to some of the oldest educational institutions, such as Colored High, the Carnegie Library, and the Gregory School. It was also home to several worshiping and religious centers, including Trinity Church, the first church for Blacks in Houston; the Antioch Baptist Church; Mt. Carmel Missionary Baptist Church; and the St. James United Methodist Church, all of which anchored themselves in the community and provided a multitude of services aimed at Black social, racial, and economic uplift.[20]

In terms of entertainment, the Fourth Ward was known as the "the Harlem of the South."[21] With places like the Lincoln Theater, considered by many to be the South's most elegant theater, it easily attracted national acts such as B.B. King and Sam "Lightning" Hopkins. As one resident described it, "It would be at these places where we got to see many of our own."[22] Dotting the landscape also would be a combination of restaurants, drinking establishments, and nightclubs such as the Rainbow Theater. A centralized location of Black cultural activity was the Pilgrim Life Insurance Building, which housed several clubrooms, ballrooms, and a rooftop roller rink.[23]

The professional sector, too, was influential within the Fourth Ward. During the early part of the twentieth century, most African American lawyers, dentists, and medics were based out of this community. Later, many medical professionals established Union Hospital, the first medical facility for Blacks in the city. Additionally, the area would have several Black-owned businesses and institutions, from mom-n-pop shops to chain-like groceries. These local businesses suggest that the region's economic activity was booming with prosperous entrepreneurial enterprises such as Frierson's, Adams' Ice Cream, and Sam and Rosa Wilson's Barber Shop. As a result, the Fourth Ward quickly became the center of African American economic, educational, religious, cultural, and professional activity. From ditch diggers to doctors, the Fourth Ward had it all. Barbershops, furniture stores, dry goods stores, groceries, tailors, and professionals all called the Fourth Ward home, as did the first high school for Blacks in Houston.[24]

Constructed in 1892, Booker T. Washington is the oldest and longest-running high school for African Americans in the city. The first school building was a two-story brick structure with about ten rooms.[25] Enrollment grew steadily so that by 1927, a new building was built on the same site to accommodate the demand. Unlike the other Houston schools for Blacks, it was noteworthy for its generic name, "Colored High."[26] When the name was changed to Booker T. Washington High, parents, teachers, and administrators made a conscious effort to stake a claim of the institutions within their neighborhood. Moreover, the name change reflected the way educators envisioned their school as a reconceptualized space designed to empower students, another CRT principle.

In 1959, another new Booker T. Washington High School was constructed, this time in Independence Heights, an area northwest of downtown Houston and the first Black incorporated city in Texas. The move was not without its issues, however. For some, figuratively taking a historic school out of the Fourth Ward was problematic. For them, the high school was synonymous with the area, and many felt a sense of estrangement, having to see it situated in a different part of the city. For others, it was a blessing, mainly since many students of the high school lived in Independence Heights and found their commutes unwelcoming. Ellen Dickey, for example, lived in that area and attended Booker T. Washington. Independence Heights became incorporated in 1915 and remained independently incorporated until 1928, when Houston annexed it. Before that, Independence Heights was already an area densely populated by former slaves. When news of freedom reached Texas on June 19, 1865, persons of color from several farms and fields poured into Houston. Like Freedman's Town in the Fourth Ward, the first settlers of Independence Heights were also able to take advantage of the assistance provided to them via Reconstruction, and many families, therefore, were also able to acquire some property.[27]

As a community, Independence Heights thrived with a Black population of homeowners, entrepreneurs, and professionals who established their institutions. Among the first to emerge were schools, including the Independence Heights School and Mrs. Susie Horton Booker's Kindergarten School (presently called Williams Academy). Also appearing in the area was an abundance of church houses such as the New Hope Missionary Baptist, the Green Chapel African Methodist Episcopal, and the St. Paul Colored Methodist Episcopal. Businesses also dotted the landscape. For example, there was a cooperative store, several small grocery stores, and cafes. There were also several drugstores, restaurants, ice cream parlors, a tailor, a barber, and a blacksmith. People even grew their fruits and vegetables and then traded with each other. With the "sharing of resources" and "an active base of goods and services," Independence Heights became an autonomous community that met the people's needs.[28] "Just about everything we needed for a city was here," recalled a resident.[29]

But what began as a small community quickly grew into nearly unmanageable numbers. In 1914, there were about 400 residents in the area. The next year there were 600 residents. By 1920 Independence Heights had a population of 715 and showed no signs of slowing down. The growth was concerning to city leaders who, despite their self-sufficiency, were unable to keep up with the pace of a growing population. In response to this, city leaders voted to become a part of Houston by the end of the 1920s. Their thinking was that Independence Heights might receive more services such as paved roads and improved plumbing structures. Regrettably, they did not get all that they had hoped. Like most Black neighborhoods, Independence Heights found itself neglected and lacking still many city services. In 1940, for example, only about 23 percent of Black-occupied homes had running water. Despite that, Independence Heights remained an autonomous Black community that continued to have a sizable number of Black homeowners, entrepreneurs, professionals, and skilled workers. And in 1959, they now had one of Houston's most historic educational centers for African Americans, Booker T. Washington High School.[30]

The Curriculum

Due to entrenched segregationist laws that prevented African Americans from enrolling in institutions of higher learning, many Black schools provided students with a curriculum they believed prepared them for gainful employment such as home economics, mechanics, and agriculture. For Booker T. Washington High School, that meant its curriculum consisted of English, Mathematics, Science, History, and Latin and specialized classes such as Domestic Science, Manual Training, Mechanical Drawing, and Supernumerary.[31]

During the 1940s, 1950s, and 1960s, administrators at Booker T. Washington expanded their industrial education course offerings, adding classes to the curriculum, including Boy's Commercial Cooking, Beauty Culture, Radio Technology, Shorthand, Typing, Landscape Gardening, Horticulture, and Home Nursing. They even reinstituted adult education programming. Initially established in 1911, the Night School Program provided instruction to anyone, free of charge, seeking a high school education. The program was staffed by African American teachers such as O'Neta Pink Cavitt, who taught a millinery class for those interested in making hats for a living and aimed at equipping Blacks with skills that could help them find gainful employment.[32]

Known as "industrial education," many Black school leaders enthusiastically endorsed this curriculum. They trusted that General Hampton of the

Hampton Institute, the brainchild of industrial education, along with his most famous pupil, Booker T. Washington, knew what they were doing. However, industrial education also faced fierce opposition from several national leaders from within the African American community who believed that type of curriculum restricted Black students to semiskilled or agricultural work. Also suspicious was how many White school officials supported providing "colored" children with an education that prepared them for work in the service industry instead of preparing them for college. The fight over the most appropriate curriculum for Black school-aged kids continued throughout the decades.[33]

In 1974, Booker T. Washington became home to the city's first magnet program and was dubbed the "High School for Engineering Professions." Magnet programs helped school districts such as the Houston Independent School District (HISD) achieve integration as they often attracted students from several communities onto a specific campus that students typically would not attend. In doing so, that campus would immediately become a tri-ethnic school. This program has been on campus for forty-six years and has provided students with real-world engineering experiences in collaboration with the National Aeronautics and Space Administration. As part of the program, students participate in several innovative projects, from producing alternative energy sources to designing and building self-guided robots and launching rockets. The Magnet program indicates that the curriculum at Booker T. Washington has evolved over the decades from industrial education courses to classes that focus on STEM and STEAM.[34]

Booker T. Washington also supported an array of extracurricular clubs and organizations, and students always had a large pool of choices from which to select. Students still found themselves busy with things outside the classroom, from cheerleading to Band, to Orchestra, or working for the school newspaper. There was also Choir and the Math and Debate Teams, which would participate in several competitions every year and win numerous awards. The Band also played a significant role in the school, establishing itself as an acclaimed program since the 1930s. Ultimately, these clubs and organizations fostered a great deal of pride and contributed to the community's sense of autonomy.[35]

Athletic clubs and sporting events similarly engendered neighborhood pride. Traditionally, the school's athletic teams competed only against other Black schools. In the decade after *Brown*, however, integrated competitions became more frequent in Texas. Having a chance to compete on an integrated field, the players at Booker T. Washington strove to do their best, proving themselves to be formidable, especially in football, winning the state championship in 1968. But victories, no matter how significant or otherwise, took on several meanings. First, they further implanted racial and territorial pride, and second, they challenged long-held perceptions of Black inferiority. Additionally, they also cemented the sense of autonomy and self-determination of the community.[36]

To expand students' academic experience, school leaders and parents worked tirelessly at getting the entire community involved. They knew well that community-wide participation was crucial for enriching student learning; thus, they formed the Mother's Club, a predecessor to the Parent-Teacher Association (PTAs), which raised money to sponsor school events.[37] Community involvement was crucial for student success, and the "role of communities of color in shaping the direction" of their school was "paramount."[38] As a result, parents and teachers worked tirelessly to make the high school an academically enriching institution that benefited from a nurturing community.

The Graduation Pipeline

While going to college for Black students throughout the decades proved difficult, it was nevertheless pursued. Despite being very limited with their own formal education, many having only completed the eighth grade, parents stressed the importance of going to college. The first graduating classes were small, but over the years, they grew, as did the number of students enrolling in colleges and universities. Before long, they were attending multiple institutions of higher learning such as Texas Southern University, University of Texas, Prairie View A&M University, University of Saint Thomas, Wiley College, University of Chicago, University of North Texas, Howard University, Columbia University, Bishop College, Tillotson College (now Huston-Tillotson University), and University of Houston. Geraldine Pittman, class of 1944, with a $50 scholarship, enrolled in Liston College but then transferred to Texas Southern University for a short stint where she took courses in Education before relocating to Tillotson College. After graduating in 1949, she spent the next forty years working for HISD.

Other students followed career paths in Nursing, Pharmacy, Education, Theological Studies, Public Administration, and Law. Most found employment as engineers, educators, counselors, business people, politicians, and school administrators. Victor Keys, for example, became one of the vice principals of the school that shaped him. Hazel B. McCullough found work at the Franklin Beauty School following graduation. And after becoming manager, she actively recruited students from the high school, connecting them to other professionals within the field of Cosmetology. Carl Walker Jr. attained his Doctor of Juris Prudence in 1955 from Thurgood Marshall School of Law and established his practice in Houston.[39]

Many other graduates obtained degrees that offered them the opportunity to work for their former Alma Mater. For example, Sandra Wilson graduated in 1953 and enrolled at Lincoln University in Jefferson City, Missouri, where she majored in Journalism. After graduation, she returned to Houston and accepted an English faculty position at her old high school. Ms. Johnnie Hart Brooks also came back. After graduating, she attended Fisk University, Texas Southern University, and the University of Texas for postgraduate work before returning to Houston to teach at Booker T. Washington. James "Bo" Humphrey graduated in 1948 and returned to teach and coach at the high school for about twelve years. Additionally, countless alum established organizations such as the National Association of Black School Educators, the Independence Heights Super Neighborhood Council, and the Booker T. Washington High School Alumni Association, which allowed them to give back to their Alma Mater. The Alumni Association, for example, sponsored athletic activities, offered scholarship opportunities, provided services for retiring teachers, and donated to the school's treasury.[40]

THE FIGHT OVER INTEGRATION

In 1954, the *Brown* decision compelled states to end the practice of school segregation. But despite the court order, many districts either refused to comply or integrated at a languid pace. HISD, for example, in the first two years after the rendering of the *Brown* decision, proposed several plans that continue to maintain segregated facilities. Because a segregationist board controlled the district, HISD continuously fought to stymie integration efforts. At the state level, legislatures, fearing a crisis like that of Little Rock, threatened to close schools if the military forced them to integrate. This opposition filtered down the local school boards, including HISD, which still had not integrated a single campus, making it the most segregated school system in the country. In *Brown II* (1955), the Supreme Court ordered that desegregation occurs at a much faster rate, but HISD again found ways to circumvent that ruling. In response to that, the NAACP's Houston chapter filed a separate lawsuit (*Ross v. HISD*) in 1956 to force HISD to speed up its integration plans. The district responded with something called the freedom-of-choice plan, where it integrated one grade at a time and worked as designed, slow and doing "little to desegregate the schools."[41]

It would not be until 1960 that HISD officially commenced with integration. That year, twelve students across three schools were integrated into the first grade. And over the next five years, that number increased to over 1,300 across eight campuses. Still, HISD's approach was too slow. Additionally, it prevented desegregation by imposing zoning patterns that matched residential segregation or initiated student transfer plans that kept African American students in all-Black schools. These tactics prompted protests throughout the city and, ultimately, forced the Justice Department to intervene. In 1969, following a report from the Texas Education Agency (TEA) which revealed that about 92 percent of African American students in HISD still attended segregated schools, the Department of Health, Education, and Welfare (HEW) became involved in the district's so-called "desegregation plan" and ordered them to achieve integration once and for all. While HISD complied, another study conducted in 1978 found that 42 percent of Houston schools remained "one-race schools."[42]

HISD also had a method of building new schools in a way that further increased racial segregation. In 1957, the district commenced building several new schools for African Americans and placed them in historically Black neighborhoods, including Kashmere (1957), Worthing (1958), a new Booker T. Washington high school (1959), and Lincoln (1966). And while these neighborhoods certainly needed new schools, many integrationists, like Dr. John Reuben Sheeler, Chair of the History Department at TSU, felt that HISD constructed these schools in a way that maintained racial segregation. Because Independence Heights was an isolated African American community, building a new Booker T. Washington high school in that neighborhood would undeniably ensure that it remains all-Black. Accordingly, this was deliberate and part of a broader strategy by HISD to avoid integrating.[43]

Integration, unexpectedly, concerned some African Americans. Students, for example, worried what their classrooms would look like integrated. Faculty and staff wondered if their jobs were at stake. Community members felt as though one of their most cherished institutions was being taken away from them. While many activists pushed toward the destruction of segregated schools, others continued to support their separation. For them, segregation was a way to preserve and protect one of their most beloved institutions, Booker T. Washington High School, and integration threatened that.[44]

It would not be until 1972 that HISD was finally forced to make significant changes toward destroying its segregated facilities. That year, following the ruling from a case known as *The United States v. The State of Texas*, the district received news that TEA would oversee all integration plans throughout the state and that HISD would no longer supervise that process. This case stems from investigations in the 1960s by HEW into discriminatory practices in several small school districts in East Texas. Lacking enforcement power, HEW referred the matter to the Department of Justice, which was at the height of its efforts to desegregate schools. After several hearings, William Wayne Justice, the chief judge of the U.S. District Court for the Eastern District of Texas, ordered TEA to assume responsibility for desegregating all Texas public schools. TEA was to conduct annual reviews of school districts that had campuses with a 66 percent or higher minority enrollment to determine compliance with federal desegregation law. If violations were found, then TEA imposed sanctions on those districts, including the denial of accreditation. The ruling impacted HISD and all its schools, including Booker T. Washington, as it, too, had to comply with the judge's orders and become a 60–40 percent school. In other words, it now had to house a student population that was 60 percent African American and at least 40 percent non-Black.[45]

To meet desegregation orders, students from Booker T. Washington found themselves bused to other high schools. Integration, however, also applied to faculty and staff and meant that many teachers from Booker T. Washington were reassigned to other schools to serve different populations. So while achieving integration was something worth applauding, there is a "poverty of progress" that came with these changes. Perhaps most important was that the ruling made it more challenging to hire a school faculty that lived locally: integration disrupted the deep-rooted sense of educational and community autonomy. Furthermore, other kinds of problems emerged with integration, including difficulties redrawing district boundaries, bussing students, and complications around achieving racial balance in schools. Ultimately, integration did not translate into a better educational experience for African American students.[46]

THE FIGHT FOR HISTORIC PRESERVATION

In 2010, Booker T. Washington High School received a Texas Historical Marker recognizing it as a significant part of Texas' history. A major push behind this designation was the Alumni Association's efforts, which, in addition to many things, was also the leading body for the preservation of the high school's history and legacy. Countless others would also play essential roles in preserving the school's history, traditions, and values. In 2015, however, plans for constructing a new $51.7 million high school were underway. More than 100 parents, students, staff, alumni, and community members attended the groundbreaking ceremony, all eager to see the launching of their new 180,000 square-foot building. For the most part, the new facility received strong support since it promised to showcase the school's engineering program with state-of-the-art technology, specialized engineering and science labs, and flexible learning spaces. However, even for those who supported a modern building, the pressing concern was the district's plan for what to do with the current high school, which was to tear it down.[47]

In 2018, the new school became operational, and the former saw its demolition. For many, its destruction was problematic because flattening the old structure also meant removing a significant historical space. Additionally, the high school was more than just a building for the community. It was where neighborhood meetings took place, where the people voted, learned to organize, and served as the center of Black cultural activities. The school did more than provide students with rigorous academic training; it unified, empowered, and nurtured a community too often neglected by city leaders. So, while ushering a new schoolhouse to continue the legacy of educational achievement remains necessary, it was thought that there must also be a better plan for preserving the school's historical legacy. Perhaps converting it into a museum to protect its century-long history is a workable solution.[48]

Similarly, the Fourth Ward has also undergone massive change, giving way to enormous gentrification and urban renewal projects displacing long-term residents. Real estate agents, corporations, and redevelopers taking advantage of revitalization projects are rapidly tearing down people's homes, and city officials, believing that the Fourth Ward lacks any historical significance, refuse to intervene. Some structures have survived, mainly since the city created a "historic district" within the Fourth Ward; however, much of it "is nearly gone except for the street layout, a park with remnants of a church, and bricks handmade by former slaves that residents had to fight to keep."[49]

In response to this, community members, historians, and activists are presently fighting to ensure that the historical legacy of the Fourth Ward remains intact. Assisting in this endeavor is the Rutherford B. H. Yates Museum, a nonprofit neighborhood preservation group that has taken the lead on the Fourth Ward's archaeological and historical research. Indeed, this and other kinds of groups are essential because, as historian Tomiko Meeks argues, gentrification has diminished the Fourth Ward's cultural and historical legacy. While city planners, private developers, and corporations believe that what they are doing is in the best interest of the city, the truth is that this kind of paternalistic and colonial-minded thinking is resulting in the erasure of the history of Houston's oldest African American neighborhood. Stated differently, the Fourth Ward is undergoing a gentrification process, which, on the one hand, promises to push it into the twenty-first century, but on the other, threatens to displace the people and destroy some of its most historic and cherished structures, leaving in its wake buildings "devoid of any historical significance."[50]

The same is true for Independence Heights, which "is on the cusp of the same kind of change that has stripped away much of [its] historic character."[51] In 1989, Independence Heights received the designation as a Historical Site. Eight years later, it was designated as a historic residential district. While both markers have gone a long way toward historically preserving the area, rapid change remains uninterrupted. Compounding this change was the flight of affluent African American families whose departure forced the community to lose a thriving business sector leaving in its place an abandonment of homes, buildings, and other structures. Additionally, their parting also paved the way for the arrival of townhomes, which have forced property taxes to skyrocket, further displacing working-class families. To date, "Burgess Hall is the only original public building left standing in the community," recalls longtime resident Vivian Hubbard Seals.[52]

Further complicating the situation is the Texas Department of Transportation's plan to initiate a highway expansion project through this neighborhood, threatening by extension to remove an additional thirty-one homes. In response to this, longtime residents of the area like Tanya Debose have developed historical revitalization plans, including restoring the region's homes and recovering, preserving, and promoting its rich history. Additionally, Debose and others have introduced something known as a heritage tax exemption to the state legislature, hoping to help older residents evade home displacement. Also assisting is the Historic Independence Heights Neighborhood Council, which has laid out plans for erecting a museum dedicated to its history.[53] At present, Booker T. Washington High School, Independence Heights, and the Fourth Ward continue working toward learning how to juggle changing demographics, gentrification, and historic preservation effectively.

CONCLUSION

Educational autonomy remains the most effective tool for challenging the discriminatory practices of the American school system. As Derrick Bell contends, "autonomy has long been thought essential . . . to . . . the quality of the educational process."[54] In the case of Booker T. Washington High School, parents, teachers, and administrators possessed an entrenched sense of educational autonomy, which helped them fight against inequitable school experiences and, by extension, helped their students excel. The school certainly had its problems, but it had its success as well, which speaks volumes and reflects the work of all those committed to ensuring the educational uplift of a student population historically segregated and neglected in schools across the state. Other schools in other communities traditionally had more resources and were better funded. Despite that, Booker T. Washington successfully educated "high-risk" students for over a century, creating a graduation pipeline to several higher learning institutions.

Similarly, community autonomy remains the most effective tool for protecting historic neighborhoods against gentrification. At present, both the Fourth Ward and Independence Heights—two historic African American communities, one a neighborhood, the other a former incorporated township—are undergoing massive changes because of gentrification, destroying many historic structures, and displacing scores of residents. Regrettably, this change is replacing both regions' history and culture, stripping them of their historic character. In response, however, residents from those communities have taken up the fight against urban renewal projects to ensure that their historical legacies remain intact. Additionally, they have initiated several plans for historical revitalization and preservation. The fight is psychologically taxing and seemingly unwinnable, but the people push on. Their deep-rooted sense of autonomy and community control sustains the battle against gentrification.

Today, Booker T. Washington High School leaders and teachers take great pride in knowing that for over a century, they have provided students a rigorous and competitive academic experience and have simultaneously offered services to the families that live in the community as well. The high school celebrates the fact it served two historically African American neighborhoods and that, at present, it has faculty and staff that reflects a changing student population. The lesson to be learned is that those who control the schools can determine who succeeds in them. In Booker T. Washington, historically, African Americans managed the school, and students performed beyond expectations as a result. Likewise, when schools are academically enriching, inclusive of parents, and culturally sensitive of the community, there are no limits to the academic achievements of their student population. Additionally, when schools are surrounded and nourished by autonomous neighborhoods, the fight to "eliminate all forms of oppression can be more fully actualized," putting everyone a step closer toward eliminating "racial inequities in society" as a whole.[55]

NOTES

1. Howard Beeth and Cary D. Wintz, *Black Dixie: Afro-Texan History and Culture in Houston* (College Station: Texas A&M University Press, 1992), 180.
2. William Henry Kellar, *Make Haste Slowly: Moderates, Conservatives, and School Desegregation in Houston* (College Station: Texas A&M University Press, 1999), 146; Vivian Hubbard Seals, Lota McCullough Charles, and Leona Walls, "Independence Heights: A Portrait of a Historic Neighborhood." Historical Independence Heights Neighborhood Council, 1985, www.historicindependenceheights.org.
3. Tim O'Brien, "Fourth Ward: A Conversation with Stephen Fox," *The Houston Review* 3:2 (2006): 49.
4. Payne Hiraldo, "The Role of Critical Race Theory in Higher Education," *The Vermont Connection* 31 (2010): 55.
5. Richard Delgado and Jean Stefancic, *Critical Race Theory: An Introduction* (New York: New York University Press, 2017), 25.
6. Hiraldo, "The Role of Critical Race Theory," 54.

7. Derrick A. Bell Jr., "Brown v. Board of Education and the Interest-Convergence Dilemma," *Harvard Law Review* 93:3 (1980): 518.

8. María C. Ledesma and Dolores Calderón, "Critical Race Theory in Education: A Review of Past Literature and a Look to the Future," *Qualitative Inquiry* 2:3 (2015): 208.

9. Ibid., 210.

10. Alwyn Barr, *Black Texans: A History of African-Americans in Texas, 1528–1995* (Norman: University of Oklahoma Press, 1996), 101, 156–57, 205.

11. Ledesma and Calderón, "Critical Race Theory in Education," 212.

12. Barr, *Black Texans*, 156–60, 205; Dwight Watson, *Race and the Houston Police Department, 1930–1990* (College Station: Texas A&M University Press, 2005), 32.

13. Barr, *Black Texans*, 156–57, 206; Watson, *Race and the Houston Police Department*, 32.

14. Barr, *Black Texans*, 156.

15. Bell, "Brown v. Board of Education," 525.

16. Ibid., 522.

17. Ruben Donato, *Mexicanos and Hispanos in Colorado Schools and Communities, 1920–1960* (New York: State University of New York Press, 2007), 124.

18. Bell, "Brown v. Board of Education," 532.

19. Ibid., 532.

20. Deborah Tedford, "Removal of Bones Sought at APV Site/Housing Authority Asks for Federal Order," *Houston Chronicle*, February 28, 1998, 30; McCullough Family Collection, MSS.0016, African American Library at the Gregory School, Houston Public Library, Houston, Texas; Scott Stabler, "Free Men Come to Houston: Blacks During Reconstruction," *The Houston Review* 3:1 (2015): 43, 74; Thelma Scott Bryant, "In the Name of Old Colored High," Thelma Scott Bryant Collection, MSS.0013, Box 3, Folder 16, African American Library at the Gregory School, Houston Public Library, Houston, Texas; Patricia Pando, "Two Worlds A Mile Apart: A Brief History of the Fourth Ward," *Houston History* 8:2 (2011): 39–40; Daniel E. Monsanto, *Houston* (Chicago: Arcadia Publishing, 2009), 9; Ronald E. Goodwin, *African Americans in Houston* (Charleston, SC: Arcadia Publishing, 2013), 34; J. Reuben Sheeler, "Education of Blacks in Houston," 1, in J. Reuben Sheeler Collection, Houston Metropolitan Research Center, Houston Public Library, Houston, Texas; E.O. Smith, "Colored Schools of Houston," in *The Red Book of Houston: A Compendium of Social, Professional, Educational and Industrial Interests of Houston's Colored Population* (Houston: Sotex Publishing Company, 1915), 15; Cary D. Wintz, "Fourth Ward, Houston," *Handbook of Texas Online* (2012): http://www.tshaonline.org/handbook/online/articles/hpf01.

21. Tomiko Meeks, "Freedmen's Town, Texas: A Lesson in the Failure of Historic Preservation," *Houston History* 8:2 (2011): 42.

22. Bryant, "In the Name of Old Colored High."

23. Thelma Scott Bryant Interview, August 3, 2007, Houston, Texas, in Thelma Scott Bryant Collection, MSS.0013, Box 3, Folder 15. African American Library

at the Gregory School, Houston Public Library, Houston, Texas; O'Brien, "Fourth Ward," 51; Wintz, "Fourth Ward, Houston."

24. Wintz, "Fourth Ward, Houston"; Bryant, "In the Name of Old Colored High"; Pando, "Two Worlds A Mile Apart," 39, 41; Bryant, Interview; Meeks, "Freedmen's Town," 42; O'Brien, "Fourth Ward," 49.

25. The Booker T. Washington Alumni Association Historical Journal of Memories, 1893–2014. African American Library at the Gregory School, Houston Public Library, Houston, Texas.

26. Smith, "Colored Schools of Houston," 15.

27. Booker T. Washington Alumni Association Historical Journal of Memories; Ellen Dickey Interview, November 21, 2013. African American Library at the Gregory School, Houston Public Library, Houston, Texas; *The Red Book of Houston*, 107; McCullough Family Collection.

28. Seals, Charles, and Walls, "Independence Heights."

29. Vivian Hubbard Seals, "Independence Heights, TX," *Handbook of Texas Online* (June 2010), http://www.tshaonline.org/handbook/online/articles/hri07.

30. Seals, "Independence Heights, TX"; Seals, Charles, and Walls, "Independence Heights."

31. Goodwin, *African Americans in Houston,* 42; *The Red Book of Houston*, 91; Smith, "Colored Schools of Houston," 14; E.L. Blackshear, "The Capability of the Negro Race," in *The Red Book of Houston*, 184–5; Michael R. Heintze, "Black Colleges," *Handbook of Texas Online,* http://www.tshaonline.org/handbook/online/articles/khb01.

32. Booker T. Washington Alumni Association Historical Journal of Memories; Sheeler, "Education of Blacks in Houston," 3; Roscoe Cavitt Collection, MSS.0026. African American Library at the Gregory School, Houston Public Library.

33. Goodwin, *African Americans in Houston*, 42; *The Red Book of Houston*, 91; Smith, "Colored Schools of Houston," 14; Blackshear, "The Capability of the Negro Race," 184–5; Heintze, "Black Colleges."

34. Texas Education Agency 2018–19 School Report Card, Booker T. Washington High School, https://www.houstonisd.org/domain/41893; Booker T. Washington Alumni Association Historical Journal of Memories; Barr, *Black Texans*, 239; Booker T. Washington High School and the High School for Engineering Professions, http://www.houstonisd.org/domain/18413.

35. Sandra Wilson Collection, MSS.0050, African American Library at the Gregory School, Houston Public Library; Booker T. Washington Alumni Association Historical Journal of Memories.

36. Ronald E. Marcello, "The Integration of Intercollegiate Athletics in Texas: North Texas State College as a Test Case, 1956," *Journal of Sport History* 14:3 (1987): 286; Booker T. Washington Alumni Association Historical Journal of Memories.

37. Sheeler, "Education of Blacks in Houston," 4.

38. Ledesma and Calderón, "Critical Race Theory in Education," 219.

39. The first graduate of Colored High was a young man by the name of Wright Munger, who received his diploma in 1896. The next year Colored High had fourteen

graduates. Throughout the decades graduating classes remained small. Booker T. Washington Alumni Association Historical Journal of Memories; Geraldine Pittman Wooten Interview, February 5, 2013, African American Library at the Gregory School, Houston Public Library, Houston, Texas; Bryant, "In the Name of Old Colored High"; Hazel McCullough Collection, MSS. 0001, African American Library at the Gregory School, Houston Public Library; Carl Walker Jr. Collection, MSS.0025, African American Library at the Gregory School, Houston Public Library.

40. Wilson Collection; Jonnie Hart Brooks Collection, MSS.0027, African American Library at the Gregory School, Houston Public Library; James Humphrey Interview, February 8, 2013, African American Library at the Gregory School, Houston Public Library, Houston, Texas; Booker T. Washington Alumni Association Historical Journal of Memories.

41. Robert D. Bullard, *Invisible Houston: The Black Experience in Boom and Bust* (College Station: Texas A&M University Press, 1987), 129; Ward Gary Schmidt, "A History of the Desegregation of the Houston Independent School District, 1954–1971" (Master's Thesis, University of Houston, 1972), v–vi, 158–59; Max Berger and Lee Wilborn, "Education," *Handbook of Texas Online*, http://www.tshaonline.org/handbook/online/articles/khe01; Barr, *Black Texans*, 208.

42. Barr, *Black Texans*, 208, 210, 239; Kellar, *Make Haste Slowly,* 155.

43. Sheeler, "Education of Blacks in Houston," 6; Goodwin, *African Americans in Houston,* 15.

44. Booker T. Washington Alumni Association Historical Journal of Memories.

45. Frank R. Kemerer, "United States v. Texas," *Handbook of Texas Online*, http://www.tshaonline.org/handbook/online/articles/jru02.

46. Booker T. Washington Alumni Association Historical Journal of Memories; Bell, "Brown v. Board of Education," 530–31; Kemerer, "United States v. Texas."

47. "Celebrating A Century of Educational Excellence: Booker T. Washington High School 100th Anniversary Celebration." August 1993, African American Library at the Gregory School, Houston Public Library, Houston, Texas; Booker T. Washington Alumni Association Historical Journal of Memories; Betsy Denson, "Demo Begins to Make Way for a New Booker T. Washington High School," *TheLeaderNews.com*, April 2, 2015; Jonathan Garris, "HISD Breaks Ground on New Booker T. Washington High School Facility," *TheLeaderNews.com*, April 13, 2016.

48. Bryant, "In the Name of Old Colored High."

49. Sarah Smith, "The First Black City in Texas is on the Verge of Losing its Identity," *Houston Chronicle*, September 25, 2019; Bryant, "In the Name of Old Colored High"; Meeks, "Freedmen's Town," 42; O'Brien, "Fourth Ward," 49, 51.

50. Meeks, "Freedmen's Town," 43; O'Brien, "Fourth Ward," 51.

51. Smith, "The First Black City in Texas."

52. Seals, "Independence Heights, TX"; Smith, "The First Black City in Texas."

53. Seals, Charles, and Walls, "Independence Heights"; Smith, "The First Black City in Texas."

54. Bell, "Brown v. Board of Education," 526.

55. Ledesma and Calderón, "Critical Race Theory in Education," 206; Hiraldo, "The Role of Critical Race Theory," 53.

BIBLIOGRAPHY

African American Library at the Gregory School, Houston Public Library, Houston, Texas.

Barr, Alwyn. *Black Texans: A History of African-Americans in Texas, 1528–1995*. Norman: University of Oklahoma Press, 1996.

Beeth, Howard and Cary D. Wintz. *Black Dixie: Afro-Texan History and Culture in Houston*. College Station: Texas A&M University Press, 1992.

Bell, Jr., Derrick A. "Brown v. Board of Education and the Interest-Convergence Dilemma." *Harvard Law Review*, vol. 93, no. 3 (1980): 518–533.

Berger, Max and Lee Wilborn. "Education." *Handbook of Texas Online*. http://www.tshaonline.org/handbook/online/articles/khe01.

Blackshear, E.L. "The Capability of the Negro Race." In *The Red Book of Houston: A Compendium of Social, Professional, Educational, and Industrial Interests of Houston's Colored Population*. Houston: Sotex Publishing Company, 1915.

Booker T. Washington High School and the High School for Engineering Professions. http://www.houstonisd.org/domain/18413.

Bryant, Thelma Scott. Interview by Patricia Smith Prather. August 3, 2007, Houston, Texas. Thelma Scott Bryant Collection, MSS.0013, Box 3, Folder 15. African American Library at the Gregory School, Houston Public Library, Houston, Texas.

Bullard, Robert D. *Invisible Houston: The Black Experience in Boom and Bust*. College Station: Texas A&M University Press, 1987.

Carl Walker Jr. Collection, MSS.0025, African American Library at the Gregory School, Houston Public Library.

"Celebrating A Century of Educational Excellence: Booker T. Washington High School 100th Anniversary Celebration." August 1993, African American Library at the Gregory School, Houston Public Library, Houston, Texas.

Delgado, Richard and Jean Stefancic, *Critical Race Theory: An Introduction*. New York: New York University Press, 2017.

Denson, Betsy. "Demo Begins to Make Way for a New Booker T. Washington High School." *TheLeaderNews.com*, April 2, 2015.

Dickey, Ellen. Interview by Adrienne Cain. November 21, 2013. African American Library at the Gregory School, Houston Public Library, Houston, Texas.

Donato, Ruben. *Mexicanos and Hispanos in Colorado Schools and Communities, 1920-1960*. New York: State University of New York Press, 2007.

Garris, Jonathan. "HISD Breaks Ground on New Booker T. Washington High School Facility." *TheLeaderNews.com*, April 13, 2016.

Goodwin, Ronald E. *African Americans in Houston*. Charleston.: Arcadia Publishing, 2013.

Heintze, Michael R. "Black Colleges." *Handbook of Texas Online*. http://www.tshaonline.org/handbook/online/articles/khb01.

Hiraldo, Payne. "The Role of Critical Race Theory in Higher Education." *The Vermont Connection*, vol. 31 (2010): 53–59.

Houston Metropolitan Research Center, Houston Public Library, Houston, Texas.

Humphrey, James. Interview by Adrienne Cain. February 8, 2013, African American Library at the Gregory School, Houston Public Library, Houston, Texas.

Kellar, William Henry. *Make Haste Slowly: Moderates, Conservatives, and School Desegregation in Houston*. College Station: Texas A&M University Press, 1999.

Kemerer, Frank R. "United States v. Texas." *Handbook of Texas Online*. http://www.tshaonline.org/handbook/online/articles/jru02.

Ledesma, María C. and Dolores Calderón. "Critical Race Theory in Education: A Review of Past Literature and a Look to the Future." *Qualitative Inquiry*, vol. 2, no. 3 (2015): 206–222.

Marcello, Ronald E. "The Integration of Intercollegiate Athletics in Texas: North Texas State College as a Test Case, 1956." *Journal of Sport History*, vol. 14, no. 3 (1987): 286–316.

Meeks, Tomiko. "Freedmen's Town, Texas: A Lesson in the Failure of Historic Preservation." *Houston History*, vol. 8, no. 2 (Spring 2011): 42–44.

Monsanto, Daniel E. *Houston*. Chicago: Arcadia Publishing, 2009.

O'Brien, Tim. "Fourth Ward: A Conversation with Stephen Fox." *The Houston Review*, vol. 3, no. 2 (Spring 2006): 49–51.

Pando, Patricia. "Two Worlds A Mile Apart: A Brief History of the Fourth Ward." *Houston History*, vol. 8, no. 2 (Spring 2011): 37–41.

Schmidt, Ward Gary. "A History of the Desegregation of the Houston Independent School District, 1954–1971." Master's Thesis, University of Houston, 1972.

Seals, Vivian Hubbard. "Independence Heights, TX." *Handbook of Texas Online*. http://www.tshaonline.org/handbook/online/articles/hri07.

Seals, Vivian Hubbard, Lota McCullough Charles, and Leona Walls. "Independence Heights: A Portrait of a Historic Neighborhood." Historical Independence Heights Neighborhood Council. www.historicindependenceheights.org.

Smith, E.O. "Colored Schools of Houston." In *The Red Book of Houston: A Compendium of Social, Professional, Educational and Industrial Interests of Houston's Colored Population*. Houston: Sotex Publishing Company, 1915.

Smith, Sarah. "The First Black City in Texas is on the Verge of Losing its Identity." *Houston Chronicle*, September 25, 2019.

Stabler, Scott. "Free Men Come to Houston: Blacks During Reconstruction." *The Houston Review*, vol. 3, no. 1 (Fall 2015): 40–43, 73–76.

Tedford, Deborah. "Removal of Bones Sought at APV Site / Housing Authority Asks for Federal Order." *Houston Chronicle*, February 28, 1998.

Texas Education Agency 2018–19 School Report Card, Booker T. Washington High School. https://www.houstonisd.org/domain/41893.

The Red Book of Houston: A Compendium of Social, Professional, Educational and Industrial Interests of Houston's Colored Population. Houston: Sotex Publishing Company, 1915.

Watson, Dwight. *Race and the Houston Police Department, 1930–1990*. College Station: Texas A&M University Press, 2005.

Wintz, Cary D. "Fourth Ward, Houston." *Handbook of Texas Online*. http://www.tshaonline.org/handbook/online/articles/hpf01.

Wooten, Geraldine Pittman. Interview by Adrienne Cain. February 5, 2013, African American Library at the Gregory School, Houston Public Library, Houston, Texas.

Part II

AFRICAN AMERICANS AND EDUCATION

Introduction

Intersections between Education and Critical Race Studies

Jonathan Chism

Educational scholactivists such as Gloria Ladson-Billings, William Tate, Adrienne Dixson, Marvin Lynn, and Jessica Decuir have influenced critical race theory (CRT) to develop a firm footing in the field of education.[1] Since the 1990s, race crits in education have striven to grapple with racism and other intersecting oppressions in educational institutions and to propose strategies for addressing inequity. CRT has been a topic of deliberation at meetings of the American Educational Research Association (AERA) and the Critical Race Studies in Education Association (CRSEA). Educational scholars' attraction to CRT seems inevitable and unsurprising given early legal scholars' acute focus on school desegregation and the import and meaning of the *Brown v. Board of Education* ruling. Derrick Bell's interest convergence thesis contended that the Supreme Court decision did not remedy long-standing racial inequities in public schools because the ruling ultimately centered on serving the interests of Whites rather than marginalized Black students.[2] However, it was not until a few decades after CRT developed in the legal academy that educational theorists began to adopt a CRT framework for education. In what follows, I briefly discuss educational scholars' employment of CRT and review three key arguments advanced in their initial works. Further, I explain ways that the chapters in this part of the volume build on the foundational scholarship of critical race theorists in education.

Pedagogical theorist Gloria Ladson-Billings and sociologist William F. Tate were instrumental in advancing CRT in education. While serving as members of the faculty at the University of Wisconsin, they presented a paper at the AERA in 1994 in which they critiqued scholars of education who focused on ways gender and class affected the education of students for offering inadequate explanations of "raced" education.[3] As they called for scholars to devote more explicit attention to race, Ladson-Billings and Tate acknowledged trailblazing theorists of race in education such as the historian Carter G. Woodson and sociologist William E. B. Du Bois whose work challenged White supremacy in society within the academy. Du Bois and Woodson were among the first African Americans to obtain a Doctor of Philosophy from Harvard University during the early twentieth century.

Woodson's most popular book, *The Miseducation of the Negro,* explained how schools perpetuated inequality and a sense of inferiority among African American students by teaching them to despise and shun their African American culture and to praise and adopt European and Greco-Roman thought and ideals. Woodson contended that educated Blacks who have been influenced to have an "attitude of contempt toward their own people" and who have been "taught to admire the Hebrew, the Greek, the Latin and the Teuton and to despise the African" had been *miseducated.*[4] Asseverating that African American educators should inspire Blacks to become autonomous thinkers and to develop an understanding and appreciation of their culture and history, Woodson founded the Study of Negro Life and History and served as editor of the *Journal of Negro History.*

Du Bois was one of the first academics of color to theorize the African American experience of race. His theory of double consciousness, "this sense of always looking at one's self through the eyes of others, of measuring one's soul by the tape of a world that look[s] on in amused contempt and pity," has frequently been cited by race scholars.[5] Du Bois wrote several texts throughout his long, extensive academic career that examined race and education including but not limited to *The Talented Tenth* (1903), "What Intellectual Training is Doing for the Negro" (1904), "Atlanta University" (1905), "The Field and Function of a Negro College" (1933), and "The Freedom to Learn" (1949).[6] Similar to Woodson, he admonished scholars working in the field of African American studies "to utilize continental and diaspora African history and culture as their foundation and grounding point of departure."[7] Additionally, he was cognizant of the intersections between racism, sexism, and classism before critical race feminists introduced the term "intersectionality." Educational theorist Reiland Rabaka refers to Du Bois as a "classical critical race theorist."[8]

While Ladson-Billings and Tate acknowledged the theoretical groundwork early race scholars such as Woodson and Du Bois established, their aim in 1994 was to advance a "critical race theoretical perspective in education analogous to that of critical race theory in legal scholarship."[9] That is to say their work signaled deep appreciation for the legal foundations of CRT. They were adamant that educational scholars should strive to understand the writings and key tenets of CRT as espoused by the pioneering legal scholars. Educational scholars have drawn on CRT's critiques of property, liberalism, and adopted CRT's method of storytelling and counternarratives to understand a host of persisting educational inequities including grappling with why White schools have been better funded, have had more "certified and prepared" teachers, have had more students in gifted and talented programs or honors classes, and have an overall enhanced reputation compared to schools that serve predominantly Black and Brown communities.[10]

Applying a CRT critique of property to education, Ladson-Billings and Tate insist that the aforementioned disparities and others exist because Whites in positions of power have designed laws to safeguard the property and material interests of White people as well as whiteness itself, which Cheryl Harris refers to as "the ultimate form of property."[11] Since the genesis of the American republic, Whites have been generally afforded privileged status and given opportunities denied to those who are not White. Ladson-Billings and Tate also argue that educational inequities tie directly to funding formulas that center on property ownership and property taxes. Affluent Whites that have paid high taxes compared to Blacks due to the higher value of their homes have often expressed resentment for funding "a public school system whose clientele is largely nonwhite and poor."[12] They feel that governmental revenue from their taxes should go toward schools in their neighborhoods. Their discontent connects to the history of White flight, a phenomenon that historian Kevin Kruse discusses at length. Whites fled urban spaces in Atlanta following the end of legal segregation because they erroneously believed they paid higher taxes relative to African Americans.[13] Their argument against desegregation was that most African Americans were freeloaders who paid little taxes and that it was unjust to permit African Americans to have equal access to quality schools, parks, recreation centers, streets, and other public spaces that hardworking Whites funded. The tax revolt was a cause that many White conservatives embraced to defend racial segregation and to subtly preserve White supremacy in the post-civil rights period.[14] Race crits in education recognize and emphasize that schools that serve Black and Brown students need access to funding to support and sustain quality educational programs. Revolting against paying taxes to fund schools in urban communities, calling for improved "educational standards," and beckoning for more parental responsibility are slick maneuvers to circumvent fair and equitable funding of schools and a means of maintaining the status quo.[15]

Ladson-Billings and Tate also explain contemporary educational inequalities by employing CRT to pinpoint flaws with multicultural education, an educational paradigm that aims to promote diversity along the lines of race, ethnicity, sex, gender, ability, and sexual orientation. Race crits in education have acknowledged that though there are concerns, which are outlined below, the multicultural education paradigm contributed to the sprouting of Ethnic Studies and Women and Gender Studies Programs at various colleges and universities throughout the United States during the post-Civil Rights period.

Furthermore, those committed to this approach have earnestly sought to encourage appreciation of diversity through facilitating programming that aims to help students broaden their cultural horizons, including creating opportunities for students to come to appreciate Hip-Hop music and to enjoy Soul Food or perhaps Jamaican cuisine. Employing CRT, race crits in education insist that this approach fails to facilitate a sincere understanding of diversity and inclusion among students and upholds unjust arrangements and norms. This paradigm did not push students to think deeply and critically about "the contradictions of US ideals and lived realities" that contribute to socioeconomic disparities.[16] The multicultural educational paradigm unwittingly reifies colorblind racism by failing to help students recognize that authentic diversity centers on respecting the humanity of others, dismantling oppressive systems and structures, and creating policies necessary to advance equality and equity.

Besides seeking to understand the connection between race and property as well as explain the flaws of the multicultural education program, educational scholars have also adopted CRT's method of storytelling and counternarratives to expose and challenge racial inequity in education.[17] Race crits employ stories in various forms such as poetry, fiction, and autobiographical reflection to trace and illuminate racial contradictions in American society and civil rights laws. Derrick Bell used narratives to make complex legal discussions understandable to an audience untrained in the law and to indicate how Whites in power have been committed to placating to the interests of Whites instead of advancing justice for all.[18] For example, in *And We Are Not Saved,* Bell developed ten "chronicles" to explain racial injustice in American law and society.[19] Geneva Crenshaw, a fictional Black woman who served as Bell's doppelganger within the narrative and the central character, provides commentary regarding trends relating to civil rights laws. In one chronicle, Geneva journeyed back in time to the Constitutional Convention in Philadelphia in 1787. Introducing herself as an African American woman from the future, she endeavored to warn delegates about the negative ramifications of slavery and to persuade them not to compromise. Dismissing her arguments, the constitutional delegates still elected to "compromise the rights of Blacks on the basis of national economic interests and White unity."[20]

Rather than merely raving and complaining about individual occurrences of racism, critical race theorists employ stories and counternarratives to illuminate systemic racism and policies that bolster inequity.[21] Counterstories expose and encourage reflection on structural racism in society. They provide the marginalized a means of going against the grain and bucking the "stock stories" that the hegemonic establishment tell to uphold and validate claims to power and reify the status quo.[22] Counterstories "open new windows into reality" and help the oppressed see and imagine alternate ways of being and living undetermined by the bounds of whiteness.[23] They have the capacity to help oppressors become conscious of their taken for granted racist assumptions, biases, and prejudices about African Americans and people of color. Race crits in education have particularly used counternarratives to explain persisting racial inequities and to illuminate how school programming and curriculums are often dictated by White administrators and teachers who advance "a White supremacist master script" that promotes whiteness and discounts, diminishes, and devalues blackness through neglecting to include Black perspectives or speak truthfully about the Black experience.[24]

Despite the extensive scholarship race crits have published in the legal academy and in the field of education, long-standing inequities remain because racism is endemic to American society. It is akin to an incurable cancer. Facing this difficult reality in a straightforward manner, scholactivists in education remain firm in their commitment to enhancing their understanding of racism, striving for justice and equity, and working to improve the life options and chances of the oppressed. In this vein, over the past twenty years, race crits in education have employed CRT to expose the racist underpinning of standardized tests and various measures of academic achievement, school curriculums, pedagogical methods and practices, zero tolerance policies, the school-to-prison pipeline, and various efforts to oppose affirmative action such as *Fisher v. University of Texas at Austin*.[25]

The scholactivists in this part of the volume aim to build on the scholarship and work race crits in education have done and to strive to advance social justice through utilizing CRT methods and frameworks, especially through engaging African Americans' voices, experiences, and stories "as teachers, parents, administrators, students and community members."[26] Darius Benton presents the narratives of African American teachers and administrators who endured the desegregation of public schools during the 1960s and 1970s. Felicia Harris and Nina Barbieri discuss "good" pedagogy, asking that educators consider their methods for teaching and whether they merely continue to perpetuate the status quo or are actively educating their students to prepare them to transform a society which is shaped by systemic racism. LeAnna Luney presents the stories of Black women students at the University of Colorado and explains how they developed community networks to cope with marginalization as they strive to overcome oppression.

NOTES

1. William F. Tate, "Critical Race Theory and Education: History, Theory, and Implications," *American Educational Research Association*, 22 (1997): 197.
2. Derrick A. Bell Jr., "Brown V. Board of Education and the Interest Convergence Dilemma," *Harvard Law Review,* 93, no. 3 (January 1980): 518, 523.
3. Adrienne D. Dixson, Celia K. Rousseau, and Jamel K. Donner, eds. *Critical Race Theory in Education: All God's Children Got a Song* (New York: Routledge, 2017), 1; Tate, "Critical Race Theory and Education," 195.
4. Carter G. Woodson, *The Mis-Education of the Negro* (Suwanee, GA: 12th Media Services, 2017, orig. 1933), 5.
5. W.E.B. Du Bois, *The Souls of Black Folk* (New York: Dover Publications, 1903), 2–3.
6. Reiland Rabaka, "W.E.B. Du Bois's Contributions to Critical Race Studies in Education: Sociology of Education, Classical Critical Race Theory, and Pro-Critical Pedagogy," Cited in *Handbook of Critical Race Theory in Education,* Marvin Lynn and Adrienne D. Dixon, eds. (New York: Routledge, 2013), 74.
7. Ibid., 76.
8. Ibid., 72.
9. Gloria Ladson-Billings and William F. Tate, "Toward a Critical Race Theory of Education," *Teachers College Record*, 97, no. 1 (Fall 1995): 47.
10. Gloria Ladson-Billings, "Just What Is Critical Race Theory and What's It Doing In a Nice Field Like Education," *International Journal of Qualitative Studies in Education*, 11, no. 1 (1998): 21; Ladson-Billings and Tate, "Toward a Critical Race Theory of Education," 54, 59–60.
11. Cheryl Harris, "Whiteness as Property," *Harvard Law Review*, 106, no. 8 (1993): 1707–09.
12. Ladson-Billings and Tate, "Toward a Critical Race Theory of Education," 53.
13. Kevin M. Kruse, *White Flight: Atlanta and the Making of Modern Conservatism* (Princeton, NJ: Princeton University Press, 2005), 126.
14. Ibid.
15. Ladson-Billings and Tate, "Toward a Critical Race Theory of Education," 54.
16. Ladson-Billings, "Just What Is Critical Race Theory," 22.
17. Dixson et al., *Critical Race Theory in Education*, 3.
18. Tate, "Critical Race Theory and Education," 218.
19. Ibid., 212; Derrick A. Bell, *And We Are No Saved: The Elusive Quest for Racial Justice* (New York: Basic Books: 1987).
20. Ibid.
21. Dixson et al., *Critical Race Theory in Education*, 38.
22. Richard Delgado, "Storytelling for Oppositionists and Others: A Plea for Narrative," *Michigan Law Review,* 87 (1989): 2414.
23. Tate, "Critical Race Theory and Education," 220.
24. Ladson-Billings, "Just What Is Critical Race Theory," 18.
25. Ibid., 19–20.

26. Ladson-Billings and Tate, "Toward a Critical Race Theory of Education," 58.

BIBLIOGRAPHY

Bell, Derrick A. *And We Are No Saved: The Elusive Quest for Racial Justice.* New York: Basic Books, 1987.

Bell, Derrick A. "Brown V. Board of Education and the Interest Convergence Dilemma." *Harvard Law Review,* 93, no. 3 (January 1980): 518–533. https://doi.org/10.2307/1340546.

Decuir, Jessica T. and Adrienne D. Dixson. "'So When It Comes Out, They Aren't That Surprised That It Is There': Using Critical Race Theory as a Tool of Analysis of Race and Racism in Education." *Educational Researcher*, 33, no. 5 (2004): 26–31.

Delgado, Richard. "Storytelling for Oppositionists and Others: A Plea for Narrative." *Michigan Law Review,* 87 (1989): 2411–2441.

Dixson, Adrienne D., Celia K. Rousseau, and Jamel K. Donner, eds. *Critical Race Theory in Education: All God's Children Got a Song*. New York: Routledge, 2017.

Du Bois, W.E.B. *The Souls of Black Folk.* New York: Dover Publications, 1903.

Harris, Cheryl. "Whiteness as Property." *Harvard Law Review*, 106n no. 8 (1993): 1707–1791.

Kruse, Kevin M. *White Flight: Atlanta and the Making of Modern Conservatism.* Princeton: Princeton University Press, 2005.

Ladson-Billings, Gloria. "Just What Is Critical Race Theory and What's It Doing In a Nice Field Like Education." *International Journal of Qualitative Studies in Education*, 11, no. 1 (1998): 7–24. https://doi.org/10.1080/095183998236863.

Ladson-Billings, Gloria and William F. Tate. "Toward a Critical Race Theory of Education." *Teachers College Record*, 97, no. 1 (Fall 1995): 47–68.

Lynn, Marvin and Adrienne D. Dixon, eds. *Handbook of Critical Race Theory in Education*. New York: Routledge, 2013.

Tate IV, William F. "Critical Race Theory and Education: History, Theory, and Implications." *American Educational Research Association*, 22 (1997): 195–247. https://doi.org/10.2307/1167376.

Woodson, Carter G. *The Mis-Education of the Negro.* Suwanee: 12th Media Services, 2017, orig. 1933.

Chapter 4

"Getcha Lesson"

Gleaning Wisdom from African American K–12 Educators Who Endured the Desegregation of Public Schools

Darius M. Benton

As a child growing up in Charlotte, North Carolina, in the 1990s, I spent a lot of time after school at my great-aunt Thelma's house. One of the phrases I remember her repeating is, "Getcha lesson!" At the time, I understood this phrase as her encouraging me to do my homework. Little did I know that there was greater meaning behind this phrase for herself and others of her generation. As a "Negro" woman born in rural South Carolina in the early 1920s, she and many of her peers did not have the opportunity to attend school beyond the eighth grade as that was all the formal education available to them. This was possibly an improvement from what was accessible to the preceding generation. However, these limitations were not apparent to those she met. Aunt Thelma's demeanor, class, and life-bred wisdom served her and those around her well. Although she did not obtain a college degree or take the national teacher's exam, she was an educator. She impacted many children, including her nieces and nephews and the children of her White employers. Rather than teaching subjects such as English, Algebra, or Social Studies, she taught the "secrets" to life. Her lessons continue to guide me as I navigate life's challenging times. Aunt Thelma's words, "Getcha Lesson!" reminds me of the value and necessity of engaging African American educators who have preceded us, and intentionally gleaning the wisdom that they have to share. Their lessons can help contemporary educators in the post-Civil Rights period meet the needs of students from underserved communities as well as inspire teachers to thrive professionally in their careers even as they continue to struggle with White supremacy and other societal challenges.

Storytelling is an important methodology within critical race theory.[1] Narratives are commonly used in critical race scholarship to highlight perspectives otherwise unheard or undervalued. Counter-storytelling is a critical race methodology that "provides a tool to 'counter' deficit storytelling . . . [and a] space to conduct and present research grounded in the experiences and knowledge of people of color."[2] This chapter is the product of my interviews with ten African American educators who participated in desegregating K–12 public schools in different regions of the United States during the 1960s and 1970s. The data gathered brings to the forefront voices and experiences of African American educators whose contributions might otherwise be lost in the historical landscape.[3]

This work highlights a cultural shift, as their historical positioning and vocation required these trailblazers to assist in altering educational and wider cultural norms. Throughout the chapter, I will discuss timeless lessons learned from conversations with educators and administrators who were called upon to implement the desegregation of public schools, one of the most significant institutional cultural changes in history. African American educators had not been equipped or trained for this task. This chapter aims to add to emerging scholarship regarding Critical Race praxis in K–12 education by sharing African American educators' reflections on their stories and experiences during desegregation and seeks to present some practical tools that may help contemporary educators, especially educators of color, adapt to the ineluctable cultural and organizational challenges they will encounter including but not limited to systemic racism.[4] These stories and their corresponding lessons offer essential strategies and coping mechanisms for current K–12 educators to successfully instruct students and advance in their careers regardless of the oppression they may face.

A HISTORICAL OVERVIEW OF THE DESEGREGATION OF PUBLIC SCHOOLS

Prior to the *Brown v. Board of Education* (1954) Supreme Court decision, public schools in the United States were divided on the basis of race, supporting the "separate but equal" doctrine established by the *Plessy v. Ferguson* (1896) Supreme Court decision. Following the *Brown v. Board of Education* decision, a radical shift slowly occurred in the United States as public schools were eventually forced to make major changes in their culture and operations in order to comply with the court decision. Different than the desegregation of buses, trains, and parks, school integration promoted "racial mixing" rather than nondiscrimination in access to facilities.[5] This period of change was met by protest and was a very difficult and terrifying era for many

African American youth who integrated into White public schools. Better-known examples include Ruby Bridges (New Orleans, LA), Dorothy Counts (Charlotte, NC), or the "Little Rock Nine" (Little Rock, AK), who not only became the face of public school desegregation in media but also experienced harsh daily treatment as they aimed to learn and survive each day.[6]

The Supreme Court's failure to provide a clear plan for the desegregation of public schools, southern resistance to the ruling, White citizenship councils, and other racist ploys prolonged the implementation of the *Brown* decision across the country.[7] Furthermore, the racial oppression derived from Jim Crow society and lack of impartiality in educational funding is the basis of academic deficits.[8] This is significant to consider as many of the stronger Black teachers were removed from their segregated schools and assigned to teach at predominately White schools upon the start of integration efforts, while many Black-serving schools, although effective, were closed.[9] Across the southern United States, school boards dominated by White members, closed Black high schools while allowing White schools to remain open.[10]

In 1965, the U.S. Congress passed the *Elementary and Secondary Education Act*, authorizing the removal of federal aid to school systems "practicing *de jure racial segregation.*"[11] This served as a motivator for school districts across the country to move toward actively integrating public schools, nearly ten years after the *Brown* decision. De Facto segregation however did remain a significant issue in many communities as integration attempts were made.[12] Associations such as the NAACP, Black Churches, and the National PTA-assisted in advancing desegregation efforts.[13] Although differing in their motive, approach, and impact, their contribution is significant toward the successful achievement of public school desegregation.

Even as schools began to desegregate there was misalignment between "educational improvement as the appropriate goal of school desegregation" and the subsequent "state of law."[14] This prompted the need for more oversight, leading school systems to respond to court cases following *Brown* by balancing student and teacher populations by race in each school, eradicating one-race schools, redesigning school assignment zones, and implementing transportation strategies to attain racial equilibrium.[15] This however did not guarantee Black children a better education than they were receiving pre-*Brown.*[16] Although children of all races were provided access and opportunity once denied them, "poor integration implementation policies and widespread white backlash presented problems for many Black students and teachers."[17] Also, many Black children and teachers found themselves in environments where their cultural identity was not understood nor celebrated.

It is important to note that segregated Black schools typically were not schools that failed students. Walker states, "Segregation-era [B]lack educators set the groundwork for an equitable and aspirational education system for all."[18] One student recounts, "Good teachers and good teaching were central elements to Black students' excelling in all-Black schools."[19] The thought persists that "integration destroyed something uniquely valuable to African Americans in the South."[20] There were also cases where the "Negro schools" in a city were considered better than White schools.[21] As students recount the dedication of Black teachers that compensated for the "material deficiencies of the schools," the main issue leading many to fight segregated schooling is the notion that the schools were not equal due to the "inequality in the provision of educational resources to African American children and all-Black public schools that condemned them to inferiority."[22] For clarity, the issue in legally segregated schools was not the quality of educators, but the equality of the resources provided.

Since the *Brown* decision and the integration of public schools in the United States, there has been a noteworthy decrease of Black teachers in the United States.[23] This is likely due to the numerous opportunities now available to Black professionals that were once unavailable prior to the desegregation era.[24] However, one must not discount the fact that throughout the decades following *Brown*, particularly in rural areas and smaller cities, "[B] lack teachers and administrators would suffer job loss, demotion, and harassment or displacement during the desegregation of the nation's schools.[25] This occurrence is unfortunate as the experiential and professional contributions of African American educators are essential to the success of African American students in school.[26] Often, the experiences of the period are told from the perspective of the student or with the student as the subject. As stated by Ledesma and Calderón, the voices of critical educators are essential to "engage White supremacist ideology prevalent across pedagogy" as both student and teacher counter-narratives are an indispensable element of critical race theory in Education.[27] This project attends to the narratives and counter-narratives of African American educators.

LESSONS FROM AFRICAN AMERICAN EDUCATORS

The educators interviewed spanned the country inclusive of service during the public school desegregation era in Florida, South Carolina, North Carolina, Virginia, Michigan, Massachusetts, and Rhode Island. Every educator interviewed for this project was taught in segregated public schools and colleges.[28] One of the educators interviewed stated, "to be a college educated Black person during this period was a great feat."[29] This premise is important because as indicated at the beginning of the chapter, in some regions of the country, education for Black (or Negro) Americans was limited. Many were unable to attend high school, or even complete primary school, making it impossible to attend college. The Black educators of this period, both male and female, were elite, privileged, considered themselves to be fortunate, and were often admired and appreciated by the communities for which they served.[30] Almost all of the educators interviewed also acquired graduate degrees. They eventually became teachers or administrators in integrated schools as districts began to relocate administrators and teachers of both races, to fulfill legal requirements. For many, this was their first integrated experience with the exception of the male educators interviewed that served in the military prior to their teaching career.

Mrs. J was an elementary educator in Rhode Island during the desegregation era. The school district recruited her after she graduated from a Historically Black College in North Carolina. The district was intentional about hiring Black teachers as a response to student protests following the assassination of Rev. Dr. Martin Luther King Jr. due to the absence of Black teachers in the area. She served the same school district in Rhode Island for thirty-one years, only taking a year off to teach in Nigeria at an international school at the beginning of her career. When asked about the training teachers may have received to support integration efforts, she shared the following story:

> No [we didn't get any additional training], just threw us out there. In the 70s they recruited you from the south, and that was true. No, there was no training, but what helped us is we went to Black churches, we got together [socially], sorority, and some of my friends got together to talk out our situation if there was a problem. No one came together to say, "you come from the south and you're going to experience this." So you know we basically did that on our own by coming together.[31]

Because there was no formal training to assist in her transition, Mrs. J and other teachers in her community had to find or develop outlets for support, which assisted her in her career and transition to a new city. One of the lessons gained from my conversation with her was to *find or create a supportive community*. This lesson points to the idea of intentionality in creating socio-emotional support. Without the formation of this circle of support, it is likely that Mrs. J may not have successfully adapted and survived this transitional period.

Mr. M was a teacher, school board member, and administrator in Michigan during public school integration. After being educated in segregated schools in South Carolina and graduating from a Black college in Atlanta, GA, he entered the military. His career as a teacher began in a segregated high school in North Carolina prior to relocating to Detroit where his integration journey began. When asked if there were any "safe spaces" for African American teachers and students, he shared the following story:

> It depends on how vocal you were I guess. You could hide, I remember how there were so many people that avoided me like the plague. If you wanted to be successful you would stay away from people like me then you'd move on up. But if you were bold and confident, I won't say arrogant but confident, and you didn't knuckle under, you always would have challenges. And have people who would try to keep you in your place and convince you of who you really are.[32]

Mr. M struggled with the idea of having to "stay in his place" or "become humble" in order to advance his career. He did not believe he should have to hide his skills or qualifications, but this did not always work to his advantage. The lesson gained from the conversation was to *be prepared for consequences when you choose to speak up for what's right.* As Mr. M indicated, some that he served with were afraid of consequences and remained quiet, avoiding "troublemakers" and directly challenging White supremacy. He was not afraid to suffer the consequences endured throughout his career as from his perspective, it was imperative to moving the cause forward. This direct approach was significant to Mr. M because he was not content with minimizing himself for the comfort of others.

Dr. R was a librarian, English teacher, and school administrator employed during this period in both school districts and colleges. She worked in both segregated and integrated schools in North Carolina and South Carolina with a career in education that spanned over fifty years. When asked what she would change about her experience during the desegregation period, she shares the following story:

> So by the end of my career I had learned diplomacy. I had also learned that sometimes you need teamwork. You can't do it all by yourself you have to have collaborators.
>
> I know that I didn't get a particular job because I was too blunt, I didn't play the game. There is a political game you have to play and that doesn't mean you have to compromise your virtues or anything like that. I applied for a job recruiting teachers for the school district. The question was, "What would you do if a principal objected to a recommendation you made?" My question was, "Well, who is his boss?" I would not have stopped if that was the most qualified person. I would fight for the most qualified person. But that was not the most politically correct address at the time. I should have said, "I would refer to the principal and work to get that person placed in another position." If I really thought they were qualified. So instances like that when I just hold my britches. That was an instance that I lost out because of my mouth and not being diplomatic.[33]

Dr. R highlights the notion that Black educators of the period had to acknowledge that there was a system at work within a system. Recognizing the invisible system and how to find success within it is a valuable key to achievement one can glean from this period. The lesson from the conversation is to *"Play the game" but don't compromise your values or virtues.* Similar to the previous lesson, this one emboldens the need to understand one's environment and the power dynamics within to be successful without sacrificing self-concept. By employing this tactic, one is able to achieve organizational goals and maintain personal worth.

Mrs. W was an educator employed in Florida during this era for over thirty-five years serving both as a teacher and elementary school principal. When asked to describe an experience of the beginning of her career, she shared the following story of personal development she encountered as a beginning teacher in her mid-twenties:

> Living in Boston, burning the bras and all that, I became a person they referred to as militant. Moving to Florida, I saw a vast difference in the way people were thinking at that particular time so there was a difference in my thinking after getting there. But I didn't see that in [the FL city], and I didn't see that passion there so at that particular point in time there were some changes in my thought pattern and some change in me personally if I wanted to develop into where I would be economically secure and safe.
>
> I thought I could be a part of a movement that could change things. It wasn't until the Malcolm X kind of thing, I got to be one of those persons that realized too that being Black was problematic for me, and basically coming into being when you yourself haven't accepted the fact that you were a Black person in America. It was Malcolm X that kinda put something into my mind and being was that basically, "what is it about yourself that you really don't like?" And you had to come into that feeling of knowing that you like yourself and always had self-esteem, so why was I trying to change and wear my hair straight, and I didn't for a while. I stopped all of that trying to be, and accepted myself as I was.[34]

Mrs. W, like many educators of the period, found herself in a personal identity struggle. Was she to embrace the fullness of herself, and present as a sign of resistance and self-love, or was she to adapt to her environment in a way that she could maintain safety and security within her new career? She found a way to stand in the truth of self while maintaining professionalism to advance rather than lose her career. The lesson gained from this conversation with her is to *accept yourself as you are and be who you are.* In today's landscape diversity is discussed more frequently, and it appears that many are finding value in differences; however, the application of this lesson continues to be a struggle for many who wrestle with acceptance, beginning with self. Mrs. W reminds us to embrace evolution and accept yourself along the way.

Dr. J was also an educator and school administrator in Florida during this era. His career advanced quickly into school administration and district-level leadership. When asked to describe one of his most memorable experiences, he had this to say:

> Seeing youngsters achieve and being able to convince them to enjoy learning. I found out that a lot of the youngsters didn't like school because it had been kind of a bad place for them because learning was not made fun or pleasant for them. But once I was able to get them to see the joy in learning it made it a lot easier and the idea is really to give youngsters as much success as you can and once you do that they will gravitate toward becoming better students.
>
> As a teacher I wished I could have convinced parents of the importance of nurturing your kids in their formative years. It seems as though many parents relied on the schools to do the educating, not realizing that if you don't work with kids during the formative years they're going to be behind. I use an example with parents when doing a workshop, I say, "if you tied your child's legs and say when he gets to school they'll teach him how to run or if you don't talk to your child and say when he gets to school they'll teach him how to talk that child will come and will be disadvantaged. It would be very difficult to teach that child. You see, children have the innate ability to learn to read if they are read to. No child learns to talk by having a lesson in talk. You just talk to a child. Children have the ability to learn to read if you read to them. Trying to teach reading is much more difficult to a youngster that doesn't understand the fundamental that print is speech written on paper. And so once a child makes that connection it's easy to facilitate learning, or learning to read.[35]

My conversation with Dr. J reinforced the notion of Black educators being completely invested in student success. He held students, parents, teachers, and himself responsible for the educational outcomes of the "youngsters" he was responsible for educating. The lesson learned from him was to "*give youngsters as much success as you can.*" As educators work diligently to close the achievement gap, activating Dr. J's advice is paramount and speaks not only to the success of the student but the educator. As students find themselves in classrooms where they know they can be a success, these experiences extend beyond the moment.

Mr. P was an educator and school administrator in South Carolina during integration. Following active duty military service, he began teaching at a segregated Black high school until it was closed resulting in the relocation of staff and students to the local White high school. When asked what he liked and disliked about the schools he served during this time, he shared these thoughts:

> There were smart kids, there were kids that lacked and didn't work as hard but by and large my relationship with them was good and because I taught [subject] and a lot of kids didn't choose to take that, I came in contact with kids that had purpose, and I didn't teach kids across the spectrum. But once we integrated of course most of the kids were white, I had no problems with them, and of course teaching advanced sciences you're getting kids who are in most cases making preparations for post high school education. I had no difficulties with them. I found them to be just like the other kids. You know, you take them for who they are and where they are, you treat them decently, they treat you decently, and of course you just move from there.
>
> I really can't think of anything I disliked. Of course when you're in a school situation there are things that go well and things that don't but most of it has to do with your involvement and of course I was a classroom teacher (at this time) so I had a responsibility for the things I did there, and came in contact with the people that were teaching [subject]. You have to be open-minded and accept things as they are and try to make things good for everybody. Of course when you do that, you usually don't have any problems.[36]

The optimistic attitude presented by Mr. P revealed that in remaining professional and continuing to be a source of inspiration for others, he was able to make a positive impact on the school community, even in what promised to be a challenging time for the community at large. A major lesson from this conversation is to "stay open-minded and make things good for everybody." His story also illuminated the fact that he was teaching advanced or college preparatory courses in both settings; however, once schools were integrated, there were fewer Black students enrolled in these courses. Were the Black students that would have been enrolled suddenly incapable of success in such a class, or were there power structures in place that would prevent them from experiencing the success once experienced in the segregated setting? Despite this apparent injustice, as did many African American educators, he continued to remain open-minded, efficient, and professional, making a direct impact.

Mrs. P spent most of her career as an elementary educator in South Carolina. When asked about the school community, she had this to share:

> A lot of the people that taught there had gone to school there, or their parents had gone to school there. And the thing that is so amazing about it, students that I taught, and this was my philosophy from the first time, I said, you know, I'm going to do my best with these young folks because when I get old these will be people making decisions about my life. Alright, I had some knee surgery, I went to the hospital, two RNs, little girls I had in the 4th grade were there and they said, "Mrs. P do you remember me?" A few years later I went to rehab following

a fall and there was another girl that came to me and asked if I remembered her. She told me what her name was. She was a physical therapist and she helped me to walk. They turn up. I have run into young men and women that I taught many years ago that are doing wonderful things in life and they always pick me out. So, you know, my advice to anyone is to be yourself and people will like you or not but you can't be anybody else. My philosophy was to do your best by these children because these children are going to have to come back and take care for you one of these days.[37]

Mrs. P's story highlights the long-lasting cyclical and communal impact of African American educators supporting the idea that Black educators offer valuable contributions to students of all races. The respect she showed to her students returned to her later in life by some of the same students she had the opportunity to teach. The lesson gained from my conversation with her can be summarized in her comment, "I was respected because I was respectable." This speaks to the character and intent of educators like Mrs. P., which appears to be common among Black educators of the period. Her respectability, even with fourth-grade students, paid off for herself and the community at large.

Mr. C served in the military, later attended college, then became a high school teacher and administrator in Virginia's newly integrated schools. When asked about professional expectations of educators this is what he had to say:

No, they weren't the same (across races) but they didn't do it obviously like I said, they would go home and call them (White teachers) or talk to them at a friend's house Friday night or something you know. Where I worked was it that obvious? No. I do know people who were working in schools as a teacher who got wrote up for coming in late or not doing what they thought they should be doing and my philosophy has always been that you won't hear that. But, in my opinion, as I stated earlier, most of them needed information or needed words on how to work with us rather than us knowing how to work with them. You see, we made ways, we found ways to work with them. I never went to school with a white kid in my life, never had a white teacher in my life. We found ways to make it work. That's just part of our personalities to talk and be friendly. They're not.[38]

The appreciated candor of my conversation with Mr. C highlighted the idea that expectations and experiences were different between the different races of educators; however, he and other Black educators did what was necessary to yield results, although they understood that they were not equally treated. As it is commonly stated, "we have to be twice as good to get half as much."

One of the lessons gained from my conversation with him was to "find ways to make things work." Adaptability is an essential trait of educators, particularly African American ones. Mr. C reminds us that each day as challenges arise, even when they may seem unfair, your duty as an educator is to figure it out and make it work.

Mrs. D was a junior high school teacher in Michigan during this era that began her career as a substitute, leading her into becoming a full-time teacher. When asked about assistance provided to struggling teachers, she had this to say:

> Eventually my supervisor was pulling me out of my class and out of my school to go to other schools and work with teachers who were having difficulty with discipline in the class. I was like, I don't want to do this. I don't want to do anything in the school system but teach. But one of my assistant principals kept trying to urge me to be a principal. I wasn't interested, I just wanted to teach. I enjoyed the kids and when they got to know me they just loved me. I was the type of person that demanded respect.
>
> Back then in the early 70s we could spank kids. This is quite comical, I had this kid, he was one little pistol. Every time I looked up he was skipping class, going out of the school, so I said the next time you skip your seventh hour class I'm going to spank you. "My mama don't let nobody spank me!" I said, ok, I'll tell you what, try me! And of course he did. I put him across my lap, oh, he boo hooed. I told him, I don't ever want you to leave this school again because it's dangerous. I am responsible for you for six and a half hours a day. To make a long story short, his mother and I ended up becoming good friends. She even gave me a going away party when I relocated and even called to try to get me to let him come stay with me. That was thirty years ago and his mom still calls me, we still communicate.[39]

Black educators are often leaned on to maintain order in the school and discipline students of all races. Mrs. D was no exception. One of the lessons gained from my conversation with her was that Black educators should *be prepared to be the disciplinarian.* Although undesirable for many, when this role is embraced, the impact on a child's life is paramount. When a person who understands cultural paradigms and cares for the child disciplines a student, he or she is likely to be amenable to correction and redirected toward student success.

Mrs. S is a dedicated high school teacher selected to move from an all-Black school to a predominantly White school in North Carolina during this era, experiencing overt racism and discrimination. While sharing her experience of transitioning into the new high school, she shared these words:

> I was given a class based on, I'm assuming my ability to teach, because I was given "low level" students to teach. And because of that I made it my concerted

effort that if you think I can't teach, I'm going to show you. And I think that was the starting point I guess of my rough exterior, and I'm going to use this because I was determined because if you think these youngsters can't learn, I'm going to show you.

They had advanced, regular, and basic classes. I only got "basic" students, I went in at the beginning of a year and I asked why I only got "basic" students, and what race would they be? They were Black. That's why I said it was never integrated, it was segregation in an attempt to mix races. I had the lowest level of students. I insisted that I spent most of the time teaching in a way that most benefited the student.

I need to tell you about my credentials so you will understand why I was so dissatisfied with the fact that I only had "basic" students. I had earned a master's degree with an emphasis on education along with postgraduate studies in guidance counseling and taught college freshmen prior to going to this high school. I was also offered a job at several colleges but turned them down because I wanted to send well educated, well prepared students to college rather than trying to unlearn the unteachable students I found teaching college freshmen who had not successfully mastered the content.[40]

Mrs. S story reinforces the passion for excellence that Black educators of the period required from their students. Her disappointment and concern for her safety in response to the difficulties within the environment did not prohibit her from ensuring that these "basic" students learned, exceeded expectations, sending many of them to college and on to successful careers. The lesson gained from my conversation with her was to *show them all kids can learn* without taking offense when you are given the worse of the bunch. Educators can take this lesson as a personal challenge. In this scenario, she was offered a situation that would have caused many to walk away; instead, she chose to survive and persevere. Her success was also her students' success.

It appears that these educators took different approaches to the challenges they faced. During this period, there was no right or wrong way of approaching each day as the scenario was new for all, and there were no instructions to accomplish the task. As a result, we are now privileged to learn from their experiences as we engage contemporary challenges. This project gleans ten tools that may be implemented to reinforce not only our understanding of this period, but a record that can strengthen the acumen of current and future public school educators, as changing and challenging times will always persist in one form or another. The table here provides a brief summary of the simple but valuable lessons that may be gleaned from the experiences of educators who worked during the period of school desegregation.

These lessons share one central theme, that quitting is not an option. These educators chose to persist through these challenging, and for some

Table 4.1 Lessons Learned from African American Educators Who Taught During the Desegregation of Public Schools in the 1970s

Educator	Lesson
Mrs. J, elementary educator	*Find or create a supportive community.*
Mr. M., teacher, school board member, and administrator	*Be prepared for consequences when you choose to speak up for what's right.*
Dr. R., librarian, English teacher, and school administrator	*"Play the game" but don't compromise your values or virtues.*
Mrs. W, a teacher and elementary school principal	*Accept yourself as you are and be who you are.*
Dr. J., educator and school administrator	*Give youngsters as much success as you can.*
Mr. P., educator and school administrator	*Stay open-minded and make things good for everybody.*
Mrs. P., elementary school teacher	*I was respected because I was respectable.*
Mr. C, high school teacher and administrator	*Find ways to make things work.*
Mrs. D, junior high school teacher	*Be prepared to be the disciplinarian.*
Mrs. S, high school teacher	*Show them all kids can learn.*

life-threatening moments, in order to continue in their mission as educators and world changers. One may consider that these educators were not volunteering for activism or as social justice pawns when they chose their career, but the historical landscape led them this way. It is unknown if educators in the future will ever have to navigate a cultural shift of this magnitude; however, changing and challenging times are almost guaranteed in one form or another as the world continues to exist. Regardless of the moment, these stories and their corresponding lessons, be it one or all, can serve as a source of accountability, inspiration, and encouragement to educators of the present and future.

GLEANING WISDOM FOR THE FUTURE

Although these stories may not fully reflect the volatile nature that one may expect, they express the professional nature and survival tactics of African American educators within racially exasperating circumstances. Though most of these educators shared positive reflections on their experiences of events occurring over fifty years ago, these stories were often rooted in trauma and pain of the period however soothed by the fruit of joy brought about from their ability to live to tell the tale and reflect on the outcome of their sacrifices. The offerings of these educators were on the forefront of one of the most pivotal moments of U.S. history. For many, like those interviewed, their presence and ability to show up to work each day was in itself an act of resistance to oppressive societal norms and to systematic racism of the period.

The events and experiences shared in these narratives are noteworthy as they assist in establishing the foundational work required to understand the important role that African American educators of this period played in establishing the work of Critical Race Praxis, "an analysis of racial, ethnic, and gender subordination in education that relies mostly upon the perceptions, experiences and counter-hegemonic practices of educators of color."[41] Stories like the ones presented in this work provide the groundwork for critical conversations surrounding educational praxis of African American educators over time.

Concerning the permanence of racism in American society, Derek Bell wrote: "Black people will never gain full equality in this country . . . This is a hard-to-accept fact that all history verifies. We must acknowledge it, not as a sign of submission, but as an act of ultimate defiance."[42] Since educational inequity may persist for the foreseeable future, it is important that African American educators learn effective strategies and coping mechanisms to employ while educating students and pursuing career advancement.

Some may consider issues of race in education to be a concern of the past. This is inaccurate as school districts across the country, particularly those in urban areas, continue to fight for equity in providing educational necessities to children of color. Critical race theory further provides the "tools" to understand and oppose racism in "the classroom, in the context of policy, and in community work."[43] As today's educators develop and respond to policy and curriculum supporting reform in K–12 public schools, it is imperative to reflect on historical incidents to understand how future cultural shifts may be best implemented without silencing the voices of those involved and affected. From these conversations, it is fair to say that the African American educators interviewed in this study and others who lived during the period of desegregation have added value to the educational and professional experiences of the schools for which they desegregated. African American educators must continue to be included in addressing issues of inequity in regards to multiple social factors, inclusive of race when making decisions related to educational praxis.

The adaptability of these educators in the midst of cultural changes in the country, inclusive of their workplaces, serves as another example of African Americans' struggle to persist as they fight to overcome oppressive circumstances. The stories they shared provide applicable lessons that any educator can apply, especially African American educators, who seek to defy institutional racism. The voices and counternarratives of these educators provide wisdom and insight to contemporary African American educators who continue to face oppressive circumstances and inequities in education.

Despite decades of critical race scholarship, the educational playing field has not been leveled, inequity persists, and as Derek Bell noted, "we are still not saved."[44] Experiencing racism on the front lines during the period of desegregation, the educators interviewed in this chapter were trailblazers. There is much that current and future educators can learn from them and from their stories.

However, as Aunt Thelma would say, it is incumbent upon us to "Getcha lesson!" This means that we must reflect on the wisdom of our elders who paved the way for us. These educators' stories have reminded me of the privilege and responsibility that I have been afforded as a teacher in multiple K–12 public school districts and now as a university professor. As I meet challenges, both personally and professionally, the educators interviewed here remind me not to give up. Being an educator is more than a vocation, it is a mission. As we continue to face White supremacy, African American educators must embrace their cultural differences, strive to maintain a positive disposition, and be creative and flexible. We must show doubters that all students can learn regardless of their background or circumstance. We must strive to provide our students with daily opportunities for success against the odds.

NOTES

1. Gloria Ladson-Billings, "Chapter 1: Just What Is Critical Race Theory, and What's It Doing in a Nice Field Like Education?" In *Race Is . . . Race Isn't: Critical Race Theory & Qualitative Studies in Education* (New York: Taylor & Francis Ltd, 1999), 2.
2. Maria Ledesma and Dolores Calderón, "Critical Race Theory in Education: A Review of Past Literature and a Look to the Future," *Qualitative Inquiry* 21, no. 3 (2015): 209.
3. Ledesma and Calderón, "Critical Race Theory in Education," 209; Daniel G. Solórzano and Tara J. Yosso, "Critical Race Methodology: Counter-Storytelling as an Analytical Framework for Education Research," *Qualitative Inquiry* 8, no. 1 (February 2002): 23.
4. Marvin Lynn and Laurence Parker, "Critical Race Studies in Education: Examining a Decade of Research on U.S. Schools," *The Urban Review* 38, no. 4 (November 2006): 282–83.
5. Derrick Bell, "Serving Two Masers: Integration Ideals and Client Interests in School Desegregation Litigation," *The Yale Law Journal*, 85, no. 4 (March 1976): 471.
6. James Patterson, *Brown v. Board of Education: A Civil Rights Milestone and Its Troubled Legacy* (New York: Oxford, 2001), 105–112.
7. Ibid., xvii.

8. Dionne Danns, "Separate and Superior: Perspectives on African-American Secondary Education," *Journal of African American History* 100, no. 4 (2015): 672.

9. Jennifer L. Martin and Jennifer N. Brooks, "Turning White: Co-Opting a Profession through the Myth of Progress, An Intersectional Historical Perspective of Brown v. Board of Education," *Educational Considerations* 45, no. 2 (January 2020): 6.

10. Kathryn Palmer, "Losing Lincoln: Black Educators, Historical Memory, and the Desegregation of Lincoln High School in Gainesville, Florida," *The Florida Historical Quarterly* 95, no. 1 (2016): 27.

11. Patterson, *Brown v. Board of Education*, xxi.

12. Adah Ward Randolph and Dwan V. Robinson. "De Facto Desegregation in the Urban North: Voices of African American Teachers and Principals on Employment, Students, and Community in Columbus, Ohio, 1940 to 1980," *Urban Education* 54, no. 10 (December 2019): 1403–30.

13. Adam Fairclough, "The Costs of Brown: Black Teacher and School Integration," *Journal of American History* 91, no. 1 (June 2004): 43–55; Sarah E. Heath, "'Lubricating the Machine of Social Change': The National PTA and Desegregation Debates, 1950–1970," *Peace & Change* 39, no. 1 (January 2014): 49–72.

14. Bell, "Serving Two Masters," 447.

15. Derrick A. Bell, "Brown v. Board of Education and the Interest-Convergence Dilemma," *Harvard Law Review* 93, no. 3 (1980): 530.

16. Ibid., 530–31.

17. Mallory Lutz, "The Hidden Cost of Brown v. Board: African American Educators' Resistance to Desegregating Schools," *Online Journal of Rural Research & Policy* 12, no. 4 (October 2017): 1.

18. Vanessa Siddle Walker, "What Black Educators Built," *Educational Leadership* 76, no. 7 (April 2019): 13.

19. H. Richard Milner IV, "Fifteenth Annual AERA Brown Lecture in Education Research: Disrupting Punitive Practices and Policies: Rac(e)Ing Back to Teaching, Teacher Preparation, and Brown," *Educational Researcher* 49, no. 3 (April 2020): 154.

20. Fairclough, "The Costs of Brown," 43.

21. Lutz, "The Hidden Cost of Brown v. Board," 6.

22. Fairclough, "The Costs of Brown," 44; Danns, "Separate and Superior," 672.

23. Martha Lash and Monica Ratcliffe, "The Journey of an African American Teacher Before and After Brown v. Board of Education," *The Journal of Negro Education* 83, no. 3 (2014): 327.

24. Ibid., 327.

25. Sonya Ramsey, "'We Will Be Ready Whenever They Are': African American Teachers' Responses to the Brown Decision and Public School Integration in Nashville, Tennessee, 1954–1966," *The Journal of African American History* 90, nos. 1–2 (January 1, 2005): 39.

26. Lash and Ratcliffe, "The Journey of an African American Teacher . . . ," 328.

27. Ledesma and Calderón, "Critical Race Theory in Education," 209.

28. Pseudonyms are used to describe the participants in compliance with IRB and consent requirements.

29. Mr. M (False Name), Retired Educator, interviewed by author July 2020.

30. April L. Peters, "Desegregation and the (Dis)Integration of Black School Leaders: Reflections on the Impact of 'Brown v. Board of Education' on Black Education," *Peabody Journal of Education* 94, no. 5 (January 1, 2019): 521.

31. Mrs. J (False Name), Retired Educator, interviewed by author July 2020.

32. Mr. M (False Name), Retired Educator, interviewed by author July 2020.

33. Dr. R (False Name), Retired Educator, interviewed by author July 2020.

34. Mrs. W (False Name), Retired Educator, interviewed by author July 2020.

35. Dr. J (False Name), Retired Educator, interviewed by author July 2020.

36. Mr. P (False Name), Retired Educator, interviewed by author July 2020.

37. Mrs. P (False Name), Retired Educator, interviewed by author July 2020.

38. Mr. C (False Name), Retired Educator, interviewed by author July 2020.

39. Mrs. D (False Name), Retired Educator, interviewed by author July 2020.

40. Mrs. S (False Name), Retired Educator, interviewed by author July 2020.

41. Marvin Lynn, "Inserting the 'Race' into Critical Pedagogy: An Analysis of 'Race-Based Epistemologies,'" *Educational Philosophy & Theory* 36, no. 2 (April 2004): 154.

42. Derek Bell, *Face at the Bottom of the Well: The Permanence of Racism* (New York: Basic Books, 1993), 12.

43. Ledesma and Calderón, "Critical Race Theory in Education," 207.

44. Derrick Bell, *And We Are Not Saved: The Elusive Quest for Racial Justice* (New York: Basic Books, 1989).

BIBLIOGRAPHY

Bell, Derrick A. *And We Are Not Saved: The Elusive Quest for Racial Justice.* New York: Basic Books, 1989.

Bell, Derrick A. "Brown v. Board of Education and the Interest-Convergence Dilemma." *Harvard Law Review* 93, no. 3 (1980): 518–33.

Bell, Derrick A. *Faces at the Bottom of the Well: The Permanence of Racism.* New York: Basic Books, 1993.

Bell, Derrick A. "Serving Two Masters: Integration Ideals and Client Interests in School Desegregation Litigation." *The Yale Law Journal* 85, no. 4 (1976): 470–515.

Danns, Dionne. "Separate and Superior: Perspectives on African American Secondary Education." *Journal of African American History* 100, no. 4 (2015): 672–80.

Fairclough, Adam. "The Costs of Brown: Black Teacher and School Integration." *Journal of American History* 91, no. 1 (June 2004): 43–55.

Heath, Sarah E. "'Lubricating the Machine of Social Change': The National PTA and Desegregation Debates, 1950-1970." *Peace & Change* 39, no. 1 (January 2014): 49–72.

Ladson-Billings, Gloria. "Chapter 1: Just What Is Critical Race Theory, and What's It Doing in a Nice Field Like Education?" In *Race Is . . . Race Isn't: Critical Race Theory & Qualitative Studies in Education*. New York: Taylor & Francis Ltd, 1999.

Ladson-Billings, Gloria. "The Evolving Role of Critical Race Theory in Educational Scholarship." *Race, Ethnicity & Education* 8, no. 1 (March 2005): 115–19.

Lash, Martha and Monica Ratcliffe. "The Journey of an African American Teacher Before and After Brown v. Board of Education." *The Journal of Negro Education* 83, no. 3 (2014): 327–37.

Ledesma, Maria and Dolores Calderón. "Critical Race Theory in Education: A Review of Past Literature and a Look to the Future." *Qualitative Inquiry* 21, no. 3 (2015): 206–22.

Lutz, Mallory. "The Hidden Cost of Brown v. Board: African American Educators' Resistance to Desegregating Schools." *Online Journal of Rural Research & Policy* 12, no. 4 (October 2017): 1–30.

Lynn, Marvin. "Inserting the 'Race' into Critical Pedagogy: An Analysis of 'Race-Based Epistemologies.'" *Educational Philosophy & Theory* 36, no. 2 (April 2004): 153–65.

Lynn, Marvin and Laurence Parker. "Critical Race Studies in Education: Examining a Decade of Research on U.S. Schools." *The Urban Review* 38, no. 4 (November 2006): 257–90.

Martin, Jennifer L. and Jennifer N. Brooks. "Turning White: Co-Opting a Profession through the Myth of Progress, An Intersectional Historical Perspective of Brown v. Board of Education." *Educational Considerations* 45, no. 2 (January 2020): 1–20.

Milner IV, H. Richard. "Fifteenth Annual AERA Brown Lecture in Education Research: Disrupting Punitive Practices and Policies: Rac(e)Ing Back to Teaching, Teacher Preparation, and Brown." *Educational Researcher* 49, no. 3 (April 2020): 147–60.

Palmer, Kathryn. "Losing Lincoln: Black Educators, Historical Memory, and the Desegregation of Lincoln High School in Gainesville, Florida." *The Florida Historical Quarterly* 95, no. 1 (2016): 26–70.

Patterson, James. *Brown c. Board of Education: A Civil Rights Milestone and Its Troubled Legacy*. New York: Oxford, 2001.

Peters, April L. "Desegregation and the (Dis)Integration of Black School Leaders: Reflections on the Impact of 'Brown v. Board of Education' on Black Education." *Peabody Journal of Education* 94, no. 5 (January 1, 2019): 521–34.

Ramsey, Sonya. "'We Will Be Ready Whenever They Are': African American Teachers' Responses to the Brown Decision and Public School Integration in Nashville, Tennessee, 1954–1966." *The Journal of African American History* 90, nos. 1–2 (January 1, 2005): 29–51.

Siddle Walker, Vanessa. "What Black Educators Built." *Educational Leadership* 76, no. 7 (April 2019): 12–18.

Solórzano, Daniel G. and Yosso, Tara J. "Critical Race Methodology: Counter-Storytelling as an Analytical Framework for Education Research." *Qualitative Inquiry* 8, no. 1 (February 2002): 23–44.

Ward Randolph, Adah and Dwan V. Robinson. "De Facto Desegregation in the Urban North: Voices of African American Teachers and Principals on Employment, Students, and Community in Columbus, Ohio, 1940 to 1980." *Urban Education* 54, no. 10 (December 2019): 1403–30.

Chapter 5

"Good" Pedagogy

Arguments for Critical Pedagogy in Higher Education

Felicia L. Harris and Nina Barbieri

In March 2020, the now late Congressman John Lewis made a surprise appearance at a march commemorating the fifty-fifth anniversary of "Bloody Sunday" in Selma, Alabama. During his remarks, Lewis urged attendees to get into "good trouble," echoing the refrain that has come to characterize his activism and career. According to Lewis, "good" trouble, or necessary trouble, is trouble that is required to create lasting change for some of society's most pressing issues.

Later, in a CNN interview on that same day, Lewis said, "We got to make America better for all of her people. When no one is left out or left behind, because of their race, their color, because of where they grew up, or where they were born."[1] Lewis's comments and hallmarked phrase serves as a call to interrogate the nature of goodness, and to challenge existing notions of what is agreeable for the status quo while discounting the experiences of some of the most vulnerable among us. Lewis's activism around racism and voter rights serves as a model for scholactivists who seek to openly trouble and resist notions of "good," or good *enough*, that fail to account for the lived experiences of the most vulnerable within our disciplines and the institutions in which we research, teach, and serve.

In higher education, the most vulnerable among us include students of color and those from historically excluded backgrounds. According to the National Center for Education Statistics, over 16 million students enrolled in an undergraduate program in fall of 2018.[2] Of these, 20 percent were Hispanic/Latinx and 12 percent Black/African American. These numbers show a 148 percent increase in enrollment for Hispanic/Latinx students and 73 percent increase for Black/African American students during the last two decades. While this upward enrollment trend demonstrates a step in the right direction, the numbers only tell part of the story. Black/African American college students are the least likely to successfully graduate within a four-year period, and the second least likely to graduate within a six-year period.[3] This indicates a glaring error on the part of higher education: we are simply not doing a "good" job at retaining and graduating students of color.

As scholars and educators, we approach this error as an opportunity to explore viable strategies for advancing equity and justice within our classrooms, beginning with norms that govern our perspectives on teaching and learning. Although there are several confounding factors that contribute to student success, in this chapter, we argue that an understanding of "good" pedagogy for college and university educators must be expanded to include critical frameworks that contribute to classroom experiences that are better suited for all of our students. In particular, we put forth the notion that as a reflection of the continued growth of historically excluded student populations, twenty-first-century educators and institutions of higher learning should be cognizant of the impact of various pedagogical strategies, particularly as they relate to matters of inclusivity, intersectionality, accessibility, dissenting voices, and sociopolitical matters.

However, we acknowledge that, in ways similar to Lewis, crossing the bridge that moves us from status quo teaching practices that leave many behind to more critical approaches may be met with resistance within and outside of the classroom. In this, we adopt Lewis's mindset and mantra, and embrace the discomfort of being an agitator that advocates for a better quality of teaching and learning that does not leave anyone out or behind. This intentional perspective on instruction should reflect a larger commitment to inclusive pedagogy across institutions for the betterment of *all* students and demonstrate our ability to be reflective in much the same way we expect our students to be while in our classroom.

CRITICAL CONVERSATIONS: PEDAGOGY CONCERNS FOR POSTSECONDARY EDUCATORS

Today, many college students and educators may have a knee jerk response to the words "left behind," a phrase that was central to the No Child Left Behind Act of 2001, the controversial federal policy governing much of K12 education from 2002 to 2015. Under No Child Left Behind, rigorous protocols were put into place to increase student success in primary and secondary education regardless of factors that had previously correlated with achievement gaps, such as race or socioeconomic status. According to Ladd, the No Child Left Behind policy had three fundamental flaws in its design, despite its admirable goals: (1) a narrow view of accountability that focused primarily on testing as an indicator of student achievement; (2) unrealistic and counterproductive standards that deemed many schools who failed to meet such standards as failures; and (3) an overwhelming pressure-based system that did not provide support for schools to reach the desired goals. Instead, incentives were offered for schools that, almost magically, achieved the primarily unattainable achievement outcomes.[4]

Although the controversial policy was phased out shortly before our arrival to the University of Houston-Downtown as college educators, we discovered that the challenges inherent in these fundamental flaws in efforts to improve student achievement—particularly for students from historically excluded backgrounds and marginalized groups—persist in postsecondary institutions.[5] In lieu of standardized testing, today's colleges and universities are governed by measurable outcomes such as retention and graduation rates among first-time freshmen, while benchmarks of post-graduation success are often reduced to statistics for job placement and salary data. These statistics and formulae continue to influence much of higher education policy and decision-making, even though research has demonstrated that many of these numerical values are related to a number of both institutional and individual factors.[6] Therefore, whereas student success appears most influenced by academic preparedness, financial assistance, and class size, these relationships are undoubtedly bolstered by a number of confounding variables and individual factors that may not be explicitly examined, such as engagement, involvement, connectedness to topics of study or learning materials, and the overall classroom experience.

Persistent gaps in student achievement in spite of institutional interventions are evidence that systemic issues in higher education require comprehensive and multidimensional solutions, of which methods and practices of teaching become an important site of intervention. It remains an enigma, then, why postsecondary educators spend little time meditating on teaching methods that do not (consistently and predictably) leave some students behind. In higher education, and in graduate schooling, the primary focus is on research and not quality teaching and classroom instruction. This disjunction leads to a further threat to students most in need of quality student engagement within the classroom, due in part to their lack of preparedness for college success.

One advantage that primary and secondary educators have in ongoing efforts to mitigate errors in student achievement is a rigorous meditation on *how* to teach. Unlike our K12 counterparts, who undergo years in teaching education and are often required to have standard certification, postsecondary educators spend most of our graduate years acquiring knowledge and skills that guide us on *what* to teach. We are groomed to become content experts and knowledge creators in environments where producing scholarship is paramount. As a result, many have argued that pedagogy is an under examined element of higher education.[7] Even at the University of Houston-Downtown, where teaching accounts for 50 percent of tenured and tenure-track faculty workload, it is the quality and quantity of our scholarship that spurns many concerns around the tenure and promotion process. As such, graduate programs that require students to engage in intentional, sustained conversations around pedagogy are a rare deviation from the norm.[8] Even still, the level of engagement within those programs on pedagogical issues account for a mere fraction of a student's program of study, while actual teaching experience can most often be summed up as sink or swim lectures and hours of grading experience gained through teaching assistantships. Then, we are off to teach in the ivory towers.

Upon our arrival, not only do we need to learn how to teach, but we must also grapple with what it means to teach *well*. In faculty orientations, we are introduced to our campus centers for teaching and learning, offered handouts on high-impact practices like service learning and undergraduate research, and encouraged to think deeply about our use of technology in the classroom.[9] However, such tried and true approaches make assumptions about the uniformity of student experiences in classrooms and/or disciplines. Rarely are we presented with larger contextual data on the robust and intersectional factors that influence our students' learning and overall success, such as race or ethnicity, socioeconomic status, and academic preparedness. All too often, this means that we are on our own if we desire to learn how to expand our teaching in such a way that acknowledges the intersectional experiences and challenges our students face within and beyond the classroom. As college educators, we are routinely confronted with what it means to have students who are "left behind," but left perplexed by what it might mean to ensure that those same students forge ahead.

Ultimately, the classroom experience has a substantial impact on a student's overall success. Previous research has shown that effective teachers can advance a K12 student the equivalent of a full grade level.[10] This demonstrates the importance of taking teaching seriously. In particular, it is evident that what a quality education means to diverse student groups varies widely and is hard to reduce to numerical and statistical benchmarks. Unfortunately, this is a premise that appears to be more widely accepted by K12 educators. For example, Urban Education exists as an area of study that prioritizes and explores the challenges of education (of all disciplines) within the social contexts and student populations often, but not always or solely, encountered in urban areas. Such challenges include limited resources, teacher qualification, and lack of academic preparation.[11] And, although the merits of the No Child Left Behind Act and its successor the Every Student Succeeds Act can be debated, both pieces of legislation establish not only legal precedent, but also financial incentives and punitive consequences that indicate a level of teaching oversight that theories of academic freedom in higher education often circumvent. It should come as no surprise, then, that K12 educators are leading the conversation when it comes to incorporating critical theory and frameworks into an understanding of what "good" pedagogy is, or is not. Groundbreaking texts such as *We Want to do More than Survive* by Bettina Love and *For White Folks Who Teach in the Hood . . . and the Rest of Y'all Too* by Chris Emdin speak to the level of engagement that K12 educators possess when it comes to thinking deeply about what it means to be a twenty-first-century educator for a diversifying student population.

That deep contemplation on the methods and practices of teaching *for all* are not requirements for postsecondary educators, and in particular those who teach students from historically excluded and disenfranchised groups, is a norm that must be widely and fiercely resisted. This belief is what led us to partner with our university's Center for Teaching and Learning Excellence (CTLE) during the 2019–2020 academic year to host a series of workshops focused on critical pedagogy titled *Critical Conversations*. Over the course of the year, we planned and executed sessions on themes ranging from incorporating critical pedagogy in any classroom to teaching through "hot-button" topics, or topics that may be highly emotional or politically charged. As facilitators, two fundamental challenges stuck out to us the most. For one, many of our colleagues were largely unfamiliar with critical pedagogy. And, second, our colleagues consistently lamented that our time together was never enough. We were overwhelmed by comments and concerns during our discussion groups and rarely suffered from a lack of questions during Q&A. In fact, the interest in this continued conversation was so considerable that the CTLE embraced the theme of Inclusive Teaching as a recurring area of training interest for subsequent years and our administration adopted a modified version of one of our sessions for new faculty orientation. In spite of receiving minimal pushback from a handful of colleagues—some verbal through program assessment and some nonverbal through lack of support or indifference—we maintain that deep thinking about the methods and practices of teaching that best serve our twenty-first-century student population is essential. Furthermore, we believe this contemplation must include a meditation on critical theory and frameworks.

A CRITICAL PEDAGOGY FRAMEWORK

In the introductory session of our *Critical Conversations* series, we asked our colleagues to respond to the discussion prompt, "What is good pedagogy?" To which, they offered responses that most college and university educators would share: they discussed flipped classroom models, responsive lecture styles, name pronunciation strategies, and noted that it helps when you can connect what students are learning to how much of a salary they will earn in the real world. Our question and answer activity was meant to draw our colleagues into a discussion on critical pedagogy frameworks as a tool better suited to deal with increasingly diverse and nontraditional classrooms. We argued that as a Minority- and Hispanic-Serving Institution, our methods and practices of teaching cannot ignore the realities of race and racism.

We then went directly into a conversation about the unique composition of the student population at the University of Houston-Downtown. With a more than 60 percent female student population, our student body is roughly 50 percent Hispanic, 21 percent Black, and 9 percent Asian. However, nearly half of our students are enrolled part-time, and many of them work full-time or are full-time caregivers for loved ones. Furthermore, more than half of our students are age twenty-five or older, with our average student age hovering around twenty-seven years old.[12] Many of our students would be considered "nontraditional" because they come from groups that have been historically excluded from higher education.[13] As a result, our students may encounter a number of unique and intersectional challenges throughout their collegiate career. In light of our discussion on our unique student population, we then challenged our colleagues to consider how such students, in particular, are served or not served by "good" pedagogy.

In this regard, critical race theory (CRT) serves as a useful starting point for understanding the practicality of educators adopting critical perspectives on teaching. In his theoretical discourse on CRT in education, Tichavakunda summarizes five central tenets that CRT scholars use to inform their thinking on education: "(1) the centrality of racism and the interconnected nature of forms of oppression (e.g., classism or sexism), (2) the challenge to dominant ideology, (3) a commitment to social justice (4) the valuation of experiential knowledge, and (5) an interdisciplinary approach."[14] Also referring to this as "a racial realist perspective" in higher education, Tichavakunda argues that by centering race and racism, and their intersections with other identities and forms of oppression, CRT allows educators to imagine and respond to a wider array of student experiences by beginning from a place of the affirmative on questions such as the impact of race in higher education.[15] When we begin from a place that acknowledges that educational inequalities do, in fact, exist among racial lines, we can find the footing to take one step toward adopting methods and practices of teaching that do not assume the uniformity in student experience and discipline-specific learning that more traditional forms of pedagogy engage.

One of the most prominent arguments of those who advocate for critical pedagogy is the notion that, within the frameworks of popular forms of "good" pedagogy, learning somehow becomes a simplified process that occurs within the context of the classroom in a way that assumes students are able to leave the experiences that influence their learning, and lives, at the door. It is almost as if, as a result of "good" pedagogy—because you learned students' names and assessed their comprehension at the end of every class—students can somehow turn off life and tune into the lesson of accounting, or advertising, or political science, and become effective learners. But, we know that is not the case.

On the contrary, critical pedagogy combines education with critical theory, a social philosophy that explores the power structures that maintain oppression and social inequity. The combination of the two offer educators a framework for thinking about teaching in a way that enables students to take control of their own learning, encourages them to question authority, and empowers them to strive to transform the world into a better place. Although there are numerous takes on critical pedagogy in higher education literature, our experiences with our colleagues and other college educators suggest these perspectives remain underexplored. Here, we offer a brief introduction of a few widely circulated tenets that make this framework distinct from how educators are traditionally taught how to teach.

Critical pedagogy is often related to the seminal text *Pedagogy of the Oppressed*, in which Paulo Freire offers a metaphor of traditional education as a "banking" concept in which teachers are depositors and students are viewed solely as depositories.[16] This concept closely aligns with the sink or swim lecture-style that is the entry point of many college educators into teaching. Professors are the experts, and we have something to say (and students better listen and take notes!). As such, students are limited by a lack of creativity, transformation, dialogue, and knowledge in a way that mimics the lack of empowerment and freedom often encountered "in the real world." In order to free students (and ourselves) of what he refers to as an "oppressor consciousness," Freire posits that educators should empower students through humanizing practices built on dialogue and by fostering a learning environment where students and teachers serve as co-creators. In this model, students are encouraged to become active participants not only in their own education but also in their own liberation.

When we embrace a radical sense of humility and teach in such a way that decenters our roles as content experts and centers students as problem-solvers in a world that is burdened by hierarchical power structures and inequalities, students are empowered both within and beyond the classroom.[17] Freire's notion that many students who land in our classrooms are oppressed is echoed in CRT's stance that race, racism, and other forms of oppression are central to educational experiences. Thus, as educators, the driving factor in our pedagogical choices becomes less about content and more about creating and sustaining educational spaces where students experience liberation that allows them to freely inquire and fully access the expertise we desire to share. In this regard, the question of *how* to teach is expanded to consider *who* we are teaching and what conditions have influenced their ability to fully participate in the learning process.

In *Teaching to Transgress*, bell hooks extends Freire's argument that education is a practice of freedom. In addition, she reiterates the premise that our students can best aspire to freedom in environments where teachers commit to a self-actualization process that explores our relationships with power and ideology, and how the interplay between both can manifest in our students' lives outside of the classroom and as an unjust exercise of domination and power over students within it.[18] Unfortunately, hooks argues, educators are often rewarded for upholding this status quo, and are indoctrinated in a teaching culture that leads to a fear of making mistakes. This leads to a lack of willingness to confront or explore complex real-world issues around social identity and experiences in our efforts to remain harmonious. Once again, the temptation exists to simply go in and teach, and leave all the messiness out. Yet, this approach in light of increasingly diverse student populations is inherently limiting and oppressive for students. Alternatively, when teaching is embraced as a site of resistance, progressive educators make attempts to make transformations to curriculum, diversify their course content to be representative of their students' bodies, and explore ideas and practices of social justice beyond discipline-specific courses.[19]

Some of the most common inquiries that we encountered from colleagues who attended our *Critical Conversations* series was that of "How do I do this?" and "What happens when I do this?" These questions point to the fear of making mistakes and the notion of the harmonious classroom that critical pedagogy calls in question. Adopting a critical framework for methods and practices of teaching goes beyond calculating the perfect ratio of lecture time to time on task. Instead, a critical perspective toward education beckons college and university educators to take a step back and reframe their teaching as one aspect within a much larger overarching system of domination and oppression, particularly for students from marginalized groups. In this, a suitable "how to" guide does not exist. We simply must begin the self-actualization process and repeat it again and again. By doing so, we allow ourselves to question not only the content we teach but to also question if our methods of teaching are suitable and cognizant of our students as complete humans with lives and a wide range of experiences. Furthermore, we make space to explore that wide range of experiences in a way that creates meaning in the classroom and in the real world.

A useful starting point is to consider the extent to which the methods and practices that govern our pedagogical approaches and overall classroom experience maintain or contribute to the systemic oppression of students. This could include, but is not limited to, classroom and syllabus policies, the acknowledgment of varying gender identities and pronouns, the modality of course assignments, or the flexibility (or lack thereof) of assignment deadlines and timelines. When we begin to question our relationships to power and ideology in the classroom, our perspectives on what agreeable or "good" pedagogy is radically change. While the outcomes of our efforts to undermine the status quo are not predictable, we can and should brace ourselves to be met by resistance from students and colleagues alike.

POLITE OR POLITICAL? MANAGING DISSENSION IN THE CLASSROOM

An underlying premise of CRT, Freire, hooks, and other critical scholars is that education is inherently political. As such, when teaching is embraced as a form of resistance and a means of liberation for students, we are bound to face accusations of being political. Furthermore, discussions around the appropriateness of our desires to sustain education as a site of transformation and liberation are bound to be contested. Students may openly challenge your decisions to "make everything about race," while your colleagues purport that "those political ideas" have no bearings on math/science/research/fill-in-the-blank. Oftentimes, even the term "political" is used politically and thrown around as a negative descriptor in student opinion surveys or performance evaluations. Such resistance fails to acknowledge that not being "political" is, in fact, a political stance in itself. When educators shy away from difficult conversations, or from those that challenge the majority group's perceptions or experiences, it diminishes the learning experience of everyone in the classroom.

As a child that experienced racial integration firsthand, bell hooks expresses particular discontent at the hegemonic power structure and need for obedience in the integrated, and now White-dominated, schools.[20] Particularly in higher education, excitement is equated with disruption. The belief that classrooms should be ordered, structured, and taught with a clear authoritative figure at the head of the class discounts the ongoing realities of our students. When we as college educators shirk from an uncomfortable truth or an alternative narrative, we devalue the very real experiences of those that lived and continue to live such narratives and thwart the ability of our students to exercise their budding sense of social agency.

Social agency can be viewed as one's commitment to political or social involvement. Unfortunately, the exercise of social agency—whether respectful or impassioned—within college classrooms is often avoided, or tamed at best, in order to avoid student resistance and adhere to accepted notions of classroom management. However, research demonstrates that minority students develop social agency when diverse issues are explored within the classroom or among peers, and when faculty are able to engage with students around those issues. More specifically, Hispanic/Latinx students developed increased social agency and commitment to social change when enrolled in ethnic or women studies programs, diversity-related coursework, and dialogues, or were able to connect with a professor as a mentor.[21] This illustrates the reality that the classroom is perhaps the most important place for a student to grow, not just intellectually, but holistically.

The resistance of instructors, and students, to engage in these sorts of conversations could be rooted in a variety of reasons. According to Souza and Noah, a few of the more salient reasons why college educators, in particular, may be reluctant to engage in the difficult conversations that a critical pedagogy framework invites include cognitive dissonance, cognitive simplification, fragility, decentering, topic taboo, blame/guilt, and belief in superiority.[22] Here, we offer brief descriptions of each reason for reluctance along with examples to understand what reluctance may look like in action.

Cognitive Dissonance

Tavris and Aronson refer to cognitive dissonance as the "engine that drives self-justification."[23] This is when an individual holds two inconsistent ideas, beliefs, or opinions simultaneously. Living in this state of duality can result in an individual feeling tense or uncomfortable. As it relates to difficult and challenging conversations, an educator may grapple with their own personal beliefs (i.e., not being a racist or homophobe) and actively resist when information is presented that may challenge that self-identity. Not only are these beliefs socially undesirable, but if confronted with the reality that something you said or did was offensive—and that does not coincide with how you self-identify—you may engage in a series of mental gymnastics to separate these two opinions. You don't *feel* racist, so how could you *be* racist? Further, this could be an artifact of the recognition that racism is real, but it is a thing of the past. An example of cognitive dissonance as a form of resistance could be if as a professor you acknowledge the reality of racism, classism, sexism, and so forth, but rarely engage in these sorts of conversations in your classroom. You rationalize this disjunction by telling yourself, "These are difficult conversations and it's not my place to talk about them." Or "I'm sure they're hearing about this in another class, at home, or on TV, so it's fine."

Cognitive Simplification

Cognitive simplification is the tendency to oversimplify complicated and difficult concepts. It encompasses the belief that the status quo is the easiest way to proceed because to change course would be too difficult, things will not change, or people are bad. This source of resistance preemptively stops any conversations and self-reflections from being had because we expect discomfort and are not willing to move through it. An example of cognitive simplification can be found in those who make claims such as, "When I look at you, I do not see you as a person of color, just a person." Such claims minimize a person's holistic self and the totality of their experiences.

Fragility

Robin DiAngelo describes fragility as the result of living in segregated societies, which have largely shielded White people from experiencing any forms of racial discomfort.[24] As such, when any conversation is had regarding race or racism, Whites are emotionally and mentally unprepared for the unpleasantness and respond defensively and/or dismissively. An example of fragility would be if while conversations are being had about racism, classism, sexism, among others, someone asks, "Why do we always have to talk about race?" or laments, "My family never owned slaves or placed Japanese-Americans into internment camps!" These responses seek to preserve the emotional comfort of majority groups as opposed to unpacking and dismantling harmful truths.

Decentering

Similar to fragility, decentering is when individuals who are used to being at the center of the narrative are exposed to alternative realities and respond to this discomfort with attempts to "recenter" the spotlight. This may be best evinced in one's quest to be "colorblind." By minimizing differences in an attempt to promote similarities, educators systematically eliminate as problematic and uncomfortable. In practice, decentering can look like a faculty member responding to an administration's initiative to hire more diverse and representative faculty across the entire institution by asking questions like, "Shouldn't we instead just focus on their qualifications? Why should race or gender matter? We're all equal."

Topic Taboo

For many individuals, the status quo is that we *not* engage in certain conversations (particularly as it relates to race and racism). As such, we are unfamiliar with the pervasiveness of current racial experiences, we are uncomfortable talking about them (see: *fragility*), and we are unprepared to be confronted with realities that differ or challenge our own experiences with society and social systems. In some ways similar to "colorblindness," avoiding conversations on these matters is only possible because of privilege afforded to Eurocentrism. A person who may be reluctant to discussing taboo topics may make statements such as, "Growing up, we were not talked to about racism, classism, sexism, etc., As such, I avoid discussing these matters myself."

Blame/Guilt

Derald Wing Sue, in his book *Race Talk and the Conspiracy of Silence,* discusses how engaging in dialogue regarding race can trigger a variety of powerful emotions, including fear, anger, frustration, guilt, and embarrassment, among others.[25] This range of emotions can be the result of discomfort given any of the aforementioned reasons, but the result is the same: reluctance to engage in critical conversations and missed opportunities to learn and grow from a potential learning experience. Such emotional responses are exemplified in the following scenario: During a department meeting, a new employee mentions an experience in which they felt treated differently because of some physical characteristic. Several colleagues begin fidgeting around, growing visually uncomfortable; another gets up and walks out of the room. By the end of the day, all of the colleagues who avoided the conversation have apologized to their new colleague, stating that they were scared to hear they may have been the one who offended, or were guilty of engaging in such a behavior before.

Belief in Superiority

We would be remiss to exclude the reality that some individuals refrain from engaging in conversations on the totality of our students' lived experiences because of innate beliefs of superiority and privilege. This outright dismissal may be rooted in intentional and conscious racist, classist, sexist, and such beliefs, but they may also be rooted in the belief that you are smarter than others. As a result of feeling more intellectually superior, one may believe their knowledge or insight on any particular matter is more accurate. Despite its origination, the result is a dismissal of one's lived experience as being truthful, valid, and significant. Superiority beliefs are evidenced by statements such as, "Of course there are more men in STEM fields. Men are inherently better at math and hard sciences."

In addition to the reasons outlined above, there are several other ways in which important critical and inclusive conversations are met by reluctant or resistant faculty or students: remaining silent, diverting the topic to something "safer," dismissing or deflecting away from the importance of the topic, implementing course policies that restrict topics or concepts, speaking about race and/or racism from a global and impersonal perspective and, lastly, by tabling the conversation to potentially be discussed at some later date, if at all.[26] Sue argues this resistance is rooted in the need to follow politeness and academic protocols (see: *topic taboo*) in which discussing race and racism is viewed as improper, impolite, and divisive. Perhaps we are fearful of being perceived as racist, of uncovering we are in fact racist, of uncovering our privilege, or being tasked with being personally responsible for ending racism or other social justice issues. Whatever the case, reluctance to engage in the difficult conversations or frameworks that account for each of our students' lived experiences is a key factor that undermines our ability to be effective teachers for all.

WHO'S INCLUDED? CONSIDERING INCLUSIVITY AND INTERSECTIONALITY

In our roles as college and university educators, we are the final step in a student's preparation to move into diverse spaces as they pursue their personal career goals; "good" pedagogy should allow for students to become reflective, independent, critical thinkers, able to recognize other people's experiences and the larger role of sociopolitical contexts because they themselves have been taught in a similar manner.[27] Adopting a critical pedagogy framework means that we as educators must be reflective of the skills we intend to instill in our students. To do this, we must continually acknowledge shared and divergent cultural and political experiences. It might go without saying that CRT and other forms of critical pedagogy acknowledge that race and racism are not the only social identities tethered to experiences of domination and oppression. As Tichavakunda notes, a CRT approach to education embraces Kimberly Crenshaw's premise of intersectionality and explores how race and racism intersect with identities of gender, class, sexuality, and more.[28] To disentangle these from the education experience is impossible.

The embracing of critical and inclusive strategies must be intentional and cross-disciplinary. Multiple historical, cultural, structural, and political viewpoints should be included in all aspects of instructional design regardless of discipline or content area. According to Freire, the classroom is a space for empowerment, for teachers and students to come together and co-create dialogue and facilitate knowledge.[29] Further, bell hooks challenges educators to incorporate the impact of social and historical constructs.[30] A multitude of all factors function simultaneously and interdependently; the ability to truly understand one's holistic self cannot be understood when looking through a singular lens of gender, or race, or socioeconomic status. Instead, we must facilitate a space for the combined realities of our students to be heard and valued in order to set the stage for effective teaching and learning.

Take, for example, Dr. Bettina Love's abolitionist approach.[31] One of her major arguments is that the education system is not culturally affirming. She explains, "We teach students about their oppression, but we don't teach them how their ancestors resisted."[32] A "good" pedagogy is one that allows educators to be culturally sensitive and able to understand how racism is deeply rooted within social systems and institutions and creates opportunities for students to acknowledge, understand, and dismantle such systems. In order to do this, educators must be reflective of the pedagogical strategies they use, and were taught, as they may likely need to be modified in order to meet the unique needs of students. Educators should consider the following questions:

- Do I continually acknowledge the shared and divergent cultural and political experiences of my students and colleagues?
- Do I intentionally include multiple historical, cultural, structural, and political viewpoints in all aspects of instructional design?
- Do I facilitate a space for the combined realities of our students, where we all create dialogue and facilitate knowledge?
- Do I incorporate discussions on the impact and intersectionality of social and historical constructs relating to a variety of identities (i.e., gender, sex, race, ethnicity, among others)?
- Do I maintain cultural sensitivity and an ability to understand how racism is deeply rooted in all social systems?

When we teach about concepts or experiences that are inherently rooted in historic racism, sexism, classism, and other forms of oppression, but refrain from engaging in actual conversations about oppression or developing classroom strategies to mitigate oppression, we are teaching from a neutral standpoint in order to maintain our own emotional comfort. In summary, as you reflect on our arguments for including critical pedagogy in higher education, we challenge you to consider these best practices and ask yourself, "Is my pedagogy 'good' or 'good *enough*'?"

NOTES

1. Devan Cole, "John Lewis Urges Attendees of Selma's 'Bloody Sunday' Commemorative March to 'redeem the soul of America' by Voting," CNN, March 1, 2020, https://www.cnn.com/2020/03/01/politics/john-lewis-bloody-sunday-march-selma/index.html.

2. "Undergraduate Enrollment," National Center for Education Statistics, last updated May 2020, https://nces.ed.gov/programs/coe/indicator_cha.asp.

3. "Indicator 23: Postsecondary Graduation Rates," National Center for Education Statistics, last updated February 2019, https://nces.ed.gov/programs/raceindicators/indicator_red.asp.

4. Helen F. Ladd, "No Child Left Behind: A Deeply Flawed Federal Policy," *Journal of Policy Analysis & Management* 36, no. 2 (Spring 2017): 464–67.

5. Harris arrived to UHD in 2015; Barbieri arrived in 2016.

6. Meghan Millea, R. Wills, A. Elder, and D. Molina, "What Matters in College Student Success? Determinants of College Retention and Graduation Rates," *Education* 138, no. 4 (Summer 2018): 310.

7. Ethan S. Ake-Little, "What K-12 and Higher Education Can Learn From Each Other," *Education Week,* September 19, 2018, https://www.edweek.org/ew/articles/2018/09/19/what-k-12-and-higher-education-can-learn.html; Gail O. Mellow, Diana D. Woolis, Marisa Klages-Bombich, and Susan Restler, *Taking College Teaching Seriously: Pedagogy Matters!* (Sterling, VA: Stylus Publishing, LLC, 2015), 2.

8. Colleen Flaherty, "Online Conversation Shines a Spotlight on Graduate Programs That Teach Students How to Teach," *Inside Higher Ed*, December 13, 2019, https://www.insidehighered.com/news/2019/12/13/online-conversation-shines-spotlight-graduate-programs-teach-students-how-teach.

9. George D. Kuh, *High-Impact Educational Practices: What They Are, Who Has Access to Them, and Why They Matter* (Washington, DC: Association of American Colleges & Universities, 2008); José Antonio Bowen, *Teaching Naked: How Moving Technology out of Your College Classroom Will Improve Student Learning* (San Francisco, CA: Jossey-Bass, A Wiley Imprint, 2012).

10. Mellow et al., *Taking College Teaching Seriously,* 13.

11. H. Richard Milner, "But What Is Urban Education?" *Urban Education* 47, no. 3 (2012): 556.

12. *University of Houston Downtown Fact Book*, University of Houston-Downtown, accessed September 18, 2020, https://www.uhd.edu/administration/institutional-research/Documents/Fact_Book_2019-2020.pdf.

13. Previously, Markle defined a nontraditional student as, "those who meet any one of the following characteristics: are 25 years of age or older or have a 5-year gap between enrollment in high school and college, are employed part-time or full-time, or serve in the role of spouse, domestic partner, parent, or caretaker." See: Gail Markle, "Factors Influencing Persistence Among Nontraditional University Students," *Adult Education Quarterly* 65, no. 3 (August 2015): 267–85.

14. Antar A. Tichavakunda, "An Overdue Theoretical Discourse: Pierre Bourdieu's Theory of Practice and Critical Race Theory in Education," *Educational Studies: Journal of the American Educational Studies Association* 55, no. 6 (January 1, 2019): 651–66.

15. Ibid., 653.

16. Paulo Freire, *Pedagogy of the Oppressed* (New York: Bloomsbury Publishing USA, 2018), 45.

17. Ibid.

18. bell hooks, *Teaching to Transgress: Education as the Practice of Freedom* (New York: Routledge, 1994), 41.

19. Ibid.

20. Ibid.

21. Marcela G. Çuellar, "Latina/o Students as Agents of Change: The Influence of Cultural Assets and College Experiences," *Race Ethnicity and Education* (2019): 1–22.

22. Tasha Souza and T. Noah, "Facilitating Meaningful Conversations about Diversity," Teaching Professor Conference (June 1, 2018), Atlanta, GA.

23. Carol Tavris and E. Aronson, *Mistakes Were Made (But Not by Me): Why We Justify Foolish Beliefs, Bad Decisions, and Hurtful Acts* (Boston: Mariner Books, 2015).

24. Robin DiAngelo, *White Fragility: Why It's So Hard for White People to Talk about Racism* (Boston: Beacon Press, 2018).

25. Derald Wing Sue, *Race Talk and the Conspiracy of Silence: Understanding and Facilitating Difficult Dialogues on Race* (Haboken, NJ: Wiley, 2015).

26. Souza and Noah, "Facilitating Meaningful Conversations."

27. Alana B. Barton, Karen Corteen, Julie Davies, and Anita Hobson, "Reading the Word and Reading the World: The Impact of a Critical Pedagogical Approach to the Teaching of Criminology in Higher Education," *Journal of Criminal Justice Education* 21, no. 1 (March 2010): 24–41.

28. Tichavakunda, "An Overdue Theoretical Discourse."

29. Freire, *Pedagogy of the Oppressed.*

30. hooks, *Teaching to Transgress.*

31. Bettina L. Love, *We Want to Do More Than Survive: Abolitionist Teaching and the Pursuit of Educational Freedom* (Boston: Beacon Press, 2019).

32. Cierra Kaler-Jones, "When SEL is Used as Another Form of Policing," *Medium*, May 7, 2020, https://medium.com/@justschools/when-sel-is-used-as-another-form-of-policing-fa53cf85dce4.

BIBLIOGRAPHY

Ake-Little, Ethan S. "What K-12 and Higher Education Can Learn From Each Other." *Education Week*, September 19, 2018. https://www.edweek.org/ew/articles/2018/09/19/what-k-12-and-higher-education-can-learn.html.

Barton, Alana, Karen Corteen, Julie Davies, and Anita Hobson. "Reading the Word and Reading the World: The Impact of a Critical Pedagogical Approach to the Teaching of Criminology in Higher Education." *Journal of Criminal Justice Education* 21, no. 1 (March 2010): 24–41.

Bowen José Antonio. *Teaching Naked: How Moving Technology out of Your College Classroom Will Improve Student Learning*. San Francisco, CA: Jossey-Bass, A Wiley Imprint, 2012.

Cole, Devan. "John Lewis urges attendees of Selma's "Bloody Sunday" commemorative march to 'redeem the soul of America' by voting," CNN, March 1, 2020.

https://www.cnn.com/2020/03/01/politics/john-lewis-bloody-sunday-march-selma/index.htm.

Cuellar, Marcela G. "Latina/o Students as Agents of Change: The Influence of Cultural Assets and College Experiences." *Race Ethnicity and Education* (2019): 1–22. https://doi.org/10.1080/13613324.2019.1579184

DiAngelo, Robin. *White Fragility: Why It's So Hard for White People to Talk about Racism.* Boston: Beacon Press, 2018.

Flaherty, Colleen. "Online Conversation Shines a Spotlight on Graduate Programs That Teach Students How to Teach." *Inside Higher Ed*, December 13, 2019. https://www.insidehighered.com/news/2019/12/13/online-conversation-shines-spotlight-graduate-programs-teach-students-how-teach.

Freire, Paulo. *Pedagogy of the Oppressed.* New York: Bloomsbury Publishing USA, 2018.

hooks, bell. *Teaching to Transgress: Education as the Practice of Freedom.* New York: Routledge, 1994.

Kaler-Jones, Cierra. "When SEL is Used as Another Form of Policing." *Medium*, May 7, 2020. https://medium.com/@justschools/when-sel-is-used-as-another-form-of-policing-fa53cf85dce4.

Kuh, George D. *High-Impact Educational Practices: What They Are, Who Has Access to Them, and Why They Matter.* Washington, DC: Association of American Colleges and Universities, 2008.

Ladd, Helen F. "No Child Left Behind: A Deeply Flawed Federal Policy." *Journal of Policy Analysis & Management* 36, no. 2 (Spring 2017): 461–69.

Love, Bettina L. *We Want to Do More Than Survive: Abolitionist Teaching and the Pursuit of Educational Freedom.* Boston: Beacon Press, 2019.

Markle, Gail. "Factors Influencing Persistence among Nontraditional University Students." *Adult Education Quarterly* 65, no. 3 (August 2015): 267–85.

Mellow, Gail O., Diana D. Woolis, Marisa Klages-Bombich, and Susan Restler. *Taking College Teaching Seriously: Pedagogy Matters!* Sterling, VA: Stylus Publishing, LLC, 2015.

Millea, Meghan, R., Wills, Anastasia Elder, and Danielle Molina. "What Matters in College Student Success? Determinants of College Retention and Graduation Rates." *Education* 138, no. 4 (Summer 2018): 309–22.

Milner, H. Richard. "But What Is Urban Education?" *Urban Education* 47, no. 3 (2012): 556–561.

National Center for Education Statistics. "Indicator 23: Postsecondary Graduation Rates." Last updated February 2019. https://nces.ed.gov/programs/raceindicators/indicator_red.asp.

National Center for Education Statistics. "Undergraduate Enrollment." Last updated May 2020. https://nces.ed.gov/programs/coe/indicator_cha.asp.

Souza, Tasha and T. Noah. "Facilitating Meaningful Conversations about Diversity." Teaching Professor Conference (June 1, 2018), Atlanta, GA.

Sue, Derald Wing. *Race Talk and the Conspiracy of Silence: Understanding and Facilitating Difficult Dialogues on Race,* Haboken, NJ: Wiley, 2015.

Tavris, Carol and E. Aronson. *Mistakes Were Made (But Not by Me): Why We Justify Foolish Beliefs, Bad Decisions, and Hurtful Acts.* Boston: Mariner Books, 2015.

Tichavakunda, Antar A. "An Overdue Theoretical Discourse: Pierre Bourdieu's Theory of Practice and Critical Race Theory in Education." *Educational Studies: Journal of the American Educational Studies Association* 55, no. 6 (January 1, 2019): 651–66.

University of Houston-Downtown. *University of Houston Downtown Fact Book.* Accessed September 18, 2020. https://www.uhd.edu/administration/institutional-research/Documents/Fact_Book_2019-2020.pdf.

Chapter 6

Surviving the Wild West

A Critical Race Feminist Analysis of African American Women Students' Experiences with Gendered Racism at the University of Colorado-Boulder

LeAnna T. Luney

Before the U.S. government established federal law in Western territories, like the geographic region now known as Colorado, local municipalities enacted law. This lack of an established federal governance inferred that Western territories were places and spaces of lawlessness where people were left to fend for themselves to survive the dangers of nature and violence from other human beings. African Americans, Indigenous Americans, Mexicans, and Chinese immigrants were particularly targeted in such violence.[1] In 2020, the temperament of the Wild West prevails throughout liberal, higher education institutions that appear as progressive enclaves. Yet, a lack of oversight and critical inspection around race and gender evokes the persistence of clandestine and aggressive violence rooted in gendered racism against Black women. This chapter explores undergraduate African American women's experiences in racially antagonistic environments at the University of Colorado Boulder (CU Boulder), a predominantly white institution (PWI) in the American West. Drawing on qualitative interviews with undergraduate African American women at CU Boulder and employing a critical race feminist conceptual framework, I contend that communal networks are essential to help Black women survive racism, classism, and heteropatriarchy at PWIs in the American West.

Compared to eastern and mid-western regions in the United States, there have been a dearth of studies exploring African Americans and their lived experiences in the West, especially African American women in higher education. Only two previously known articles situate how Black women college students cope in the western United States. Corbin, Smith, and Garcia explore tensions in how Black women college students maneuver microaggressions based on stereotypes of the Strong and Angry Black Woman. Rooted in the *white gaze*, these images influence the silencing of Black women at colleges and universities and causes them to experience racial battle fatigue and other types of psychological distress.[2] Szymanski and Lewis's study similarly addresses the relationship between gendered racism and psychological distress for Black women college students.[3] They set out to find how gender and racial identity centrality mediates gendered racism and discrimination for Black college women. The authors found that gender and racial identity centrality do not mitigate gendered racism for Black college women, and that there are various engagement and disengagement coping strategies that Black college women employ instead.

While these authors make significant interventions to literature on Black women college students' psychological realities of mitigating gendered racism, neither of the articles expound upon the West's unique racial climate. Corbin, Smith, and Garcia's study takes place at a PWI in the West. Szymanski and Lewis include findings on one participant that attends a PWI in the West. The scholars have given limited attention to the coping strategies of African American women within the context of anti-Black settler colonialism in the Western United States. Furthermore, the authors do not engage Black feminist theory and conceptualizations of power and difference in the academy.

Black feminism and critical race feminism provide a conceptual framework for this analysis. The goal of Black feminism is for women and girls of the African diaspora to reflect on their unique experiences and to politically understand their diverse lives in relation to white supremacy, heteropatriarchy, and capitalism as well as to navigate and resist unequal power dynamics. Black feminism seeks to empower and foster sisterhood among Black women.[4] Critical race feminism is "an embryonic effort in legal academia that emerged at the end of the twentieth century to emphasize the legal concerns of a significant group of people—those who are both women and members of today's racial/ethnic minorities, as well as disproportionately poor."[5] Major tenets of critical race feminism are a committed struggle for human rights through legal systems; the social construction of race, as racism is foundational to U.S. society; critical questioning on the persistence of racism and framing racial progress as cyclical; rejecting colorblind racism; storytelling and narrative as method; multidisciplinarity or interdisciplinarity; evolving theory into praxis; and antiessentialism, intersectionality, and multiplicative identities.[6]

Conceptually, this chapter also employs intersectional analysis, a key methodology of critical race feminism. Coined by critical race theorist

Kimberlé Crenshaw, intersectionality provides a way to read and examine various structures of dominance affecting Black undergraduate women's lives. Scholars of Black feminism have employed an intersectional method to analyze Black women's *herstorical* experiences with and resistance of multiple oppressions including but not limited to racism, sexism, and classism.[7] An intersectional methodology provides a way to examine how racialized, capitalist, heteronormative structures of dominance in institutions of higher learning affect Black college students' lives. The intersectional approach accents students' voices and agency in their own destinies.[8] Going beyond heteropatriarchal, White supremacist ways of knowledge production that prioritize positivist and objective research perspectives, a Black and critical race feminist, and intersectional approach upholds researchers' and participants' multiple sites of oppression and privilege and admonishes introspective self-reflection.

AN OVERVIEW OF THE STUDY

To explore how African American women cope at CU Boulder, I utilized a qualitative research design, including interviews and participant-observation. I conducted two semistructured focus group interviews with seven African American undergraduate students, ranging from sophomores to seniors during the Spring 2020 semester. Four students—Assata, Milan, Florence, and Shirley—attended the first semistructured focus group and three students—Regina, Bell, and Anna—attended the second focus group.[9] Both focus group interviews were conducted via Zoom video, an online platform for virtual calls and meetings. I also conducted a thirty-minute in-person, joint interview with two self-identified African American undergraduate first-year women attending CU Boulder—Marya and Jazmine. I asked students questions regarding their perceptions of CU Boulder, their overall well-being, and their favorable and unfavorable experiences at the institution. Although I heavily draw on the group interviews in the forthcoming analysis, participant observation informed how I conducted the interviews, the questions asked, and my analysis of the local context of CU Boulder. As a participant-observer during the fall 2019 and spring 2020 semesters, I spent one to two hours a week observing African American students engaging in common spaces on campus and meetings both in-person and online. Some of these spaces were the Center for Inclusion and Social Change (CISC), affinity spaces, and political demonstrations that pertain to Black lives.

Concerning my role and positionality, I have held various positions at CU Boulder, including the following: Black Student Alliance (BSA) member, teaching assistant, part-time instructor, staff member at the CISC, and mentor for the Onyx program. These roles enabled me to establish a rapport with the student participants. I consider myself an outsider from the students because of my education status, place of origin, socioeconomic status, experience with attending a small liberal arts undergraduate institution, and the power dynamics between students and me. Alternatively, my status as a Black woman matriculating through the CU education system very much makes me an insider with experiential knowledge about how African American students are treated in this education system.

WELCOME TO THE WILD WEST: THE HISTORICAL CONTEXT OF THE UNIVERSITY OF COLORADO BOULDER

Many African Americans migrated to the American West as freedmen pre-Reconstruction and to escape the Jim Crow South during and after Reconstruction.[10] They migrated to the West with hopes to find economic stability and racial equity. By the late 1800s, many African Americans began to establish Black communities and a Black middle-class in Denver, Colorado, and surrounding areas. Populated with Indigenous Americans, Mexicans, Black Americans, and Chinese and European immigrants, Denver was more ethnically diverse than many southern cities. Hence, African American residents in Denver were not subjected to the intense anti-Black racism that persisted in the American South.[11]

Historians point to interracial interactions between white and Black folks to discuss white people's tolerance of African Americans in the West during the late eighteenth and early nineteenth centuries.[12] Dismally, white acceptance of Black people in the West was predicated on a racial hierarchy that valued African Americans' humanity more than that of Indigenous Americans, Mexicans, and Chinese immigrants. Settler colonialism is at the center of this racial hierarchy and is responsible for the tolerance that white Westerners had for Black Americans. Because Indigenous Americans, Mexicans, and Chinese immigrants were also a part of the West's geopolitical context, White people viewed African Americans as less "foreign" and more American, and thus, more worthy of respect on the basis of cultural and linguistic familiarity. Nevertheless, African Americans remained critical of racism in the West, and racial violence persisted against Black people in all regions of the United States.[13] Because of this, ideologies of white superiority still dominated Western culture and relegated Black Westerners as second-class denizens.

In the West, Whites' acceptance of African Americans, which oftentimes emanates as liberalism, is not based on the recognition of Black people's humanity, dignity, nor an understanding of oppression and white privilege.

Instead, it is based on the dehumanization of other non-White Westerners such as Indigenous Americans, Mexicans, and Chinese immigrants. This type of tolerance of African Americans persists in higher education institutions in the West such as CU Boulder. It is unequivocally and largely due to liberal administrators' lack of critical approaches to racism in the academy.

African American students account for only 1.6 percent of CU Boulder's undergraduate population of over thirty thousand students. In fact, in 2018, only fifty-three African American freshmen enrolled for the fall semester. The number of African Americans has not grown, although White and Latinx student populations have grown since 2016.[14] Of the African American undergraduate students attending CU Boulder, 39 percent are first generation, 45 percent receive federal Pell grants, 70 percent pay in-state tuition as Colorado residents, and half identify as women and half as men.[15]

A 2014 campus climate survey shows that African American students feel less welcome, valued, and supported than the rest of the CU Boulder student population. This survey also indicates that African American students feel less intellectually stimulated at the institution and are not as proud to attend the institution when compared to the overall student population. CU Boulder's Black student population is less likely to perceive CU Boulder as diverse. African American students reported experiencing more microaggressions on campus than the rest of the student population as well. A compelling finding of the survey is that Black students were less likely to report a sense of community and that they have made friends. In the classroom, African American students expressed that instructors tolerate the use of stereotypes, prejudicial comments, or ethnic, racial, and sexual slurs or jokes. Black students are less likely to feel that instructors help students to understand the different perspectives of diverse cultures and social groups as well. Additionally, Black students are less likely to feel that instructors successfully manage discussions about sensitive or difficult topics, treat students with respect when they voiced positions or opinions, and provide a supportive classroom environment in other ways.[16]

Many African American students attend CU Boulder under the pretense that the university is a prominent public teaching and research institution.[17] Boulder, Colorado, is one of the most liberal cities in the Western United States, and CU Boulder by proxy is also a "liberal bastion."[18] Regardless of having an overwhelmingly White (87.85 percent) and affluent ($83,755 median income) population, people in the city are politically left-leaning with most registered as Democrats based on voting data.[19] Yet, despite being a "liberal bastion," the qualitative interview data indicates that African American undergraduate women experience gendered racism at CU Boulder.

The CU Boulder administration has attempted to address racism on campus through establishing the Center for Inclusion and Social Change (CISC).

Formed in 2018, the CISC is a conglomeration of affinity spaces for non-White, LGBTQ+, women and femme, and first-generation college students to exist together at the behest of the Office of Diversity, Equity and Community Engagement (ODECE).[20] Other administrative efforts to address racism on campus includes reserving Hallett Hall, a residential dormitory, for students interested in equality, social justice, and identity development.[21] Three living and learning communities (LLC) at Hallett Hall focus on these aspects from different perspectives. The Lucille B. Buchanan LLC targets students of the African diaspora and allies; the Multicultural Perspectives LLC targets students of any race who are interested in social justice, civil rights, and identity development; and the Spectrum LLC targets LGBTQIA+ students and allies. Black students who frequent the CISC or are interested in living in Hallett Hall's LLCs share these spaces with non-African American students who identify as women or as LGBTQ+. Considering that anti-Black prejudice and racism persist in marginalized communities—like people identifying as women, LGBTQ+, or non-White—Black students at CU Boulder may share these affinity spaces with racist white students or prejudiced non-White students.[22] Unfortunately, CU Boulder's "social justice" settings, like the CISC and Hallett Hall LLCs, do not cater to the nuances within marginalized groups and thus fail to effectively create a space where students benefit equally from these settings. In turn, Black women may face anti-Black and gendered prejudice and racism recurring in these spaces from non-Black students who hold other marginalized identities.

BLACK COLLEGE WOMEN COPING WITH RACISM THROUGH ENGAGING COMMUNITY

African Americans cope differently with racism than other racial-ethnic groups based on the types of discrimination they face and the culturally specific coping strategies they learned and passed on throughout generations.[23] For African American college students, racial-ethnic socialization during childhood determines the techniques used to cope with racial hostility at predominantly white higher education institutions.[24] More specifically, African American students raised in families that promote cross-racial relationships, who learn strategies to navigate racism, take pride in their culture, and are taught about their heritage and cultural values are less likely to suffer from psychological problems like John Henryism—a detrimental coping strategy in which African Americans (and other non-White people, typically) expend high levels of effort to combat prolonged exposure to discrimination-based stressors. Consequently, African American college students experience physiological and psychological enervation.[25]

According to Black feminist scholars, Black women hold deep-rooted connections with one another and combine their "oppositional knowledges" to create a collective wisdom used to challenge injustices.[26] In praxis, Black feminism's concepts of oppositional knowledges and sisterhood speak to African Americans' psychological coping experiences at predominantly higher education white institutions, which is illustrated by cultural connections, community, and the collective coping strategies African American women use (e.g., sister-friends, sister circles, and support networks).[27] The qualitative interview data presented below suggests that undergraduate African American women at CU Boulder understand and demonstrate community as a coping strategy through forming friendships with people of the same race and ethnicity and with people of different races and ethnicities, through engaging with cultural organizations and spaces, and through becoming involved in community organizing and activism.[28]

Friendships, Community, and Coping

The two different types of friendship used to cope include friends of the same race and ethnicity of students, and friends of different races and ethnicities than students. Friendships with people of the same race and ethnicity emerged as a theme when I asked students about the strategies they employ to cope with racism on campus. Considering that 70 percent of African American students attending CU Boulder are in-state students,[29] some established these friendships before attending the institution as a coping strategy after hearing about race relations at CU Boulder. Regina explains this when she states that being in community with her friends—many of whom she has known since before being a student at CU Boulder—mitigates stresses of having to be in the presence of white peers. She says,

> I've had a community since I was a freshman, so my roommates were my friends from back in Aurora [a city near Denver] and the people that we hung around with, we were always together. And another thing was that I feel like, because I was in ASA [African Student Association] [and] BSA, I was participating in those activities which consist of 99.9% Black of people. And so when I wasn't around [them], like when I was in class and stuff, I would become dependent on my friends to kind of make me feel any sort of happiness 'cause being around all these white people all the time in my classes just really, just mentally was not it. It wasn't it.[30]

As Regina's excerpt describes, she had developed friendships with other African American students prior to attending CU Boulder, building her own community of Black people. Participating in groups with mostly African

American students is another example of how Regina mitigates gendered racism which persists as being in predominantly white classes.

The same theme emerged in my joint interview with Marya and Jazmine. Jazmine said,

> I feel like I'm grateful. I grew up in Boulder, so [I've] definitely been around white people my entire life. But when I came to CU, I feel very blessed, gifted, with a group of friends that all share the same ethnic background as I did. And being friends with other Black people, being involved with cultural events, makes me feel like I have a space and have my community. So I feel like a lot of the time it's just knowing I can go to my friends and knowing that I can go to these people that I've been grateful enough to have these connections with.[31]

Similar to Regina, Jazmine noted the significance of having African American friends in her community, which makes here "grateful," especially as a Black woman who grew up in predominantly white spaces.

Later in our dialogue, Marya expressed, "Ways that I deal with it [racism] after [racist events] is BSA and just being able to talk to my friends about it because I'm also very grateful to have a group of friends who share the same ethnicity as me and all that."[32] This was Marya's response after I had asked what coping strategies she employs after she had experienced racism on campus. As she indicates in the excerpt, Marya dialogues with her African American friends to cope with gendered racism on campus and is "grateful" to have these friends in times of dealing with racial antagonism.

These interview segments speak to how Black women in college understand and value friendship to cope with racially hostile experiences while attending CU Boulder. Not only do Regina, Marya, and Jazmine speak about relying on their friends, but they also center friendships with people of the same race and ethnicity as them, which emphasizes the role of race and ethnicity in how they understand community and how they psychologically navigate racial hostility.[33]

In addition to developing friendships with members of their own racial group, students also spoke about their relationships with non-African American students in the two focus groups and the joint interview. Additionally, participant observation reveals that an overwhelming number of non-Black allies attend BSA meetings and engage in the struggle toward racial equality at CU Boulder. These included relationships with White and non-White allies. Florence notes this when she talks about joining a sorority in which most members do not identify as African American to cope with racism on campus and to establish a sense of community. Most students explaining relationships with people of different races and ethnicities talk about other non-White students as friends. Florence said, "I even have a group of friends who don't have the same ethnicity but are considered allies or just understand the problems that me and other African Americans, People of Color, go through. So, just being able to be surrounded by a lot of people at this school who are able to help me, and we can all help each other get through everything together."[34] Florence also explains the role of having non-White friends in her processes of coping when she says, "Being in Boulder, I can't be on campus a lot. I actually had to be with my friends of color to help cope and help me mentally. Because of CU, the academics, just the whole education and then just how it is." She continues by saying, "I realized I wasn't coping properly when it came to situations like this [gendered racism]. So, I would surround myself with, of course, my friends of color, people who understood me."[35]

As Florence's narrative underscores, undergraduate African American women maintain more friendships with non-White students of different races and ethnicities than them because they understand the precarity around occupying a racially marginalized position while attending CU Boulder. Perhaps this sense of understanding stems from the fact that students are navigating and fighting similar networks of power in higher education.[36] Although non-White students—African American, Asian American, Indigenous, and Latinx—have distinct histories with power, the state, and empire, a common ground between their experiences remains. This common ground is the manifestation of state power and empire on college campuses in the forms of interpersonal and institutional racism. Therefore, undergraduate African American women's friendships with other non-White students transpires as a plausible coping strategy at CU Boulder.

Cultural Organizations and Spaces, Community, and Coping

Students mentioning the social support the BSA provides and having cultural events emphasizes how culturally affirming spaces assist students in battling racism and developing collective consciousness to fight injustices, as scholars have previously suggested.[37] Interestingly, like Regina, Marya, and Jazmine explained, many students mentioned that joining cultural groups led them to establishing friendships with people of the same race and ethnicity. Students spoke to the importance of cultural groups and its connection with making friends of the same race and ethnicity at all points of data collection—both focus group interviews, participant observation, and the joint interview. Students even found ways to form friendships with Black women participating in groups outside of CU Boulder. As Assata explains that "I think generally, what I like to do and what I think I thrive in for coping is being in community. I find myself in very weird and awkward places when I try and isolate and handle things by myself. And that's something that I'm learning is to just be in community as much as I can. So, I have this [B]lack femme writing group that I go to in Denver every Monday and we write, we talk it out and it's kind of like my own therapy in a weird, unorthodox way."[38]

The significance of cultural groups is that they provide space for marginalized people to meet and interact with others with similar marginalized statuses. As Assata mentioned in her focus group, "If you weren't intentional about who you kept around you, like from the Black community, you could go three weeks without seeing another Black person. And that's just the way that CU is set up."[39] Because CU Boulder is predominantly White and rarely fosters spaces that are exclusive to Black students, students had to intentionally seek out and create Black spaces. Like Assata, students' engagement with cultural organizations and spaces is particularly important for coping with gendered racism at CU Boulder's predominantly white campus for African American women obtaining their undergraduate degrees.

Community Organizing Networks and Coping

Undergraduate African American women expressed that community organizing helps them to cope as they matriculate through CU Boulder. Examples of community organizing occurring on campus before stay-at-home orders due to the impact of Covid-19 included "Tones" —a space Assata created for African Americans to perform poetry, songs, and dance once a month—and the Onyx program—a space Angela (self-identified as a gender nonconforming femme) created for African Americans across campus to commune and contribute to a summer program for high school students to visit campus. After I asked about strategies that assist students in coping and the impact of these coping strategies, Assata stated,

> I think to go off of it [community organizing], the impact [is] to be seen and filled up by the work. Because when you're going through it, it sucks. I'm not even going to front, it's f – cking terrible. When you're actually in the thick of organizing and all of those other things. But I think [the] work fills you up. Well it fills me up afterwards and seeing that you really did make a difference in somebody's life. I dunno, even from the BSA thing, I can't say that the entire community of CU has changed. That would be false to say, but the individuals that have come up to me specifically after the event or felt that they had someone that they could relate to or knew that was fighting for them, that really kept me going and it fueled me to do all of these other projects. And I think that that's where the impact is felt for me for community organizing. Just having more fuel to run off of to create and organize more.[40]

Assata's excerpt reveals that she feels more whole when engaging in community organizing due to the possibility of impacting others' lives.

Findings reveal that community organizing instills a sense of purpose for students to continue their efforts to create change. Subsequently, community organizing makes students feel whole, or "filled up," by knowing that they have changed people's lives. Assata's excerpt also emphasizes the inimical aspects of community organizing when she refers to being "in the thick" of organizing. This relates to being an African American student within the Black Lives Matter (BLM) era and the downside of universities employing Black bodies—Black women's bodies particularly—to fight racial injustices on campus and foster community between African Americans.[41] This exists in contention with the positive impacts of community organizing as coping that were previously referenced, such as having a sense of purpose and changing people's lives.

Another project Assata had been working on was to create a festival to celebrate Blackness and to build community between CU Boulder's Black students and Black communities in the Denver-Aurora area. Assata decided to resign from her role on the festival planning committee, which she had participated on for several months. During an afternoon walk, she explained to me that the organizing work was becoming overwhelming and unduly stressful. Assata felt that she needed to devote time to self-care and other community initiatives that were dear to her and perhaps easier to execute such as serving unhoused communities and working with Tones.[42]

Assata exhibits contradictory sentiments about the impact of community organizing on undergraduate African American women's well-being. From a Black feminist lens, the complexity in how Assata understands the positives and negatives of community organizing and its ability to ease stressors or contribute to them indicates the contentions of using community organizing as a coping strategy. Milan's experience with community organizing to cope illustrates this contention as well:

> Tied onto the whole community organizing thing. I think the impact of that . . . I think maybe why it was not as good as a coping mechanism for me was because it was very much out in the open and not for myself, so it allowed a lot of other people to put all these responsibilities on my shoulders almost like, "Oh, you're a leader so you should do this." Or "Oh, you did this with BSA, so can you do this too with us?" (Gotcha). Community organizing was great and I'm very passionate about my activism. But it's only a coping mechanism if it works for yourself and not when other people are telling you to do it. And putting all of these big responsibilities [on us] when as Black women, we already carry a lot of weight as we walk in the world. So that [community organizing] was really harmful for me.[43]

Milan's excerpt illustrates community organizing as a burden when others expected her to take on additional responsibilities. In this case, community organizing is not a communal coping mechanism but is an additional hardship for some Black women undergraduate students at CU Boulder.

Ultimately, community organizing as a coping strategy is not beneficial for everyone and oftentimes generates more stress and responsibility in addition to the constant racism and sexism African American undergraduate women face. Expectations of Black women as saviors within the BLM era perpetuate the pressure undergraduate women experience in their efforts toward racial justice and equity. My argument here is not that Black women are incapable of leading the way, but that expecting them to take on additional initiatives prove to be debilitating to their well-being even when community organizing is a way for them to cope.

Figure 6.1, pictured below, provides an overview of the different types of community that African American women engage to cope with gendered racism at CU Boulder. Each arrow in the figure points from more specific community coping strategies to overarching community coping strategies, until they all pinpoint the central theme of African American women engaging community to cope with gendered racism. The figure starts with three main community coping strategies which are shown and labeled as "(a) cultural organizations and spaces"; "(b) community organizing"; and "(c) friends." Subcategories of how African American women cope using friendship are "(d) friends of same race and ethnicity"; and "(e) friends of different race and ethnicity." All of these coping strategies constitute ways that African American women engage community to cope with gendered racism, labeled as "(f)" in the center of the figure. Figure 6.1 illustrates and the findings in this study indicate that community, in its various forms, is central to African American undergraduate college women coping with gendered racism.

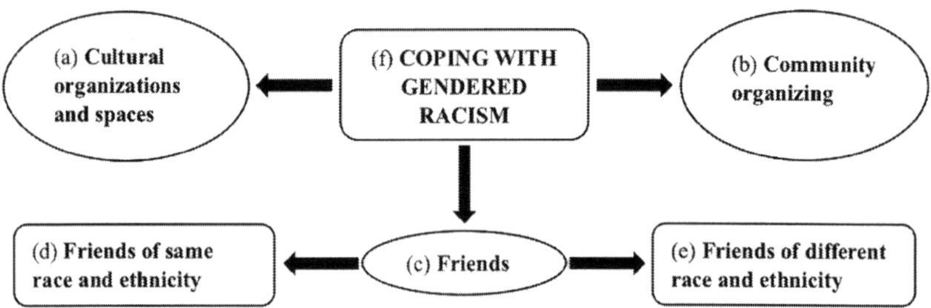

Figure 6.1 Community Coping Strategies for Undergraduate African American Women at the University of Colorado-Boulder. *Source*: Courtesy of LeAnna T. Luney.

IMPLICATIONS AND CONCLUSION

Academic institutions by and large do not welcome Black women with progressive political stances or those who critique and speak boldly against universities' oppressive policies and practices.[44] University administrators demonstrate this with their lack of efforts to eradicate gendered and racial hostility and microaggressions on campuses like CU Boulder, a "liberal bastion" that is symbolically progressive but has failed to create a campus climate conducive for Black women and other non-White people to learn, socialize, and live in environments free of gendered racism. To maintain their well-being and dignity and to navigate the university's "business as usual" racial hierarchies and politics, African American women adopt coping mechanisms including establishing friendships, joining cultural organizations and hanging out in cultural spaces, and participating in local community organizing efforts.[45]

Anti-Black settler colonialism is part of the undergirding background for Black college women coping at CU Boulder. African American college students' experiences are situated within the larger context of higher education institutions as mediums of state power and control over racial formations.[46] Deeming colleges and universities as dominant actors in networks of power, Roderick A. Ferguson analyzes how the state used them to suppress the dynamism of social movements in the 1950s, 1960s, and 1970s because the movements were adversarial to hegemonic constructions of difference.[47] Ferguson demonstrates how power enlisted the university as a site of difference to pacify racial tensions by arguing that "hegemonic power denotes the disembodied and abstract promotion of minority representation without fully satisfying the material and social redistribution of minoritized subjects, particularly where people of color are concerned."[48] On this accord, protests motivated hegemonic power to shift the intent of student activists from a call for redistribution and disruption of inequality, to an empty call for racial and ethnic representation. As a result, the academy never redistributed power dynamics to appease student activists' protests. Instead, they ideologically conflated power with bringing more non-White people into the academy, claiming that a growing number of non-White folks indicates a shift of power and access within higher education. This phenomenon is what Ferguson refers to as *institutionality*. Ferguson explains that universities have interest in race and ethnicity to propel hegemonic power over racial difference for capitalist gain, instead of genuine concern to advance racially equitable higher education institutions.[49]

In his interest convergence thesis, critical race theorist Derrick Bell explains that institutions holding power in the United States inherently resist racial progression, and only improve racial dynamics for their own gain.[50] The same occurred as student movements of the 1960s and 1970s elicited public and political support for the inclusion of non-White students at U.S. colleges and universities. This is what Brigitta R. Brunner refers to as the "smoke-screen of diversity."[51] Not only does the hegemonic establishment use the university as a means to surveil and police student demands for racial and ethnic inclusion and radical social movements by proxy, it also promotes shallow understandings of diversity without allowing its true purpose to come into fruition. This is done under the guise of welcoming "minority" difference. Moreover, within the context of globalization and economic ties between the university and global capitalist agencies, colleges, and universities serve as paternalist pipelines strategically enforcing hegemonic means of production. In other words, the academy maintains control over how race and ethnicity are understood, keeping radical movements at bay through imperialist ventures globally. In this way, the academy mirrors state and capitalistic hegemonies as an extension of racist and colonial dominance over the subaltern.[52]

Anti-Blackness and the perception of Black bodies as property at PWIs further demonstrate colonial remanences and how they aid in understanding the contradiction of "minority" difference in academic spaces. In their assessment of anti-Blackness in higher education institutions during a BLM era, T. Elon Dancy, Kirsten T. Edwards, and James Earl Davis urge U.S. colleges and universities to address their persistent conceptualizations of Black bodies as property.[53] Dancy, Edwards, and Davis highlight how constructed theories of settler colonialism and anti-Black ideologies "(re)interpret" arrangements and relationships between people of African descent and PWIs.[54] The authors maintain that PWIs' political agendas consist of employing the Black body as property which is deeply rooted in U.S. colleges' and universities' policy, practice, and culture.[55] The sentiment that Black bodies are property stems from Cheryl Harris' concept of whiteness as property, which states that in order for whiteness as a signifier of humanity to exist, African Americans are perpetually deemed as property due to the history of racial enslavement and free labor.[56] In other words, the Black body must be understood as subordinate and as inferior for white people to gain citizenship and rights in the United States. In higher education, notions of the Black body as property results in the dehumanization of Black students, faculty, and staff. PWIs must not merely promise to value Black life and commit to racial progress when it benefits their interest. Given the endemic nature of institutional racism and whites people's propensity toward pursuing their interests, racism may likely persist at many PWIs for years to come. Be that as it may, being attentive to Black students' stories about their experiences with racism on campus is an important step in helping African American students in general and African American women college students in particular navigate and survive racism in PWIs.

Researchers should consider conducting more qualitative studies that welcome students to share their experiences with coping with racism at PWIs. Furthermore, this qualitative approach should complement predestined and closed-question campus climate surveys that enable students to be open and honest about their experiences with racism and other forms of oppression. Such qualitative research should incorporate a critical race feminist framework and not merely focus on racism but should also acknowledge African American undergraduate women's experiences with sexism and other forms of oppression.

NOTES

1. Tracy O. Patton and Sally M. Schedlock, "Let's Go, Let's Show, Let's Rodeo: African Americans and the History of Rodeo," *The Journal of African American History* 96, no. 4 (2011): 503.

2. Nicola A. Corbin, William A. Smith, and Roberto J. Garcia, "Trapped between Justified Anger and Being the Strong Black Woman: Black College Women Coping with Racial Battle Fatigue at Historically and Predominantly White Institutions," *International Journal of Qualitative Studies in Education* 31, no. 7 (2018): 626–43.

3. Dawn M. Szymanski and Jioni A. Lewis, "Gendered Racism, Coping, Identity Centrality, and African American College Women's Psychological Distress," *Psychology of Women Quarterly* 40, no. 2 (2016): 229–43.

4. Patricia Hill Collins, *Black Feminist Thought: Knowledge, Consciousness, and the Politics of Empowerment* (New York: Routledge Classics, 2009); Patricia Hill Collins, *Intersectionality as Critical Social Theory* (Durham, NC: Duke University Press, 2019), 158; bell hooks, *Feminist Theory: From Margin to Center* (New York: Routledge, 2015); Jennifer C. Nash, *Black Feminism Reimagined: After Intersectionality* (Durham, NC: Duke University Press), 5.

5. Adrien Katherine Wing, *Critical Race Feminism: A Reader* (New York: New York University Press, 2003), 1.

6. Ibid., 5–7.

7. Distinct from "historical," "herstorical" centers a feminist perspective of history. "Herstory" can be broken down as "her story" to assert women's agency in creating and telling their own stories; Patricia Hill Collins and Sirma Bilge, *Intersectionality (Key Concepts)* (New York: Polity, 2020), 82.

8. Collins and Bilge, *Intersectionality*, 14; Kimberlé Crenshaw, "Mapping the Margins: Intersectionality, Identity Politics, and Violence Against Women of Color," in *Critical Race Theory: The Key Writings that Formed the Movement*, ed. Kimberlé Crenshaw et al. (New York: The New Press, 1995), 357–83; Kimberlé Crenshaw, "Demarginalizing the Intersection of Race and Sex: A Black Feminist Critique of Antidiscrimination Doctrine, Feminist Theory and Antiracist Politics," in *Critical Race Feminism: A Reader*, ed. Adrien K. Wing (New York: New York University Press, 2003), 7, 23–33.

9. I use pseudonyms to withhold the students' identities throughout this chapter.

10. Polly E. Bugros McLean, *Remembering Lucille: A Virginia Family's Rise From Slavery and a Legacy Forged a Mile High* (Boulder, CO: University Press of Colorado, 2018); Patton and Schedlock, "Let's Go, Let's Show, Let's Rodeo."

11. William M. King, *Going to Meet a Man: Denver's Last Legal Public Execution, 27 July 1886*. 1st edn (Niwot, CO: University Press of Colorado, 1990); McLean, *Remembering Lucille*.

12. McLean, *Remembering Lucille*; Jesse T. Moore, "Seeking a New Life: Blacks in Post-Civil War Colorado," *Journal of Negro History* 78, no. 3 (Summer 1993): 167.

13. McLean, *Remembering Lucille*; Patton and Schedlock, "Let's Go, Let's Show, Let's Rodeo."

14. "Undergraduate Profile: Fall 2019," Office of Data Analytics, University of Colorado Boulder, accessed July 6, 2020, https://www.colorado.edu/oda/sites/default/files/attached-files/ugprofilefall19.pdf; "2018–19 Diversity Report," System Office of Institutional Research, University of Colorado, accessed July 7, 2020, https://www.cu.edu/doc/oaareportdiversity-2018-19pdf;

15. CU Boulder follows state and federal guidelines for reporting gender (and race), which means students are classified on a male-female binary for gender. CU Boulder provides the opportunity for gender nonconforming and nonbinary students to report as such in internal identification records.

16. "CU-Boulder Undergraduate Student Social Climate Survey: Fall 2014 Findings Summary," University of Colorado Boulder, accessed July 6, 2020, https://www.colorado.edu/oda/sites/default/files/attached-files/ugsocialclimatesurvey2014web.pdf. This campus climate study is distributed every four years since 1994 but skipped in 2018 because of a university system-wide campus climate survey distributed in November 2019. An official report of 2019 findings are expected to be released in July 2020.

17. "University of Colorado Boulder," Data USA, accessed July 6, 2020, https://datausa.io/profile/university/university-of-colorado-boulder/; "The CU Boulder Difference," University of Colorado Boulder, accessed July 6, 2020, https://www.colorado.edu/about; "University of Colorado—Boulder," Best Colleges, U.S. News and World Report, accessed July 7, 2020, https://www.usnews.com/best-colleges/university-of-colorado-boulder-1370.

18. The term "liberal" indicates people and groups supporting seemingly progressive institutional reform. Such reform results in the institutionalization and co-optation of radical politics and promotes state-sanctioned oppression; Collins and Bilge, *Intersectionality*, 132. Liberals fail to seriously challenge racism, and other types of oppression in society. Venus Evans-Winters, *Black Feminism in Qualitative Inquiry: A Mosaic for Writing Our Daughter's Body (Futures of Data Analysis in Qualitative Research)* (Abingdon-on-Thames: Routledge, 2019), 57; Hillary Amma Potter (Associate Dean for Inclusive Practice), Interview with LeAnna T. Luney, Denver, CO, November 24, 2019.

19. "Quick Facts," Boulder City, Colorado, U.S. Census Bureau, accessed July 6, 2020, https://www.census.gov/quickfacts/fact/table/bouldercitycolorado,US/PST045219.

20. "Center for Inclusion and Social Change," Office of Diversity, Equity, and Community Engagement, University of Colorado Boulder, accessed July 6, 2020, https://www.colorado.edu/cisc/.

21. "Hallett Hall," Housing and Dining Division of Student Affairs, University of Colorado Boulder, accessed July 6, 2020, https://www.colorado.edu/living/housing/residence-halls/hallett-hall.

22. Michael Omi and Howard Winant, *Racial Formations in the United States* (New York: Routledge, 2015), 130.

23. Sah'Kema M. Blackmon et al., "Linking Racial-ethnic Socialization to Culture and Race-specific Coping among African American College Students," *Journal of Black Psychology* 42, no. 6 (2016): 549–76, 10.1177/0095798415617865; Cynthia Garcia Coll et al., "An Integrative Model for the Study of Developmental Competencies in Minority Children," *Child Development* 67, no. 5 (1996): 1891–914, 10.2307/1131600; Alfrieda Daly et al., "Effective Coping Strategies of African Americans," *Social Work* 40, no. 2 (1995): 240–48, 10.1093/sw/40.2.240; Deborah J. Johnson, "Parental Characteristics, Racial Stress, and Racial Socialization Processes as Predictors of Racial Coping in Middle Childhood," in *Forging Links: African American Children Clinical Developmental Perspectives*, ed. A. M. Neal-Barnett, J. M. Contreras, and K. A. Kerns (Westport, CT: Greenwood Press, 2001), 57–74; Lionel D. Scott, "The Relation of Racial Identity and Racial Socialization to Coping with Discrimination among African American Adolescents," *Journal of Black Studies* 33, no. 4 (2003): 520–37, 10.1177/0021934702250035; Shawn O. Utsey, Eve P. Adams, and Mark Bolden, "Development and Initial Validation of the Africultural Coping Systems Inventory," *Journal of Black Psychology* 26, no. 2 (2016): 194–215, 10.1177/0095798400026002005.

24. Coll et al., "An Integrative Model for the Study of Developmental Competencies in Minority Children," 1891–914; Johnson, "Parental Characteristics, Racial Stress, and Racial Socialization Processes as Predictors of Racial Coping in Middle Childhood," 57–74; Scott, "The Relation of Racial Identity and Racial Socialization to Coping with Discrimination among African American Adolescents," 520–37.

25. Blackmon et al., "Linking Racial-ethnic Socialization to Culture and Race-specific Coping among African American College Students," 549–76.

26. Audre Lorde, *Sister Outsider* (Berkeley, CA: Crossing Press, 2007), 151; Collins, *Black Feminist Thought*, 12.

27. Martinique K. Jones and Thomandra S. Sam, "Cultural Connections: An Ethnocultural Counseling Intervention for Black Women in College," *Journal of College Counseling* 21, no. 1 (2018): 73–86, 10.1002/jocc.12088; Christine E. Smith and Reginald Hopkins, "Mitigating the Impact of Stereotypes on Academic Performance: The Effects of Cultural Identity and Attributions for Success among African American College Students," *Western Journal of Black Studies* 28, no. 1(2004): 312–21; Veronica J. Smith et al., "Implicit Coping Responses to Racism Predict African Americans' Level of Psychological Distress," *Basic & Applied Social Psychology* 30, no. 3 (2008): 264–77, https://doi-org.colorado.idm.oclc.org/10.1080/01973530802375110; Jioni A. Lewis et al., "'Ain't I a Woman?' Perceived Gendered Racial Microaggressions Experienced by Black Women," *The Counseling Psychologist* 44, no. 5 (2016): 758–80, 10.1177/0011000016641193.

28. Race is rooted in biological processes of categorizing people based on physical attributes like skin color and/or hair texture, whereas ethnicity is a process of categorizing people based on their cultural expression and identification (M. Andersen, *Race in Society: The Enduring American Dilemma* (Louisville, CO: Roman & Littlefield Publishers, 2017)). Although distinctions between race and ethnicity prominently exist, some students throughout the focus group and joint interviews used the terms interchangeably, while others specifically refer to race or ethnicity.

29. "University of Colorado IR."

30. Regina (student) in discussion with the author, April 2020.

31. Jazmine (student) in discussion with the author, April 2020.

32. Marya (student) in discussion with the author, April 2020.

33. Joseph A. Baldwin, "African Self-Consciousness and the Mental Health of African Americans," *Journal of Black Studies* 15, no. 2 (1984): 177–94, https://www.jstor.org/stable/2784007; Jones and Sam, "Cultural Connections," 73–86; Wade W. Nobles, "Extended Self: Rethinking the So-called Negro Self-concept" (Speech: National Association of Black Psychologists Convention, 1974); Smith and Hopkins, "Mitigating the Impact of Stereotypes on Academic Performance," 312–21; Smith et al., "Implicit Coping Responses to Racism Predict African Americans' Level of Psychological Distress," 264–77.

34. Florence (student) in discussion with the author, April 2020.

35. Florence (student) in discussion with the author, April 2020.

36. Roderick A. Ferguson, *The Reorder of Things: The University and Its Pedagogies of Minority Difference* (Minneapolis, MN: University of Minnesota Press, 2012).

37. Jioni Lewis et al., "Coping with Gendered Racial Microaggressions among Black Women College Students," *Journal of African American Studies* 17, no. 1 (2012): 51–73; Collins, *Black Feminist Thought.*

38. Assata (student) in discussion with the author, April 2020.

39. Assata (student) in discussion with the author, April 2020.

40. Assata (student) in discussion with the author, April 2020.

41. T. Elon Dancy II, Kirsten T. Edwards, and James Earl Davis, "Historically White Universities and Plantation Politics: Anti-Blackness and Higher Education in the Black Lives Matter Era," *Urban Education*, 53, no. 2 (2018): 176–95, https://doi.org/10.1177/0042085918754328.

42. LeAnna T. Luney's Fieldnotes, February 20, 2020.

43. Milan (student) in discussion with the author, April 2020.

44. Patricia Hill Collins, "Learning from the Outsider Within: The Sociological Significance of Black Feminist Thought," *Social Problems* 33, no. 6 (December 1986): 14–32; Olivia N. Perlow, "Gettin' Free: Anger as Resistance to White Supremacy Within and Beyond the Academy," in *Black Women's Liberatory Pedagogies: Resistance, Transformation, and Healing Within and Beyond the Academy*, ed. Olivia N. Perlow, Sharon L. Bethea, Durene I. Wheeler, BarBara M. Scott (New York: Springer International Publishing, 2018), 101–23.

45. Jones and Sam, "Cultural Connections," 73–86; Lewis et al., "Coping with Gendered Racial Microaggressions among Black Women College Students," 51–73;

Teresa Ramos, "Managing Racial Risk in the U.S. University of the Twenty-first Century: Racial Theme Parties, Administrative Management, and Strategic Resistance" (PhD diss., University of Illinois, 2012); Teresa Ramos, "Critical Race Ethnography of Higher Education: Racial Risk and Counter-storytelling," *Learning and Teaching* 6, no. 3 (2013): 64–78, https://doi.org/10.3167/latiss.2013.060306.

46. Lewis et al., "Coping with Gendered Racial Microaggressions among Black Women College Students," 51–73; Jioni Lewis and Helen A. Neville, "Construction and Initial Validation of the Gendered Racial Microaggressions Scale for Black Women," *Journal of Counseling Psychology* 62, no. 2 (2015): 289–302, 10.1037/cou0000062; Lewis et al., "'Ain't I a Woman?'" 758–80; Dancy, Edwards, and Davis, "Historically White Universities and Plantation Politics," 176–95; Ferguson, *The Reorder of Things*.

47. Ferguson, *The Reorder of Things*.

48. Ibid., 7–8.

49. Ibid., 49.

50. Derrick Bell, "Brown V. Board of Education and the Interest Convergence Dilemma," in *Critical Race Theory: The Key Writings that Formed the Movement*, ed. Kimberlé Crenshaw et al. (New York: The New Press, 1995), 22.

51. Brigitta R. Brunner, "Student Perceptions of Diversity on a College Campus: Scratching the Surface to Find More," *Intercultural Education* 17, no. 3 (2006): 311–17, https://doi.org/10.1080/14675980600841751.

52. Ferguson, *The Reorder of Things*.

53. Dancy, Edwards, and Davis, "Historically White Universities and Plantation Politics," 176–95.

54. Ibid.

55. Ibid., 180.

56. Cheryl Harris, "Whiteness as Property," in *Critical Race Theory: The Key Writings that Formed the Movement*, ed. Kimberlé Crenshaw et al. (New York: The New Press, 1995), 276–91.

BIBLIOGRAPHY

Andersen, M. *Race in Society: The Enduring American Dilemma*. Louisville, CO: Roman & Littlefield Publishers, 2017.

Baldwin, Joseph A. "African Self-Consciousness and the Mental Health of African Americans." *Journal of Black Studies* 15, no. 2 (1984): 177–194.

Bell, Derrick. "Brown V. Board of Education and the Interest Convergence Dilemma." In *Critical Race Theory: The Key Writings that Formed the Movement*, edited by Kimberlé Crenshaw, Neil Gotanda, Gary Peller, and Kendall Thomas, 357–383. New York: The New Press, 1995.

Blackmon, Sah'Kema M., Laura D. Coyle, Sheron Davenport, Archandria C. Owens, and Christopher Sparrow. "Linking Racial-ethnic Socialization to Culture and Race-specific Coping among African American College Students." *Journal of Black Psychology* 42, no. 6 (2016): 549–576. 10.1177/0095798415617865.

Brunner, Brigitta R. "Student Perceptions of Diversity on a College Campus: Scratching the Surface to Find More." *Intercultural Education* 17, no. 3 (2006). 10.1080/14675980600841751.

Collins, Patricia Hill. "Learning from the Outsider Within: The Sociological Significance of Black Feminist Thought." *Social Problems* 33, no. 6 (1986): 14–32.

Collins, Patricia Hill. *Black Feminist Thought: Knowledge, Consciousness, and the Politics of Empowerment.* New York: Routledge Classics, 2003.

Collins, Patricia Hill. *Intersectionality as Critical Social Theory.* Durham, NC: Duke University Press, 2019.

Collins, Patricia Hill and Sirma Bilge. *Intersectionality (Key Concepts).* New York: Polity, 2020.

Corbin, Nicola A., William A. Smith, and J. Roberto Garcia. "Trapped between Justified Anger and being the Strong Black Woman: Black College Women Coping with Racial Battle Fatigue at Historically and Predominantly White Institutions." *International Journal of Qualitative Studies in Education* 31, no. 7 (2018): 626–643.

Crenshaw, Kimberlé, Neil Gotanda, Gary Peller, and Kendall Thomas, eds. *Critical Race Theory: The Key Writings that Formed the Movement.* New York: The New Press, 1995.

Daly, Alfrieda Daly, Jeanette Jennings, Joyce O. Beckett, and Bogart R. Leashore. "Effective Coping Strategies of African Americans." *Social Work* 40, no. 2 (1995): 240–248. 10.1093/sw/40.2.240.

Dancy II, T. Elon, Kirsten T. Edwards, and James Earl Davis. "Historically White Universities and Plantation Politics: Anti-Blackness and Higher Education in the Black Lives Matter Era." *Urban Education* 53, no. 2 (2018): 176–195. https://doi.org/10.1177/0042085918754328.

Data USA. "University of Colorado Boulder: Doctoral Universities." Accessed July 6, 2020. https://datausa.io/profile/university/university-of-colorado-boulder/.

Evans-Winters, Venus E. *Black Feminism in Qualitative Inquiry: A Mosaic for Writing Our Daughter's Body (Futures of Data Analysis in Qualitative Research).* Abingdon-on-Thames: Routledge, 2019.

Ferguson, Roderick A. *The Reorder of Things: The University and Its Pedagogies of Minority Difference.* Minneapolis, MN: University of Minnesota Press, 2012.

Harris, Cheryl. "Whiteness as Property" Critical Race Theory: The Key Writings that Formed the Movement, edited by Kimberlé Crenshaw et al., 276–291. New York: The New Press, 1995.

hooks, bell. *Feminist Theory: From Margin to Center.* New York: Routledge, 2015.

Johnson, Deborah J. "Parental Characteristics, Racial Stress, and Racial Socialization Processes as Predictors of Racial Coping in Middle Childhood." In *Forging Links: African American Children Clinical Developmental Perspectives*, edited by Angela M. Neal-Barnett, Josefina M. Contreras, and Kathryn A. Kerns, 57–74. Westport, CT: Greenwood Press, 2001.

Jones, Martinique K. and Thomandra S. Sam. "Cultural Connections: An Ethnocultural Counseling Intervention for Black Women in College." *Journal of College Counseling* 21, no. 1 (2018): 73–86. 10.1002/jocc.12088.

King, William M. *Going to Meet a Man: Denver's Last Legal Public Execution, 27 July 1886*. Vol. 1st ed. Niwot, Colo: Chicago Distribution Center [CDC Presses], 1990. https://search-ebscohost-com.colorado.idm.oclc.org/login.aspx?direct=true&db=nlebk&AN=281&site=ehost-live&scope=site.

Lewis, Jioni A. and Neville, Helen A. "Construction and Initial Validation of the Gendered Racial Microaggressions Scale for Black Women." *Journal of Counseling Psychology* 62, no. 2 (2015): 289–302. 10.1037/cou0000062.

Lorde, Audre. *Sister Outsider*. Berkeley, CA: Crossing Press, 2017.

McLean, Polly E. Bugros. *Remembering Lucile: A Virginia Family's Rise From Slavery and a Legacy Forged a Mile High*. Boulder, CO: University Press of Colorado, 2018.

Moore, Jesse T. "Seeking a New Life: Blacks in Post-Civil War Colorado." *The Journal of Negro History* 78, no. 3 (1993): 166–187.

Nash, Jennifer, C. *Black Feminism Reimagined: After Intersectionality*. Durham, NC: Duke University Press, 2019.

Nobles, Wade W. "Extended self: Rethinking the So-called Negro Self-concept." Speech, National Association of Black Psychologists Convention, 1974.

Omi, Michael and Winant, Howard. *Racial Formations in the United States*. New York: Routledge, 2015.

Patton, Tracy Owens and Schedlock, Sally M. "Let's Go, Let's Show, Let's Rodeo: African Americans and the History of Rodeo." *The Journal of African American History* 96, no. 4 (2011): 503.

Perlow, Olivia N., Durene I. Wheeler, Sharon L. Bethea, and BarBara M. Scott. *Black Women's Liberatory Pedagogies: Resistance, Transformation, and Healing within and Beyond the Academy*. 1st 2018 edition.. Cham: Springer International Publishing, 2018.

Potter, Hillary Amma. "Liberal Bastion." Interview by LeAnna T. Luney. November 24, 2019.

Ramos, Teresa. "Managing Racial Risk in the U.S. University of the Twenty-first Century: Racial Theme Parties, Administrative Management, and Strategic Resistance." PhD diss., University of Illinois, 2012.

Ramos, Teresa. "Critical Race Ethnography of Higher Education: Racial Risk and Counter-Storytelling." *Learning and Teaching* 6, no. 3 (2013): 64–78. https://doi.org/10.3167/latiss.2013.060306.

Scott, Lionel D. "The Relation of Racial Identity and Racial Socialization to Coping with Discrimination among African American Adolescents." *Journal of Black Studies* 33, no. 4 (2003): 520–537. 10.1177/0021934702250035.

Smith, Christine E. and Reginald Hopkins. "Mitigating the Impact of Stereotypes on Academic Performance: The Effects of Cultural Identity and Attributions for Success among African American College Students." *Western Journal of Black Studies* 28, no. 1 (2004): 312–321.

Szymanski, Dawn M. and Jioni A Lewis. "Gendered Racism, Coping, Identity Centrality, and African American College Women's Psychological Distress." *Psychology of Women Quarterly* 40, no. 2 (2016): 229–243.

Tabuleau Public. "University of Colorado Boulder IR—Profile." Accessed July 7, 2020. https://public.tableau.com/profile/university.of.colorado.boulder.ir#!/.

United States Census Bureau. "Quick facts." Access July 6, 2020. https://www.census.gov/quickfacts/fact/table/bouldercitycolorado,US/PST045219.

University of Colorado Boulder. "Center for Inclusion and Social Change." Accessed July 6, 2020. https://www.colorado.edu/cisc/.

University of Colorado Boulder. "The CU Boulder Difference." Accessed July 6, 2020. https://www.colorado.edu/about.

University of Colorado Boulder. "CU-Boulder Undergraduate Student Social Climate Survey Fall 2014 Findings Summary." Accessed July 7, 2020. https://www.colorado.edu/oda/sites/default/files/attached-files/ugsocialclimatesurvey2014web.pdf.

University of Colorado Boulder. "Housing and Dining Division of Student Affairs." Accessed July 6, 2020. https://www.colorado.edu/living/housing/residence-halls/hallett-hall.

University of Colorado Office of Data Analytics. "Undergraduate Profile: Fall 2019." Accessed July 7, 2020. https://www.colorado.edu/oda/sites/default/files/attached-files/ugprofilefall19.pdf.

University of Colorado System Office of Institutional Research. "University of Colorado 2018–19 Diversity Report." Accessed July 7, 2020. https://www.cu.edu/doc/oaareportdiversity-2018-19pdf.

U.S. News & World Report. "Overview of University of Colorado—Boulder." Accessed July 7, 2020. https://www.usnews.com/best-colleges/university-of-colorado-boulder-1370.

Utsey, Shawn O., Adams, Eve P., and Bolden Mark. "Development and Initial Validation of the Africultural Coping Systems Inventory." *Journal of Black Psychology* 26, no. 2 (2016): 194–215. 10.1177/0095798400026002005.

Wing, Adrien Katherine. *Critical Race Feminism: A Reader.* New York: New York University Press, 2003.

Part III

AFRICAN AMERICAN LITERARY AND CULTURAL STUDIES

Introduction

Intersections between African American Literature, Cultural Studies, and Critical Race Studies

Vida Robertson

Many of the foundational tenets of critical race theory emerge from the fertile, interdisciplinary fields that comprise the humanities. More precisely, philosophical, literary, cultural, and ethnic studies have profoundly shaped the formation and evolution of critical race theory. Humanists interrogate the underlying institutional and aesthetic processes requisite for the formation of racialized, gendered, class-oriented, sexually prescribed and able-bodied subjects. Ethnic, cultural and literary representations serve as societal repositories for these ideological configurations. Representation and narrative are indispensable tools employed by all cultures and social groups. The investigation of sociocultural narratives fosters deep insights into the imperceptible principles shaping the social order. In the words of Nobel and Pulitzer Prize-winning African American novelist Toni Morrison, "Narrative is radical, creating us at the very moment it is being created."[1] It is from this radical perspective that Professor Derek Bell ushers critical legal studies into counter-storytelling which challenge the racist myths that epitomize and reinforce racial dynamics. Richard Delgado in a seminal article entitled "Storytelling for Oppositionists and Others: A Plea for Narrative" explains:

> Counterstories, which challenge the received wisdom . . . can open new windows into reality, showing us that there are possibilities for life other than the ones we live. They enrich imagination and teach that by combining elements from the story and current reality, we may construct a new world richer than either alone. Counterstories can quicken and engage conscience . . . They can show that what we believe is ridiculous, self-serving, or cruel. They can show us the way out of the trap of unjustified exclusion. They can help us understand when it is time to reallocate power.[2]

For Delgado and Bell, the ability to analyze and understand the reflexive operation narrative serves in justifying the subjugation of non-white peoples is indispensable to critical race theorists. The critical interrogation of the structural, procedural, and aesthetic elements of individual and societal narratives provides ideological access into the interpellation of race.[3]

Unlike other academic fields of inquiry, philosophy, humanities, and literary criticism share certain theoretical lines of inquiry which explore questions of individual and relational subjectivity central to critical race theory. The humanistic disciplines focus on the intricate and multifaceted nature of the individual and the community. Ghanaian philosopher and cultural theorist Kwame Anthony Appiah would refer to the bifurcation of subject formation as one's racial identity and racial identification.[4] African American and Black philosophers, cultural critics, and literary scholars beginning in the mid-nineteenth century served as intellectual predecessors and scholactivists of critical race concepts and frameworks.

Critical race theory differentiates itself from other forms of critical theorizing by methodically scrutinizing the process of racialization, the justifications for racism, and the systemic inequity sustained by it. Although interdisciplinary in scope, critical race theory is deeply indebted to the theorizations of Karl Marx, Antonio Gramsci, Michel Foucault, and Jacques Derrida. The materialist and poststructuralist approach of these European intellectuals informs the structuralist assessments and ideological considerations of a critical race analysis of systemic oppression. Dialectical materialism and deconstructionism comprise the skeletal apparatus undergirding Derek Bell's conceptions of racial realism and interest convergence theory.[5] Moreover, Marx and others maintained an earnest commitment to move beyond thought into action. Karl Marx famously explained, "The philosophers have only interpreted the world, in various ways. The point, however, is to change it."[6] Marx foreshadows critical race theory's principle commitment to alleviate oppression through research that strives for social justice reform.

One of the earliest examples of scholactivism in the humanities is found in the works of African American abolitionist, physician and newspaper editor Martin Delany. Delany integrated his medical education and Black nationalist sensibilities into a biopolitical refutation of White supremacy. In his 1879 publication of *Principia of Ethnology: The Origin of Races and Color*, he reimagines the basis and import of Black racial identity.[7] By supplanting European skin complexions as the default human phenotype with the racial neutrality of the albinic body, Delany attempts to dismantle the eugenics argument for White supremacy and establish a record of Black artistic and scientific ingenuity. Martin Delany's social constructionist idea of racial identity would inform the writings of iconoclast and scholactivist W. E. B. DuBois. DuBois would openly refute the racist proponents of eugenics in his essay "The Conservation of Races" in which he argues that the essentialist characterization of racial identity is a farce. The stereotypical depictions and categorizations of racial difference purported by propagandistic pseudoscientists do not align with statistical and historical fact. DuBois concedes that the diversity of "physical characteristics are patent enough, and if [the physical characteristics and racial categorizations] agreed with each other it would be very easy to classify mankind. Unfortunately for scientists, however, these criteria of race are most exasperatingly intermingled."[8] Or as he would say more simply in his autobiography "It is easy to see that scientific definition of race is impossible."[9] Like Delany, W. E. B. DuBois used his talent as a writer, cultural critic, and racial theorist to disprove essentialist notions of African American inferiority and establish institutions dedicated to Black liberation.[10] In his groundbreaking anthology *The Souls of Black Folk*, DuBois offers a structural critique of the nation's unique brand of racialized capitalism as well as provides exceptional insight into the "double consciousness" trauma of the African American experience. For both DuBois and Delany, race is a sociohistorical phenomenon superimposed onto the population by the deterministic forces of the nation's Eurocentric legal and economic systems.[11] The liberation of the African American community demands direct and institutional acknowledgment of the overt and covert systems which buttress racial hierarchies.

With the advent of the Civil Right Movement, African American novelist, essayist, and activist James Baldwin emerges as another forebear of critical race theory by further expanding the theoretical footprint of counterstories into arenas of racialized gender and sexuality. In the midst of the turbulent 1960s, James Baldwin artfully highlighted the cruel anti-Black sentiment of American society which violently commandeered African American life. Just prior to the 1963 March on Washington, Baldwin publishes *The Fire Next Time,* a letter written to his nephew commenting on the 100th anniversary of the Emancipation Proclamation. In the letter, Baldwin writes, "You were born where you were born and faced the future that you faced because you were Black and for no other reason . . .You were born into a society which spelled out with brutal clarity, and in as many ways as possible, that you were a worthless human being."[12] Baldwin sketched the centrality and permanence of racism in U.S. society in his essays, speeches, and debates. The clarity and precision of his analysis are echoed in the pioneering work of fellow civil rights activist Derek Bell in *Faces at the Bottom of the Well: The Permanence of Racism.* Moreover, James Baldwin's avant-garde scholactivism necessitates a comprehensive understanding to African American liberation that appreciates the overlapping oppression of race, gender, and sexuality that predates the intersectional scholarship of the notable critical race theorist, Kimberlé Crenshaw.[13]

However, it is the contemporary literary and cultural criticisms of Toni Morrison that best exemplify the incorporation of critical race theory in the humanities. Renowned author and literary critic, Toni Morrison argues that the American literary imagination, exemplified in the works of Mark Twain, William Faulkner, and Earnest Hemingway, was fashioned over and against an intangible African presence which outlines the constitutive borders of whiteness. In *Playing in the Dark: Whiteness and the Literary Imagination*, Morrison incorporates racial constructionism as a critical lens to explore the racist implications of mainstream American literary conventions, linguistic strategies, and racial idioms. The rugged, masculine, individuality of whiteness expressed in the novels denotes the inferiority and subordination of all identities. She sharpens and builds upon this line of literary criticism in *The Origins of Others*. Here Morrison traces the dehumanizing practice of "othering" through nineteenth-century eugenics records to the literary allusions documented in the novels of Ernest Hemingway and Harriet Beecher Stowe. In this exceptional rebuttal to the disavowal of authentic portrayals of African American life, Morrison generously offers her own literary characters as more suitable counterstories and complex representations of the African American experience.

One of the most recent additions to the chorus of voices in the genre of cultural criticism and ethnic studies is African American journalist, essayist, and novelist Ta-Nehisi Coates. Coates is most notably known for his highly acclaimed bestseller *Between the World and Me*. In this essay length letter to his son, Coates adopts the racial realism, anti-essentialism, and pervasive brutality described in critical race theory to relay the tragic embodiment of African American life under the logic of White supremacy. He unambiguously explains to his son who is recently traumatized by the lack of police accountability for the brutal murder of Michael Brown that "white supremacy—serves to obscure that racism is a visceral experience, that it dislodges brains, blocks airways, rips muscle, extracts organs, cracks bones, breaks teeth. You must never look away from this."[14] By gracefully interweaving American history, memoir, racial theory, and cultural criticism, Coates provides brilliant insight to the way that race exerts an unrelenting and deadly force on the lives of African Americans. The cloak of White supremacy is unveiled to provide a stark criticism of American culture and faintly transcendent vision of what it means to "be a conscious citizen of this terrible and beautiful world."[15]

By and large, the well-established symbiotic relationship of the humanities and critical race theory has fostered an intellectual partnership which emphasizes the importance of identifying and theorizing the socio-economic, cultural, and legal exigencies that contour the way authors and readers experience and respond to racism. Cultural critics, literary scholars, and social theorists understand literature, speeches, film, legal documents, and other cultural artifacts as evidence of the society's shared values and beliefs. As such, the humanities help identify and dismantle systemic racism by making visible the iterative linguistic, cultural, historical, and political operations used to produce them. As scholactivists, researchers in the humanities have often deployed critical race theory to investigate racism a theoretical, historical, and intensely personal experience.

The three chapters in the literature and culture section of this text participate in the ongoing interplay of cultural criticism and critical race theory. Ordner Taylor explores Toni Morrison's novel *Beloved* as an emancipatory counter-narrative in the chapter entitled "Rememory and Toni Morrison's *Beloved*: A Counter-Narrative to Forgetting America's Past." In this chapter, Taylor adroitly intersects the historical life of Margaret Garner and Morrison's literary representation of Sethe Suggs to provide his readers with a more nuanced understanding of the last four hundred years of the African American life. Taylor argues that Morrison's concepts of rememory grants humanity and dignity to the enslaved African American men and women whose lives fueled the American Dream. In "The Unscripted Script of Black YouTube (BYT): The Working Identities of African American Family Vloggers," Jenean A. McGee interrogates hegemonic force of White middle-class politics of respectability. She documents the aesthetic and material influences of American capitalism on the YouTube (re)presentation of the African American family. McGee challenges the antiracist, postracial, color-blind rhetoric of the Obama era by highlighting pervasive manner that supposedly egalitarian spaces like the Internet are governed by interest convergence. Finally, Khyree Davis examines the sexualized violence of gay and queer African American men during the emergence of the 1980s HIV/AIDS pandemic. Davis adroitly situates this latest demonstration of state-sanctioned violence in a long history of distinctly salacious racialized oppression enacted on Black communities beginning with the chattel enslavement and the Middle Passage. According to Davis, the African diaspora have historically, strategically, and creatively positioned their bodies to thwart the dominant logics of anti-Blackness, sexual conquest, and reproductive control. By reimagining the geographies of African American gay and queer struggle, Khyree Davis details their resilience and opposition to the Eurocentric and homophobic response of the U.S. government during one of the greatest health crises of the twentieth century.

NOTES

1. Toni Morrison, "Nobel Lecture 1993," *World Literature Today* 68, no. 1 (Winter 1994): 5.

2. Richard Delgado, "Storytelling for Oppositionists and Others: A Plea for Narrative," *Michigan Law Review* 87, no. 8 (1989): 2414–15.

3. Interpellation is a term coined by Louis Althusser (1918–1990) which maintains that certain societal ideas are so well inculcated into our social worldview that we believe they are innate, natural, and real. Interpellation is the psychosocial procedure through which subjects encounter their communal beliefs and internalize them. See Louis Althusser, *Lenin and Philosophy and Other Essays* (New York: Monthly Review Press, 2001, orig. 1971).

4. Kwame Anthony Appiah establishes this distinction in several places but most notably in Kwame Anthony Appia, Amy Gutmann et al., *Color Conscious: The Political Morality of Race* (Princeton, NJ: Princeton University Press, 1996), 75–76.

5. Derrick Bell, *Faces at the Bottom of the Well: The Permanence of Racism* (New York: Basic Books, 1993); Derrick A. Bell, *And We Are No Saved: The Elusive Quest for Racial Justice* (New York: Basic Books: 1987).

6. "Theses on Feuerbach" was first published as an appendix to *Ludwig Feuerbach and the End of Classical German Philosophy* in 1888. Robert C. Tucker, ed., *The Marx-Engels Reader*, 2nd edition (New York: W.W. Norton and Company 1978).

7. Martin Robison Delany, *Principia of Ethnology : The Origin of Races and Color: With an Archeological Compendium of Ethiopian and Egyptian Civilization, From Years of Careful Examination and Enquiry* (Philadelphia: Harper and Brother, 1879).

8. David Levering Lewis, *W.E.B. DuBois: A Reader* (New York: Henry Holt and Company, Inc. 1995).

9. W.E.B. Du Bois, *Dusk of Dawn: An Essay toward an Autobiography of a Race Concept* (New York: Schocken Books, 1940), 137.

10. W.E.B. DuBois was a proponent of the Niagara Movement and cofounder of the National Association for the Advancement of Colored People (NAACP). He served as editor of several literary magazines including *The Crisis*. He also helped organize the Pan-African Congresses which was dedicated to the emancipation of African colonies from European rule.

11. W.E.B. Du Bois, *Black Reconstruction in America: An Essay toward a History of the Part which Black Folk Played in the Attempt to Reconstruct Democracy in America, 1860–1880* (New York: Harcourt Brace, 1935).

12. James Baldwin, *The Fire Next Time* (New York: Dial Press, 1963), 7.

13. James Baldwin and Quincy Troupe, *The Last Interview and Other Conversations* (Brooklyn, NY: Melville House, 2014).

14. Ta-Nehisi Coates, *Between the World and Me* (New York: Spiegel & Grau, 2015), 10.

15. Ibid., 108.

BIBLIOGRAPHY

Althusser, Louis. *Lenin and Philosophy and Other Essays*. New York: Monthly Review Press 2001, orig. 1971.

Appia, Kwame Anthony, Amy Gutmann, and David B. Wilkins. *Color Conscious: The Political Morality of Race*. Princeton, NJ: Princeton University Press, 1996.

Baldwin, James. *The Fire Next Time*. New York: Dial Press, 1963.

Baldwin, James and Quincy Troupe. *James Baldwin: The Last Interview and Other Conversations*. Brooklyn, NY: Melville House, 2014.

Bell, Derrick A. *And We Are No Saved: The Elusive Quest for Racial Justice*. New York: Basic Books: 1987.

Bell, Derrick. *Faces at the Bottom of the Well: The Permanence of Racism*. New York: Basic Books, 1993.

Coates, Ta-Nehisi. *Between the World and Me*. New York: Spiegel & Grau, 2015.

Delany, Martin Robison. *Principia of Ethnology: The Origin of Races and Color : with an Archeological Compendium of Ethiopian And Egyptian Civilization, From Years of Careful Examination and Enquiry*. Philadelphia: Harper and Brother, 1879.

Delgado, Richard. "Storytelling for Oppositionists and Others: A Plea for Narrative." *Michigan Law Review* 87, no. 8 (1989): 2411–41. https://repository.law.umich.edu/mlr/vol87/iss8/10.

Du Bois, W.E.B. *Black Reconstruction in America : An Essay toward a History of the Part Which Black Folk Played in the Attempt to Reconstruct Democracy in America, 1860–1880*. New York: Harcourt, Brace, 1935.

Du Bois, W.E.B. *Dusk of Dawn: An Essay toward an Autobiography of a Race Concept*. New York: Schocken Books, 1940.

Levering, David Lewis. *W.E.B. DuBois: A Reader*. New York: Henry Holt and Company, Inc. 1995.

Morrison, Toni. "Nobel Lecture 1993." *World Literature Today* 68, no. 1 (Winter 1994): 4–8. doi:10.2307/40149835.

Tucker, Robert C., ed. *The Marx-Engels Reader,* 2nd edition. New York: W.W. Norton and Company 1978.

Chapter 7

Rememory and Toni Morrison's *Beloved*

A Counter-Narrative to Forgetting America's Past

Ordner W. Taylor, III

David Omotoso Stovall in *Born Out of Struggle: Critical Race Theory, School Creation, and the Politics of Interruption* (2016) interprets Charles Laurence III to state that critical race theory (CRT) situates the marginalized voices of people of color in historically relevant and politically valid spaces of significance. Stovall further argues that historical and political omissions—unintentional or otherwise—compel "the activist/scholar to intentionally engage the political space to tell our story."[1] As such, CRT gives space for the author—who has been a representative or metonym of an oppressed group—to provide a counter-narrative to the tale that is told about her/him. By providing a counter-narrative, the individual who has been discussed by the oppressive voice shifts from object to subject, from a kind of flat literary character in a third-person narration to a first-person omniscient narrator of the entire work. When Kimberly W. Benston in "I yam what I yam the topos of un(naming) in Afro-American Literature" discusses former slaves who procured freedom and became authors, she notes that they felt "the need to resituate or displace the literal master/father by a literal act of unnaming."[2] These people of newly acquired freedom extricated themselves from the final elements of bondage by engaging in a practice of autonaming by rejecting their former surnames—which were often the surnames of their owners. This unaming/autonaming couplet action seems to serve as an early example of individuals intentionally engaging the political space to tell their stories. By renaming themselves, they—especially in the cases of Frederick Douglass and William Wells Brown—claim by force a humanity and personhood taken from them through violence. By writing their stories, one a slave narrative and the other, the first work of African American fiction, these authors intentionally positioned their previously marginalized voices in the historical and political locus of significance.

It is therefore arguable that some of the first examples of CRT praxis predate even the formulation of its lexicon. As such, CRT and its constituent parts function descriptively rather than prescriptively, and CRT applications can thus be applied to a myriad of situations as seen by Douglass's slave narrative which is literary and autobiographical in nature and Brown's novel which is literary and fictional in nature. Brown's 1853 *Clotel: or the President's Daughter* changed the literary and historical landscapes of both the American and African American societies in part because his historical fiction directly confronted the complicated relationship between Whites and African Americans in the United States during the nineteenth century. While his theme was both bold and provocative, his use of the novel as his medium was the most indelible part of his legacy. Brown used the novel to discuss the very well-known secret of Thomas Jefferson, his slave Sally Hemings, and their biracial family. This novel presents an amazing example of the tragic mulatta whose fortunes turn when her beauty ceases to serve her. More importantly, this novel speaks to the lengths that Black mothers went to protect their children and preserve their homes. Because slave narratives limited writers to the veracity of autobiography or memoir, the novel liberated authors to explore and explain the elements of the African American experience including villainy, heroism, and justice from the vantage point of African Americans. The African American novel became a dynamic vehicle that allowed many authors to produce some of the most important literature that America and the world would come to know, and it became one of the most important tools in helping to construct and retain African American culture—a cultural reservoir for Black experiences. Because the American experience and the African American experience are undivorceable from one another, the successes and failures that either has reflects upon the other. As such, among the great novels that illuminate or reflect America are the works from unforgettable African American authors. Brown's engagement of Black America's challenges with the White South became a seminal theme in African American literature that could easily be seen throughout in the lineage of the African American novel with examples from DuBois's *The Quest of the Silver Fleece* (1911), Zora Neale Hurston's *Their Eyes Were Watching God* (1937), Gayle Jones's *Corregidora* (1975), and Toni Morrison's *Beloved* (1987).

Of the many authors who used the power of the African American novel, Toni Morrison's work stands out as uniquely exceptional. Her lyrical language and serious subjects articulate the vast array of African Americans' emotions inside and outside of DuBois's veil in *The Souls of Black Folk*

(1903). Morrison's eleven novels directly treat themes ranging from contemporary colorism to mythical flying Africans, and within that canon, one sees Morrison's exploration of the immediate and long-term effects of African captivity in America. Readers can easily see how Morrison's works contribute to the world's understanding of the cultural and historical arc of the African American, and *Beloved* functions as the exemplar text. By comparing the biography of the real-life Margaret Garner with the fictional life of Sethe Suggs, Morrison used *Beloved* to offer a trifurcated view of the past, present, and future of African Americans, contribute to the cultural reservoir, and add to the richness of CRT with her selection of counter-narrative while masterfully presenting the arc of the African American experience in America from the era of slavery to contemporary times through what she identifies as rememory.

Margaret Garner's story predicates the counter-narrative of *Beloved*. Just as Douglass and Brown rename themselves and tell their own stories—stories that stand at odds with the American master narratives (as identified by Jean-François Lyotard), Morrison opts for an individualized narrative that counters the master narratives by utilizing rememory as the literary narrative tool and the CRT counter-narrative device (in the CRT sense).[3] Morrison herself wrote that:

> It was in *Beloved* that all of these matters coalesced for me in new and major ways. History versus memory, and memory versus memorylessness. Rememory as in recollecting and remembering as in reassembling the members of the body, the family, the population of the past. And it was the struggle, the pitched battle between remembering and forgetting, that became the device of the narrative.[4]

Morrison later noted that:

> Nobody in the book can bear too long to dwell on the past; nobody can avoid it. There is no reliable literary or journalistic or scholarly history available to them, to help them, because they are living in a society and a system in which the conquerors write the narrative of their lives. They are spoken of and written about—objects of history, not subjects within it.[5]

Beloved brings the experience of rememory of slavery to America because this experience is a part of the American legacy that continues to haunt America and her citizens. Where Sethe Suggs is the rememory of American slavery, Margaret Garner's biography is the original trauma.

Beloved is a fictional work that uses the real-life events of Margaret Garner, a twenty-two-year-old slave, wife, and the mother of four children, living in Kentucky who ran for freedom in 1856, as its point of departure.

On January 27, 1856, Margaret, her twenty-one-year-old husband Robert Garner, and their children were determined to escape the Gaines Plantation where they lived. So they stole a horse-drawn sled from their master, traveled about twenty miles in the Kentucky cold to the Ohio River where they met up with other members of their party who had come from the nearby Maplewood Plantation. Together, all of the escaped slaves traveled across the Ohio River's six-inch-solid surface from slavery to freedom.

Once in Ohio, the group separated, and the Garner family—Margaret, Robert, their four children: Thomas, age six; Samuel, age four; Mary, age two; and Priscilla/"Cilla," age nine months, and Robert's parents—Simon and Mary—took refuge in the home of Elijah Kite,[6] a former slave and Margret's paternal uncle. The freedom in the Kite home was short-lived because Archibald Gaines, the slave master, had discovered their location and intended to take the Garner family back to Kentucky with him. But the Garners had no intentions of returning, and they resisted vehemently. When Gaines arrived at the Kite home, he attempted to force the door of the home open, and his attempt was met with gunfire from a weapon that Robert used. Robert's resistance prompted Gaines to seek the aid of the U.S. Marshals. Gaines returned with the Marshals, who stormed the small home in an effort to restore law and order, but their actions actually brought more chaos and destruction.

During breakfast, as the Marshals burst through the door, Margaret realized that her freedom was being stolen from her, and she acted. Margaret took a carving knife from the table, and she nearly severed the head of her older daughter from its body.[7] Next, she smashed the head of her youngest daughter with a heavy shovel. Lastly, she attempted to kill her two sons.[8] While Margaret Garner took astonishing measures to keep her children from returning to slavery, what happened afterward was even more unexpected—the trial of Margret Garner.

For two weeks, the country's attention was drawn to Ohio where there were reports of a slave woman who had killed her child rather than allow her to reenter slavery; the trial became a symbol for the cause of antebellum abolitionists. The idea, that the degradations of the institution were so bad that a mother would kill her own child to prevent the experience to continue, provided fuel for the intellectually and emotionally united group of abolitionists. Where one might have expected the trial to have been focused on the facts that Mary Garner died and Margaret was directly responsible for her death, the trial became a case about determining Margaret Garner's status as slave or free person. If Margaret and Mary were free—because the child had the status of the mother—then it would have been a trial about murder. If Margaret were chattel, then she could not be convicted of murder because she was not human, and neither was Mary Garner.

The courts never ruled on this matter because Archibald Gaines did not return Garner to stand trial as he had promised. Instead, Gaines shifted the Garner family from place to place and employed different leasing options for their labor before finally selling them to a Mississippi family. History records that Margaret Garner died in the summer of 1858 after reportedly contracting typhoid fever in Mississippi. Her husband Robert escaped slavery, joined the Colored Infantry, and fought in the Siege of Vicksburg in 1863. Her sons reportedly remained in Mississippi where they worked as farmers.[9]

Margaret Garner's story voiced the vile reality of the slave condition and the victimization of slave women in a way that slave narratives—the autobiographical narratives of slaves—in general, did not, and especially in ways that male voices from previous slave narratives could not. When Toni Morrison discovered Margaret Garner's story while researching and editing *The Black Book* (1974), it does not seem difficult to understand why Margaret Garner's story would have captured her imagination. It is easy to ponder and perform the intellectual and spiritual exercises of one asking "'Are there any circumstances when/where could I see myself doing that?' and/or 'Was this woman a good mother or a bad mother for killing her own child?'" It appears that Toni Morrison's engagement with these mental and emotional calisthenics manifested itself in the creation of the 1987 novel *Beloved*—through which Morrison took a single event that resulted from a series of historic tragedies and articulated much of the pain and despair of Black people.

When Garner and Sethe are confronted with the reality that they and their young children will be forced back into slavery, they respond by nearly decollating one child and advancing to kill another. Beyond those events, *Beloved* becomes a fictional work of art—a neo-slave narrative—that explores what happens after the death of Sethe's child. Morrison's approach is innovative—especially for literature in the African American canon—because she tells Sethe's story with two distinct narrative approaches: split narrative technique and magical realism. Within the novel, readers encounter a character, Beloved—presumably the incarnated adult child whom Sethe has killed earlier in her life—who metamorphizes from a baby who haunts the house that Sethe and her family occupy, to exist as an occupying adult force who continues to haunt and disrupt the daily, common experiences of the Suggs family.

Morrison's split narrative allows the reader to understand the unique circumstances that have led Sethe to her seemingly instant choice to kill her child and the repercussions that result from that choice. When readers first encounter Sethe, she is in the isolated home of 124, Bluestone Road that is haunted by her child, in large part, because Sethe has become a pariah within her community. Sethe's status within the community is challenging to understand because the reader must determine if the community isolates Sethe because it views her as a bad mother who has killed her child or if there is something else at work. Nevertheless, the baby's haunting has driven Sethe's sons away, and it has all but slowly killed her mother-in-law who has lived with her. As the tale progresses, readers discover how Sethe's past life on the Kentucky plantation of Sweet Home, where she has experienced a horrific sexual assault while pregnant at the hands of the plantation's owner's White employees, solidifies her decision to escape slavery.

Readers also meet the wandering Paul D, a former Sweet Home slave, who finds Sethe—unaware of her history—and begins a romantic relationship with her. Denver Suggs, Sethe's daughter who has remained in the ostracized and quasi-excommunicated Cincinnati dwelling, functions as the one constant contact to Sethe, 124, and outside world. She sees the haunting ghost as a friend, but the neighborhood children see Denver as strange and as a coowner of her mother's guilt. For a time, Sethe, Denver, and Paul D exist together at 124 Bluestone Road as a makeshift family until a strange woman named Beloved who also comes to reside in the home interrupts them.

Eventually, the house becomes too small for all of its residence, and Paul D finds himself (re)moved from 124. While he is away, he discovers Sethe's history, and he confronts her about the choices of her past. Their conversation leads to an almost irreparable divergence of the two, and Sethe chooses to return to Beloved, whom she identifies as an adult version of the ghost that once haunted her home; Sethe takes her to be the adult materialization of the child she murdered many years prior. While Beloved has the size and shape of an adult, she has the social, intellectual, and emotional development of a toddler. As such, she becomes continuously more demanding to the point that she consumes and nearly destroys everything connected with 124 including Sethe, whom she claims to love. As Denver approaches womanhood, she recognizes that Sethe and Beloved's toxic cohabitation is proving to be fatal to all of them because they lack a purpose for living along with the means by which to continue living. Denver musters the courage to leave the life-in-death world of 124 to enter the world of the living beyond 124's gates. She leaves, finds friends, finds support—emotional and financial—and she sets the stage for a moment of atonement for Sethe and her Cincinnati community.

With the help of Denver and the women of community, Beloved is exorcized from 124, and Sethe slowly returns to the community of the living. Having confronted her past, and having dealt with her present, Sethe spends her last days in the company of Paul D—who like she—survives the experience with the last demons of the Sweet Home plantation. It is both Sethe and Paul D together who have each other because no one else from the town—with good or bad intentions—can truly understand the(ir) Sweet Home experience. It is they alone who can truly understand each other's pain, if only in small measures, because the tragedies that they bear as cherry trees growing from their backs are born from the same sorrow and sadness of the hellish Kentucky Plantation soil. The "too thick" love that Paul D declares and Sethe embraces by saying, "Love is or it ain't. Thin love ain't love at all."[10] This type of love is something that only they can comprehend, and they do—together.

In the end, readers see Paul D return to 124 where he finds Sethe emotionally and mentally exhausted from Beloved's stay and departure. While Sethe seems to want to give up, Paul D insists that she live, and he reminds her of the many things for which she has to live.[11] Sethe seems to perseverate in a place plagued by the painful memories of her youth. All Sethe knows is that she has done everything that she can to protect the beloved child whom she sees as the best of her. But Paul D reminds or informs her that, "You your best thing, Sethe. You are."[12] With these words, Paul D puts into action his desire to "put his story next to hers" because, as he says, "me and you, we got more yesterday than anybody. We need some kind of tomorrow."[13] It seems that Paul D's tender, affirming words and gentle touch slowly begin to bring Sethe back to the land of the living. As Paul D's words begin to clear the clouds of doubt away, Sethe responds to his "best thing" comment with a question, "Me? Me?"

This is the last of their personal narrative, and it is the last that the reader hears those two communicate with each other. From there, the omniscient narrator offers a denouement. Readers see how Beloved has come and gone, how Sethe has been a part of and apart from the community of the living, and how slavery has touched all of their lives in one way or another. Readers twice are told that "It was not a story to pass on" and then they are finally told that "This is not a story to pass on."[14] It is arguable that the story did not need to be passed on because it, just as Sethe, Baby Suggs, Denver, Paul D, and the many people from the town—even the good White people, never get away from it. Slavery and its effects are akin to what Paul D says about walking into a "pool of pulsing red light" whose sadness feels like a "wave of grief" that soaks one so thoroughly that it makes a person want to cry.[15]

In the novel, readers witness a conversation between Sethe and Denver when Sethe tries to explain rememory. Sethe remarks:

> If a house burns down, it's gone, but the place—the picture of it stays, and not just in my rememory, but out there, in the world. What I remember is a picture floating around out there outside my head. I mean, even if I don't think it, even if I die, the picture of what I did, or knew, or saw is still out there. Right in the place where it happened.
>
> "Can other people see it?" asked Denver.
>
> "Oh, yes. Oh yes, yes, yes. Someday you be walking down the road and hear something or see something going on. So clear. And you think it's you thinking it up. A thought picture. But no. It's when you bump into a rememory that

> belongs to somebody else. Where I was before I came, that place is real. It's never going away if you go there and stand in the place where it was, it will happen again; it will be there for you waiting for you.[16]

Sethe speaks of rememories as one's (re)connection(s) with past events in such a way that the individual can (inter)act with those past experiences in the present in ubiquitous and inescapable ways. Additionally, rememories are not limited to the individual who performed the inciting incident; people can experience the experiences of others. Paul D's experience with the pool of red light early in the text serves as the reader's first encounter with rememory. In that passage, the reader has an engagement with the occurrence that predates it lexicon.

It is arguable that the novel *Beloved* functions as Sethe's thought picture or a rememory of Margaret Garner's choice during those late January days in 1856. In a 1992 interview with Elissa Schappell, Morrison explained that she did not know all of Margaret Garner's story when she wrote *Beloved* but concluded that Garner's life was much worse than depicted in the novel, saying that "if I had known all there was to know about her, I would not have written it . . . there would have been no place in there for me."[17] It appears that Morrison, with and through *Beloved*, exposes the world to one metonymical rememory of the slave woman's experience. Sethe's rape reveals a feature (not a defect) in the master narrative that Morrison addresses by focusing specifically on Margaret Garner's abuse. Morrison humanizes the experience of slave rape by inversion. This is not the story of many faceless women; this is the story of one woman. *Beloved* becomes a (petit récits) a small, singularly, and locally situated tale that intentionally engages the political space to show how slave women who endured rape from slave masters, direct abuse or tacet acceptance of abuse of others from slave mistresses, and the kidnapping and theft of their slave children were often forced to choose between slavery's insanity and impossibility. Margaret Garner, in her early twenties, was already a mother to four children. Mary, the dead child, was so fair skinned that she was almost White, and her living sister Cilla, who was light enough for reds to be seen in her cheek, were likely the children of rape (Archibald Gaines or another White man on the plantation most probably fathered those children).[18] Margaret was one of these many slave women—raped, abused, or ignored, and about to have her children stolen from her; she was also one who found herself making a choice that no parent would ever want to have to make.

It would seem that Morrison, like Paul D, walked into that "pool of pulsing red light" that made her want to cry when she discovered the Garner story. But Morrison did not simply do nothing; she did not let history take and bury Garner's life; Morrison told the singular story of Sethe Suggs in *Beloved* for Margaret Garner and the "Sixty Million and more" to whom or for whom those opening words of the novel are presumably meant.[19] Marilyn Sanders Mobly says it best; "it is in *Beloved* that history simultaneously becomes both theme and narrative process . . . *Beloved*, dramatizes the complex relationship between history and memory by shifting from lived experiences . . . to remembered experiences."[20] With *Beloved*, Morrison intentionally synergizes the angst, pain, horror, and sorrow of the African and African American ancestors. She shows which women Harriet Jacobs in *Incidents in the Life of a Slave Girl* (1861) was engaging when Jacobs said, "I do earnestly desire to arouse the women of the North to a realizing sense of the condition of two millions of women at the South, still in bondage, suffering what I suffered, and most of them far worse."[21] Margaret Garner was one of the women who suffered far worse.

Beloved offers a counter-narrative to the master narrative of American slavery using rememory. No other voice in American letters was better able or more willing to tell the story of the past as Toni Morrison did (through the life of Sethe Suggs). The impossible and insane still plague African Americans centuries after their first ancestors arrived as slaves in the Americas. The legacy of Africans in America is comprised within Morrison's canon. From sexually assaulted girls in her *Bluest Eye* (1970) and *Beloved* to abused and murdered women along with neglected and discarded men in *Jazz (1992)* and *Paradise* (1997), Morrison captured them all. While, the tales of slavery that include flying Africans who would not endure bondage in *Song of Solomon* (1977) and the mother who would not subject her daughter to the horrors of the plantation torture are the stories that the omniscient narrator of *Beloved* warns not to be passed on, by Jean-François Lyotard would encourage that the small stories (petit récits) be used to engage the public, political, and historical discourse to ensure that the true stories are accurately told.

Governing all of this is the concretization of a Morrisonian truth. She is credited with saying, "If there's a book that you want to read, but it hasn't been written yet, then you must write it." Not only did Toni Morrison write the book that she wanted to read—she also wrote the books that needed to be read, to be written, and she told the stories that needed to be remembered. Her contributions to African Americans and humanity are unparalleled, and her true greatness will come as future generations come to appreciate her masterpieces which are unapologetically Black. Her canon of narratives and counter-narratives will prove her to be one of the literary giants within the immortality of the greatest ones.

NOTES

1. David Omotoso Stovall, *Born Out of Struggle: Critical Race Theory, School Creation, and the Politics of Interruption* (Albany: State University of New York Press 2016), 4.

2. Kimberly W. Benston, "I Yam What I Yam: The Topos of Un(naming)," in *Black Literature & Literary Theory*, edited by Henry Louis Gates Jr. (New York: Routledge 1984), 15.

3. Claire Nouvet et al., *Minima Memoria in the Wake of Jean-François Lyotard* (Stanford: Stanford University Press), xvi.

4. Toni Morrison, "'I Wanted to Carve Out a World Both Culture Specific and Race-Free': An Essay by Toni Morrison," *The Guardian*, Thu August 8, 2019, retrieved from https://www.theguardian.com/books/2019/aug/08/toni-morrison-rememory-essay.

5. Ibid.

6. Steven Weisenburger, *Modern Medea* (New York: Hill and Wang, 1999), 52.

7. Steven Weisenburger, "Margaret Garner," in *Toni Morrison Encyclopedia*, edited by Elizabeth A. Beaulieu (Westport: Greenwood Press, 2003), 134.

8. Weisenburger, *Modern Medea*, 74–75.

9. Weisenburger, "Margaret Garner," 135.

10. Toni Morrison, *Beloved* (New York: Knopf, 1987), 165.

11. Ibid., 271.

12. Ibid., 273.

13. Ibid.

14. Ibid., 274–75.

15. Ibid., 9.

16. Ibid., 36.

17. Elissa Schappell, "Toni Morrison: The Art of Fiction," in *Toni Morrison Conversations*, edited by Carolyn C. Denard (Jackson: University Press of Mississippi, 1992), 90.

18. Levi Coffin, *Reminiscences of Levi Coffin, The Reputed President of the Underground Railroad* (Cincinnati: Western Tract Society, 1876), 563.

19. Morrison, *Beloved*, vii.

20. Marilyn Sanders Mobley, "A Different Remembering: Memory, History, and Meaning in *Beloved*," in *Toni Morrison: Critical Perspectives Past and Present,* edited by Henry Louis Gates and Kwame Anthony Appiah (New York: Amistad Press, 1993), 357.

21. Harriet Jacobs, *Incidents in the Life of a Slave Girl* in *Norton Anthology of African American Literature vol 1*, edited by Henry Louis Gates, Jr. and Nellie Y. McKay (New York: Norton, 1996), 224.

BIBLIOGRAPHY

Benston, Kimberly W. "I Yam What I Yam: The Topos of Un(naming)," in *Black Literature & Literary Theory*, ed. Henry Louis Gates Jr. New York: Routledge 1984.

Coffin, Levi. *Reminiscences of Levi Coffin, the Reputed President of the Underground Railroad,* Cincinnati: Western Tract Society, 1876.

DuBois, W.E.B. "*The Souls of Black Folk*," in *Writings*, ed. Nathan Irvin Huggins, 357–584. New York: Literary classics of the United States, 1986.

Jacobs, Harriet. "*Incidents in the Life of a Slave Girl*," in *Norton Anthology of African American Literature vol 1*, eds. Henry Louis Gates, Jr. et al. 224–260. New York: Norton, 1996.

Mobley, Marilyn Sanders. "A Different Remembering: Memory, History, and Meaning," in "*Beloved*" *Toni Morrison: Critical Perspectives Past and Present*, eds. Henry Louis Gates Jr. and Kwame Anthony Appiah. New York: Amistad Press, 1993.

Mobley, Marilyn Sanders. "Toni Morrison," in *The Oxford Companion to African American Literature*, eds. William L. Andrews, Frances Smith Faster, and Trudier Harris. New York: Oxford University Press, 1997.

Morrison, Toni. *Beloved*. New York: Knopf, 1987.

Morrison, Toni. *The Bluest Eye*. New York: Knopf, 1970.

Morrison, Toni. "'I wanted to carve out a world both culture specific and race-free': An Essay by Toni Morrison," *The Guardian*, Thu August 8, 2019. Retrieved from https://www.theguardian.com/books/2019/aug/08/toni-morrison-rememory-essay.

Schappell, Elissa. "Toni Morrison: The Art of Fiction," in *Toni Morrison Conversations*, ed. Carolyn C. Denard. Jackson: University Press of Mississippi, 1992.

Smith, Valerie and Toni Morrison. *African American Lives*, eds. Henry Louis Gates, Jr. and Evelyn Higginbottom. New York: Oxford University Press, 2004.

Snyder, Terri L. "Suicide, Slavery, and Memory in North America." *Journal of American History* 97, no. 1 (2010): 39–62.

Stovall, David Omotoso. *Born Out of Struggle: Critical Race Theory, School Creation, and the Politics of Interruption*. Albany: State University of New York Press, 2016.

Washington, James M. *I Have a Dream: Writings and Speeches that Changed the World*. New York: Harper Collins Publishers, 1992.

Weisenburger, Steven. "Margaret Garner," in *Toni Morrison Encyclopedia*, ed. Elizabeth A. Beaulieu. Westport, CT: Greenwood Press, 2003.

Weisenburger, Steven. *Modern Medea*. New York: Hill and Wang, 1999.

Chapter 8

The Unscripted Script of Black YouTube (BYT)

The Working Identities of African American Family Vloggers

Jenean A. McGee

Historically, African Americans have had limited control over how their image is projected into the national consciousness. White supremacy's popular culture and media campaigns, like blackface, and the nightly news have constructed the identity of African Americans as a deviant group of people. On the reverse of the negative portrayal, there has been an influx of African American life being promoted in ways that highlight successful and exceptional African Americans in the 1980s, 1990s, and 2000s. From the sitcoms such as *Cosby Show, A Different World, Fresh Prince of Belair, My Wife and Kids, Black-ish, Mixed-ish,* and *#blackAF* to 2000s reality shows such as *Runs House, The Real Housewives of Atlanta, Snoop Dogg's Fatherhood, T.I. and Tiny's: Family Hustle,* and *The Braxton's* mainstream media presents the world with prosperous African American life, which is centered around African American wealth and/or respectability. In the era of color-blind liberalism, people enjoy seeing "previously" marginalized groups achieve what many believe to be the American Dream of financial stability and a loving family. Television shows often promoted a false sense of economic prosperity of the African American community by strategically highlighting African American assimilation and class stability. These two very important socioeconomic dynamics, assimilation and class stability, coincide with postracial, color-blind neoliberal promotions of equality and equity through negating the ongoing systemic racial issues in the United States. In other words, mainstream media shows the "color-blind" United States what it needs to see, in order to project a prosperous and progressive national image.

In the twenty-first century, this promotion of African American prosperity and progress is further incorporated into mainstream media through social media platforms such as YouTube. Social media has allowed for individual and corporate users to produce and distribute their content through Web 2.0, a "user-led revolution," where Internet-users produce and create their content for a variety of entertainment and educational purposes. Platforms like YouTube gained mass popularity due to their user-produced content that captures the imagination of the public.[1] Theoretically, Web 2.0 provides a platform for ordinary people to express themselves. In order to market and brand various aspects of their lives, this phenomenon places the power of Black representation in the hands of ordinary African Americans. However, the "ordinary" African American life promoted on YouTube is often centered around middle-class African Americans who reinforce and perform the politics of respectability.

Through a critical examination of two African American family vlogs[2] (AAFV)—The Daily Davidsons (DD) and GabeBabeTV (GB TV)—this chapter examines how respectability politics in African American family vlogs assist in promoting the myth of an equitable color-blind United States. Building on two theories that have come out of Critical Race Theory (CRT)—Working Identity (Carbado and Gulati 2000) and Interest Convergence (Derrik Bell 1995), African American family vlogs that successfully secure brand sponsorship follows "the U.S. family script," which adheres to hegemonic White middle-class values. DD and GB have been able to garner brand sponsors by appealing to U.S. hegemonic social norms. The working identities that are performed by DD and GB work to benefit their respective families, as well as their brand sponsors. Thus, these African American family vloggers—regardless of intent—are inadvertently being utilized by corporations to promote antiracist, postracial, color-blind rhetoric which highlights social inclusivity and racial progress. This lucrative demonstration of corporate "inclusivity" disproportionately highlights African American affluence, while distorting the effects of systemic racism on African American life.

COLOR-BLIND AND POSTRACIAL RHETORIC

U.S. color-blind ideologies reach as far back as the inception of the country itself. The coded language is embedded in founding documents, such as the Declaration of Independence and the Constitution, as well as legislative discourse.[3] The rhetoric of color-blind ideologies in the United States is so pervasive because it uses the guise of humanist philosophies, such as liberalism and democracy, to promote White supremacy. In discussing the functions of color-blind rhetoric, critical race scholar George Lipsitz articulates,

> Colorblindness pretends that racial recognition rather than racist rule is the problem to be solved. Colorblindness does not do away with color, but rather reinforces whiteness as the unmarked norm against which difference is measured . . . Even its most zealous proponents cannot explain how simply not noticing and not mentioning the decidedly unequal distribution of opportunities and life chances in U.S. society can possibly lead to closing the racial wealth gap or the racial health gap.[4]

Such postracial rhetoric is seductive and intoxicating because it alludes to models of responsibility and equity that are far outside the scope of its capacity. Racial parity prevails as a social mantra rather than a political and economic priority. By ignoring racialized categories, color-blind liberals imagine that they have dismantled the destructive effects of racism.

In the post-Civil Rights movement era not recognizing one's race is understood to many as being "progressive." Proponents of race evasive ideologies distort ideas of the 1960s Civil Rights movement to push the "progressive" narrative of moving beyond race in the name of equality. Employing Dr. King's 1963 speech where he expresses his hope that one day his children will not be judged based on the color of their skin, but by the content of their character,[5] proponents of color-blind ideologies push a liberal narrative that focuses on merit-based individualism. This rhetoric promotes a superficial understanding of positionality, where one's individual "character" is taken up rather than their racial position in a White supremacist society.

While color-blind rhetoric has been embedded within the foundational ideologies of the country, the backlash from the Civil Rights movement that surfaced in the 1990s saw a conservative push for the resurgence of this rhetoric. The resurgence was ushered in through right-winged political projects that opposed policies of affirmative action and voting rights.[6] The color-blind rhetoric of the 1990s did not garner attraction from moderates and liberals.[7] However, Kimberlé Crenshaw argues that the ushering in of the Obama era as postracial allowed for color-blind ideologies to be embraced across political lines. She states:

> [p]ostracialism brought rock star marketability to colorblindness's legitimizing project, rebranding it with an internationally recognized symbol attached to its conservative rhetorical content. While the celebratory dimension of the "Obama phenomenon" pulled countless people into its orbit, the colorblind rhetoric of racial denial stripped ongoing efforts to name and contest racial power of both legitimacy and audience.[8]

Counterintuitively, the Obama Administration generated fresh opportunities to legitimize the longstanding color-blind rhetoric and racialized oppression that typifies U.S. history. The first Black president suggests to many that the United States had overcome its racist past and entered a "postracial" era. This rhetoric of the color-blind, postracial, progress coincides with the rise of the user-led revolution of Web 2.0 and YouTube.

YOUTUBE

The social media platform YouTube was created in 2005 by three young men—Jawed Karim, Steven Chen, and Chad Hurley. However, one year after its launch, in October 2006, YouTube was purchased by the Internet conglomerate Google for 1.65 billion dollars. That same year, YouTube's slogan became "Broadcast Yourself," which aligned with the "new era" of Web 2.0.[9] In 2020, YouTube's slogan still reminds "Broadcast Yourself," stating that their mission is to "give everyone a voice and show them the world."[10] YouTube articulates that their values are based on four essential freedoms: Freedom of Self Expression, Freedom of Information, Freedom of Opportunity, and Freedom to Belong.[11]

By focusing on various freedoms, YouTube gives its user a sense of liberty and equality. It suggests that regardless of who you are, YouTube will assist in protecting your freedoms. In the context of U.S.-based users, this resonates with neoliberal national ideologies of individuality, liberty, justice, and profit. YouTube states,

> We believe people should be able to speak freely, share opinions, foster open dialogue, and that creative freedom leads to new voices, formats and possibilities . . . We believe everyone should have easy, open access to information and that video is a powerful force for education, building understanding, and documenting world events, big and small. . . We believe everyone should have a chance to be discovered, build a business and succeed on their own terms, and that people—not gatekeepers—decide what's popular. . . We believe everyone should be able to find communities of support, break down barriers, transcend borders and come together around shared interests and passions.[12]

Essentially, YouTube suggests that people who use their platform are "free" to not conform to what is popular or the status quo and be themselves, they are "free" to be discovered by corporations, and they are "free" to make money. Anyone—who has access to the technology—has an equal chance to produce and profit off their production. They create an image of an equitable democratic society where "the people" are in control over what is successful, not the established order. The notion that "the people" cannot be gatekeepers themselves play into this notion of equal opportunity, and individualism.

The statements present the platform as a utopia for organic creativity, that is outside the confines of the hegemony. However, the platform operates within societies that are steeped in racist, classist, sexist, homophobic, transphobic, ableist oppressive systems. The oppressive systems of U.S. hegemony inform how people consume and engage with content. Consumers must want to watch the content, and financial sponsors have to feel as if the content fits their image.

YouTube has a large variety of genres of content. From gaming, beauty, lifestyle, DIY, to videos on "Van Lifers," "Tiny House" enthusiast, product reviews, the list is extensive. Like genres of any sort, certain agreed-upon conventions develop overtime. To fit within a genre, conventions must be met. The genre of family vlogs is no different from any other genre, some rules and conventions regulate it.

According to *Time Magazine,* time spent watching family vlogs grew 90 percent in 2017.[13] The popularity may be attributed to the array of content that the genre allows for, giving viewers the option to choose what they are interested in most. Family channels have a wide variety of content, some focus on pranking and challenges, others focus on showing their daily lives, from their morning and nighttime routines to shopping trips, cleaning routines, daily outings, and family vacations. To fit into the genre of family vlogs, vlogs must document family life in some fashion. While a lot of content can fit within the realm of family vlogs, not all family vloggers can make a profit off their content through brand sponsors. To earn money through these platforms, channels must brand themselves in a way that signifies to their audiences and potential sponsors who they are, and how their values align with those of the viewer and potential sponsors. The families must convey an idolized lifestyle that viewers want—in some capacity—to recreate or engage. In order to secure brand sponsorships with corporations such as Walmart, Johnson & Johnson, Pampers, and Playtex, these families must adhere to the family scripts that emphasize the hegemonic, color-blind rhetoric, and values that corporate sponsors demand.[14]

FAMILY SCRIPT AND RESPECTABILITY POLITICS

The family script often employed by these content providers resembles the structure of the quintessential White middle-class family. In the U.S. context, the average family is a Caucasian, two-parent, patriarchal, heteronormative household consisting of a mother, father, and children. Such families are finically stable, suburban homeowners, who express their economic position through the consumption of the latest material goods. Growing up in the United States with access to mainstream television, many Americans have experienced such families on television shows like the 1950s *Leave it to Beaver* and myriad commercial advertisements. This commercial prototype saturates television airways. The script conveys to audiences the 'ideal family' and the products they should value.

The concept of politics of respectability was coined in 1993 by African American scholar Evelyn Brooks Higginbotham. It refers to a political movement that African American Baptist women took to combat the racial stereotypes White patriarchal society ascribes to them. Such politics lean heavily on ability to assimilate and conform to the norms, manners, and morals of mainstream American society, which oppose idleness and vice and celebrate the "hard work ethics."[15]

According to Higginbotham, politics of respectability "did not reduce to an accommodationist stance toward racism, or compensatory ideology in the face of powerlessness. Nor did it reduce to a mindless mimicry of White behavior or a 'front' without substance or content. Instead, the politics of respectability assumed a 'fluid and shifting position along a continuum of African American resistance.'"[16] Thus, the politics of respectability function to utilize methods of conformity and assimilation while simultaneously maintaining a radical position[17] of social justice for African Americans. However, while the Baptist women of the early ninetieth and twentieth centuries were seen as radical in regards to social justice for African Americans, they still situated themselves within the larger U.S. hegemonic framework and social norms.[18] African American Baptist women of the early nineteenth century were up against the media's negative stereotyped image of them, "[m]edia such as—films, school textbooks, art, newspapers—produced and disseminated rhetoric of violence."[19] Therefore,

> [b]y claiming respectability through their manners and morals, poor black women boldly asserted their will and agency to define themselves outside the parameters of prevailing racist discourses . . . Baptist women's appeals to respectable behavior . . . were also explicit rejections of Social Darwinist explanations of blacks' biological inferiority to [W]hites. Respectability was perceived as a weapon against such assumptions, since it was used to expose race relations as socially constructed rather than derived by evolutionary law or divine judgment.[20]

Respectable manners for African American Baptist meant rejection and policing of what they consider improper manners, which included gum chewing, loud talking, gaudy colors, jazz, littered yards, and other "perceived improprieties."[21] They also focused on the cleanliness of one's home.[22] Because "blackness" was under constant surveillance by the White gaze, the goal of adhering to these manners was to act as a distancing defense from racist stereotypical images.[23] In other words, the Baptist women of the late nineteenth and early twentieth centuries utilized politics of respectability to validate themselves as worthy of respect and dignity.

Early forms of politics of respectability were inclusive of socioeconomic classes within the African American community, but were more concerned with one's behavior and manner, over one's socioeconomic class position. However, as African Americans, both women and men began attending college and becoming more affluent, notions of respectability became more interlocked with materialism. E. Franklin Frazier in his book *Black Bourgeoise* argues that as this more affluent middle and secular class grew, "respectability became less a question of morals and manners and more a matter if the external marks of a high standard of living."[24] As new generations came into power notions of politics of respectability, which were hyper-focused on cleanliness, manners, and religion also became transfixed within social uplift through materialism. The successful YouTube families', like the DD and GB TV, performance is reflective of twenty-first century constructs of Higginbotham's concept of politics of respectability.

THE CHANNELS/FAMILIES

It is important to keep in mind that the analysis of the families is based on what a viewer could assume while watching the families' daily vlogs. My analysis of these two YouTube channels is strictly based on what the Youtubers share with their audiences. A critical interrogation of their respective performances exhibit a troubling neoliberalist color-blind African American representation and postracial rhetoric.

The DD features an African American family, the father (TJ), the mother (Tiffany), and four children Jayden, Chance, Carter, and Nova. GB TV is an interracial family vlog made up of White father (Chad Sr.), African American Mother (Gabrielle), and two biracial children (Chad Jr. and Reagan). Both have a similar audience set, began their channels around the same time, have a similar number of followers, and are maintained by the profit generated by their content.

Both the DD and GB TVwere created by young African American women, Tiffany and Gabrielle, in the early 2000s—DD (2009) and GB TV (2010). Both women initially used the platform to share their lives with the world. Most of the early video consisted of the women sitting stationary in front of the camera.[25] The domain names of both channels changed when the content of the channel shifted to be centered around the heteronormative family. In 2011 and 2012, both channels shifted to incorporate a family dynamic. For Tiffany, in 2012, she began producing daily vlogs that featured her fiancé

TJ and toddler son Jayden. Gabrielle's channel shifted in 2011 to incorporate her husband, Chad. While both channels shifted to incorporate a family aspect, the women continued to utilize the channel to produce content that was centered on themselves as African American women. In 2013 and 2014, the women incorporated more family content and rebranded their family vlog channels. For both the DD and GB TV, the expansion of content included reimaging the channel's brands.

For both channels, the rebranding shifted what was featured in their video content. Where the original channel domains feature diary-like and informative vlogs, the expanded family channels move to incorporate daily life vlogs. The new daily vlogs are focused around consumer culture—going to the grocery store, department stores, the mall, as well as using consumer goods—which have become centralized features. Many of the daily vlogs feature the families being consumers and buying products. "Traditional" U.S. heteronormative family milestones such as, having a child, purchasing a house, getting married in vlogs function as avenues to express normativity while simultaneously representing capitalist consumption.

When the channels began centrally featuring their heteronormative families, they represented themselves as working class. For example, both families were living in modest apartments. However, as their channels grew, their consumer capital, lifestyles, and houses improved as well. Initially, both families did not rely on YouTube and the brand sponsors as a primary income source. Before the rebranding of the channels, it appeared that both families relied on the income of the male-head of the household. For example, during the early period of the family vlogs, the male heads of households presumed work outside of the home in the public sphere, whereas the women occupied life within the domestic sphere where they maintained their homes and cared for their biological children. The husbands of both channels initially had full-time jobs, working outside of the home, before both being laid off; TJ Davidson was an engineer, and Chad Rader Sr. was an ex-military vet and a production manager. The men's incomes were presumably the family's main source of financial revenue. However, over the last four years, there has been a correlation with the introduction and increase of corporate brand sponsorships and a shift in socioeconomic status. YouTube and other social media platforms have become a career for these families. Their lives have now become a brand that is intertwined with their incomes.

Within the phenomena of Web 2.0, self-branding is key for one to make it to the position of an influencer.[26] AAFVs—the DD and GB TV—form of self-branding appeals to hegemonic U.S. social norms to gain success on YouTube, through respectability politics, they perform versions of themselves that are palatable to a middle-class, African American audience as well as mainstream corporate sponsors. Their lives promote a corporate

White supremacist narrative of color-blind merit-based success. This narrative encourages perseverance, hard work, and adherence to the hegemonic script of American life. It propagates the notion that hardships occur to those who are lazy and "uncultured." The development of their channels conveys a story of entrepreneurship and bootstrap determination. DD and GB covey that two young African American women can succeed in the United States. Such success also portrays both YouTube and the U.S. society as benevolent protectors of opportunity and liberty. What is lost in their narratives are the concessions—conscious or unconscious—of their success.

For vlog families such as the DD and GB, their income and lifestyles are largely dependent upon the number of subscribers, video views, video likes, and maintaining the interest of brand sponsors. For YouTubers such as the DD and GB TV, corporate brand sponsors function as their employers. Both channels hit YouTube's milestone marker of one hundred thousand subscribers, directly after their reimaging. As of 2020 GB TV has 340k subscribers with an average of 36k views per video, and the DD has 27.1k subscribers with an average of 31k views per video.[27] Being that African Americans have historically suffered from negative racial stereotypes, these families' brands contribute extra labor in appealing to their audience and brand sponsors. DD and GB have secured corporate brand sponsors from major brands—such as Walmart, Johnson & Johnson, Pampers, Playtex, Audible, Hershey, Hallmark, LeapFrog, Motts, Popsicle, Crest, McDonald's, the Pacers, Kids Bop, Netflix, U.S. Virgin Islands, Visit Florida—just to name a few. The brands solicit these families because of their large following, influence, and focus on conventional U.S. family values.

WORKING IDENTITIES AND RESPECTABILITY POLITICS

The corporate sponsors that the DD and GB TV work with depend on the coercive assimilation rhetoric of United States to obtain their ideal African American influencers. In their article "Working Identity," Devon Carbado and Mitu Gulati argue that employees are often forced to engage in "a continual process of negotiating and performing identity." This negotiation is between the employee's understanding of identity and the identity they perform for their employer.[28] As employees seeking success, these families adopt strategies that signal to their employer that they fit very well into the already established work environment. Their performances demonstrate they are worthy of employment and promotion.[29] Carbado and Gulati argue:

> [Some] employees engage in a continual process of negotiating and performing identity. The choice of how to perform identity is a negotiation to the extent that it reflects a conflict resolution. The employee seeking advancement has an incentive to resolve the conflict between his sense of his identity and his sense of identity he needs to project to signal to his employer that he exhibits the characteristics the employer values.[30]

While the AAWFVs do not occupy a traditional workspace, their vlogs negotiate the challenging racial dynamic of marketing their Blackness in a White supremacist society. The DD and GB TV utilize politics of respectability to perform their working identities. Through their daily vlogs, both families portray as well-to-do, well-groomed, and "respectable." One of the best examples of this is through their vernacular and the way both the parents pay close attention to the grooming of their children and homes.

Mother Gabrielle, of GB TV, pays close attention to aspects of her appearance such as her hair, clothing, nails, and eyebrows. This is conveyed in the vast amount of footage of her discussing the maintenance of her appearance and almost biweekly nail appointments, and monthly eyebrow appointments, as well as the consistent conversation and videos about the maintenance of her hair. Another example can be seen in one vlog of GB TV. Gabrielle's mother had cornrowed her son's (Chad Jr.) hair while she was babysitting him overnight. Gabrielle's response to her son's hair being groomed in cornrows highlights her attempt to distance her family from racist notions of African American poverty and criminality. Her mother asks her if she likes the way she styled her son's hair, and through their interaction, Gabrielle is not pleased with the way Chad Jr.'s hair is styled. While Gabrielle is polite to her mother, the tone of her voice is skeptical. Gabrielle responds to her mother's question by stating "umm I am not a big fan." Her mother, who can sense her daughter's discomfort, then states, "it's different." To which Gabrielle responds, "it's very different."[31] Gabrielle's response, "I am not a big fan" and "It's very different," puts her and her son in direct opposition to the negative stereotypes that are associated with cornrows. Gabrielle's body language, comments, and tone of voice convey resistance to the Afrocentric and "lower"-class hairstyle of cornrows. To viewers she expresses a level of discomfort with her son's hair not appealing to social Eurocentric norms.

The Daily Davidson also struggle with postracializing their family image as well. The Davidsons parade their wealth through the ornamentation of their home. While politics of respectability's origins were originally centered around manners, Higginbotham also relays that the campaign's focus shifted to include one's ability to express their American identity through the consumption of material goods.[32] As the DD garnered more wealth, they could purchase a larger home and adorn that home with material goods. A common genre of YouTube is house reveals/tours, both unfurnished and furnished. Working within the genre, the DD present their five-bedroom, three-bathroom house complete with two offices, a filming room, and large bonus room. The house is immaculately clean and is custom decorated from floor to ceiling.[33] This display of wealth also conveys the Daily Davidson's standard of living as Americans who occupy the middle/upper-middle class. Such prominent performances of respectability make it easy for brands to sponsor their content. Ultimately, these two families undermine the challenges of disadvantaged African American communities through their willing distortion of the destructive effects of Eurocentric hegemony and racialized of capitalism.

INTEREST CONVERGENCE

Web 2.0 has provided corporations both large and small a platform where they can further promote their respective brands. Large corporations are utilizing what Derrick Bell calls "interest convergence" to further gain capital while satisfying the current "color-blind" neoliberal needs of the U.S. nation-state. African American social media influencers need to be cautious when aligning themselves with certain brands. Bell articulates that "'interest convergence' provides the interest of Blacks in achieving racial equality will be accommodated only when it verges with the interests of [W]hites."[34] While Web 2.0 has allowed for African Americans and other marginalized groups representation within media, corporate sponsors are utilizing the large audience network and influential power that some African American influencers, like the DD and GB TV, to market and sell their product. Major corporations have been able to utilize Web 2.0 to find marginalized groups to endorse their brands with having to do little labor in the production other than providing a paycheck. By having African American families and mixed-race families as brand ambassadors, brands can present themselves as antiracist. Companies solicit these families with compensation to promote their brands and increase their companies' profits through influencer-based advertisements. Not only do families get economic capital and social mobility by endorsing these brands, but they also receive social capital by being seen as influential enough to have brand deals. Within the racial history of the United States, it appears that African Americans have been able to break another glass ceiling because now "ordinary" African Americans are now being more utilized in marketing by brands. In turn, the companies and brands, who employ African American spokespersons, are seen in the public eye as proponents of equality progress.

By promoting and aiding African Americans who have made it, corporations like Walmart are able to deflect how they treat working class and working poor African American employees, as well as non-White factory workers who produce their products. These corporations are using "assimilated" African American content producers to benefit their interests. They are able to make money while simultaneously projecting as racially progressive. African Americans have been forced to appeal to U.S. hegemonic social norms through utilizing politics of respectability to garner "success" within the Eurocentric capitalistic structure. Therefore, the "authentic" image of the families has already been coursed by dominant U.S. social norms. By adhering to said social norms, DD and GB simultaneously perform a working identity that matches their various corporate sponsors' brand. The corporations do not need to tell these vloggers how to present themselves because society and corporate branding has already shown them that assimilation is profitable.

CONCLUSION

Taken at face value, the image of African American "success" through monetary means presents as racial progress. However, a closer analysis of how African American success is recognized within media exposes a latent White supremacist narrative; one that is fraught with continual coercion and concessions. Many in the United States understand racial progress through media's racial campaigns that highlight "exceptional" and "successful" African American life. However, it is curial that we look behind the velvet curtain of "progress" to understand what is hidden backstage. The image of successful African American family vloggers—DD and GB—further perpetuates a post-racial neoliberal U.S. narrative. A narrative that illustrates U.S. racial progressivism through both capitalism and consumerism. What is often hidden in the underbelly of these success narratives are generational assimilation survival tactics that have forced African Americans to discard parts of their cultural identities, and the ongoing systemic oppression that African Americans face daily.

The construction of African American life in the U.S. imaginary has always been closely tied to the media. For African Americans, the advent of Web 2.0 seemed to be a promising escape from White supremacy's media control over our images. However, our images are still often controlled by White supremacy and capitalism. As African American content creators and content consumers, it is important for us to understand the power of our images in order to regain it.

NOTES

1. Jean Burgess and Joshua Green, "The Entrepreneurial Vlogger: Participatory Culture Beyond the Professional Amateur Divide," in *The YouTube Reader*, eds.

Snickars, Pelle and Patrick Vonderau, Vol. 12 (Stockholm: National Library of Sweden, 2009), 89.

2. Video blogs are referred to as vlogs.

3. Burgess and Green, "The Entrepreneurial Vlogger: Participatory Culture Beyond the Professional Amateur Divide," 25.

4. George Lipsitz, "The Sounds of Silence: How Race Neutrality Preserves White Supremacy," in *Seeing Race Again Countering Colorblindness Across the Disciplines*, ed. Crenshaw, Kimberlé Williams (Berkeley: University of California Press, 2019), 24.

5. Martin Luther King, "March on Washington," *March on Washington*, accessed July 15, 2020, https://www.archives.gov/files/press/exhibits/dream-speech.pdf.

6. Kimberlé Williams Crenshaw, "How Colorblindness Flourished in the Age of Obama," in *Seeing Race Again Countering Colorblindness Across the Disciplines*, ed. Crenshaw, Kimberlé Williams (Berkeley: University of California Press, 2019), 129.

7. Ibid.

8. Ibid.

9. Jean Burgess and Joshua Green, *YouTube: Online Video and Participatory Culture* (Cambridge and Malden, MA: Polity, 2009), 1.

10. YouTube, "About YouTube," *YouTube*, accessed November 3, 2018, https://www.youtube.com/yt/about/.

11. Ibid.

12. Ibid.

13. Belinda Luscombe, "The YouTube Parents Who Are Turning Family Moments into Big Bucks," *Time USA*, May 18, 2017, https://time.com/4783215/growing-up-in-public/.

14. Not all family that secure brand sponsorship has to adhere to this script directly, however, adhering to the script does put people in better positions to be a sponsor.

15. Evelyn Brooks Higginbotham, "The Politics of Respectability," in *Righteous Discontent: The Women's Movement in the Black Baptist Church 1880–1920* (Cambridge, MA: Harvard University Press, 1993), 187.

16. Ibid., 187.

17. The radical position being soliciting their humanity and rights in a white supremacy nation-state.

18. Higginbotham, "The Politics of Respectability," 187.

19. Ibid., 189.

20. Ibid., 192.

21. Ibid., 195.

22. Ibid., 202.

23. Ibid., 196.

24. Ibid., 210.

25. GabeBabeTV, "Saying Hello," *YouTube*, March 7, 2010, video, 1:00, https://www.youtube.com/watch?v=ALDELSr5llA; Tiffany Davidson, "Welcome to My Vlog," *YouTube*, November 5, 2009, video, 1:08, https://www.youtube.com/watch?v=4XHqkjN9LqY.

26. An influencer is a person who brands solicit to promote their product through social media.

27. The top family vlogs on YouTube in 2020 are the Ace Family and Roman Atwood have 19 million and 15 million subscribers.

28. Devon Carbado and Mitu Gulati, "Working Identity," in *Critical Race Theory: The Cutting Edge*, eds. Delgado, Richard and Stefancic, Jean (Philadelphia: Temple University Press, 2013), 224.

29. Ibid.

30. Ibid., 225.

31. GabebabeTv, "What Happened to Your Hair?!" *YouTube,* video, 15:02, accessed March 9, 2019, March 23, 2015, https://youtu.be/VlFzayh4ZLo.

32. Carbado and Gulati, "Working Identity," 210.

33. Daily Davidsons, "House Tour!!! (Finally)," *YouTube,* video, 11:40, accessed March 9, 2019, October 26, 2017, https://youtu.be/awaCrIXts2c.

34. Derrick Bell, "Brown V. Board of Education and the Interest Convergence Dilemma," in *Critical Race Theory: The Key Writings that Formed the Movement*, edited by Kimberlé Crenshaw et al. (New York: The New Press, 1995), 22.

BIBLIOGRAPHY

Bell, Derrick. "Brown V. Board of Education and the Interest Convergence Dilemma." In *Critical Race Theory: The Key Writings that Formed the Movement*, edited by Kimberlé Crenshaw, et al., 20–28. New York: The New Press, 1995.

Burgess, Jean and Joshua Green. "The Entrepreneurial Vlogger: Participatory Culture beyond the Professional Amateur Divide." In *The YouTube Reader*, edited by Pelle Snickars and Patrick Vonderau. Vol. 12. Stockholm: National Library of Sweden, 2009.

Burgess, Jean and Green Joshua. *YouTube: Online Video and Participatory Culture.* Malden, MA, Polity, 2009.

Carbado, Devon and Gulati Mitu. "Working Identity." In *Critical Race Theory: The Cutting Edge*, edited by Richard Delgado and Jean Stefancic. Philadelphia: Temple University Press, 2013.

Crenshaw, Kimberlé Williams. "How Colorblindness Flourished in the Age of Obama." In *Seeing Race Again Countering Colorblindness Across the Disciplines*, edited by Crenshaw, Kimberlé Williams Crenshaw. Berkeley: University of California Press, 2019.

Daily Davidsons. "100,000k Subscriber Celebration," *YouTube*, January 16, 2015, video, 8:14, https://www.youtube.com/watch?v=G2vi_1ZrxZ8.

Daily Davidsons. "House Tour!!! (Finally)." *YouTube,* video, 11:40. Accessed March 9, 2019, October 26, 2017. https://youtu.be/awaCrIXts2c.

Daily Davidsons. "Welcome to My Vlog," *YouTube*, November 5, 2009, video, 1:08, https://www.youtube.com/watch?v=4XHqkjN9LqY.

Eaton, Kyleigh. "Top 10 Family Channels on YouTube: NeoReach Blog," NeoReach, November 26, 2019, https://neoreach.com/top-family-channels-youtube/.

GabeBabeTV. "Saying Hello," *YouTube*, March 7, 2010, video, 1:00, https://www.youtube.com/watch?v=ALDELSr5llA.

GabeBabeTV. "Thank You," *YouTube*, October 2, 2014, video, 8:57, https://www.youtube.com/watch?v=OkADYvkJf4k.

GabeBabeTV. "What Happened to Your Hair?!" *YouTube,* Video, 15:02. Accessed March 9, 2019, March 23, 2015. https://youtu.be/VlFzayh4ZLo.

Higginbotham, Evelyn Brooks. *Righteous Discontent: The Women's Movement in the Black Baptist Church 1880–1920*. Cambridge, MA: Harvard University Press, 1993.

King, Martin Luther. "March on Washington," *March on Washington*. Accessed July 15, 2020, https://www.archives.gov/files/press/exhibits/dream-speech.pdf.

Lipsitz George. "The Sounds of Silence: How Race Neutrality Preserves White Supremacy." In *Seeing Race again Countering Colorblindness across the Disciplines,* edited by Kimberlé Williams Crenshaw. Berkeley: University of California Press, 2019.

Luscombe, Belinda. "The YouTube Parents Who Are Turning Family Moments into Big Bucks," *Time USA*, May 18, 2017, https://time.com/4783215/growing-up-in-public/.

YouTube. "About YouTube," YouTube. Accessed November 3, 2018, https://www.youtube.com/yt/about/.

Chapter 9

HIV/AIDS, Sexualized Anti-Blackness, and Bodily Geographies of Struggle

Khyree Davis

Four-hundred years have passed since the first enslaved Africans arrived on the shores of what would become the settler-colony nation of the United States. It has been forty years since HIV/AIDS was first diagnosed within the U.S. populace.[1] While scholars across various fields of study have explored the transatlantic slave trade and the system of chattel slavery as well as examined the anti-Blackness of the HIV/AIDS pandemic and state responses to it, these historical moments have not often been comparatively juxtaposed despite their convergences, parallels, and overlaps. This chapter will show that in both the cases of chattel slavery and HIV/AIDS state and social violences enacted onto Black people and Black communities are distinctly sexual and/or sexualized in their character. Consequently, I offer the concept of sexualized violence as a recognition of both the sexual violence—rape, sexual assault, sexual exploitation, and so on—faced by Black people and communities during the Middle Passage and on plantations. Concurrently, sexualized violence is also an acknowledgment of the sexualized representations of Black non-heterosexual/queer and non-cisgender/trans communities that the hegemonic establishment upholds to facilitate the perpetuation of violence on Black people. Both chattel slavery and the HIV/AIDS pandemic-created conditions for sexualized violence to thrive in particularly anti-Black contexts. Yet, subjugation within these violent contexts does not wholly reflect Black psychic or material conditions at any point in the historical timeline. Resistance and resilience do important work to co-characterize Black communities alongside these violent ruptures.

This chapter embraces a transdisciplinary methodological and theoretical approach. History contextualizes and grounds this chapter's early discussions of violence. By "reading along the bias grain," I recuperate histories and lives which absented from the official record yet hyper-present in the narrative construction of various archival sources.[2] Additionally, sociology provides crucial documentation regarding violences and material conditions central to this chapter's analysis. Finally, the critical interdisciplinary field of Black studies, which includes the subfields of Black queer and trans studies, Black feminist thought, critical race theory, and Black geographies, helps to contextualize and emphasize Black agency, struggle, and resilience in the face of anti-Black violence.

Beginning the chapter, I consider histories of anti-Black violence in the makings of and throughout the duration of slave societies. I position the violences within these histories as distinctly and crucially sexual in their implication and enactment, before considering the ways in which Black persons suffering these conditions of sexualized anti-Blackness strategically manipulated their own racial-sexualization to alternatively navigate geopolitical terrains. Then, the chapter turns toward an analysis of the initial state and social responses to the AIDS crisis, which positioned AIDS as an issue of sexual morality as opposed to a pandemic. Offering an alternative reading of media coverage of the AIDS pandemic, I show that the history of AIDS is not only grounded in discourse about sexuality but also implicitly attached to histories of racism and racialization in American public discourse. Naming these strategies *bodily geographies of struggle*, the chapter then situates Black gay men's responses to HIV/AIDS and the shifting geographies its pandemic produces as aligned within the histories of Black people's alternative use of racial-sexual mischaracterization to produce alternative spaces and strategies within and against violent geopolitical atmospheres. Ultimately, this chapter argues that Black populations have creatively deployed sexuality and their bodies to resist dominating logics of White supremacy even while constrained by and within such logics.

HISTORICAL VIOLENCE: BLACKNESS AS HYPERSEXUAL—BLACK RESISTANCE

The violence that constructs the foundation of a slave society such as the United States and its preceding settler-colonies have been discussed at length by various scholars.[3] The transatlantic slave trade, chattel slavery on the plantation, Jim and Jane Crow, as well as the expansion of the carceral complex into an industry post-1865 have had their many violences against Black persons and communities documented and scrutinized. Here, I insist that the linkage between these historical acts of anti-Black violence and the state-society violence of HIV/AIDS is not solely racial, but simultaneously racial and sexualized. An exploration of these different yet interconnected historical moments unveils the co-constitutive formation of racialization and sexualization in the enactment and persistence of anti-Black violences underneath systems and processes of settler-colony and nation-state building in the Americas.

In her interventive essay "Black Atlantic, Queer Atlantic: Queer Imaginings of the Middle Passage," literary scholar Omise'eke Natasha Tinsley offers her critique of a Black studies tendency to solely metaphorize sex and sexuality rather than attend to the many historical and material ways in which sex and sexuality play out in the construction of Black lives and anti-Black conditions.[4] Her work dissects literary histories in order to highlight how sexuality intersected with racialization processes of the Middle Passage and slave societies. Tinsley interrogates explicitly sexualized processes of captivity which structured the transatlantic slave trade such as the employment of sex-segregated holds to enforce the violence of deprivation in accordance with Euro-normative/heteronormative sexual assumptions. She notes that sex-segregated holds also became a space in which potential insurgency arose both in the form of violent uprising among same-sex holdmates and even erotic resistance between same-sex holdmates coming together in care—sexual and nonsexual—of each other.[5] Tinsley explains that "the emergence of intense shipmate relationships in the water-rocked, no-person's-land of slave holds created a Black Atlantic same-sex eroticism: a feeling of, feeling for the kidnapped that asserted the sentience of the bodies that slavers attempted to transform into brute matter."[6] She further emphasizes the co-constitutive nature of racialization and sexualization through her recovery of these Black queer Atlantic histories. Critical attention to these recoveries reveals sexualization and racialization as intimate and intrinsic geopolitical forces which co-structured the material and psychic life of Black persons both through the violence of slavers and in the resistance of captive Black persons. This centering of Black queer subjectivity within the canon of Black studies lore discloses the central role sexualization plays in early modern Black histories by expanding the resulting critical lens beyond the slave ship and onto the shores of colonized lands.

The violence experienced through the sexualization of Black persons worked to define and confine Blackness in slave societies. Within plantation economies, Black life and Black death were tied to slavability, defined here as the processes, ideologies, and conditions which understand Blackness as capital, and subsequently, work to render Black persons and their bodies as usable, transferable, and transactional—independent of the agency and autonomy of Black people. Crucially, the move to render Blackness as capital necessarily deploys intensive and distinctive sexualization of the racialized Black persons and their bodies. Many slave narratives situate the sexualized processes of chattel slavery. For example, Harriet A. Jacobs's *Incidents in the Life of a Slave Girl* is, perhaps, most aligned in contemporary consciousness with the sexual violence faced by enslaved Black women and men. Jacobs discusses Luke, a young enslaved man who faced sexual violence not unsimilar with which she was confronted during her life.[7] Rape and the control of reproduction for enslaved Black populations both function as sexualizing tools which understand sex and sexuality as mechanisms for enshrining White supremacist power. The logics of sexual conquest and control over Black populations necessarily imagine enslaved Black persons as sexually promiscuous and available. This logic legalized the inhumanity of Black persons and effectively marked Black people's bodies as sites to be violated without consequence.

While the sexualization of Blackness and Black people under chattel slavery was undeniably violent, the use of these White and Western sexual (mis)understandings of Blackness allowed Black folk to assert differential and contextual resistance. Harriet Jacobs's own recounting of her enslaved years reveals her manipulation of sex and sexuality in the service of her own agenda.[8] Jacobs's narrative indicates how she maneuvers race, gender, and sexuality in a variety of ways throughout her life. Having recognized her slave master's increasing interest in exerting sexual power over her, Jacobs sought a sexual relationship with a different White man who she had some measure of influence with—enough to garner promises from him that he would purchase the freedom of her own children later in life.[9] Perhaps, the more striking example of the simultaneous manipulation of racialization and sexualization comes in the form of Jacobs's racial-gender transgressions in the midst of her first escape attempt. Recounting her steps, Jacobs wrote, "I wore my sailor's clothes, and had blackened my face with charcoal. I passed several people whom I knew. The father of my children came so near that I brushed against his arm; but he had no idea who it was."[10] This much referenced passage has been the subject of several critical engagements within Black studies, including C. Riley Snorton's *Black on Both Sides: A Racial History of Trans Identity* (2017).[11] My discussion engages as well as extends these analyses of Jacobs. In both her strategic choice of sexual partner and skin-darkening, gender-transgressing disguise, Jacobs's actions and her recounting of them suggest a willful playing with or manipulation of racialized and sexualized scripts of desire. Making careful use of the racial dynamics, gender hierarchies, and compulsory heteronormativity of American society, Jacob moves past her lover and the father of her children undetected. Jacobs's bold and proactive moves allow her to temporarily and limitedly maneuver the violent landscape of a plantation slave society.

These examples of sexual violence aboard slave ships and on plantations reveal a sexual fascination with Blackness and Black persons' bodies located within chattel slave histories. Critical works considering the sexual legacies of the Jim Crow era insist that obsessive sexualization of Black bodily forms persists alongside the mythology of the Black male rapist and the sexually violable/rape-able Black jezebel. For example, Angela Davis's "Rape, Racism and the Myth of the Black Rapist" in *Women, Race, and Class* (1983) details the afterlives of plantation racial-sexual violence. Davis emphasizes the sociopolitical expediency of the cultural narrative of the Black male rapists during the post-emancipation period as a uniquely gendered tool of racial domination, one which allowed for the targeted death of Black men and boys while aiding in the obfuscation of the continued rape and sexual abuse of Black women and girls.[12] Yet, in many of these cases, as Black feminist and/or Black queer-trans scholars who have studied violence in the context of slave ships and the plantation acknowledge how sexually oppressed Black populations have appropriated the mechanics and logics of racialization and sexualization to resist constraining violence. Refusals, contestations, and affirmations are all made accessible within inhospitable spaces of anti-Black violence through Black knowledge, intimate engagements, and creative deployment of their bodies. This intimate usage of the Black body through a knowledge of self demonstrates a bodily geography of struggle.

THE STATE, AIDS, AND BLACK [IN]VISIBILITY

On October 15, 1982, journalist, Rev. Lester Kinsolving, asked Deputy Press Secretary of the Reagan administration, Larry Speakes, for Reagan's reaction to the CDC announcement that AIDS is officially an epidemic.[13] Unearthed video recordings discovered by Scott Calanic and produced into short film, "When AIDS Was Funny," reveal multiple years of the Reagan administrations ambivalent responses regarding the outbreak of HIV/AIDS.[14] All responses in the documentary happen during White House press briefings or conferences which mark them as official comments from the Reagan administration. This particular response to Kinsolving was met with assertions from Speakes that he does not know what AIDS is followed by his own laughter and that of other members of the press when Kinsolving explains "it's known as gay plague . . . it's a pretty serious thing."[15] Speakes went on to avoid answering the question posturing that he did not have the disease while suggesting that perhaps Kinsolving had it as potential reasoning for his question. When pushed to comment whether or not the president or anyone in the White House knows about the AIDS crisis, Speakes responds, "I don't think so . . . I don't think there's been any . . . there's been no personal experience here Lester."[16] Speakes's response was callous and dismissive. The CDC had been tracking statistics on HIV/AIDS since 1981[17] and both Speakes and Reagan later admit that the then-president had been advised on public health matters from the CDC that pertain to AIDS. Speakes's responses read less as a statement of fact, and more as an antagonistic attitude concerning a "gay plague." This position highlights the incredulity with which the Reagan administration viewed suggestions that fighting AIDS could or should be prioritized by the executive body of a state. This response coupled with the knowledge that the Reagan administration had been advised on AIDS positions the deputy press secretary's response as one of willful ignorance. Such blatant disregard of a pandemic expressed by state officials constitutes indirect violence against populations suffering from the pandemic outbreak and spread. When paired with antagonistic anti-gay accusations aimed at a journalist asking how the state intends to respond to the crisis of pandemic, the state must be read as permitting the death of gay men.

A closer look at CDC data reveals how antagonism toward treating AIDS as a pandemic rendered racialized, specifically anti-Black, violence. CDC data collection dating back to the early 1980s reveals that despite initial diagnoses of HIV/AIDS registering the pandemic as one in which White persons were in the majority, trends in the data showed a steady increase in Black diagnoses until they became the majority in 1996.[18] Given that the government was advised on AIDS at nearly every jurisdictional level, this data was available to the state and its agents in the executive administration. It is questionable whether they were knowingly conscious of Black vulnerability to HIV/AIDS or had not delved deep enough into the briefings to learn about Black vulnerability to the virus. Yet, without a doubt, their actions jesting at or castigating HIV/AIDS victims, debating funding, and considering limiting public accessibility for persons with AIDS were functionally anti-Black and structurally racist. The actions and inactions of state officials led to the mass death and systemic neglect of many people within Black [queer] communities in the United States.

Still, media archives suggest that connections between HIV/AIDS, state response, and Black populations were not so far removed from public consciousness. In 1985, Los Angeles-based journalist, Robert Shogan wrote, "[t]he deadly new scourge of AIDS is recasting one of democracy's oldest and thorniest political dilemmas—the conflict between the rights of the minority and the welfare of the majority."[19] In this opening line to an article which positioned Black populations in the United States as a group which "used to" be subjected to this debate, Shogan—despite his failure to read rights-based struggle as actions which Black communities were continuing to endeavor toward—invokes collective American public memory and consciousness by linking the maintenance of normalcy among White majorities at the expense of the lives, safety, and well-being of a Black minority population. Shogan, then, reframes the minority rights versus majority welfare debate in an HIV/AIDS context writing, "The minority, in this case, is the nation's male homosexual population . . . [t]he majority is the rest of the citizenry, including many who see gays not just as potential victims of AIDS but also as potential carriers."[20] Once again, Shogan elides any substantial acknowledgment of the ways race produces varying experiences of the violence captured by this debate. And yet, his framing of the debate, when placed over and against the backdrop of anti-Blackness, ushers Black gay men and other nonheterosexual Black persons to the center stage of this discussion. When employing Fuentes's notion of reading "along the bias grain" for the unspecified yet underwritten presence within textual archival sources, one sees that Black gay men's subjecthood emerges in the social context of the article despite their explicit elision from the text. Shogan's piece largely focused on (White) male "homosexuals" and portrayed Black communities in a nondescript fashion presuming that African Americans (including the nonheterosexual) no longer struggled against White supremacy either in general or specifically in the context of HIV/AIDS.

Beyond these verbal and written responses to HIV/AIDS, race factors significantly into the geographies of funding and medical research/response to the crisis. *Los Angeles Times* journalist Robert Steinbrook's 1989 article, "AIDS Trials Shortchange Minorities and Drug Users," reveals Black and Hispanic[21] AIDS patients in clinical drug trials.[22] Steinbrook's investigative research revealed an extremely disproportionate number of Black and Hispanic AIDS patients were being excluded from drug trials. Additionally, these numbers only looked more dismal when factoring in class and geography.[23] These statistics suggest that clinical trials were not serving areas with higher Black and Latino populations nor were they made accessible to poor and un[der]insured populations. In effect, trials aimed at reducing the mortality rate associated with AIDS were not provided to Black communities. In doing so, African Americans were systemically excluded resulting in Black queer communities being denied the material advantage of drug trials. These discoveries highlight that the fundamental operations of violence in the United States have historically occurred in the context of anti-Black power relations and the vulnerabilities anti-Black logics produce.

BODILY GEOGRAPHIES OF STRUGGLE: BLACK QUEER ACTION IN THE MIDST OF AIDS

What do bodies have to say about space? How are geographies found within the body? Black feminist geographer and Canadian scholar, Katherine McKittrick, discusses bodily geographies, stating: "While geographies of black women are certainly not always about flesh, or embodiment, the legacy of racism and sexism demonstrates how social systems organize seeable or public bodily differences."[24] As previously noted, racism and homoantagonism conspire to organize Black gay/queer men's seeable and sexualized bodily differences as markers of moral failing and/or hypersexuality and, thus deserving of AIDS and, ultimately, death.

Black gay/queer men have been and continue to be hyperaware of their location at the intersection of state violence and social marginalization. Social marginalization is an apt term, as it communicates the ways in which sociality figures movements—both bodily and ideological—across the spaces in which social interaction and transaction occur. In the particular case of Black gay/queer men, social marginalization operates where the gayness/queerness, or nonheterosexuality and nonheteromasculine gender performance, of Black men and boys is pushed out of the ideologic public within exclusively and predominantly Black social landscapes. Early insistences that HIV/AIDS was exclusively a gay disease or "gay plague"[25] as well as the disproportionate rates of HIV infection and AIDS-related death among Black gay and bisexual men[26] conspire to mark Black gay/queer men as risks within Black communities. This contributed to the ideological pushing of Black gay/queer men further into the social margins. As social distance from larger communities became increasingly more common, the HIV/AIDS pandemic, as well as the resulting state violence, continued to restrict Black gay/queer men's geographic mobility and access to resources. Consequently, strategies which best embraced the reality of AIDS, as a public bodily signifier of difference and violence, were developed out of Black gay/queer men's own bodily knowledges and autonomy. Thus, Black gay men's collective experiences with HIV/AIDS—whether through seroconversion or its threat—conjured a collective strategy of interrogating and integrating the body as a site of insurgency and reclamation of possibility. As a strategy, this response is ethically and historically aligned within the tradition of bodily geographies of struggle embraced by previous generations of African diasporas resisting anti-Black sexualized violence.

Texas-born filmmaker and Black gay poet, Marlon Riggs, offers an example of such strategies in his 1989 documentary, *Tongues Untied*, through a poetry piece co-performed with Black gay poet and political theorist, Essex Hemphill:

What legacy is to be found in silence? (How many lives lost . . .)
What future lies in our silence? (How much history lost . . .)
So seductive, its grip. (This silence.)
Breaks it. (Our silence.)
Loose the tongue! (Testify.)
Let's end the silence, baby. (Together? Now?)[27]

Riggs's lines—written without parentheses—and Hemphill's—written within the parentheses—collaborate to re-contextualize Black gay men's presence within the public consciousness of the United States. Black gay histories are not publicly taught, thus Riggs's questioning of "legacy" within "silence" emphasizes long-absented yet ever-present Black gay lives, which Hemphill's accompaniment line reads as having been lost to history alongside the loss of Black lives to the ongoing Black AIDS crisis in the moment of its original airing. This poetic section of the film embraces the body as a site of struggle in its linguistic emphasis on the tongue as a tool which can disrupt the silence on and silencing of Black gay lives. The geographies of Black gayness/queerness are called upon through this examination. The silence Riggs speaks of in this poem is produced. Black gay men are not so much *silent* in Riggs's conceptualization here, as they are *silenced* as a result of their exclusion from public and social discourse. The multiple silences of the state obscure the violences of the state by making them geographically unlocatable. At the same time, Riggs's refocusing of the tongue evokes images on Black queer male sexual practices and makes hyper-visible the resounding clamor of their silencing. Here, Riggs's focus on the tongue reinterprets this vehicle for oral and anal sexual stimulation—moral condemnation of homo-sex sexual acts often structured calls for not investing in health resources for HIV/AIDS—as a usable source of bodily struggle. In this way, state-social fascination with Black sexuality and the violence that accompanies it is deployed in an effort to re-spatialize Black gay men. Through this effort, Black gay men's lives and their deaths are strategically reframed in the public consciousness. This move is not solely rhetorical. The images which move in conjunction with the poem display Riggs's nude Black gay male form contorting his own body in forms which casually move him through both shadows and light in the frame. Literally, Riggs's body comes out of the shadows, and at varying moments, insists his figure into the frame, always partially obscured yet, at times, more visible than before. Juxtaposed with the poem, Riggs's body reads as struggling against the darkened space which parallels his examination of silence and the Black gay death silence produces. Riggs shows his viewers how Black gay men's presence are organized literally within the margins of spaces dominated by sexualized anti-Blackness. At the same time, he demonstrates his intimate awareness of his own racialized and sexualized self. His body works to subvert and resist popular geographic narratives which insist on the totality of racialized and sexualized domination.

In our contemporary moment, Black gay men have continued to understand bodily engagement and intimate knowledges as essential to navigating hostile racial-sexual geographies. Black queer studies scholar, Marlon M. Bailey's, work on Black gay men, HIV, and raw sex offers crucial perspectives on Black gay men's uses and understandings of their own bodies. In his 2019 study, "Whose Body Is This? On the Cultural Possibilities of a Radical Black Sexual Praxis," Bailey discusses homosex-normative discourse and its failure to critically examine Black gay men's sexual subjectivities.[28] Coined by Bailey, homosex-normativity refers to discourse which emphasizes that HIV prevention should be the primary and prevailing sexual logic which informs decision-making during sexual encounters.[29] Bailey's work intervenes homosex-normativity, insisting that a broad, clinical, and uncritical application of such logics onto Black gay men's sexual practices fails to contend with Black gay men's differential relationship to state-social power and violence when compared with other racialized groups of gay men. Of his interlocutors expressed interests in raw sex, Bailey writes: "I do not suggest that Black gay men do not think about or fear seroconversion and that HIV never plays a role in their sexual decision-making; instead, I suggest that other needs and priorities such as sexual pleasure, intimacy, connection, and satisfaction are also key factors and, in some cases, more important ones."[30] Bailey's informants' interests in raw sex directly contradict the homosex-normative logics which prevail within current public health discourse. From a public health perspective, such positions might seem counterproductive to resisting the legacy of HIV/AIDS as sexualized anti-Black violence perpetuated by state-society inaction at its outset and beyond. However, a Black (queer) studies perspective can situate this position—which prioritizes varying forms of affective connection, care, and pleasure for Black gay men and their bodies—differently. Tinsley's research concerning affective resilience on the slave ship reveals,

> During the Middle Passage, as colonial chronicles, oral tradition, and anthropological studies tell us, captive African women created erotic bonds with other women in the sex-segregated holds, and captive African men created bonds with other men. In so doing, they resisted the commodification of their bought and sold bodies by feeling and feeling for their co-occupants on these ships.[31]

Refracted through a Black (queer) studies lens, Black gay men's refusal to unilaterally forego raw sex as a possibility might be more wholly explained as keeping with the logics of bodily geographies of struggle expressed as early as the slave ship, in which Black folks embrace intimacy with one another and intimate knowledge of their own bodies as a means of navigating some rewarding and/or sustainable space within the context of direct and fundamentally sexualized anti-Black violence. By embracing the Black gay HIV-positive body as a site of continued erotic encounter, Black gay men resist the geographic logics of public health discourse which insist Black gay men regulate their desires and, consequently, their mobility. Without accusing the slave ship and HIV/AIDS as producers of analogous geographies, I want to suggest that Black gay men do, in fact, understand the depth and breadth of their vulnerability to HIV seroconversion. However, Black gay men understand this vulnerability as linked to their geopolitical condition underneath the continued logics of sexualized anti-Blackness. In understanding their seroconversion as potentially inevitable, these men seek out pleasurable connections which allow them to alternatively navigate hostile geographies.

CONCLUSION: WHAT WE MAKE OF ALTERNATIVE/ALTERABLE GEOGRAPHIES

Katherine McKittrick's notion of "more humanly workable geographies" helps to consider how geography is not a fixed nor universally experienced logic of the world.[32] Stories and histories which insist on a singular, White supremacist/Western understanding of spaces and places fail to recognize the importance of understanding how domination and power figure logics of human existence within those spaces and places. As such, these perspectives do not wholly contend with the ways in which subaltern populations interpret and experience their own movements within and across space. By embracing parallel Black sexual geographies, one acknowledges that space is humanly alterable, and also that place can be alternatively, even simultaneously, experienced. Black sexual geographies show us how citing, siting, and sighting Black sexualities, bodies, and intimacies unveils histories through which differential understandings of Blackness and Black resistance mark insurgent practices of spatial reworking.

NOTES

1. I express thanks to my close friends, Joy, Justin, and Jocelyn, as well as my grandmother, Nancy, for listening to me flesh out my thoughts on this subject for hours on end in the midst of the current Covid-19 pandemic. Their time and care were essential to my being able to complete work concerning an ongoing global pandemic for Black people while in the beginnings of another global pandemic with disproportionate impact of Black populations.

2. Marisa Fuentes, *Dispossessed Lives: Enslaved Black Women, Violence, and the Archive* (Philadelphia: University of Pennsylvania Press, 2016), 7.

3. The following recommendations are not exhaustive but do inform this study in part: Fuentes, *Dispossessed Lives*, 2016; Katherine McKittrick, *Demonic Grounds: Black Women and the Cartographies of Struggle* (Minneapolis: University of Minnesota Press, 2006); Angela Davis, *Are Prisons Obsolete?* (New York: Seven Stories Press, 2003); Saidiya Hartman, *Scenes of Subjection: Terror, Slavery, and Self-Making in Nineteenth Century America* (New York: Oxford University Press, 1997).

4. Omise'eke Natasha Tinsley, "Black Atlantic, Queer Atlantic: Queer Imaginings of the Middle Passage," *GLQ: A Journal of Lesbian and Gay Studies* 14, nos. 2–3 (2008): 191–215.

5. Ibid., 198.
6. Ibid., 199.
7. Additionally, other narratives such as Elizabeth Keckly's *Behind the Scenes, or, Thirty Years as a Slave, and Four Years in the White House* and Frederick Douglass's *Narrative of the Life of Frederick Douglass, an American Slave* also speak to the ways in which reproductive exploitation conditioned the lives of Black women, children, and men.
8. Harriet Jacobs, *Incidents in the Life of a Slave Girl: Written by Herself* (London: Hodson and Son, 1862).
9. Ibid.
10. Ibid., 172.
11. Snorton offers a compelling case out of this passage which advocates an understanding for the transness of Blackness and the Blackness of transness. He argues Blackness has always existed in excess and, thus, outside of Western/White conceptualizations of gender. He asserts Black people have been transcending gender in their practices of freedom, resistance, and resilience throughout Black modern histories.
12. Angela Davis's "Rape, Racism and the Myth of the Black Rapist," in *Women, Race, and Class* (New York City: Vintage Book, 1983); I also find Patricia Hill Collin's chapters, "Assume the Position: The Changing Contours of Sexual Violence," in *Black Sexual Politics* and "Mammies, Matriarchs, and Other Controlling Images," in *Black Feminist Thought* useful in considering the extensions of racial-sexual logics outside of the plantation both temporally and geographically. Patricia Hill Collins, *Black Sexual Politics: African Americans, Gender, and the New Racism* (New York: Routledge, 2005); Patricia Hill Collins, *Black Feminist Thought: Knowledge, Consciousness, and the Politics of Empowerment*, 2nd edition (New York City: Routledge, 2000).
13. Scott Calanic, "When AIDS was Funny: Reagan Administration's Chilling Response to the AIDS Crisis," Filmed December 2015. Video, 7:43, https://youtu.be/yAzDn7tE1lU.
14. Ibid.
15. Ibid.
16. Ibid.
17. "First Report of AIDS," CDC, accessed June 24, 2020. https://www.cdc.gov/mmwr/preview/mmwrhtml/mm5021a1.htm#:~:text=First%20Report%20of%20AIDS,homosexuals%22%3B%20two%20had%20died.
18. "HIV and AIDS—United States, 1981–2000," CDC, accessed November 1, 2019. https://www.cdc.gov/mmwr/preview/mmwrhtml/mm5021a2.htm.
19. Robert Shogan, "AIDS Threatens to Be 'Biggest Political Issue': Welfare of Majority vs. Rights of Minority," *Los Angeles Times*, December 1, 1985, ProQuest Historical Newspapers.
20. Ibid.
21. Hispanic, here, is drawn from the article which makes use of this state-medical designation for categorization. I recognize the limited usefulness of this term as protested by those who have advocated, instead, for the use of terms like Latina/o, Latinx, and Latine.

22. Robert Steinbrook, "AIDS Trials Shortchange Minorities and Drug Users," *Los Angeles Times*, 1989. ProQuest Historical Newspapers.

23. Ibid.

24. McKittrick, *Demonic Grounds*, 46.

25. Calanic, "When AIDS was Funny."

26. CDC, "HIV and African American Gay and Bisexual Men," accessed July 8, 2020, cdc.gov/hiv/group/msm/bmsm.html.

27. Marlon Riggs, *Tongues Untied*, performed by Marlon Riggs and Essex Hemphill (San Francisco: Frameline, 1989), documentary film, transcription mine.

28. Marlon M. Bailey, "Whose Body Is This? On the Cultural Possibilities of a Radical Black Sexual Praxis," *American Quarterly* 71, no. 1 (2019): 161–69.

29. Marlon M. Bailey, "Black Gay Sex, Homosex-Normativity, and Cathy Cohen's Queer of Color Theory of Cultural Politics," *GLQ: A Journal of Lesbian and Gay Studies* 25, no. 1 (January 2019): 162–68.

30. Bailey, "Whose Body Is This?" 168.

31. Tinsley, "Black Atlantic, Queer Atlantic," 192.

32. McKittrick, *Demonic Grounds*, xxv.

BIBLIOGRAPHY

Bailey, Marlon M. "Black Gay Sex, Homosex-Normativity, And Cathy Cohen's Queer of Color Theory of Cultural Politics." *GLQ: A Journal of Lesbian and Gay Studies* 25, no. 1 (January 2019): 162–168.

———. "Whose Body Is This? On the Cultural Possibilities of a Radical Black Sexual Praxis." *American Quarterly* 71, no. 1 (2019): 161–169.

Calanic, Scott. "When AIDS was Funny: Reagan Administration's Chilling Response to the AIDS Crisis." Published December 2015. Video, 7:43. https://youtu.be/yAzDn7tE1lU.

CDC. "First Report of AIDS." Accessed June 24, 2020. https://www.cdc.gov/mmwr/preview/mmwrhtml/mm5021a1.htm#:~:text=First%20Report%20of%20AIDS,homosexuals%22%3B%20two%20had%20died.

———. "HIV and African American Gay and Bisexual Men." Accessed July 8, 2020. cdc.gov/hiv/group/msm/bmsm.html.

———. "HIV and AIDS—United States, 1981–2000." Accessed November 1, 2019. https://www.cdc.gov/mmwr/preview/mmwrhtml/mm5021a2.htm.

Collins, Patricia Hill. *Black Feminist Thought: Knowledge, Consciousness, and the Politics of Empowerment*, 2nd edition. New York City: Routledge, 2000.

______. *Black Sexual Politics: African Americans, Gender, and the New Racism.* New York City: Routledge, 2005.

Davis, Angela. *Women, Race, and Class.* New York City: Vintage Books, 1983.

Fuentes, Marisa. *Dispossessed Lives: Enslaved Women, Violence, and the Archive.* Philadelphia: University of Pennsylvania Press, 2016.

Jacobs, Harriet A. (Linda Brent). *Incidents in the Life of a Slave Girl: Written by Herself.* Edited by L. Maria Child. London: Hodson and Son, 1862.

McKittrick, Katherine. *Demonic Grounds: Black Women and The Cartographies of Struggle.* Minneapolis: University of Minnesota Press, 2006.

Riggs, Marlon. *Tongues Untied.* Performed by Marlon Riggs and Essex Hemphill. San Francisco: Frameline, 1989. Documentary film.

Shogan, Robert. "AIDS Threatens to Be 'Biggest Political Issue': Welfare of Majority vs. Rights of Minority." *Los Angeles Times*, December 1, 1985. ProQuest Historical Newspapers.

Snorton, C. Riley. *Black on Both Sides: A Racial History of Trans Identity.* Minneapolis: University of Minnesota Press, 2017.

Steinbrook, Robert. "AIDS Trials Shortchange Minorities and Drug Users." *Los Angeles Times*, 1989. ProQuest Historical Newspapers.

Tinsley, Omise'eke Natasha. "Black Atlantic, Queer Atlantic: Queer Imaginings of the Middle Passage." *GLQ: A Journal of Lesbian and Gay Studies* 14, nos. 2–3 (2008): 191–215.

Part IV

AFRICAN AMERICAN PSYCHOLOGY AND AFRICAN AMERICAN RELIGION

Introduction

Intersections between African American Psychology, African American Religion, and Critical Race Studies

Stacie Craft DeFreitas and Jonathan Chism

What does critical race theory (CRT) have to do with the study of psychology, a field that studies the mind and behavior of humans or with religion, a field that examines humans' beliefs about ultimate reality and studies the rituals, practices, and institutions based on such belief systems? Psychologists and scholars of religion have devoted limited attention to CRT since it was first developed in the 1970s. This is perhaps because they deemed it to be outside of their respective discursive frameworks and germane to the legal academy. In contrast to educational theorists who adopted CRT during the 1990s and employed it to understand persisting educational inequalities (See the Introduction to the Education Section), a critical race psychology and critical race theology has not been discussed until more recently. Yet, psychologists and religious studies scholars have examined and endeavored to resist racial oppression for decades. DeFreitas and Chism discuss ways that scholactivists in psychology and religion have produced scholarship that intersects with CRT's fundamental commitment to understanding and resisting white supremacy. In the first section, DeFreitas discusses ways psychologists have aspired to advance racial justice, explains how social psychologists have recently begun to call for a critical race theoretical approach to psychology, and highlights methodological considerations for psychological researchers. In the second section, Chism discusses how Black theology has been the prevailing framework for challenging oppression in the context of American religion, especially within Protestant Christianity, the dominant religion in the United States. He maps some points of intersection between CRT and Black theology. Both scholars offer reflections on how CRT can aid scholactivists in their respective fields in challenging racist worldviews and systems that have been toxic to the mental and spiritual health of Black people.

AFRICAN AMERICAN PSYCHOLOGY AND CRT

The relationship between CRT and psychology is less solidified than in other areas of scholarship such as sociology (though educational psychology is the exception). However, the two disciplines are progressing toward a firm theoretical grounding that can be usefully implemented in psychological research as psychologists have taken up the charge posed by Glenn Adams and Phia S. Salter to use CRT to disrupt psychological conventions that maintain the current racial hierarchy.[1] Adams and Salter have spearheaded the formation of critical race psychology, which seeks to develop psychological understandings of race and racism.[2] The Turner and Turner paper in this section highlights how the tenets of CRT help us to understand racism and its impact on Black people's mental health. They note that psychologists must interrogate the common misperceptions put forth in the discipline such as the notion that mainstream European American perspectives are the only ones that create valid understandings of psychology and that racism is a primarily individual characteristic, not a systemic part of society.[3] However, CRT has grown in its application so that psychologists are also utilizing it to understand various other topics, particularly in the area of Black psychology, Liberation psychology, queer theory, and feminism. CRT is being used to understand mental health treatment, intimate partner violence, and other forms of trauma, health disparities, and the teaching of psychology among other areas.[4]

Social psychology specifically has begun embracing CRT as evidenced by the text *The Palgrave Handbook of Critical Social Psychology*.[5] This handbook is currently one of the few, if not the only, psychology books completely grounded in CRT. However, there are many psychology texts, such as *African American Psychology: A Positive Psychology Perspective*, that clearly articulate and discuss CRT, utilizing some of its framework to position their work.[6] Further, many psychologists are addressing the wide-ranging impact of systemic racism and other forms of oppression, but may not profess to utilize a CRT perspective.

One important way CRT is shaping psychology is through its use as a tool to dismantle research ideas and perspectives that have been widely perpetuated throughout psychology. For example, Signithis Fordham and John Ogbu suggested that one explanation for the Black-White academic achievement gap was due to Black students associating academic achievement with "acting White" and therefore these students chose to devalue school.[7] In *Critical Race, Psychology, and Social Policy*, Fine and Cross interrogate this perspective using CRT, highlighting the educational striving of Black people from slavery to current times, the underfunding of Black schools, and ways educational policies and procedures work to re-segregate schools and continue to perpetuate inequality.[8] Fine and Cross further examine the work of Anne

Galletta who noted how school districts, primarily led by White administrators and school boards, have been unwilling to shift the privilege granted to White schools and students, but have focused on the deficits of students of color.[9] In doing so, Galletta helps to lead psychology away from the idea of pathologizing the child and instead points at the primarily White leadership as the problem.

Not only are researchers and theorists using CRT to challenge psychological notions that have been put forth about Black people, CRT is shaping how psychologists conduct research and in turn influencing the knowledge that stems from said research. For example, CRT rejects the notion of the objective researcher, noting that people are not neutral, but have human biases based upon their experiences, knowledge, and objectives.[10] Psychologists utilizing CRT and other similar methodologies often ground their studies by discussing how their perspective impacts their research. This gives some of the power back to the reader as they now have more information that they can use to interpret the findings reported. Other strategies include recognition that Western assumptions of psychological reality do not apply to all people.[11] Hence, psychological scientists must note perspectives that prioritize the individual may not be valued by all cultures and that many cultural groups champion perspectives that elevate the collective or the group. Notions of who is included in "us" vary significantly. Psychologists must be particularly sensitive when doing research with African American participants due to the history of unethical treatment African Americans have experienced including the Tuskegee Syphilis Study, among others.[12] As a result of this history, many African Americans harbor mistrust against researchers. Psychological researchers and thinkers who espouse notions of CRT must consider why they are conducting research and who benefits from it.[13] They should reflectively ask: "Does this research agenda only serve my interests and aim to advance my career? Am I serving those I study, and am I aspiring to contribute to their communities and the greater good?"

Psychology scholactivists should strive to serve those they study by considering how research participants can take a more active role in the research process. For example, researchers should consider consulting participants regarding questions participants want to be answered as well as participant perspectives that the researcher may not have considered. Further, it is suggested that psychologists collect data qualitatively, allowing the voice of participants to be prioritized instead of forcing their responses into a Likert scale. In line with CRT's employment of storytelling and counter-narratives, this method of qualitative analysis strives to clearly articulate the voice and perspective of the participants. Additionally, participants should be an active part of the analysis and allowed to clarify responses. Researchers should not be left to make assumptions about what the participants intended.

Then, once the research is done, researchers should consider the best method of sharing results with participants. They are not likely to access academic journal articles; therefore, the scholars need to ask them, "What is the best way for us to let the community know what we concluded?" This is key as it shows the participants that the researcher has no desire to hide the results from them and is eager to seek their perspectives. Including community participants in research teams is one way to do some of this work, but researchers must also immerse themselves in the community they seek to understand.

The field of psychology is poised to facilitate positive change for the Black community through its impact on mental health, Black people's appraisals of self and Black culture, and various other constructs, as psychology is a wide-reaching field that interacts with many other areas including education, physical health, and religion. Psychology scholactivists should utilize their research and platform to support the growth and development of the Black community. There are various steps that psychological researchers can take to move us toward this end. Some considerations include teaching our students, K–12, undergraduate, and graduate, about the realities of systematic racism and how it interacts with the lived experience of Black people in the United States and the diaspora as well as how Black people have worked to combat this system. Psychologists should guide the representations of and ideas about Black people that are perpetrated by conducting research to edify the Black community. Psychologists must reject color-blind approaches because we recognize the value of Black culture and identity as well as the impact of racism on our society. Psychologists must then create interventions that educate and empower, opposing images of Blackness that disseminate negative stereotypes that fuel division and fear. Social scientists like psychologists reach the heart and minds of people and in this way, we can inspire a brighter future free of oppression. Psychologists must strive to examine how Blackness impacts ways of being in this world and how power hierarchies based on race, socioeconomic status, color, and other aspects of identity impact the lives of Black people in order to facilitate lasting change.

In sum, Fine and Cross note suggestions for producing critically informed psychological research, some of which are paraphrased here.[14] They suggest that before postulating ideas of deficits in Black people, researchers clearly examine the history to understand how systems may be impacting the psychological construct at hand. Further, as scholactivists, psychologists must not only examine the history that is related to oppression but address how communities have fought against those historical structures. This reminds the Black community that they are not victims, but resilient activists. Finally, researchers should examine social movements against oppression while collaborating with members of the oppressed group, highlighting the power the community wields and their progress toward their own goals.

AFRICAN AMERICAN RELIGION AND CRT

The connection between CRT and African American religious studies is inexplicit and rather indirect. Critical race theorists seldom cite religious scholarship on race in their academic writings. Anthony Cook's chapter entitled, "Beyond Legal Studies: The Reconstructive Theology of Dr. Martin Luther King Jr" was only one of twenty-seven articles in *Critical Race Theory: The Key Writings that Formed the Movement* that centered on religion.[15] None of the sixty-three articles in the expansive anthology, *Critical Race Theory: The Cutting Edge* (2000) engage the intersections between race, law, and religion. The centrality of racial realism to CRT likely explains critical race scholars' nominal interest in religion, especially Christianity.[16] Racial realism posits that white supremacy is a means of organizing society into racial hierarchies to allot entitlements and benefits toward certain groups.[17] Race crits who embrace racial realism have tended to ignore theories positing a theological and/or spiritual origin of racism because they hold that race is socially constructed and derives from humans' desire and quest for power. Many early critical race theorists embraced the Black Nationalist and Black Power Movements, which regarded Christianity as inconsequential to Blacks' struggle for justice if not outright antithetical to racial justice.[18] Black Power activists by and large distanced themselves from Christianity, including Christian activists who committed to nonviolent resistance. The Black Power Movement precipitated a *dechristianization* of the Civil Rights Movement.[19]

Religious scholars do not frequently make direct references to CRT and have published very little on CRT explicitly (See the Appendix for Readings on Race and Religion). Darrius Hills's chapter in this section utilizes Black theological ethics to challenge and oppose contemporary manifestations of racism. Hills asserts that President Donald J. Trump's "Make America Great Again" campaign platform, which was very popular among white evangelicals, is grounded in authoritarianism and a self-serving quest for power. Drawing on the work of Bernard Loomer, Howard Thurman, and Martin Luther King Jr., Hills presents a counter-narrative of greatness that centers on including the marginalized and recognizing the interconnectedness of human life throughout the globe. Hills's employment of counter theologies and ethical frameworks is inadvertently congruent with CRT method of counter-storytelling. He does not directly turn to CRT scholarship to bolster his critique of Trump's racial rhetoric because CRT is not the dominant paradigm typically adopted by religious scholars when examining white supremacy, especially within the context of religion.

Recently, Duane Terrence Loynes Sr. completed a dissertation entitled, "A God Worth Worshipping: Toward a Critical Race Theology." Though the subtitle of his dissertation included the words "critical race theology," his dissertation actually evidenced very limited engagement of CRT sources. His extensive bibliography did not reference notable critical race theorists such as Derrick Bell, Neil Gotanda, Richard Delgado, or critical race feminists such as Kimberlé Crenshaw and Adrien Wing. Rather than CRT, for Loynes, the starting point for constructing a critical race theology was Black theology or a Black theology of liberation.[20]

For decades, Black theology has provided the prevailing discursive framework that scholars within theology in particular and religious studies broadly have utilized to frame conversation about racial justice. Although there are a number of influential Black theologians of liberation, such as Albert Cleage, Major Jones, Joseph Washington, and J. Deotis Roberts, here I focus on James H. Cone, a minister in the African Methodist Episcopal Church who was the academic progenitor of Black Theology and widely regarded as its "father." In his first book from 1969, *Black Theology and Black Power,* Cone aspired to reconcile the nonviolent civil rights approach of Martin Luther King Jr. with the revolutionary philosophy of Malcolm X and demonstrate the relevance of Christianity for the empowerment of African Americans.[21] Relating the gospel to Blacks' experience of suffering, Black theology aims to persuade racially oppressed African American Christians that God and Jesus Christ support them in their struggle for liberation. Cone castigated White theologians for neglecting to address race and racism in the history of American Christianity. He argued that White churches that were silent on racial injustices in the church and society and condoned social evils such as chattel slavery, lynching, convict leasing, and segregation were not authentically Christian and were a manifestation of the antichrist in contemporary times.[22] Cone insisted Black theology was the authentic expression of Christianity, and he became the first African American theologian to develop an academic systematic theology that drew on the perspectives of Black Christians who resisted racism.[23] Although situated in separate fields of study, Black theology and CRT share the same blood, similar viewpoints, and a relatively overlapping historical development.

The Black nationalist rhetoric of Malcolm X, an African American Muslim minister, and the Black Power Movement of the late 1960s influenced both Bell and Cone's racial consciousness. Malcolm X militantly attacked Christianity as the religion of Whites, accused Black Christians of being "brainwashed," and castigated Blacks for worshipping a "blond-haired, blue-eyed Jesus" made in the image of Europeans.[24] Malcolm X insisted that African Americans should not wait patiently and contently for eternal bliss in the heavenly afterlife or pie in the sky while affluent Whites enjoy financial prosperity and material success in this life.[25] His rhetoric inspired Stokely Carmichael and young activists affiliated with the Student Nonviolent Coordinating Committee to distance themselves from King's dream of integration and Christian-centered goal of redeeming Whites. Rather than seeking to advance the spiritual reign of God, Black power activists focused on pursuing social and political liberation. The Black rebellions occurring in urban cities such as Watts and Detroit made it challenging for Cone to disregard Malcolm X's critique of white Christianity and the Black Power movement. Cone deemed that much of what Malcolm X articulated about normative white Christianity was indeed the truth.[26]

Both Derrick Bell and Cone agreed with Malcolm X's pessimistic stance concerning the intrinsic nature of racism in society. The Nation of Islam was a Black nationalist religious movement that stressed that racism was ingrained in American society. Elijah Muhammad, the long-time leader of the Nation of Islam, taught that Whites were irredeemable and that Blacks could not integrate into American society because of the entrenched nature of racism.[27] This logic of irredeemability and separation was undergirded by the Nation of Islam myth of Yacub, the story of a Black scientist who created the White race through experimenting on Black bodies about 6,000 years ago. Through this myth and the teachings to emerge from it, Muhammad aspired to explain the prevalence of white supremacy in American history and to provide a counter-narrative to Black inferiority.[28] Muhammad believed that Blacks would not be fully integrated into American society, and he encouraged Blacks to separate from Whites and to trust in Allah to execute divine judgment on America. Congruent with Muhammad and Malcolm X's skeptical view regarding Blacks' integration into mainstream American society, Bell wrote:

> Black people will never gain full equality in this country. Even those herculean efforts we hail as successful will produce no more than temporary "peaks of progress," short-lived victories that slide into irrelevance as racial patterns adapt in ways that maintain white dominance. This is a hard-to-accept fact that all history verifies. We must acknowledge it, not as a sign of submission, but as an act of ultimate defiance.[29]

Bell suggests that racism is as much a permanent feature of American life as death is of human life. Inasmuch as accepting the inevitable reality of death can enable an individual to strive to maximize his or her finite life, African Americans must accept and boldly face the uncomfortable truth of their collective marginalized status and "perceive more clearly both a reason and a means for further struggle."[30] Accepting the permanence of racism in American society is a central tenet of CRT.

Alongside Bell, Cone acknowledged the intrinsic nature of white supremacy in the United States. He held white supremacy to be "part of the spirit of the age, the ethos of the culture, so embedded in the social, economic, and political structure that white society is incapable of knowing its destructive nature."[31] He further contended that "White supremacy is so widespread and deeply internalized by its victims that many are unaware of their illness and others who are often do not have the cultural and intellectual resources to heal their wounded spirits."[32] In essence, many White Americans are unknowingly racist and fail to see white supremacy as a moral and social sickness, and many Whites who are racially conscious are incapable of jettisoning the privilege and power that whiteness affords.

Similar to CRT which focuses on the experiences of everyday people and accentuates the significance of Black resistance to oppression through using their voices to speak their truth and present a counter-narrative to the hegemonic status quo, Black theology centers on the African American experience and African American history.[33] In focusing on the collective Black experience, Cone aimed to encapsulate the entirety of Black life, including Black musical expression, art, anger, self-esteem, and sheer existence in the context of white supremacy.[34] As a theologian, he aspired to explain what the gospel of Christ means to Black people who experience "humiliation and suffering" as a consequence of racism.[35] He explains, "The Black experience is police departments adding more recruits and buying more guns to provide 'law and order,' which means making a city safe for its white populations. It is politicians telling Blacks to cool it or *else* . . . The Black experience is college administrators defining 'quality' education in the light of white values."[36] For Cone, Black history largely centers on the oppressive history of enslavement, dehumanization, and resistance of white supremacy.[37] He asserts that Black theology developed when Black ministers like Nat Turner led slave rebellions in the name of God, when Black clergy like Richard Allen during the Antebellum Period refused to accept discrimination in white churches and established independent African Methodist churches and denominations.[38] Black theology was also reflected in the prophetic witness of Martin Luther King Jr. and several African American ministers and ordinary Christian laypersons who participated in protest demonstrations during the Civil Rights Movement.

CRT and Black theology have both been subject to internal debate and criticism within their respective discursive milieus. For example, several race crits critiqued Bell's early analysis of racism within American law as preoccupied with the narrow Black-White paradigm. Their critiques provided a foundation for critical race feminism, Latino Critical Race Studies, Asian American Critical Race Studies, American Indian Critical Race Studies, Disability Critical Race Studies, and Queer Critical Race Studies. Likewise, scholars of Black religion critiqued early Black theologians' limited understanding of the Black experience. Cornel West challenged Black theologians for failing to develop a strong analysis of class and encouraged Black theologians to devote more attention to progressive Marxism and to reflect on overcoming systems of production and exploitive political powers that are well funded by big corporations at the expense of Black economic disempowerment.[39] He states, "What is critical is that [racist] practices must be linked to the role they play in buttressing the current mode of production, concealing the unequal distribution of wealth, and portraying the lethargy of the political system."[40] Engaging the work of Marxist Antonio Gramsci, West envisions Black theologians and Black religious leaders as functioning as organic intellectuals who engage in concrete political action to oppose hegemonic culture and strive for "structural social change."[41] Womanist theologians such as Katie G. Cannon and Delores Williams criticized Black theologians' inattention to the experiences of Black women in the Black Church and society. While there are multiple Black women who have critically engaged Black theology, Cannon was the first African American woman scholar to apply the "womanist" description of Black women's experiences to the work of Black women scholars of religion. Alice Walker, an acclaimed African American novelist, coined the term "womanist" to distinguish Black feminists from white feminists in 1983. In *Black Womanist Ethics* (1988), Cannon gleaned ethical lessons and moral wisdom from the Black women's literary tradition, particularly studying Zora Neale Hurston's life and literature, which reflected the everyday struggles and experiences of Black women.[42] Williams, in her 1993 *Sisters in the Wilderness*, drew on the biblical story of Hagar, an oppressed bondswoman of African descent who was pushed to be a surrogate, mother and "forced into exile" with her son by Sarai, to categorize Black women's experience as survival in the wilderness.[43] Williams argued that Hagar's experience of survival in the wilderness is a more accurate description of the Black experience in the United States than the Exodus narrative of the children of Israel. Rather than liberating Hagar, God helped her survive and secure a better quality of life. Employing CRT's intersectional method of analysis, womanist scholars of religion have focused on Black women's multiple intersecting experiences and have signaled a commitment to focusing on the most marginalized persons within Black communities who experience oppression from without and within Black communities.[44]

Other scholars like Charles Long, the historian of religions, and William R. Jones, the philosopher of religion, challenged Black liberation theologians' narrow focus on African American Christianity and neglect of other religious orientations in African American history that have endeavored to help African Americans find fulfillment. Long admonished religious scholars to deconstruct normative white theology through attending to "nontheological" modes of discourse in African American life and culture including but not limited to "folklorists, novelists, poets" and "slave narratives, sermons, the words and music of spirituals and the blues, the cycle of Brer Rabbit, and High John the

Conqueror stories."[45] These diverse sources portray how African Americans have found meaning in life in the context of racial discrimination and dehumanization in diverse ways. William R. Jones challenged Cone's Christian theological conception of a benevolent and liberating God. He argued that Black liberation theology failed to grapple with the problem of evil and suffering in history and to provide historical evidence of divine impartiality for all groups. Jones provocatively considers the possibility that the divine could be "a white racist" who has been working to uphold the interests of the prevailing racial hierarchy.[46] Concluding that there is untenable evidence in African American history to bolster the claim that God is a liberator for oppressed Blacks, Jones advances *humanocentric theism* and accentuates the importance of human agency and resistance against oppressive forces as opposed to divine strength and power.[47] Jones introduced to Black Theology "the possibility of nontheistic theologizing as organic to African American [socio-political] praxis."[48] The aforementioned scholars provide a cursory and introductory sketch of important ways African American religious scholars debated Black theology during the 1970s and 1980s. More recent discussions of Black theology are included in the Appendix.

In addition to being subject to internal debate, both CRT and Black theology have been subject to external attack and derision. Harvard legal scholar, Randall Kennedy, derided CRT scholars for accusing mainstream scholars of ignoring the work of scholars of color and for using the race card of victimization without sufficient evidence to substantiate their claims of discrimination.[49] Additionally right-wing conservatives used Obama's election as president to bolster their argument that America has entered a postracial period and that Blacks can reach the highest level of success in America. Right-wing conservatives also tried to undermine Obama's presidency by connecting him with Derrick Bell, a leading critical race theorist who taught at Harvard while Obama was in law school there.[50] As discussed in the Introduction to the volume, many persons who uphold color-blind racism, including President Donald Trump, wrongly view CRT as the problem instead of systemic racism.

Black theology came under severe criticism and scrutiny during Obama's campaign for the presidency in 2008 when a sound bite from a videotaped sermon surfaced of Obama's former pastor of Trinity United Church of Christ, Jeremiah Wright exclaiming, "God Damn America." As a student of Black theology, Wright frequently employed its prophetic critique of systemic racism in his messages to his congregation. Conservatives attempted to undermine Obama's candidacy through associating Obama with Black theology and accusing him of being an anti-White radical. Conservatives and liberals who uphold color-blind ideology have misunderstood and wrongly conceived Black theology as a message of hate and have assumed from the viral sound bite of Wright's sermon that Black theology is grotesquely un-American. Many conservatives and liberals, including President Obama who distanced himself from Wright to avoid losing political support, have failed to understand and fully appreciate the Black theology project that aims to unsettle white supremacy and ultimately advance a more equitable and just society for all.

While Black theology and CRT are both technical, academic discourses that are only beginning to interact, the issues most prominent to both discourses play out organically and simultaneously in the real-lived experiences of many scholactivists. Black theology has inspired the social justice strivings of religious scholars and seminary-trained pastors, including but not limited to religious scholactivists who have participated in Black Lives Matter protests in Ferguson, Baltimore, Waller County, Minneapolis, Louisville, and other places.[51] Chism's exposure to Black theology as a seminarian at Perkins School of Theology gave him the inspiration to establish the Path to Freedom when serving as an associate pastor at St. John's Downtown in Houston, Texas. As founder of this organization, Chism organized men and women who had served time in jail and prison and facilitated opportunities for them to return to prison to share their stories of triumph with incarcerated individuals. He also established a support program for men and women recently released from jail who experience challenges finding a job, housing, and being able to meet their material needs. In partnership with Grassroots Leadership Texas, he helped educate and train Path to Freedom members on how to share their stories in order to raise awareness about persisting inequities in the criminal justice system. Additionally, he educated volunteers on how to seek and pursue changes to policies that perpetuate injustice and decrease the life chances of persons negatively affected by the criminal justice system.

James H. Cone and other pioneers of Black theology have inspired and helped nurture the activist spirit of Chism and numerous scholars of African American religion. Still, besides Black theology, religious scholars interested in social justice should consider devoting more attention to CRT, especially as originally advanced by pioneering legal scholars. CRT can help religious scholactivists working within various religious traditions deepen their understanding of contemporary racism as they strive to oppose it. Certainly, faith moved and motivated numerous civil rights activists to dedicate and risk their lives fighting for freedom with the hope that "We Shall Overcome." Though important resources, faith and hope by themselves have proven to be insufficient to overcoming or eradicating racial oppression. As the long struggle for justice persists, CRT can help scholactivists of religion access the true nature of racism in America, possess hope grounded in reality, and sharply contest color-blind, postracial utopianism, a new form of pie in the sky that maintains the oppressive status quo.

NOTES

1. Glenn Adams and Phia Salter, "A Critical Race Psychology Is Not Yet Born," *Connecticut Law Review* 43, no. 5 (2011): 1355–77.

2. Phia S. Salter and Glenn Adams, "Toward a Critical Race Psychology," *Social & Personality Psychology Compass* 7, no. 11 (2013): 781–93, doi:10.1111/spc3.12068; Phia S. Salter and Andrea D. Haugen, "Critical Race Studies in Psychology," in *The Palgrave Handbook of Critical Social Psychology*, edited by Brendan Gough (New York: Palgrave Macmillan, 2017), 123–45.

3. Ibid.

4. Don P. Trahan and Matthew E. Lemberger, "Critical Race Theory as a Decisional Framework for the Ethical Counseling of African American Clients," *Counseling & Values* 59, no. 1 (2014): 112–24, doi:10.1002/j.2161-007X.2014.00045.x; Clare Cannon, Regardt J. Ferreira, and Fred Buttell, "Critical Race Theory, Parenting, and Intimate Partner Violence: Analyzing Race and Gender," *Research on Social Work Practice* 29, no. 5 (2019): 590–602, doi:10.1177/1049731518784181; Vanessa V. Volpe, Danyelle N. Dawson, Danny Rahal, Keadija C. Wiley, and Sianneh Vesslee, "Bringing Psychological Science to Bear on Racial Health Disparities: The Promise of Centering Black Health through a Critical Race Framework," *Translational Issues in Psychological Science, Psychological Science to Reduce and Prevent Health Disparities* 5, no. 4 (2019): 302–14, doi:10.1037/tps0000205; Mary Watkins, Nuria Ciofalo, and Susan James, "Engaging the Struggle for Decolonial Approaches to Teaching Community Psychology," *American Journal of Community Psychology* 62, no. 3/4 (2018): 319–29, doi:10.1002/ajcp.12295.

5. Brendan Gough, ed., *The Palgrave Handbook of Critical Social Psychology* (New York: Palgrave Macmillan, 2017), 123–45.

6. Stacie Craft DeFreitas, *African American Psychology: A Positive Psychology Perspective* (New York: Springer Publishing Company, 2020).

7. Signithia Fordham and John U. Ogbu, "Black Students' School Success: Coping with the 'burden of Acting White,'" *The Urban Review: Issues and Ideas in Public Education* 18, no. 3 (1986): 176, doi:10.1007/bf01112192.

8. Michelle Fine and William E. Cross Jr., "Critical Race, Psychology, and Social Policy: Refusing Damage, Cataloging Oppression, and Documenting Desire," in *The Cost of Racism for People of Color: Contextualizing Experiences of Discrimination*, edited by Alvin N. Alvarez, (Washingon, DC: American Psychological Association, 2016).

9. Ibid.

10. Salter and Haugen, "Critical Race Studies in Psychology," 128.

11. G. Bernal, E. Cumba-Avilés, and N. Rodriguez-Quintana, "Methodological Challenges in Research with Ethnic, Racial, and Ethnocultural Groups," in *APA Handbook of Multicultural Psychology, Vol. 1: Theory and Research*, edited by F. L. Leong, L. Comas-Díaz, G. C. Nagayama Hall, V. C. McLoyd, and J. E. Trimble (Washington, DC: American Psychological Association, 2014), 105–23, doi:10.1037/14189-006.

12. "About the USPHS Syphilis Study," *Tuskegee University*, 2020, https://www.tuskegee.edu/about-us/centers-of-excellence/bioethics-center/about-the-usphs-syphilis-study.

13. Bernal et al., "Methodological Challenges in Research with Ethnic, Racial, and Ethnocultural Groups," 107.

14. Fine et al., "Critical Race, Psychology, and Social Policy," 289–90.

15. Brandon Paradise, "How Critical Race Theory Marginalizes the African American Christian Tradition," *Michigan Journal of Race and Law* 20 (2014): 117. Available at: https://repository.law.umich.edu/mjrl/vol20/iss1/3. Cook wrote a book chapter entitled, "Toward a Narrative Framework of a Love-Based Community," in *Law And Religion: A Critical Anthology* (2000), *The Least of These: Race, Law and Religion in American Culture* (1997), *The Death of God in American Pragmatism and Realism: Resurrecting the Value of Love in Contemporary Jurisprudence* (1994), and *The Spiritual Movement Towards Justice* (1992).

16. Paradise, "How Critical Race Theory Marginalizes the African American Christian Tradition," 176.

17. CRT's notion of racial realism, rooted in materialism, is distinct from the biological conception of racial realism, a new form of scientific racism adopted by white nationalists to posit the distinctive inferiority/superiority complex between non-Whites and Whites. Quayshawn Spencer, "Racial Realism I: Are biological Races Real?" *Philosophy Compass* 13 (2018): 1–13, https://doi.org/10.1111/phc3.12468; Richard Delgado and Jean Stefancic, *Critical Race Theory: An Introduction* (New York: New York University Press, 2017), 21.

18. Paradise, "How Critical Race Theory Marginalizes the African American Christian Tradition," 121, 161.

19. Gayraud Wilmore, *Black Religion and Black Radicalism: An Interpretation of the Religious History of Afro-American People* (Maryknoll, NY: Orbis Books, 1983, orig. 1973), 188.

20. My assertions here are based on my training in religious studies and review of a breadth scholarship on race and religion in the field. Loynes's dissertation is by no means representative of the wide range of scholarship in the field of religion; however, his work merely reflects here the prominence of black theology in the field of religion in comparison to critical race theory. Graduate students producing work on race and religion are more likely to interact with black theology than critical race theory.

21. James H. Cone, *Black Theology and Black Power* (Maryknoll, NY: Orbis Books, 1970), 25–26.

22. James H. Cone, "The White Church and Black Power," in *Black Theology: A Documentary History, 1966–1979,* edited by Gayraud S. Wilmore and James H. Cone (Maryknoll, NY: Orbis Books, 1979), 120; Michael O. Emerson and Christian Smith, *Divided By Faith: Evangelical Religion and the Problem of Race in America* (New York: Oxford University Press, 2001), 22–49.

23. Cornel West, *Prophesy Deliverance!: An Afro-American Revolutionary Christianity* (Louisville, KY: Westminster John Knox Press, 1982), 103.

24. Cone, *Black Theology and Black Power*, 24–25.

25. Ibid.

26. James H. Cone, *Martin & Malcolm & America: A Dream or a Nightmare* (Maryknoll, NY: New York University Press, 1991), 168.

27. Stephen Jamal Leeper, "In Defense of Critical Race Theory: Islam, Race, & the Modern Public Intellectual," February 5, 2020, *Maydan*. Retrieved September 15, 2020, https://themaydan.com/2020/02/in-defense-of-critical-race-theory-islam-race-the-modern-public-intellectual/#_ftn1.

28. Ibid.

29. Derrick Bell, "Racial Realism," *Connecticut Law Review* 24 (1992): 363; Cited in Leeper, "In Defense of Critical Race Theory"; Derek Bell, *Faces at the Bottom of the Well: The Permanence of Racism* (New York: Basic Books, 1993), 12.

30. Bell, *Faces at the Bottom of the Well,* 12.

31. Cone, *Martin & Malcolm,* 87–88.

32. James H. Cone, "Theology's Great Sin: Silence in the Face of White Supremacy," *Black Theology: An International Journal* 2, no. 2 (2004): 141.

33. Mark S. Giles, "Howard Thurman, Black Spirituality, and Critical Race Theory in Higher Education," *The Journal of Negro Education* 79, no. 3 (2010): 357.

34. M. Shawn Copeland, "African American Religious Experience," cited in Katie G. Cannon and Anthony B. Pinn, eds., *The Oxford Handbook of African American Theology* (New York: Oxford University Press, 2014), 43.

35. James H. Cone, *A Black Theology of Liberation* (Maryknoll, NY: Orbis Books, 1990, orig. 1986), 23.

36. Ibid.

37. Stephen C. Finley, "African American History and African American Theology," in *The Oxford Handbook of African American Theology*, edited by Katie G. Cannon and Anthony B. Pinn (New York: Oxford University Press, 2014), 43.

38. As it relates to Black history, Dwight Hopkins, a professor of theology at the University of Chicago who did graduate work with Cone at Union Theological Seminary, has authored and edited several texts that examine slave narratives to demonstrate ways that enslaved black Christians resisted oppression such as *Down, Up, and Over: Slave Religion and Black Theology* (1999), and *Cut Loose Your Stammering Tongue: Black Theology in the Slave Narratives* (2003). In *Shoes That Fit Our Feet: Sources for a Constructive Black Theology* (1993), Hopkins also examines how the writings of W.E.B Du Bois, Toni Morrison, Martin Luther King Jr., and Malcolm X provide sources for constructing Black theology.

39. West, *Prophesy Deliverance!*, 106; Cornel West, "Black Theology and Marxist Thought," in *Black Theology: A Documentary History, 1966–1979*, edited by Gayraud S. Wilmore and James H. Cone (Maryknoll, NY: Orbis Books, 1979), 556.

40. Ibid., 558.

41. Ibid., 564.

42. Katie G. Cannon, *Black Womanist Ethics* (Atlanta, GA: Scholars Press, 1988), 90; Copeland, "African American Religious Experience," 56.

43. Delores S. Williams, *Sisters in the Wilderness: The Challenge of Womanist God-Talk* (Maryknoll, NY: Orbis Books, 1993); Copeland, "African American Religious Experience," 57.

44. Frederick L. Ware, "Methodologies in African American Theology," cited in Katie G. Cannon and Anthony B. Pinn, eds., *The Oxford Handbook of African American Theology* (New York: Oxford University Press, 2014), 132.

45. Charles H. Long, "Perspectives for a Study of African American Religion in the United States," in *Down by the Riverside: Readings in African American Religion*, edited by Larry G. Murphy (New York: New York University Press, 2000), 10, 14; Charles H. Long, *Significations: Signs, Symbols, and Images in the Interpretation of Religion* (Philadelphia: Fortress Press, 1986), 196. Cone endeavored to respond to Long's critique and included more cultural sources in his theology. In 1972, he wrote *The Spirituals and the Blues.*

46. William R. Jones, *Is God a White Racist?: A Preamble to Black Theology* (Garden City, NY: Anchor Press, 1998, orig. 1973).

47. Ibid., 202.

48. Anthony B. Pinn, "Humanism in African American Theology," cited in Katie G. Cannon and Anthony B. Pinn, eds., *The Oxford Handbook of African American Theology* (New York: Oxford University Press, 2014), 282.

49. Delgado and Stefancic, *Critical Race Theory*, 102–03.

50. Ibid., 104.

51. Eddie S. Glaude Jr., *Democracy in Black: How Race Still Enslaves the American Soul* (New York: Crown Publishing, 2017), 3–10. Religious historian Eddie Glaude discusses his activism in Ferguson, MO following the murder of Michael Brown. Additionally, I have several friends and seminary-trained colleagues who participated in the protests at the Waller County Jail following the death of Sandra Bland.

BIBLIOGRAPHY

"About the USPHS Syphilis Study," Tuskegee University, 2020. https://www.tuskegee.edu/about-us/centers-of-excellence/bioethics-center/about-the-usphs-syphilis-study.

Adams, Glenn and Phia Salter. "A Critical Race Psychology Is Not Yet Born." *Connecticut Law Review* 43, no. 5 (2011): 1355–1377.

Bell, Derek. *Faces at the Bottom of the Well: The Permanence of Racism.* New York: Basic Books, 1993.

Bell, Derrick. "Racial Realism." *Connecticut Law Review* 24 (1992): 363–379.

Bernal, George, E. Cumba-Avilés, and N. Rodriguez-Quintana. "Methodological Challenges in Research with Ethnic, Racial, and Ethnocultural Groups," in *APA Handbook of Multicultural Psychology, Vol. 1: Theory and Research,* edited by F. L. Leong et al., 105–123. Washington, DC: American Psychological Association, 2014. doi:10.1037/14189-006.

Cannon, Clare, Regardt J. Ferreira, and Fred Buttell, "Critical Race Theory, Parenting, and Intimate Partner Violence: Analyzing Race and Gender." *Research on Social Work Practice* 29, no. 5 (2019): 590–602. doi:10.1177/1049731518784181.

Cannon, Katie G. and Anthony B. Pinn, eds., *The Oxford Handbook of African American Theology.* New York: Oxford University Press, 2014.

Cone, James H. *A Black Theology of Liberation.* Maryknoll, NY: Orbis Books, 1990, orig. 1986.

———. *Black Theology and Black Power.* Maryknoll, NY: Orbis Books, 1970.

———. *Martin & Malcolm & America: A Dream or a Nightmare.* Maryknoll, NY, 1991. New York University Press, 2017.

———. "Theology's Great Sin: Silence in the Face of White Supremacy." *Black Theology: An International Journal* 2, no. 2 (2004): 139–152. https://doi.org/10.1558/blth.2.2.139.36027.

DeFreitas, Stacie Craft, *African American Psychology: A Positive Psychology Perspective.* New York: Springer Publishing Company, 2020.

Emerson, Michael O. and Christian Smith. *Divided By Faith: Evangelical Religion and the Problem of Race in America.* New York: Oxford University Press, 2001.

Fine, Michelle and William E. Cross Jr. "Critical Race, Psychology, and Social Policy: Refusing Damage, Cataloging Oppression, and Documenting Desire," in *The Cost of Racism for People of Color: Contextualizing Experiences of Discrimination*, edited by Alvin N. Alvarez. Washington, DC: American Psychological Association, 2016.

Fordham, Signithia and John U. Ogbu. "Black Students' School Success: Coping with the 'burden of Acting White.'" *The Urban Review: Issues and Ideas in Public Education* 18, no. 3 (1986): 176–206. doi:10.1007/bf01112192.

Giles, Mark S. "Howard Thurman, Black Spirituality, and Critical Race Theory in Higher Education." *The Journal of Negro Education* 79, no. 3 (2010): 354–65. https://www.jstor.org/stable/20798354.

Glaude, Eddie S. *Democracy in Black: How Race Still Enslaves the American Soul.* New York: Crown Publishing, 2017.

Gough, Brendan, ed. *The Palgrave Handbook of Critical Social Psychology.* New York: Palgrave Macmillan, 2017.

Jones, William R. *Is God a White Racist?: A Preamble to Black Theology.* Garden City: Anchor Press, 1998, orig. 1973.

Leeper, Stephen Jamal. "In Defense of Critical Race Theory: Islam, Race, & the Modern Public Intellectual." February 5, 2020, *Maydan.* Retrieved September 15, 2020. https://themaydan.com/2020/02/in-defense-of-critical-race-theory-islam-race-the-modern-public-intellectual/#_ftn1.

Long, Charles H. *Significations: Signs, Symbols, and Images in the Interpretation of Religion.* Philadelphia: Fortress Press, 1986.

Murphy, Larry G., ed. *Down by the Riverside: Readings in African American Religion.* New York: New York University Press, 2000.

Paradise, Brandon. "How Critical Race Theory Marginalizes the African American Christian Tradition." *Michigan Journal of Race and Law* 20 (2014): 117–211. Available at: https://repository.law.umich.edu/mjrl/vol20/iss1/3.

Salter, Phia S. and Andrea D. Haugen. "Critical Race Studies in Psychology," in *The Palgrave Handbook of Critical Social Psychology*, edited by Brendan Gough. New York: Palgrave Macmillan, 2017.

Salter, Phia S. and Glenn Adams. "Toward a Critical Race Psychology." *Social & Personality Psychology Compass* 7, no. 11 (2013): 781–93. doi:10.1111/spc3.12068.

Spencer, Quayshawn. "Racial Realism I: Are Biological Races Real?" *Philosophy Compass* 13 (2018): 1–13. https://doi.org/10.1111/phc3.12468.

Trahan, Don P. and Matthew E. Lemberger. "Critical Race Theory as a Decisional Framework for the Ethical Counseling of African American Clients." *Counseling & Values* 59, no. 1 (2014): 112–124. doi:10.1002/j.2161-007X.2014.00045.x.

Volpe, Vanessa V., Danyelle N. Dawson, Danny Rahal, Keadija C. Wiley, and Sianneh Vesslee. "Bringing Psychological Science to Bear on Racial Health Disparities: The Promise of Centering Black Health through a Critical Race Framework." *Translational Issues in Psychological Science, Psychological Science to Reduce and Prevent Health Disparities* 5, no. 4 (2019): 302–314. doi:10.1037/tps0000205.

Watkins, Mary, Nuria Ciofalo, and Susan James. "Engaging the Struggle for Decolonial Approaches to Teaching Community Psychology." *American Journal of Community Psychology* 62, no. 3/4 (2018): 319–29. doi:10.1002/ajcp.12295.

West, Cornel. *Prophesy Deliverance!: An Afro-American Revolutionary Christianity.* Louisville, KY: Westminster John Knox Press.

Wilmore, Gayraud. *Black Religion and Black Radicalism: An Interpretation of the Religious History of Afro-American People.* Maryknoll, NY: Orbis Books, 1983, orig. 1973.

Wilmore, Gayraud S. and James H. Cone, ed. *Black Theology: A Documentary History, 1966–1979.* Maryknoll, NY: Orbis Books, 1979.

Chapter 10

The State of Black Mental Health

Understanding Disparities through the Lens of Critical Race Psychology

Erlanger A. Turner and Tinicia C. Turner

Whereas many Americans may be stressed by life events, Black Americans may be at an increased risk compared to their White counterparts. According to the Stress in America survey, Black Americans often report higher stress levels compared to other ethnic groups due to concerns about police brutality, financial stress, and workplace discrimination.[1] The history of slavery, Jim Crow laws, dehumanization, human experimentation, racism, devaluing of Black life, and inequality also contribute to significant difficulties with mental health for many Black Americans.[2] More recently, the American Psychological Association[3] identified that COVID-19 resulted in Black people reporting higher levels of stress due to the pandemic. According to decades of research, Black and African Americans are one of the least likely ethnic groups to seek mental health treatment which may compound their difficulties with managing life stressors.[4] As a field, psychology has attempted to understand why many Black Americans are reluctant to engage in seeking mental health treatment. One potential explanation is the impact of systemic issues on treatment seeking. The focus of this chapter is to apply a critical race perspective to better understand the factors that contribute to Black people seeking mental health treatment, highlight areas of mental health concerns among this group, and conclude with considerations for addressing mental health among Black Americans through intervention.

CRITICAL RACE THEORY AND PSYCHOLOGY

Critical race theory (CRT) has been applied to multiple fields including law, education, and sociology.[5] More recently, CRT has been used to better understand psychological concepts.[6] Proponents of CRT suggest that racism and oppression are embedded within American society and therefore will continue to impact how individuals navigate life.[7] CRT scholars have described how important dynamics around race contribute to our understanding of numerous issues such as social class, wealth and income gaps, campus climate, affirmative action, immigration, and racial profiling.[8]

CRT emphasizes the extent to which racial bias in hierarchies permeate the day-to-day operations of every institution.[9] Core tenets of CRT include a belief that racism is normal and embedded within systems, that color-blind ideology attempts to mask the impact of race, that dominant groups racialize different minoritized groups in response to their needs, and that only those with lived experience as an individual from an ethnic or racial group have the competence to discuss race and racism.[10] Finally, Salter and Haugen note that "broad-based support of civil rights for people of color emerges only when it aligns with the interests of White Americans."[11] As a result, the ultimate challenge toward reducing racist practices within systems is to diminish the perceived disadvantage among White people for the sake of equality.

From the perspective of critical race psychology (CRP), a framework that integrates themes of CRT to understand race and racism, mainstream psychology often focuses on race in terms of negative bias or how individuals from ethnic and racial groups are treated differentially based on assumed ignorance among White Americans.[12] CRP finds issue with this, as these ideologies often result in difficulties acknowledging racist systems. CRP seeks to decolonize psychology by emphasizing two strategies: normalizing (provide a context-sensitive account that mainstream psychological science regards as abnormal) and denaturalizing patterns that mainstream psychological science tends to portray as standard.[13] These patterns in psychological science that are deemed "standard" often reflect preferential selection by the dominant group and reproduces an understanding based on those in power.[14] In this chapter, we apply these critical theories to our current understanding of mental health disparities.

BLACK AMERICANS AND TREATMENT BARRIERS

Research has consistently described many barriers to treatment initiation among Black people in the United States. More recently, scholars have described a model to capture the complexity of factors that may impact treatment seeking.[15] According to Turner et al., the Model of Treatment Initiation (MTI) provides an alternative way to explore the multiple factors that help explain mental health disparities among diverse populations including African Americans.[16] The MTI contains four major domains: accessibility factors that represent structural variables that may influence an individual's ability to access treatment, availability factors which examine access to culturally appropriate services, appropriateness factors that explain whether individuals view mental health problems as requiring psychiatric treatment, and acceptability factors that represent variables that may promote or hinder individuals from seeking treatment such as stigma and mistrust of mental health professionals.[17] See table 10.1 for the Domains of Treatment Initiation.

The following section briefly describes the domains of the MTI and how those variables impact treatment seeking within the Black and African American community. Refer to other sources for a more detailed discussion.[18] The *accessibility domain* explores multiple factors that contribute to the using of mental health services such as cost, availability of providers of color, and other structural barriers. These represent examples of systemic forms of racism within CRT that serve as barriers for Black Americans to receive adequate mental health care. Research documents that financial costs associated with seeking treatment may contribute to Black Americans' therapy use.[19] However, the literature also finds that costs may not be the biggest factor to consider. For example, one study found that even when Black Americans have insurance coverage, they are still less likely to seek treatment.[20] Some research also reports that Black people may face discrimination when seeking treatment. Kugelmass, found that even when African

Table 10.1 Domains of Treatment Initiation within the Context of Critical Race Theory

Domains	*Examples of Barriers*	*Examples of CRT*
Acceptability	Fears of discrimination	Systemic racism
	Concerns about medical mistreatment	Differential racialization
Availability	Lack of ethnic/racial therapists	Voice of color presumption
	Lack of provider's cultural competence	Tenets of color-blindness
Appropriateness	Limited focus on cultural practices	Tenets of color-blindness
	therapy focused on Western worldview	Interest convergence
Accessibility	Affordability of therapy	Systemic racism
	Limited health care access	Systemic racism

American clients desire to seek treatment they may be less likely to receive an appointment due to delayed follow-up by mental health professionals[21]. Another concern is access to mental health treatment in the Black community. Numerous authors have noted that a lack of availability of mental health clinics, psychiatric hospitals, and emergency room care may reduce access to mental health treatment.[22]

Within the *availability domain* variables primarily include the desire for culturally competent services. This includes both access to Black therapists and non-Black therapists that offer culturally sensitive treatment. Historically, the field of psychology has attempted to meet the needs of all individuals using evidence-based practices without regard for cultural considerations. According to CRT, this implies that science is identity-blind and does not require considerations of race or ethnicity to enhance outcomes.[23] However, Cabral and Smith published a systematic review and reported that African Americans have a strong preference for same-race therapists.[24] In addition to increasing adherence to treatment, client-therapist ethnic-matching may also influence treatment outcomes. For example, Thompson and Alexander found that African American clients that were assigned to same-race therapists reported increased self-understanding, acceptance, and belief in the utility of treatment compared to those assigned to non-Black therapists.[25]

Given the lack of diversity within the mental health profession, it is also important that Black Americans have access to culturally sensitive providers.[26] One of the challenges with engaging Black Americans in treatment is the lack of culturally competent providers. According to Thompson, Bazile, and Akbar, Black clients perceive a therapist as being more culturally competent if the therapist is comfortable discussing sensitive topics such as race and racism.[27] Black Americans may have expectations that their therapist feel comfortable discussing issues related to race, ethnicity, and culture.[28] For those therapists that shy away from these potentially difficult topics, it may come across to Black clients as not acknowledging their experiences within American society. With the recent increases in police brutality and racial protests, it may require that therapists are comfortable understanding the impact of racism on Black people's mental health and for those therapists to be able to address treatment from an anti-racist perspective. Consistent with CRP, many Black Americans' experiences of race involve being stigmatized or devalued.[29] Therefore, it is imperative that both Black and non-Black therapists improve their cultural competence by being intentional about having conversations around race in the context of therapy. Research has stressed the importance of culturally sensitive services to increase treatment engagement among diverse populations including Black Americans.[30] As psychology continues its growth as a field, cultural competence needs to be emphasized to address the needs of Black people. This includes ensuring that all providers, regardless of their ethnicity or race, understand the impact of sociopolitical influences on Black mental health.

The *appropriateness domain* identifies variables that explain Black people's preferences regarding healing practices such as working with a therapist or seeking pastoral care. A large percentage of Black people identify with having strong religious beliefs, and as a result many prefer to cope with mental health concerns by engaging in religious coping.[31] Belgrave and Allison note that prayer is an important coping strategy for many African Americans.[32] Furthermore, because many Black people adhere to collectivist cultural beliefs, they rely on social support networks for coping. This results in utilizing family members or friends to cope with life challenges as opposed to seeking mental health treatment.[33] Some research demonstrates that Black Americans that have strong religious beliefs or engage in religious practices (e.g., prayer) are less likely to suffer from mental health difficulties.[34] Given the connection to spirituality and mental health, it is beneficial for therapists to explore the importance of these factors when working with Black clients. Scholars note the significance of religion and spirituality in the lives of Black Americans across the lifespan.[35] For some individuals, endorsement of religious coping has been associated with decreased intentions to engage in seeking therapy.[36] To improve engagement in therapy, it may be important to highlight when religion is a form of social support for some Black clients.

Finally, the *acceptability domain* identifies variables that promote or hinder treatment seeking including mental health stigma and cultural mistrust. Research has reported that negative perceptions and stigma about treatment decrease treatment seeking.[37] Furthermore, the use of terms such as psychotherapy may be associated with additional stigma toward treatment.[38] In a qualitative study, the authors found that African American mothers reported that seeking mental health treatment would stigmatize their child and therefore they avoided seeking therapy to reduce negative perceptions.[39] Findings also indicate that the lack of acceptability among some Black Americans may be due to beliefs that mental health services are intended for those with severe psychological disorders such as schizophrenia.[40] Within the MTI model, factors such as cultural mistrust and perceived discrimination by providers may also hinder therapy use.[41] According to Whaley, cultural mistrust or cultural paranoia has been used to describe an African American client's adaptive cultural response style resulting from experiences with racism and oppression in American society.[42] This cultural paranoia may result in issues of trust, suspicion, and self-consciousness.[43] It is important to recognize that this mistrust could impact the initial therapy relationship and how some therapists may interpret psychological paranoia in Black clients. For example, White therapists must realize that they represent the larger White society to the

Black client, and this may result in their reluctance to engage openly early in treatment.[44]

Overall, the MTI domains describe the importance of considering how multiple variables influence treatment seeking among Black Americans. Integrating this understanding into addressing mental health among Black people requires a deep awareness of these barriers, as well as, how sociopolitical factors impact access to services. When examining disparities through the lens of CRT, it is clear that systemic issues and cultural considerations impact access to mental health treatment (see table 10.1). For example, systemic racism may influence allocation of resources in the Black community and limited training for providers of color to enter the workforce. In order to reduce mental health disparities, the field needs to engage in changes to address these systemic issues.

MENTAL HEALTH OUTCOMES

In the twenty-first century, the influence of social and political context continues to contribute to poor mental health among Black Americans. Despite these challenges many people continue to be resilient and thrive in the midst of a chaotic world. In this section, we describe several areas that may lead to psychological difficulties among Black people in America. This section is not intended to be exhaustive but aims to identify some areas of consideration when exploring mental health among Black Americans.

Psychological Adjustment and Stress

Decades of psychological studies have identified numerous outcomes associated with stress and adjustment among Black Americans.[45] Many Black Americans are at an increased risk of mental health difficulties due to marginalization and discriminatory incidents that occur within society and their communities.[46] According to Belgrave and Allison, experiences of racism in society not only increase the risk of psychological difficulties but also have a negative impact on physical health such as higher risk of chronic health conditions like cardiovascular disease.[47] In recent years, police violence and the killings of Black people have continued to be a concern. This dehumanization has increased in awareness through content being shared on social media platforms such as Instagram and Twitter. Exposure to these violent events through social media may also result in poor mental health.[48] For example, one recent study found that Black Americans reported significant stress after national events of police killings compared to White Americans.[49] Additionally, Bryant-Davis et al. noted that racial and ethnic minorities who observe or experience police brutality often experience flashbacks, nightmares, or hypervigilance.[50] Living in a society that devalues and dehumanizes your community can be stressful and have long-lasting negative effects. Particularly if individuals do not receive the necessary mental health treatment to heal from the potential stress and trauma.

Impacts of Discrimination on Mental Health

Racism and discrimination can cause mental health difficulties among Black Americans across the lifespan.[51] Utsey and Payne noted that racism is a chronic source of stress that permeates many aspects of life for Black Americans.[52] When examining the literature, research on children, adolescents, and young adults identify the negative effects of racism on mental health outcomes.[53] For example, studies among Black youth have found that those who encounter discrimination and racism often experience poor psychosocial outcomes such as low self-esteem and symptoms of depression.[54] According to Seaton, Caldwell, Sellers, and Jackson, approximately 87 percent of African American youth and 90 percent of Caribbean youth reported at least one discriminatory incident over a year time frame.[55] More seriously, the study found that these negative experiences resulted in mental health difficulties. Specifically, perceived discrimination among African American and Caribbean youth was associated with increased depressive symptoms, decreased self-esteem, and decreased life satisfaction.[56]

Research has consistently found a negative relationship between discrimination and poor mental health outcomes. However, some studies also identify that racial and ethnic socialization may serve as a protective factor to buffer against the negative effects of racism. According to one study, when parents engage in racial socialization (i.e., discuss potential to experience discrimination), youth are more likely to exhibit higher academic functioning, stronger self-efficacy, and fewer depressive symptoms.[57] This provides an opportunity for parents and therapists to collaborate to engage in behaviors to promote healthy development and foster resilience. It is important for therapists to recognize these potential challenges and directly inquire about how events in society may be additional areas for intervention.

Discrimination and racism can also take a toll on the psychological functioning of Black adults. According to studies, experiencing or witnessing racist incidents can lead to emotional difficulties and increased risk of mental illness such as posttraumatic stress disorders (PTSD).[58] Turner notes that "although research has provided evidence that exposure to discrimination can lead to symptoms of race-based traumatic stress, little is known about what aspects of racism may produce trauma."[59] The range of how Black people perceive these events may make it difficult for researchers to understand how racism may differentially impact their mental health. For example, race-based experiences can range from microaggressions (e.g., subtle forms of racism like invalidating an individual or hate speech) to blatant hate crimes and physical assault.[60] Therefore, not every Black American that experiences a racist encounter will develop race-related stress or poor mental health.[61]

Mental Health and Employment Issues

As we continue to explore the relationship between racism and mental health, we have to consider the implications of workplace discrimination and mistreatment. Similar to other social institutions, the global workforce consists of a White-dominated patriarchal system that was not created to include minorities, specifically Black Americans, who were essentially chattel used around the world for free labor. It was not until the ratification of the Fourteenth Amendment, the Civil Rights Act of 1964, that it was illegal to discriminate against someone on the basis of race, color, religion, national origin, or sex.[62] Although there are laws created to guarantee workplace and employee protection, people of color still encounter barriers that keep them out of the workforce or marginalized in work settings such as discrimination in hiring practices, harassment, and abuse on the job.

Racial discrimination in hiring practices is as prevalent today as it was twenty-five years ago. In a meta-analysis, the authors found that over the years, there have been no declines in discrimination practices toward Black Americans.[63] Given continued racial discrimination in hiring practices, there should be no surprise in the stark differences in the unemployment rate.[64] Education levels, race-based employment discrimination, and cultural norms concerning work may be to blame. Societal racism within institutions and organizations often disadvantages Black people because social systems were not designed to include them. One study of hospital employees explored workplace discrimination among diverse ethnic/racial groups in Northern California.[65] The authors noted that because hospitals are complex hierarchical organizations with potential inequities in employee power distribution, employees occupying lower status positions in those settings may face especially high emotional demands. The results of the study revealed that Black Americans endorsed more frequent workplace discrimination compared to White Americans (and other ethnic/racial groups). Furthermore, the data indicated an association between discrimination and depressive symptomology (even after controlling for job strain and general stress). According to the authors, this confirms the impact of workplace discrimination on mental health as distinguishable from other psychosocial and occupational stressors.[66]

Another study examined the relations among workplace environments to health.[67] It was noted that tokenism or numerical rarity in their work environment (i.e., working in occupations where there is a lack of diversity) elicit two forms of stress: personal self-doubt and low expectations and a sense of rejection. Similarly, racial tokenism was also found to be associated with increased stress and symptoms of depression and anxiety among Black middle-class workers.[68] Black professional women may be at higher risk of stress in the work environment due to being forced to cope with occupational stressors associated with the job and with double the discrimination due to gender and race.[69]

Within the context of critical race theories, we have to consider the implications of racial discrimination on mental health in the workforce. Incidents of daily discrimination such as ongoing feelings of judgment and mistreatment can be mentally and physically exhausting. According to some scholars, discrimination is taxing because it impedes access to opportunities and adversely affects interpersonal interactions, resulting in psychological and physiological stress responses, such as negative emotions and heightened blood pressure[70] Furthermore, findings suggest that discrimination accounts for lower job satisfaction reported by Black Americans and discrimination is a key factor in health disparities.[71] Considering the tenets of critical race theories, in order to reduce workplace issues, we must first tackle systemic issues around race. It is possible that addressing these challenges could reduce discriminatory actions and consequently decrease mental health difficulties resulting from workplace discrimination.

While psychology attempts to move the needle on mental health in people of color, it is important for employers to understand and recognize the impact of racial discrimination, lack of representation and microaggressions on mental health. Moreover, it is time for companies to not only advocate and promote racial equality but also create work spaces and communities that support mental well-being and inclusivity. This cannot happen without proper education and training. Managers and supervisors must be empowered to support and lead mental health and inclusion efforts while individually supporting each employee. As many companies step out of the shadows to support racial justice, it is paramount that they recognize mental health as a pillar to moving forward. In general, studies show that racism and discrimination can cause psychological difficulties among youth and adults regardless of the type of racism they experience directly or indirectly.[72] Given the pervasive nature of systemic racism and oppression, it is paramount that psychology as a field improve our understanding of addressing the intersection of race and other identity factors within mental health treatment.

TREATMENT CONSIDERATIONS TO REDUCE MENTAL HEALTH ISSUES

Providing treatment to Black Americans requires that therapists are aware of their stereotypes and avoid allowing those biases to negatively impacting treatment. Some Black clients may avoid seeking therapy due to their perceptions about mental health providers not being sensitive to their needs.[73] The majority of training programs for future therapists are centered around a Eurocentric philosophy. These Eurocentric values often emphasize individuality, authoritativeness, nuclear family structures, and competitiveness.[74] According to Morris, therapists trained from a Eurocentric perspective may have an "inadequate understanding of the psychological mindset of most African Americans."[75] This could result in some difficulties in the therapeutic relationship or misdiagnosis.

Black Americans are strongly influenced by their African heritage and culture.[76] Therefore, it is imperative that mental health providers incorporate aspects of their Black ethnic and cultural identity into treatment.[77] Numerous scholars and Black psychologists have described values consistent with an Afrocentric perspective.[78] Africentric values may include emphasis on the group and relationships, democratic orientation, extended family structure, interdependence orientation or communalism, social time phenomenon, spirituality, thriving under harmony or integration of all aspects of one's life, and verbal tradition.[79] Not all Black Americans come from the same cultural mind-set, not all Black Americans have the same worldviews, and not all Black Americans are at the same stage of identity development.[80] Therefore, it is important for therapist to explore ethnic identity and how certain beliefs may be important to each individual Black client.

When providers are culturally sensitive, they hold specific knowledge about diverse racial and ethnic minority groups, understand the generic characteristics of providing therapy, and possess the skills and abilities to generate a wide variety of verbal and nonverbal responses within the therapy context.[81] Chu, Leino, Pflum, and Sue provided a conceptual framework articulating the importance of cultural competency.[82] The first principle in their model is creating a contextual match with the client's lived experience. Turner notes that many African American clients may feel that some therapists do not understand their perspective—either indirectly or directly—and this may reduce the therapists' ability to recognize how contextual factors may cause the client distress.[83] Therapists must have a full understanding of the impact of external factors on Black clients' mental health (e.g., racial injustice). The second principle described by Chu et al. is that cultural competency creates an experiential match.[84] This involves ensuring that mental health providers understand how family and interpersonal relationships in the community (e.g., school, church) have a direct influence on the individual (both positive and negative). Finally, cultural competency is creating an environment where the client feels understood and empowered.[85] Scholars have noted that cultural humility allows therapists to be open to the client's beliefs, values, and worldview as opposed to viewing their own beliefs and values as superior.[86] According to Chu et al., engaging in cultural humility or empathy allows the mental health provider to effectively communicate their understanding of the client's background.[87]

From the perspective of CRT, racism is built into the fabric of American society, and despite making some progress, we will continue to navigate different forms of oppression and racism over time. To address the needs of Black Americans, therapists must enhance their understanding of African values and how these cultural considerations improve treatment seeking, as well as, how societal issues contribute to mental health outcomes. As a profession, it is the providers' ethical responsibility to facilitate psychological improvement in all clients and lack of cultural competence may hinder treatment improvement, specifically for Black Americans.

CONCLUSION

Black Americans have consistently experienced historical oppression and racism in American society. According to CRT, race and racism is embedded within society and will be a constant concern to navigate.[88] In the twenty-first century, the influence of the social and political context continues to contribute to poor mental health among Black Americans. To further advance the field of psychology and to improve mental health access for Black Americans, it is imperative that CRP be more central to our work. Critical theories, such as CRP, will allow the field to improve its understanding of issues around race and racism, and work toward decolonizing psychology to promote healing among Black Americans.

The MTI domains (accessibility, availability, appropriateness, and acceptability) represent some areas that could be addressed from the perspective of CRT and CRP. For example, if we address systemic issues around limited access to providers from diverse ethnic groups it could improve desires among Black Americans to seek therapy. When there is more access to same-race therapists, some Black Americans may be more open to seeking help.[89] Furthermore, research supports the idea that cultural sensitivity is important to treatment engagement and retention.[90] If the field is able to improve the ability to integrate African values and practice within a culturally informed approach this may also help reduce mental health disparities.

NOTES

1. American Psychological Association, "Stress and Health Disparities Report," 2017, http://www.apa.org/pi/health-disparities/resources/stress-report.aspx.

2. Phia Salter and Glenn Adams, "Toward a Critical Race Psychology," *Social and Personality Psychology Compass* 7, no. 11 (2013): 781–93; Erlanger A. Turner, *Mental Health Among African Americans: Innovations in Research and Practice* (Lanham, MD: Rowman & Littlefield, 2019), 2–5.

3. APA, "Stress in America Report: Stress in the Time of COVID-19," August 10, 2020, https://www.apa.org/news/press/releases/stress.

4. Lonnie R. Snowden, "Barriers to Effective Mental Health Services for African Americans," *Mental Health Services Research* 3, no. 4 (2001): 181–87; Erlanger A. Turner, Hsiu-Lan Cheng, Jasmín D. Llamas, Alisia G.T.T. Tran, Kyle X. Hill, Jennie M. Fretts, and Alfonso Mercado, "Factors Impacting the Current Trends in the Use of Outpatient Psychiatric Treatment among Diverse Ethnic Groups," *Current Psychiatry Reviews* 12, no. 2 (2016): 200–20; U.S. Department of Health and Human Services, "Mental Health: Culture, Race, and Ethnicity—A Supplement to Mental Health: A Report of the Surgeon General" (Rockville, MD: USDHHS, 2001).

5. Derrick Bell, "Racism: A Major Source of Property and Wealth Inequality in America," *Indiana Law Review* 34 (2000): 1261–71; Glenn E. Bracey, "Toward a Critical Race Theory of State," *Critical Sociology* 41, no. 3 (2015): 553–72; Kimberlé W. Crenshaw, "From Private Violence to Mass Incarceration: Thinking Intersectionally about Women, Race, and Social Control," *UCLA Law Review* 59 (2011): 1418; Richard Delgado and Jean Stefanic, *Critical Race Theory: An Introduction* (New York: NYU Press, 2001).

6. Salter and Adams, "Toward a Critical Race Psychology"; Bryana H. French, Jioni A. Lewis, Della V. Mosley, Hector Y. Adames, Nayeli Y. Chavez-Dueñas, Grace A. Chen, and Helen A. Neville, "Toward a Psychological Framework of Radical Healing in Communities of Color," *The Counseling Psychologist* 48, no. 1 (2020): 14–46.

7. Salter and Adams, "Toward a Critical Race Psychology," 781–93; Crenshaw, "From Private Violence to Mass Incarceration," 1418–72; Delgado and Stefanic, *Critical Race Theory: An Introduction*; Kimberlé Crenshaw, Neil Gotanda, Gary Peller, and Kendall Thomas, eds., *Critical Race Theory: The Key Writings that Formed the Movement* (New York: The New Press, 1995).

8. Bell, "Racism"; Crenshaw, "From Private Violence to Mass Incarceration"; Delgado and Stefanic, *Critical Race Theory: An Introduction*; Crenshaw, Gotanda, Peller, and Thomas, *Critical Race Theory: The Key Writings that Formed the Movement.*

9. Crenshaw, "From Private Violence to Mass Incarceration"; Delgado and Stefanic, *Critical Race Theory: An Introduction.*

10. Salter and Adams, "Toward a Critical Race Psychology"; Delgado and Stefanic, *Critical Race Theory: An Introduction*; Phia S. Salter and Andrea D. Haugen, "Critical Race Studies in Psychology," in *The Palgrave Handbook of*

Critical Social Psychology, edited by Brendan Gough (London: Palgrave Macmillan, 2017), 123–45.

11. Salter and Haugen, "Critical Race Studies in Psychology," 124.

12. Ibid.

13. Salter and Adams, "Toward a Critical Race Psychology"; Salter and Haugen, "Critical Race Studies in Psychology," 123–45.

14. Salter and Haugen, "Critical Race Studies in Psychology."

15. Turner, *Mental Health Among African Americans*; Turner, Cheng, Llamas, Tran, Hill, Fretts, and Mercado, "Factors Impacting the Current Trends in the Use of Outpatient Psychiatric Treatment among Diverse Ethnic Groups," 199–220.

16. Turner, Cheng, Llamas, Tran, Hill, Fretts, and Mercado, "Factors Impacting the Current Trends in the Use of Outpatient Psychiatric Treatment among Diverse Ethnic Groups."

17. Ibid.; Erlanger Turner, A., Celeste Malone, and Courtland Douglas, "Barriers to Mental Health Care for African Americans: Applying a Model of Treatment Initiation to Reduce Disparities," in *Eliminating Race-based Mental Health Disparities: Promoting Equity and Culturally Responsive Care across Settings* (Oakland, CA: New Harbinger Publications, 2019).

18. Turner, *Mental Health Among African Americans*, 12–30; Turner, Malone, and Douglas, "Barriers to Mental Health Care for African Americans."

19. Turner, *Mental Health Among African Americans*; Snowden, "Barriers to Effective Mental Health Services for African Americans."

20. Madonna G. Constantine, Mai. M. Kindaichi, Sheila. V. Graham, and Nicole L. Watkins, "Strategies for Reducing Disparities in African Americans' Receipt and Use of Mental Health Services," in *Toward Equity in Health: A New Global Approach to Health Disparities,* edited by B. C. Wallace (New York: Springer, 2008); John R. Weisz and Bahr Weiss, "Studying the 'Referability' of Child Clinical Problems," *Journal of Consulting and Clinical Psychology* 59, no. 2 (1991): 266–73.

21. Heather Kugelmass, "'Sorry, I'm Not Accepting New Patients' An Audit Study of Access to Mental Health Care." *Journal of Health and Social Behavior* 57, no. 2 (2016): 168–183.

22. Turner, *Mental Health Among African Americans*; Snowden, "Barriers to Effective Mental Health Services for African Americans"; Lonnie R. Snowden and Jane Holschuh, "Ethnic Differences in Emergency Psychiatric Care and Hospitalization in a Program for the Severely Mentally Ill," *Community Mental Health Journal* 28, no. 4 (1992): 281–91.

23. Salter and Adams. "Toward a Critical Race Psychology."

24. Raquel R. Cabral, and Timothy B. Smith. "Racial/ethnic Matching of Clients and Therapists in Mental Health Services: A Meta-analytic Review of Preferences, Perceptions, and Outcomes," *Journal of Counseling Psychology* 58, no. 4 (2011): 537–54.

25. Vetta L. Sanders Thompson and Hyter Alexander, "Therapists' Race and African American Clients' Reactions to Therapy," *Psychotherapy: Theory, Research, Practice, Training* 43, no. 1 (2006): 99–110.

26. Turner, *Mental Health Among African Americans.*

27. Vetta L. Sanders Thompson, Anita Bazile, and Maysa Akbar, "African Americans' Perceptions of Psychotherapy and Psychotherapists," *Professional Psychology: Research and Practice* 35, no. 1 (2004): 19–26.

28. Turner, Malone, and Douglas, "Barriers to Mental Health Care for African Americans."

29. Salter and Haugen, "Critical Race Studies in Psychology."

30. Turner, *Mental Health Among African Americans*; Nancy Boyd-Franklin, "Incorporating Spirituality and Religion into the Treatment of African American Clients," *The Counseling Psychologist* 38, no. 7 (2010): 976–1000.

31. Boyd-Franklin, "Incorporating Spirituality and Religion into the Treatment of African American Clients"; Thema Bryant-Davis and Carlota Ocampo, "Racist Incident-based Trauma" *The Counseling Psychologist* 33, no. 4 (2005): 479–500; Thema Bryant-Davis and Eunice C. Wong, "Faith to Move Mountains: Religious Coping, Spirituality, and Interpersonal Trauma Recovery," *American Psychologist* 68, no. 8 (2013): 675–84.

32. Faye Z. Belgrave and Kevin W. Allison, *African American Psychology: From Africa to America*. (Thousand Oaks, CA: Sage Publications, 2014), 137–230.

33. Turner, Cheng, Llamas, Tran, Hill, Fretts, and Mercado, "Factors Impacting the Current Trends in the Use of Outpatient Psychiatric Treatment among Diverse Ethnic Groups," 200–30; Boyd-Franklin, "Incorporating Spirituality and Religion into the Treatment of African American Clients."

34. Belgrave and Allison, *African American Psychology*, 231–300.

35. Boyd-Franklin, "Incorporating Spirituality and Religion into the Treatment of African American Clients"; Shiquina L. Andrews, James Tres Stefurak, and Sheila Mehta, "Between a Rock and a Hard Place? Locus of Control, Religious Problem-Solving and Psychological Help-Seeking." *Mental Health, Religion & Culture* 14, no. 9 (2011): 855–76.

36. Andrews, Stefurak, and Mehta, "Between a Rock and a Hard Place?"

37. Turner, Cheng, Llamas, Tran, Hill, Fretts, and Mercado, "Factors Impacting the Current Trends in the Use of Outpatient Psychiatric Treatment among Diverse Ethnic Groups"; Thompson, Bazile, and Akbar, "African Americans' Perceptions of Psychotherapy and Psychotherapists"; Stacie Craft DeFreitas, Travis Crone, Martha DeLeon, and Anna Ajayi, "Perceived and Personal Mental Health Stigma in Latino and African American College Students," *Frontiers in Public Health* 6 (2018): 49; Akihiko Masuda, Page L. Anderson, and Joshua Edmonds, "Help-seeking Attitudes, Mental Health Stigma, and Self-concealment among African American College Students," *Journal of Black Studies* 43, no. 7 (2012): 773–86.

38. Thompson, Bazile, and Akbar, "African Americans' Perceptions of Psychotherapy and Psychotherapists," 19–26.

39. Richard Thompson, Barbara L. Dancy, Tisha R. A. Wiley, Cynthia J. Najdowski, Sylvia P. Perry, Jason Wallis, Yara Mekawi, and Kathleen A. Knafl, "African American Families' Expectations and Intentions for Mental Health Services," *Administration and Policy in Mental Health and Mental Health Services Research* 40, no. 5 (2013): 371–83.

40. Thompson, Bazile, and Akbar, "African Americans' Perceptions of Psychotherapy and Psychotherapists," 19–26.

41. Turner, *Mental Health Among African Americans.*

42. Arthur L. Whaley, "Cultural Mistrust and Mental Health Services for African Americans: A Review and Meta-analysis," *The Counseling Psychologist* 29, no. 4 (2001a): 513–31.

43. Ibid.; Arthur L. Whaley, "Cultural Mistrust: An Important Psychological Construct for Diagnosis and Treatment of African Americans," *Professional Psychology: Research and Practice* 32, no. 6 (2001b): 555–62.

44. Ibid.

45. Belgrave and Allison, *African American Psychology*; Bryant-Davis and Ocampo, "Racist Incident-based Trauma"; Thema Bryant-Davis, Tyonna Adams, Adriana Alejandre, and Anthea A. Gray, "The Trauma Lens of Police Violence against Racial and Ethnic Minorities," *Journal of Social Issues* 73, no. 4 (2017): 852–71.

46. Turner, *Mental Health Among African Americans,* 25–37.

47. Belgrave and Allison, *African American Psychology*, 3–30.

48. Jacob Bor, Atheender. S. Venkataramani, David R. Williams, and Alexander C. Tsai, "Police Killings and Their Spillover Effects on the Mental Health of Black Americans: A Population-based Quasi-experimental Study," *The Lancet* 392 (2018): 302–10.

49. Ibid.

50. Bryant-Davis, Adams, Alejandre, and Gray, "The Trauma Lens of Police Violence against Racial and Ethnic Minorities."

51. Turner, *Mental Health Among African Americans*; Belgrave and Allison, *African American Psychology*; Bryant-Davis, Adams, Alejandre, and Gray, "The Trauma Lens of Police Violence against Racial and Ethnic Minorities"; Shawn O. Utsey and Yasser Payne, "Psychological Impacts of Racism in a Clinical versus Normal Sample of African American Men." *Journal of African American Men* 5, no. 3 (2000): 57–72.

52. Utsey and Payne, "Psychological Impacts of Racism in a Clinical versus Normal Sample of African American Men," 57–72.

53. Turner, *Mental Health Among African Americans*; Utsey and Payne, "Psychological Impacts of Racism in a Clinical versus Normal Sample of African American Men"; Deidre Franklin-Jackson and Robert T. Carter, "The Relationships between Race-related Stress, Racial Identity, and Mental Health for Black Americans," *Journal of Black Psychology* 33, no. 1 (2007): 5–26.

54. April Harris-Britt, Cecelia R. Valrie, Beth Kurtz-Costes, and Stephanie J. Rowley, "Perceived Racial Discrimination and Self-esteem in African American Youth: Racial Socialization as a Protective Factor," *Journal of Research on Adolescence* 17, no. 4 (2007) : 669–82; Eleanor K. Seaton, Cleopatra H. Caldwell, Robert M. Sellers, and James S. Jackson, "The Prevalence of Perceived Discrimination among African American and Caribbean Black Youth," *Developmental Psychology* 44, no. 5 (2008).

55. Seaton, Caldwell, Sellers, and Jackson, "The Prevalence of Perceived Discrimination among African American and Caribbean Black Youth," 1288–97.

56. Ibid., 1288–96.

57. Harris-Britt, Valrie, Kurtz-Costes, and Rowley, "Perceived Racial Discrimination and Self-esteem in African American Youth: Racial Socialization as a Protective Factor."

58. Janet E. Helms, Guerda Nicolas, and Carlton E. Green, "Racism and Ethnoviolence as Trauma: Enhancing Professional Training," *Traumatology* 16, no. 4 (2010): 53–62; Monnica T. Williams, Emily Malcoun, Broderick A. Sawyer, Darlene M. Davis, Leyla Bahojb Nouri, and Simone Leavell Bruce, "Cultural Adaptations of Prolonged Exposure Therapy for Treatment and Prevention of Posttraumatic Stress Disorder in African Americans," *Behavioral Sciences* 4, no. 2 (2014): 102–24.

59. Turner, *Mental Health Among African Americans*, 16.

60. Bryant-Davis and Ocampo. "Racist Incident–based Trauma," 479–500; Williams, Malcoun, Sawyer, Davis, Nouri, and Bruce, "Cultural Adaptations of Prolonged Exposure Therapy for Treatment and Prevention of Posttraumatic Stress Disorder in African Americans," 102–124.

61. Bryant-Davis and Ocampo. "Racist Incident-based Trauma," 479–500; Robert T. Carter, "Racism and Psychological and Emotional Injury: Recognizing and Assessing Race-based Traumatic Stress," *The Counseling Psychologist* 35, no. 1 (2007): 13–105.

62. U.S. Equal Employment Commission, "Title VII of the Civil Rights Act of 1964." Accessed October 9, 2020. https://www.eeoc.gov/statutes/title-vii-civil-rights-act-1964.

63. Lincoln Quillian, Devah Pager, Ole Hexel, and Arnfinn H. Midtbøen, "Meta-analysis of Field Experiments Shows no Change in Racial Discrimination in Hiring over Time," *Proceedings of the National Academy of Sciences* 114, no. 41 (2017): 10870–75.

64. Lincoln Quillian, Devah Pager, Arnfinn H. Midtbøen, and Ole Hexel, "Hiring Discrimination Against Black Americans Hasn't Declined in 25 Years." Last modified June 15, 2020, https://hbr.org/2017/10/hiring-discrimination-against-black-americans-hasnt-declined-in-25-years.

65. Wizdom Powell Hammond, Marion Gillen, and Irene H. Yen, "Workplace Discrimination and Depressive Symptoms: A Study of Multi-Ethnic Hospital Employees," *Race and Social Problems* 2, no. 1 (2010): 19–30.

66. Ibid.

67. Torsheika Maddox, "Professional Women's Well-Being: The Role of Discrimination and Occupational Characteristics," *Women & Health* 53, no. 7 (2013): 706–29.

68. Ibid..

69. Ibid., 706–719.

70. Elizabeth A. Deitch, Adam Barsky, Rebecca M. Butz, Suzanne Chan, Arthur P. Brief, and Jill C. Bradley, "Subtle Yet Significant: The Existence and Impact of Everyday Racial Discrimination in the Workplace," *Human Relations* 56, no. 11 (2003): 1299–324.

71. Ibid.

72. Turner, *Mental Health Among African Americans,* 11–20; Bryant-Davis and Ocampo. "Racist Incident–based Trauma," 485–95.

73. Turner, *Mental Health Among African Americans,* 13–21.

74. Edward F. Morris, "Clinical Practices with African Americans: Juxtaposition of Standard Clinical Practices and Africentricism," *Professional Psychology: Research and Practice* 32, no. 6 (2001): 564.

75. Ibid., 564.

76. Belgrave and Allison, *African American Psychology*, 103–30; Madge Gill Willis, "Learning Styles of African American Children: A Review of the Literature and Interventions," *Journal of Black Psychology* 16, no. 1 (1989): 47–65.

77. Turner, *Mental Health Among African Americans.*

78. Wade W. Nobles, "Psychological Nigrescence: An Afrocentric Review," *The Counseling Psychologist* 17, no. 2 (1989): 253–57; Linda James Myers, *Understanding an Afrocentric World View: Introduction to an Optimal Psychology* (Dubuque, IA: Kendall/Hunt Publishing Company, 1993); Shawn O. Utsey, Alexis Howard, and Otis Williams III, "Therapeutic Group Mentoring with African American Male Adolescents," *Journal of Mental Health Counseling* 25, no. 2 (2003): 128–30.

79. Turner, *Mental Health Among African Americans*; Belgrave and Allison, *African American Psychology*; Nancy Boyd-Franklin, *Black Families in Therapy: Understanding the African American Experience* (New York: Guilford Press, 2003).

80. Morris, "Clinical Practices with African Americans: Juxtaposition of Standard Clinical Practices and Africentricism," 563–72.

81. Stanley Sue, Nolan Zane, Gordon C. Nagayama Hall, and Lauren K. Berger, "The Case for Cultural Competency in Psychotherapeutic Interventions," *Annual Review of Psychology* 60 (2009): 525–48.

82. Joyce Chu, Amy Leino, Samantha Pflum, and Stanley Sue, "A Model for the Theoretical Basis of Cultural Competency to Guide Psychotherapy," *Professional Psychology: Research and Practice* 47, no. 1 (2016): 18–29.

83. Turner, *Mental Health Among African Americans,* 40–57.

84. Chu, Leino, Pflum, and Sue, "A Model for the Theoretical Basis of Cultural Competency to Guide Psychotherapy," 18–29.

85. Ibid.

86. Turner, *Mental Health Among African Americans,* 40–50; French, Lewis, Mosley, Adames, Chavez-Dueñas, Chen, and Neville, "Toward a Psychological Framework of Radical Healing in Communities of Color," 14–46; Bryant-Davis and Ocampo, "Racist Incident-based Trauma," 479–500.

87. Chu, Leino, Pflum, and Sue, "A Model for the Theoretical Basis of Cultural Competency to Guide Psychotherapy," 18–29.

88. Bell, "Racism"; Bracey, "Toward a Critical Race Theory of State"; Crenshaw, "From Private Violence to Mass Incarceration"; Delgado and Stefanic, *Critical Race Theory.*

89. Turner, Malone, and Douglas, "Barriers to Mental Health Care for African Americans."

90. Turner, *Mental Health Among African Americans,* 39–57; Sue, Zane, Hall, and Berger, "The Case for Cultural Competency in Psychotherapeutic Interventions," 525–48; Chu, Leino, Pflum, and Sue, "A Model for the Theoretical Basis of Cultural Competency to Guide Psychotherapy," 18–29.

BIBLIOGRAPHY

American Psychological Association. "Stress and Health Disparities Report." December 2017. http://www.apa.org/pi/health-disparities/resources/stress-report.aspx.

American Psychological Association. "Stress in America Report: Stress in the Time of COVID-19." August 10, 2020, https://www.apa.org/news/press/releases/stress.

Andrews, Shiquina L., James Tres Stefurak, and Sheila Mehta. "Between a Rock and a Hard Place? Locus of Control, Religious Problem-Solving and Psychological Help-Seeking." *Mental Health, Religion & Culture* 14, no. 9 (2011): 855–76.

Belgrave, Faye Z., and Kevin W. Allison. *African American Psychology: From Africa to America*. Thousand Oaks, CA: Sage Publications, 2014.

Bell, Derrick. "Racism: A Major Source of Property and Wealth Inequality in America." *Indiana Law Review* 34 (2000): 1261–71.

Bor, Jacob, Atheendar S. Venkataramani, David R. Williams, and Alexander C. Tsai. "Police Killings and Their Spillover Effects on the Mental Health of Black Americans: A Population-based Quasi-experimental Study." *The Lancet* 392 (2018): 302–10.

Boyd-Franklin, Nancy. *Black Families in Therapy: Understanding the African American Experience*. New York: Guilford Press, 2003.

Boyd-Franklin, Nancy. "Incorporating Spirituality and Religion into the Treatment of African American Clients." *The Counseling Psychologist* 38, no. 7 (2010): 976–1000.

Bracey, Glenn E. "Toward a Critical Race Theory of State." *Critical Sociology* 41, no. 3 (2015): 553–72.

Bryant-Davis, Thema. "Coping Strategies of African American Adult Survivors of Childhood Violence." *Professional Psychology: Research and Practice* 36, no. 4 (2005): 409–14.

Bryant-Davis, Thema, and Carlota Ocampo. "Racist Incident-based Trauma." *The Counseling Psychologist* 33, no. 4 (2005): 479–500.

Bryant-Davis, Thema, and Eunice C. Wong. "Faith to Move Mountains: Religious Coping, Spirituality, and Interpersonal Trauma Recovery." *American Psychologist* 68, no. 8 (2013): 675–84.

Bryant-Davis, Thema, Tyonna Adams, Adriana Alejandre, and Anthea A. Gray. "The Trauma Lens of Police Violence against Racial and Ethnic Minorities." *Journal of Social Issues* 73, no. 4 (2017): 852–71.

Cabral, Raquel R., and Timothy B. Smith. "Racial/Ethnic Matching of Clients and Therapists in Mental Health Services: A Meta-analytic Review of Preferences, Perceptions, and Outcomes." *Journal of Counseling Psychology* 58, no. 4 (2011): 537–54.

Carter, Robert T. "Racism and Psychological and Emotional Injury: Recognizing and Assessing Race-based Traumatic Stress." *The Counseling Psychologist* 35, no. 1 (2007): 13–105.

Chu, Joyce, Amy Leino, Samantha Pflum, and Stanley Sue. "A Model for the Theoretical Basis of Cultural Competency to Guide Psychotherapy." *Professional Psychology: Research and Practice* 47, no. 1 (2016): 18–29.

Constantine, Madonna G., Mai M. Kindaichi, Sheila. V. Graham, and Nicole L. Watkins. "Strategies for Reducing Disparities in African Americans' Receipt and Use of Mental Health Services." In B. C. Wallace (ed.), *Toward Equity in Health: A New Global Approach to Health Disparities*, 155–67. New York: Springer, 2008.

Crenshaw, Kimberlé W. "From Private Violence to Mass Incarceration: Thinking Intersectionally about Women, Race, and Social Control." *UCLA Law Review* 59 (2011): 1418–72.

Crenshaw, Kimberlé, Neil Gotanda, Gary Peller, and Kendall Thomas. *Critical Race Theory: The Key Writings that Formed the Movement.* New York: The New Press, 1995.

DeFreitas, Stacie Craft, Travis Crone, Martha DeLeon, and Anna Ajayi. "Perceived and Personal Mental Health Stigma in Latino and African American College Students." *Frontiers in Public Health* 6 (2018): 49.

Deitch, Elizabeth A., Adam Barsky, Rebecca M. Butz, Suzanne Chan, Arthur P. Brief, and Jill C. Bradley. "Subtle Yet Significant: The Existence and Impact of Everyday Racial Discrimination in the Workplace." *Human Relations* 56, no. 11 (2003): 1299–324.

Delgado, Richard, and Jean Stefanic. *Critical Race Theory: An Introduction.* New York: New York University Press, 2001.

Franklin-Jackson, Deidre, and Robert T. Carter. "The Relationships between Race-Related Stress, Racial Identity, and Mental Health for Black Americans." *Journal of Black Psychology* 33, no. 1 (2007): 5–26.

French, Bryana H., Jioni A. Lewis, Della V. Mosley, Hector Y. Adames, Nayeli Y. Chavez-Dueñas, Grace A. Chen, and Helen A. Neville. "Toward a Psychological Framework of Radical Healing in Communities of Color." *The Counseling Psychologist* 48, no. 1 (2020): 14–46.

Hammond, Wizdom Powell, Marion Gillen, and Irene H. Yen. "Workplace Discrimination and Depressive Symptoms: A Study of Multi-Ethnic Hospital Employees." *Race and Social Problems* 2, no. 1 (2010): 19–30.

Harris-Britt, April, Cecelia R. Valrie, Beth Kurtz-Costes, and Stephanie J. Rowley. "Perceived Racial Discrimination and Self-esteem in African American Youth: Racial Socialization as a Protective Factor." *Journal of Research on Adolescence* 17, no. 4 (2007): 669–82.

Helms, Janet E., Guerda Nicolas, and Carlton E. Green. "Racism and Ethnoviolence as Trauma: Enhancing Professional Training." *Traumatology* 16, no. 4 (2010): 53–62.

Kugelmass, Heather. "'Sorry, I'm Not Accepting New Patients' An Audit Study of Access to Mental Health Care." *Journal of Health and Social Behavior* 57, no. 2 (2016): 168–83.

Maddox, Torsheika. "Professional Women's Well-Being: The Role of Discrimination and Occupational Characteristics." *Women & Health* 53, no. 7 (2013): 706–29.

Masuda, Akihiko, Page L. Anderson, and Joshua Edmonds. "Help-Seeking Attitudes, Mental Health Stigma, and Self-concealment among African American College Students." *Journal of Black Studies* 43, no. 7 (2012): 773–86.

Morris, Edward F. "Clinical Practices with African Americans: Juxtaposition of Standard Clinical Practices and Africentricism." *Professional Psychology: Research and Practice* 32, no. 6 (2001): 563–72.

Myers, Linda James. *Understanding an Afrocentric World view: Introduction to an optimal psychology*. Dubuque, IA: Kendall/Hunt Publishing Company, 1993.

Nobles, W. W. "Psychological Nigrescence: An Afrocentric Review." *The Counseling Psychologist* 17, no. 2 (1989): 253–57.

Quillian, Lincoln, Devah Pager, Arnfinn H Midtbøen, and Ole Hexel. "Hiring Discrimination Against Black Americans Hasn't Declined in 25 Years." Last modified June 15, 2020. https://hbr.org/2017/10/hiring-discrimination-against-black-americans-hasnt-declined-in-25-years.

Quillian, Lincoln, Devah Pager, Ole Hexel, and Arnfinn H. Midtbøen. "Meta-analysis of Field Experiments Shows no Change in Racial Discrimination in Hiring over Time." *Proceedings of the National Academy of Sciences* 114, no. 41 (2017): 10870–75.

Salter, Phia S., and Andrea D. Haugen. "Critical Race Studies in Psychology." In *The Palgrave Handbook of Critical Social Psychology*, 123–145. London: Palgrave Macmillan, 2017.

Salter, Phia, and Glenn Adams. "Toward a Critical Race Psychology." *Social and Personality Psychology Compass* 7, no. 11 (2013): 781–93.

Seaton, Eleanor K., Cleopatra H. Caldwell, Robert M. Sellers, and James S. Jackson. "The Prevalence of Perceived Discrimination among African American and Caribbean Black Youth." *Developmental Psychology* 44, no. 5 (2008): 1288–97.

Snowden, Lonnie R. "Barriers to Effective Mental Health Services for African Americans." *Mental Health Services Research* 3, no. 4 (2001): 181–87.

Snowden, Lonnie R., and Jane Holschuh. "Ethnic Differences in Emergency Psychiatric Care and Hospitalization in a Program for the Severely Mentally Ill." *Community Mental Health Journal* 28, no. 4 (1992): 281–91.

Sue, Stanley, Nolan Zane, Gordon C. Nagayama Hall, and Lauren K. Berger. "The Case for Cultural Competency in Psychotherapeutic Interventions." *Annual Review of Psychology* 60 (2009): 525–48.

Thompson, Richard, Barbara L. Dancy, Tisha R.A. Wiley, Cynthia J. Najdowski, Sylvia P. Perry, Jason Wallis, Yara Mekawi, and Kathleen A. Knafl. "African American Families' Expectations and Intentions for Mental Health Services." *Administration and Policy in Mental Health and Mental Health Services Research* 40, no. 5 (2013): 371–83.

Thompson, Vetta L. Sanders, Anita Bazile, and Maysa Akbar. "African Americans' Perceptions of Psychotherapy and Psychotherapists." *Professional Psychology: Research and Practice* 35, no. 1 (2004): 19–26.

Thompson, Vetta L. Sanders, and Hyter Alexander. "Therapists' Race and African American Clients' Reactions to Therapy." *Psychotherapy: Theory, Research, Practice, Training* 43, no. 1 (2006): 99–110.

Turner, Erlanger A. *Mental Health Among African Americans: Innovations in Research and Practice*. Lanham, MD: Rowman & Littlefield, 2019.

Turner, Erlanger A., Celeste Malone, and Courtland Douglas. "Barriers to Mental Health Care for African Americans: Applying a Model of Treatment Initiation to Reduce Disparities." In *Eliminating Race-based Mental Health Disparities: Promoting Equity and Culturally Responsive Care across Settings*, 27–42. Oakland, CA: New Harbinger Publications, 2019.

Turner, Erlanger A., Hsiu-Lan Cheng, Jasmín D. Llamas, Alisia G.T.T. Tran, Kyle X. Hill, Jennie M. Fretts, and Alfonso Mercado. "Factors Impacting the Current Trends in the Use of Outpatient Psychiatric Treatment among Diverse Ethnic Groups." *Current Psychiatry Reviews* 12, no. 2 (2016): 199–220.

U.S. Department of Health and Human Services. Mental Health: Culture, Race, and Ethnicity—A Supplement to Mental Health: A Report of the Surgeon General. Rockville, MD: USDHHS, 2001.

U.S. Equal Employment Commission. "Title VII of the Civil Rights Act of 1964." Accessed October 9, 2020. https://www.eeoc.gov/statutes/title-vii-civil-rights-act-1964.

Utsey, Shawn O., Alexis Howard, and Otis Williams III. "Therapeutic Group Mentoring with African American Male Adolescents." *Journal of Mental Health Counseling* 25, no. 2 (2003): 126–39.

Utsey, Shawn O., and Yasser Payne. "Psychological Impacts of Racism in a Clinical versus Normal Sample of African American Men." *Journal of African American Men* 5, no. 3 (2000): 57–72.

Weisz, John R., and Bahr Weiss. "Studying the 'Referability' of Child Clinical Problems." *Journal of Consulting and Clinical Psychology* 59, no. 2 (1991): 266–73.

Whaley, Arthur L. "Cultural Mistrust and Mental Health Services for African Americans: A Review and Meta-analysis." *The Counseling Psychologist* 29, no. 4 (2001a): 513–31.

Whaley, Arthur L. "Cultural Mistrust: An Important Psychological Construct for Diagnosis and Treatment of African Americans." *Professional Psychology: Research and Practice* 32, no. 6 (2001b): 555–62.

Williams, Monnica T., Emily Malcoun, Broderick A. Sawyer, Darlene M. Davis, Leyla Bahojb Nouri, and Simone Leavell Bruce. "Cultural Adaptations of Prolonged Exposure Therapy for Treatment and Prevention of Posttraumatic Stress Disorder in African Americans." *Behavioral Sciences* 4, no. 2 (2014): 102–24.

Willis, Madge Gill. "Learning Styles of African American Children: A Review of the Literature and Interventions." *Journal of Black Psychology* 16, no. 1 (1989): 47–65.

Chapter 11

The True Measure of American Greatness

Power, Relationality, and Community in the Thinking of Bernard Loomer, Howard Thurman, and Martin Luther King Jr.

Darrius D. Hills

In the current social and political climate, national rhetoric on American "greatness" remain contested discursive spaces. This is made so, on the heels of arguably our age's major spokesman and advocate for American greatness, the former president. While interest in the idea of American greatness has taken on renewed vigor in the present, it is not necessarily a novel idea. American exceptionalism, for example, is anticipated by ideas of a "set apart" nation—the proverbial "beacon on a hill"—all rhetorical sleight of hands deployed by America's Puritan ancestors. American greatness has re-emerged in the public imagination in part due to the campaign sloganeering of President Donald Trump in 2016 and into the present. In an essay for *The Nation*, Tom Engelhardt observes that while "Making America Great Again" is among the most known and popular rallying cries of the Trump administration, it is also the one least analyzed.[1] There could be a host of reasons for this tendency, though this is not the primary concern for the reflections to follow. Of course, of some interest is the addition "Again," which has prompted many, including Engelhardt, to reflect upon the ways America has declined from greatness at all, since Trump and his administration suggested a *return* to greatness is in order.

The rhetoric and policies stemming from Trump's politics partly informed the motivation for the present topic, but my concerns extend far beyond the political arrangements of the far-right populist and alternative right political landscape. The following chapter thinks through alternative notions of (American) greatness as philosophical, religious, and ethical sites of possibility. Namely, I critique the inordinate power schemas of greatness currently at play, in order to excise its problematic and promising manifestations for social and religious life in American culture, while also proffering a different hermeneutic. Current framings of greatness as articulated by the former president at this particular social, political, and religious moment in America are bolstered by rhetoric and policies that are authoritarian, coercive, and domineering in scope and application. This conception of greatness is preoccupied with an unbridled grasp for power (over others), perpetual "winning," and obsession over size. Winning and size, in particular, in our political context, is often linked to hierarchical mechanisms of (anti)-relation that are both vulnerable to tyrannical attributes and uphold a "might-is-right" mind-set, particularly toward the most vulnerable. This disposition results in the alienation of allies, neighbors, and peers. Such narrow views that privilege the (dis)connection from others create microlevel ruptures in everyday intracommunal interactions, and run the risk of bolstering macrolevel conflicts domestically and abroad.

Utilizing philosophical ethics and Black religious thought, I propose a reframing of American greatness as a mechanism of relationality rather than an asymmetrical power grab. As I suggest above, while attaching notions of greatness to power, size, and winning may be a popular refrain in a general, quotidian sense, especially in the current political culture, I wish to pursue a different interpretation of greatness—one situated along a relational register. After examining the ethical problems of authoritarianism as a measure of power and greatness using the work of process theologian and philosopher Bernard Loomer, I discuss the religious thought of noted mystic and Black religious thinker Howard Thurman to illustrate a possible turn in the relational ethos currently at play in discourses on American greatness. I argue that the relational underscoring of the insights from Loomer and Thurman offer a useful indictment of American cultural discourses and policy formation that is hinged upon aggrandizement within a nationalist purview at the expense of those deemed "other," or those imagined to be beyond the bounds of America's values, ethos, and identity. Loomer and Thurman's understanding of greatness is centered upon mutually reinforcing growth—the expansion of social and relational openness in human beings as an enduring communal praxis. Loomer's alternate ontology of power and size reframes the category of human-to-human relational identity, in which inclusion, rather than exclusion, denotes the anchoring of notions of strength and power. Loomer's interpretive work opens up powerful interpretive possibilities when linked with Howard Thurman's insights on estrangement and separation articulated within *Jesus and the Disinherited.* Thurman expands the conversation by casting a new light on the authoritarian and adversarial relational structures that so often contour the present American social and political imagination, and its modalities of governance and leadership. Martin Luther King is an ideological heir and contemporary to Thurman. I will therefore conclude with some parting reflections on King's notion of beloved community as societal aspiration and as a way to conceive of greatness in more wholistic and affirmative terms.

RELATIONAL POWER AS RESPONSE TO AUTHORITARIANISM

Matthew MacWilliams has noted that Donald Trump's policies on immigration and the border wall, for example, resonate with supporters harboring strong leanings toward authoritarian sensibilities. For those communities, Trump's twitter-based mantras and revolving rallies feature an ethno-nationalistic thematic that strikes at the heart of his appeal: Trump's crude and unpolished jeremiads are tethered to subtle warnings about racial and religious "others" who pose a threat to America's way of life and its prosperity.[2] To this demographic of the American public, Trump represents a kind of populist *ubermensch* who can reconstruct American and Christian values over against these "others"—whether they be immigrants, Muslims, or leftists. Because Christianity is central to America's identity in the public and religious imagination, particularly among self-identified conservative voters, it would be remiss not to highlight the uneasy fusion of evangelical Christianity, (American) nationalism, and right-wing politics. Andrew Whitehead and Samuel L. Perry elaborate upon this view, offering what they refer to as the phenomenon of "Christian nationalism," a powerful explanation for the deeply divisive and polarizing climate in popular American discourse.[3] While Whitehead and Perry are clear that Christian nationalism and far-right authoritarianism are distinct from each other, they are, nonetheless, correlated. Higher measures of Christian nationalism among conservative voters tend to yield higher measures of aggressive authoritarian psychological profiles, ethnocentrism, and racial prejudice.[4]

One avenue, therefore, to understand President Trump's mindset, political rhetoric, and approach to policy formation, is through a psychological and sociological appraisal of *right-wing authoritarianism*. While the following is not an exhaustive treatment, there are a few characteristic attributes of authoritarianism that are appropriate in any analysis of Trump's political mind-set. Trump's authoritarianism accents a "might is right" dynamic grounded in control and dominion over one's enemies and/or those thought to be a threat, politically or otherwise. Psychology theorist Robert Altemeyer cites three distinctive characteristics of (right-wing) authoritarianism useful for the analysis: (1) acceptance of established authority; (2) authoritarian aggression; and (3) the unquestioning acceptance of conventional norms.[5] The second characteristic, authoritarian aggression, was particularly relevant and central to Trump's political persona. Authoritarian aggression is a "muscular" personal and attitudinal postures seeking the maintenance of power and control over the behavior and activities of imagined inferiors through disciplinary means—particularly through the sanctioning of their space, place, and identity. But the authoritarian also, says history professor Ruth Ben-Ghiat, "wants us to lose our faith in our eyes and our ears, what we read and what we observe, so that we can be more dependent" on said authoritarian and the "appropriate" worldview set forth. At the time of this writing and research, President Trump was criticized for undermining local election results featuring successful Democrat candidates—leading many to speculate whether his efforts are par for the course regarding bolstering public distrust in the 2020 general election. If Trump's repeated push to dismantle America's most heralded democratic traditions (further underscored by his narcissism, disdain for empirical data, and gleeful embrace of falsehoods) in favor of his own singular view of the world and grasp on power is any indication, it does appear that American citizens suffered a president who thrived on authoritarian politics and modes of relating.[6]

What is also unique about Trump's authoritarianism is that he often applied it toward other Americans; namely political rivals. Known for his incendiary social media messages, Trump once shared a video on *Twitter* featuring a Republican official in New Mexico commenting that "the only good Democrat is a dead Democrat," eliciting cheers from crowd.[7] One can also not avoid the deeply gendered and raced quality of Trump's authoritarian aggression, which was evident from continued insults toward women and non-White Democrats—often singling them out to diminish their appearance and intelligence, while undermining their political authority and acumen.[8] Such examples should not be discounted as mere political grandstanding and bluster. On the contrary, they reflect the psychology of someone who sees people as a mix of collective rivals and threats that are in need of control and, if possible, removal.

Obviously, one element of authoritarian sanctioning from former President Trump is rhetorical, but such indictments against whole swaths of peoples and nations can be deadly in terms of their acceleration and reifying of the sense of racial resentment and disdain for non-White communities and countries.[9] When Trump mused, for example, that "some" immigrants from Mexico were "good people"—or when he off-handedly referred to immigrants as "bad hombres"—he was not simply articulating racialized code language meant to feed into xenophobia (whether intentional or not, is debatable).[10] Rather, when considered from the standpoint of authoritarian categorization and practice, perhaps this language is also a reification of *otherness*—a way of illustrating the chasms that properly delineate who is and is not a "true" American. These rhetorical devices are also backed by specific policy platforms that heighten the "us vs. them" lacunas central to authoritarian leadership. The border wall legislation, which *separates* the United States from Mexico, is meant to stunt the perceived widespread tides of illegal immigration, despite evidence to the contrary.[11] Additionally, past and present vetting mechanisms cast against immigrants from Muslim-majority countries are supposedly meant to *shield* Americans from the threat of extremist religious terrorism, notwithstanding the fact that the more significant threat is domestic terrorism of the right-wing persuasion.[12] In looking at the general scope of these policies from a theological vantage point, it is not American interests that particularly stand out. The concern for American interests is little more than a smoke screen and is secondary to President Trump's more primordial concern. The president's proposals and policies reflect a radical disregard for neighbor premised upon inordinate power consumption. Bernard Loomer's ontology of human power and size offers a more equitable approach to modes of relating in American political culture.

In "Two Kinds of Power," Loomer distinguishes between unilateral and relational power. The former "is the ability to produce intended or desired effects in our relationship to nature or to other people," through which we can manipulate and shape them according to *our* own particular aims and purposes. The latter is a shared power that is open, receptive, and mutual between equal parties and persons. Relational power is the ability "to produce and undergo an effect . . . the capacity to both influence others *and to be influenced by others*" [italics mine].[13] Loomer laments that unilateral power is typically the philosophical modus operandi contouring national and international political approaches. Its weakness lies in its noncommunal, coercive, and manipulative "means as an end" treatment of those in our midst. The consequence of this is that the controlling and authoritative person operates in a way that is ultimately dismissive of the humanity and personhood of others. On this view, the dominant are "unaffected by the relationship" and are unresponsive to the humanity of others.[14] There is also a competitive drive underscoring unilateral power relations, in that relative strength, size, or greatness, is measured solely by the degree to which one is able to prevail over against the powers of another. It is the back-and-forth power struggle, therefore, and the correlating capacity to curtail and steer the course of others, that is the measure of unilateral power and relationality. The unilateral distinction is apt for the kind of authoritarian power that is operative in the present administration. Whether the targets for belittling and ostracization are dissenting protesters, political rivals, immigrants, or women, it seems fair to cite the present political climate and political rhetorics as examples of a culture premised upon polemical paradigms that construct power, size, and notions of greatness as rooted in the capacity to bend, control, and sanction the identities and freedoms of others to the singular focus of the unilaterally powerful.

Relational power is constitutive for human life. It is within the realm of the relation that humanity has its identity and being. Another way to describe this characteristic of the web of human life is through the lens of interdependent interrelationships, which is a primordial fact of our existence: "as individuals we are interdependent. We do not become interdependent, but rather are such from our inception."[15] While human life and existence are characterized by finitude and fragility, we are caught in this web together, and are therefore better off embracing relational self-constitution and communal exchange. Relational, or shared power, as a conceptual frame for human identity formation may strike many as a radical, and thus a deviation from how we commonly perceive ourselves as a society of individuals. Admittedly, this alternate vision of human life, engagement, and living, is radical, but the rationale driving such a turn, is hardly new. I would submit that the current historical moment is primed for a more relational praxis in our political framework. Modern conceptions of the human as a private and self-contained entity untethered to others can partly be traced to philosophical treatises within classical liberalism centered on private property as the basis of citizenship, and the centrality of the individual who pursues his or her own interests. The relational element of our existence, and our political arrangements, is therefore typically not given greater consideration. Loomer is instructive because his conception of the nature of power broadens notions of selfhood by favoring a view of human identity as shared, communal, and nonhierarchical.

Relational power, between equal persons, contributes to the rising of the "other's" stature. In the absence of hierarchy and power schemas in this kind of relationship, individuals and groups do not collapse into the mold of hegemonic power, nor are they relegated to a monolith. Rather, the alterity and distinctive identity of each is preserved and safeguarded and human dignity is held intact.[16] The disruption or truncation of relational power embeds rudderlessness into the fabric of human life. If relation is the anchoring point of human existence and is embedded into our very being, to *not* live relationally disrupts what it means to be human. The human from human—country from country—nation from nation—is ultimately an act that generates estrangement, which Loomer defines as "the brokenness of life's essential relationships."[17] In turning from Loomer, a consideration of the shape and practice of these "essential relationships" is useful. If relationality is the character that conditions human life, what resources are at our disposal to fully realize and live into this character? In raising this question, I now appeal to the religious philosophy of Howard Thurman in order to flesh out and expand the moral and ethical import of, and responsiveness to, the problem of estrangement.

THE DISINHERITED, ESTRANGEMENT, AND REAL RELIGION

What is happening in America is only symptomatic of a larger cultural, spiritual, and theological problem. If both literal and metaphorical walls are outgrowths that branch out into the world and choke authentic community, it is necessary to consider what such root causes may be, so as to identify them and offer a viable response. One such cause is best described as estrangement or separation. Estrangement is unbelonging—thus solidifying mechanisms of (un)relating in human community and personality. Entrenchment into isolated religious, racial, and cultural enclaves, rather than maintaining personal and collective openness, or what Miroslav Volf has called catholic personality—dismantles neighborliness and closes the door on any hope of relational personhood. Grappling with the themes of cultural estrangement, neighborliness, and the reconstruction of relationality and their impact on the current context is useful in articulating a new way to understand the role of authentic religious praxis.

In the foreword to *Jesus and the Disinherited*, Vincent Harding notes that preceding generations following this monumental work would find resonation with Thurman's words and insights "even if their walls are different from the ones Thurman and his grandmother knew."[18] In absorbing this observation seriously, a few things emerge for our consideration. Of course, the constant, both past and present, is the pervasiveness of intergenerational societal walls—the barriers that block the hope of authentic community. While Thurman's concern about the arbitrary erecting of walls was primarily racial; those of the present day are more intersectional. Staying with Thurman's wall motif, I press for theological interrogations of President Trump's travel ban and border wall advocacy. Summarily speaking, both policy platforms, which find great support from White evangelical communities,[19] construct more than mere physical and spatial barriers; these policies *diminish the strands of interdependent concern and relational connection to neighbor*. What results from building walls, material and/or ontological, between ourselves and our neighbors is not "American greatness." Rather, isolation from these phantom "others" who are a supposed threat, is a practice of dis-neighborly estrangement, rendering "others" unknown and unknowable. This raises another simple, but prominent question, which may reverberate within the minds of those who support nonrelational notions of greatness: why strive to *know* others? What is the point of knowing people—caring about people, for example, from the "shithole countries" that Trump castigated?[20]

Following Thurman, to know and embrace neighbors—is to reach into the depths of knowing ourselves. The key feature of estrangement as both a religious and existential problem is thus also an epistemological quandary.

Ours is a society in which truly *knowing* other peoples, nations, and communities is an afterthought. The result is a world of strangers perpetually isolated due to the refusal to embrace the humanity of all. Those who become strangers are the dispossessed and the disinherited from Thurman's observations. These are the communities perpetually "on the outs" and absent from any societal consciousness. Thurman's relational theology is premised upon privileging marginalized communities. By contrasting the social world of Jesus to that of African Americans, Thurman is able to establish a commonality between Jesus and all racial and social outcasts. Jesus, and particularly African Americans, according to Thurman, are linked vis-à-vis their minoritization and disenfranchisement in hostile social worlds dominated by the religious and racial powers; one marked by the Roman powers in antiquity, and the second marked by White, Euro-American supremacy. As he observed in his autobiography regarding the contrast between Jesus and African Americans: "the racial climate was so oppressive and affected us all so intimately that analogies between His life as a Jew in a Roman world and our own were obvious."[21]

Thurman's thinking and racial philosophy was largely influenced by Quaker mysticism, but he is also part of a larger corpus of twentieth-century liberal theologians who sought to modernize the reach, import, and meaning of Christianity in American culture.[22] Following this view, Thurman's insights provide an excellent foundation for religious and theological responses that illustrate new conceptions of relationality in our current political, religious, and economic context. In the example of Jesus, Thurman centers an embodiment of the relational model that can overcome human estrangement. Further, Jesus is the prime revelation of authentic religion. Community and relationality, says Thurman, is found when one practices true religion as exemplified in the life of Jesus. The religion of Jesus, in contrast to spiritually dead and moribund Christian doctrine and dogma, is founded upon neighborly embrace. Jesus lived and embodied an ethical and this-worldly impulse in which *neighborliness with and among those typically construed as "other"* was the ultimate measure of the link between God and humankind. In lieu of the sterile, confused, and vague nature of "conventional Christianity," and its aloofness toward the material realities of human life, the religion of Jesus is grounded in immediate identification with otherness—with those who stand with their backs against the wall. True religion, therefore, embraces, works to improve the condition, and affirms the humanity, of the "poor, the disinherited, the dispossessed"[23] by "blending the ethical and spiritual" as central to Christian praxis.[24] Real religion, thus, is relational and connective. It unites rather than divides—uplifts rather than degrades human personality—creates rather than destroys. The exclusionary barriers that underscore much of the current political climate, and as bolstered under President Trump's immigration and national security policies, betray this manifestation of authentic religious faith in action. Taking Thurman's distinction on an engaged, active, and relational religious faith with the dispossessed seriously necessitates a few important criticisms of Trump's authoritarian policy formation and mind-set.

The exclusionary and authoritarian impetus that undergirds many of Trump's policies accomplish a two-pronged goal: they often feature a "weak vs. strong" binary that isolates and excludes, and further, uphold self-aggrandizing mechanisms solely for those in power. Thurman discusses this asymmetrical relational framing of power in terms of the fixed positionality of the oppressed and excluded, and the relative mobility and freedom of the oppressor. The kind of power relations that feature the prominence and growth of the strong and powerful at the expense of the weak, is powerfully exemplified in America's legacy of segregation and Jim Crow social arrangements. Segregation, says Thurman, offers no community or relationship, because there is inequality in social relations. The exclusion of others based on race, religion, sexuality, gender, allow "the stronger to shuttle back and forth between the prescribed areas with complete immunity . . . while the position of the weaker, on the other hand, is quite defiantly fixed and frozen."[25] In exclusionary platforms, therefore, oppressive identities are reified and sedimented in place, offering no respite. The "shutting out" of communities we imagine as outside our own, such as foreign and international racial and religious groups, fixes said communities in manners that violate personhood and short-circuit human identity.[26] The Jim Crow politics of yesteryear thus finds a terrible complement with contemporary policy. The walls of Jim Crow America, for example, have been augmented with the enthusiastic embrace of border walls and immigration "vetting" mechanisms meant to exclude and keep at arm's length the racial and religious "outsiders" that encroach upon the lines, customs, and mileus of imagined White sacred space and place.[27] I would propose, in response to these exclusionary times, an *ethic of belonging* rather than expulsion. The challenge and critique of Thurman rings forth clearly in this light: if persons of faith are to be authentically religious—authentically human, then embracing and receiving the other—particularly the marginalized, is the standard for ethical and religious conduct.

The nature of belonging requires a few observations. First, following on the heels of both Thurman and Loomer, a reimagining of human personality helps to broaden notions of racialized and religious borders in American discourse. Victor Anderson has referred to this as "human enlargement."[28] This is not an enlargement that functions in a self-aggrandizing way, but rather, is a reconfiguring of human identity in a manner that further accents communal selfhood. This is a selfhood premised upon a heightened willingness to embrace and make space for the other, rather than exclude. Human enlargement toward neighborly belonging is about reconsidering what it means to be human within an inclusive context of other human selves—selves understood to have dignity, integrity, and are worthy of the fullness of material flourishing. Second, an ethic of belonging necessitates, as Thurman illustrates, a conception and praxis of shared humanity—a humanity in which we see those "strange others" as extensions of ourselves and which transcends the arbitrary borders and exclusivities that we construct. Of belonging, Miroslav Volf notes that "the will to give ourselves to others and to welcome them, to readjust our identities to make space for them," renders us better able to identify others in their humanity.[29] Willingness to invite others into this space of belonging is the ontological recognition of human worth and dignity. In intellectual and faith communities, the development of receptive and open identities, as an ongoing societal project, provides the necessary theological and ethical justification for a collective critique and indictment of American political arrangements that diminish inclusive belonging, at home or abroad. America's political culture and its reach may just be saved in the process.

CONCLUSION: A (GREAT) WORLD HOUSE

In his classic sermon, "A Tough Mind and a Tender Heart," Martin Luther King condemns the hardhearted person for their lack of a relational impetus as a guide for their conduct toward their fellows. The hardhearted person "never truly loves . . . lacks the capacity for genuine compassion . . . never sees people as people, but rather as mere objects or as impersonal cogs in an ever-turning wheel . . . [such a person] depersonalizes life."[30] Critiquing both the softminded religion that hides behind the status quo of old and is resistance toward new truths, and the harsh, dogmatic religion that embraces doctrine over love for humanity, King sought to embody and live into the "true religion" and faith articulated by Thurman and Loomer. This is a faith posture that is grounded in the embrace of peoplehood and the extension of self on behalf of neighbor, no matter the resistance—and despite the protestations of one's enemies. The enduring reconciliatory focus of King's theology and religious orientation is traced to the affirmations of Black Christianity, which held, and continues to hold, that all persons are made in God's image and therefore are kith and kin regardless of race, sex, region, social stature, or any other identity marker. As James Cone notes of the primary impact of King's faith upon his spirituality: "As God's justice is grounded in God's creative and redeeming love, so human justice is grounded in love. Neighborly love, especially love for the enemy, defines the means by which justice is established and also the goal of the struggle for freedom, namely the beloved community."[31]

King's notion of the beloved community found many expressions throughout his writings, speeches, and sermons, but of particular interest on this concept, is his elaboration of the "world house," examined in *Where Do We Go from Here: Chaos or Community?* King's world house envisioning of the fruits of authentic and real religion in which neighbor is embraced and the uplift of others is axiomatic, is a well-suited structural and institutional paradigm that can be applied to the breakdown of human relationships at the micro- and macrolevels, and within the context of a vicious political culture. A world house mind-set, says King, is open and receptive and shifts the basic human drive beyond the insulary, the isolated, the segregated, and instead embraces our human birthright as relational and connected. Says King, "In a real sense, all life is interrelated . . . We are inevitably our brother's keeper because we are our brother's brother. Whatever affects one directly affects all indirectly."[32] In looking upon the present state of our varied political discourses from the vantage points offered from Loomer, Thurman, and King, what stands out is not the sensationalism, but rather the display of anti-communal, anti-relationship, and anti-neighbor dispositions. With the vision provided from these, true greatness is measured by the collective willingness to embrace the relational, the shared, and the inclusive as primary, instead of the common tendency to render others as obstacles and objects to be overcome.

At its best, the democratic ethos and praxis of religious faith is grounded in a push to inspire people to unify themselves over against division and promote a spirit of goodwill and neighborly ties. Religion has potential to be a source of upliftment and spiritual amelioration, but sadly, it has often been bolstered and exploited by many pervasive disconnects arising from racism, sexism, and xenophobia. Unfortunately, these disconnects have been given new life and a renewed vigor with the Trump administration. While any final answer to this matrix is elusive, I do advocate what Kelly Brown Douglas has referred to as a "bifocal," self-reflexive look into what our religious faiths and communities practice, and what kinds of life options our political choices impact. We also must discern how these practices diminish wholeness and solidarity. Part of the needed soul-searching involves the development of more mutualized, nonexclusionary, and receptive individual and social identities. From this, we may begin the process of relearning how to embrace one other while also developing new mechanisms of building bridges in these deeply divisive and disconnected times.[33] Inclusion, embrace, and belonging offer far greater means of responding to the brokenness of our age than authoritarian grandstanding and the subordination of the "weak" or less powerful. Perhaps the better mode of power to be embraced is not the vanquishing of perceived or real enemies, but the inclusion of our enemies into our sense of self-constitution. *Embodied and connective reception, not deletion*, could in this manner become the true measure of American greatness. If the country and all our racial and religious communities are to thrive, we might do well to reconsider the nature of American greatness as rooted in communal and neighborly threads of belonging.

NOTES

1. Tom Englehardt, "What Trump Really Means When He Says He'll Make America Great Again," *The Nation*, April 26, 2016, https://www.thenation.com/article/archive/what-trump-really-means-when-he-says-hell-make-america-great-again/.

2. Matthew C. MacWilliams, "Who Decides When The Party Doesn't? Authoritarian Voters and the Rise of Donald Trump," *PS: Political Science & Politics* 49, no. 4 (2016): 716–21, doi:10.1017/S1049096516001463.

3. Andrew Whitehead and Samuel Perry, *Taking American Back for God: Christian Nationalism in the United States* (New York: Oxford University Press, 2020).

4. Ibid., 19.

5. Robert Altemeyer, *Right-Wing Authoritarianism* (Winnipeg: University of Manitoba Press, 1981).

6. Tom McCarthy, "Is Donald Trump an authoritarian?," *The Guardian*, November 18, 2018, https://www.theguardian.com/us-news/2018/nov/18/is-donald-trump-an-authoritarian-experts-examine-telltale-signs. John F. Harris, "Trump is an Authoritarian Weakman," *Politico*, March 26, 2020, https://www.politico.com/news/magazine/2020/03/26/trump-is-an-authoritarian-weakman-149573.

7. Aris Folley, "Trump shares video of supporter," *The Hill*, May 28, 2020, https://thehill.com/blogs/blog-briefing-room/news/499917-trump-shares-video-supporter-saying-politically-only-good-democrat-is-a-dead.

8. Elana Lyn Gross, "Ocasio-Cortez Challenges Trump to Release His College Transcripts," *Forbes*, August 13, 2020, https://www.forbes.com/sites/elanagross/2020/08/13/after-trump-calls-her-a-poor-student-ocasio-cortez-challenges-trump-to-release-his-college-transcripts/#4bc14a84b251.

9. Ibram X. Kendi, "The Day *Shithole* Entered the Presidential Lexicon," *The Atlantic*, January 13, 2019, https://www.theatlantic.com/politics/archive/2019/01/shithole-countries/580054/.

10. Michelle Mark, "Trump just Referred to One of His Most Infamous Campaign Comments," *Business Insider*, April 5, 2018, https://www.businessinsider.com/trump-mexicans-rapists-remark-reference-2018-4.

11. Jeffrey S. Passel and D'Vera Cohn, "U.S. Unauthorized Immigrant Total Dips to Lowest Level in a Decade," *Pew Research Center*, November 27, 2018, https://www.pewresearch.org/hispanic/2018/11/27/u-s-unauthorized-immigrant-total-dips-to-lowest-level-in-a-decade/.

12. Seth G. Jones, Catrina Doxsee, and Nicholas Harrington, "The Escalating Terrorism Problem in the United States," *Center for Strategic and International Studies*, June 17, 2020, https://www.csis.org/analysis/escalating-terrorism-problem-united-states.

13. Bernard Loomer, "Two Kinds of Power," *Criterion* 15, no, 1 (Winter 1976): 14, 20.

14. Ibid., 14.

15. Loomer, "The Size of God," in *The Size of God: The Theology of Bernard Loomer in Context*, William Dean and Larry E. Axel, eds. (Macon: Mercer University Press, 1987), 32.

16. Loomer, "Two Kinds of Power," 26.

17. Ibid., 27.

18. Howard Thurman, *Jesus and the Disinherited* (Boston: Beacon Press, 1996), xiii.

19. Gregory A. Smith, "Most White Evangelicals Approve of Trump Travel Prohibition," *Pew Research Center*, February 27, 2017, http://www.pewresearch.org/fact-tank/2017/02/27/most-white-evangelicals-approve-of-trump-travel-prohibition-and-express-concerns-about-extremism/. Jim Wallis, "White American Christianity is a Bubble—and Its about to Burst," *Sojourners*, May 3, 2017, https://sojo.net/articles/white-american-evangelical-christianity-bubble-and-it-s-about-burst.

20. Alan Fram and Jonathan Lemire, "Trump: Why Allow Immigrants from 'shithole countries'?" *Associated Press*, January 12, 2018, https://apnews.com/fdda2ff0b877416c8ae1c1a77a3cc425/Trump:-Why-allow-immigrants-from-%27shithole-countries%27.

21. Howard Thurman, *With Head and Heart: The Autobiography of Howard Thurman* (San Diego: Harcourt Brace & Jovanovich, 1981), 78–79.

22. Gary Dorrien, *The Making of American Liberal Theology: Idealism, Realism, and Modernity* (Louisville: Westminster John Knox Press, 2003).

23. Thurman, *Jesus and the Disinherited*, 3.

24. Dorrien, *The Making of American Liberal Theology*, 563.

25. Thurman, *Jesus and the Disinherited*, 32.

26. Ibid.

27. Kelly Brown Douglas, *Stand Your Ground: Black Bodies and the Justice of God* (Maryknoll: Orbis Books, 2015), 40–44.

28. Victor Anderson, *Creative Exchange: A Constructive Theology of African American Religious Experience* (Minneapolis: Fortress Press, 2008), 14.

29. Miroslav Volf, *Exclusion and Embrace: A Theological Exploration of Identity, Otherness, and Reconciliation* (Nashville: Abingdon Press, 2019), xxiii.

30. Martin Luther King, Jr., *Strength to Love* (Philadelphia: Fortress Press, 1981), 17.

31. James Cone, *Martin & Malcolm & America: A Dream or a Nightmare* (Maryknoll: Orbis Books, 2001), 126.

32. Martin Luther King, Jr., *Where Do We Go From Here: Chaos or Community?* from James M Washington, ed., *A Testament of Hope: The Essential Writings*

and Speeches of Martin Luther King, Jr. (New York: HarperCollins Publishers, 1991), 626.

33. Kelly Brown Douglas, *The Black Christ* (Maryknoll: Orbis Books, 1994), 98–99.

BIBLIOGRAPHY

Altemeyer, Robert. *Right-Wing Authoritarianism.* Winnipeg: University of Manitoba Press, 1981.

Anderson, Victor. *Creative Exchange: A Constructive Theology of African American Religious Experience.* Minneapolis: Fortress Press, 2008.

Cone, James. *Martin & Malcolm & America: A Dream or a Nightmare.* Maryknoll: Orbis Books, 2001.

Dean, William and Larry E. Axel, eds. *The Size of God: The Theology of Bernard Loomer in Context.* Macon: Mercer University Press, 1987.

Douglas, Kelly Brown. *The Black Christ.* Maryknoll: Orbis Books, 1994.

———. *Stand Your Ground: Black Bodies and the Justice of God.* Maryknoll: Orbis Books, 2015.

Englehardt, Tom. "What Trump Really Means When He Says He'll Make America Great Again." *The Nation.* April 26, 2016. https://www.thenation.com/article/archive/what-trump-really-means-when-he-says-hell-make-america-great-again/.

Folley, Aris. "Trump Shares Video of Supporter." *The Hill.* May 28, 2020. https://thehill.com/blogs/blog-briefing-room/news/499917-trump-shares-video-supporter-saying-politically-only-good-democrat-is-a-dead.

Fram, Alan and Jonathan Lemire. "Trump: Why Allow Immigrants from 'shithole countries'?" *Associated Press.* January 12, 2018. https://apnews.com/fdda2ff0b877416c8ae1c1a77a3cc425/Trump:-Why-allow-immigrants-from-%27shithole-countries%27.

Gross, Elana L. "Ocasio-Cortez Challenges Trump to Release His College Transcripts." *Forbes.* August 13, 2020. https://www.forbes.com/sites/elanagross/2020/08/13/after-trump-calls-her-a-poor-student-ocasio-cortez-challenges-trump-to-release-his-college-transcripts/#4bc14a84b251.

Harris, John F. "Trump is an Authoritarian Weakman." *Politico.* March 26, 2020. https://www.politico.com/news/magazine/2020/03/26/trump-is-an-authoritarian-weakman-149573.

Jones, Seth G., Catrina Doxsee, and Nicholas Harrington. "The Escalating Terrorism Problem in the United States." *Center for Strategic and International Studies.* June 17, 2020. https://www.csis.org/analysis/escalating-terrorism-problem-united-states.

Kendi, Ibram X. "The Day *Shithole* Entered the Presidential Lexicon." *The Atlantic.* January 13, 2019. https://www.theatlantic.com/politics/archive/2019/01/shithole-countries/580054/.

King, Martin Luther. *Strength to Love.* Philadelphia: Fortress Press, 1981.

Loomer, Bernard. "Two Kinds of Power." *Criterion* 15, no. 1 (1976): 11–29.

MacWilliams, Matthew. "Who Decides When The Party Doesn't? Authoritarian Voters and the Rise of Donald Trump." *PS: Political Science & Politics* 49, no. 4 (2016): 716–21. doi:10.1017/S1049096516001463.

Mark, Michelle. "Trump just Referred to One of His most Infamous Campaign Comments." *Business Insider*. April 5, 2018. https://www.businessinsider.com/trump-mexicans-rapists-remark-reference-2018-4.

McCarthy, Tom. "Is Donald Trump an Authoritarian?" *The Guardian*. November 18, 2018. https://www.theguardian.com/us-news/2018/nov/18/is-donald-trump-an-authoritarian-experts-examine-telltale-signs.

Passel, Jeffrey S. and D'Vera Cohn. "U.S. Unauthorized Immigrant Total Dips to Lowest Level in a Decade." *Pew Research Center*. November 27, 2018. https://www.pewresearch.org/hispanic/2018/11/27/u-s-unauthorized-immigrant-total-dips-to-lowest-level-in-a-decade/.

Smith, Gregory A. "Most White Evangelicals Approve of Trump Travel Prohibition." *Pew Research Center*. February 27, 2017. http://www.pewresearch.org/fact-tank/2017/02/27/most-white-evangelicals-approve-of-trump-travel-prohibition-and-express-concerns-about-extremism/.

Thurman, Howard. *With Head and Heart: The Autobiography of Howard Thurman*. San Diego: Harcourt Brace & Jovanovich, 1981.

———. *Jesus and the Disinherited*. Boston: Beacon Press, 1996.

Volf, Miroslav. *Exclusion and Embrace: A Theological Exploration of Identity, Otherness, and Reconciliation*. Nashville: Abingdon Press, 2019.

Wallis, Jim. "White American Christianity is a Bubble—and Its about to Burst." *Sojourners*. May 3, 2017. https://sojo.net/articles/white-american-evangelical-christianity-bubble-and-it-s-about-burst.

Washington, James M., ed. *A Testament of Hope: The Essential Writings and Speeches of Martin Luther King, Jr.* New York: HarperCollins Publishers, 1991.

Whitehead, Andrew and Samuel Perry, *Taking American Back for God: Christian Nationalism in the United States*. New York: Oxford University Press, 2020.

Appendix

Further Readings

AFRICAN AMERICAN HISTORY

Alexander, Michelle. *The New Jim Crow: Mass Incarceration in the Age of Colorblindness.* New York: The New Press, 2020, orig. 2010.

Anderson, Carol. *White Rage: The Unspoken Truth of Our Nation's Divide.* New York: Bloomsbury USA, 2017.

Bonilla-Silva, Eduardo. *White Supremacy and Racism in the Post-Civil Rights Era.* Boulder, CO: Lynne Rienner Publishers, 2001.

Franklin, John Hope and Evelyn Higginbotham. *From Slavery to Freedom: A History of African Americans.* New York: McGraw-Hill, 2010.

Gates, Henry Louis. *Stony the Road: Reconstruction, White Supremacy, and the Rise of Jim Crow.* London: Penguin Press, 2019.

Hinton, Elizabeth. *From the War on Poverty to the War on Crime: The Making of Mass Incarceration in America.* Cambridge, MA: Harvard University Press, 2016.

Kendi, Ibram X. *Stamped from the Beginning: The Definitive History of Racist Ideas in America.* New York: Bold Type Books, 2017.

Marable, Manning. *Race, Reform and Rebellion: The Second Reconstruction in Black America, 1945–1982.* Jackson, MS: University Press of Mississippi, 1984.

———. *How Capitalism Underdeveloped Black America: Problems in Race, Political Economy, and Society.* Chicago: Haymarket Books, 2015.

Muhammad, Khalil Gibran. *The Condemnation of Blackness: Race, Crime, and the Making of a Modern Urban America.* Cambridge, MA: Harvard University Press, 2011.

Myrdal, Gunnar. *An American Dilemma: The Negro Problem and Modern Democracy.* New York: Pantheon Books, 1975.

Painter, Nell Irvin. *The History of White People.* New York: Norton & Company, 2010.

Washington, Harriet A. *Medical Apartheid: The Dark History of Medical Experimentation on Black Americans from Colonial Times to the Present.* New York: Anchor, 2008.

Wilkerson, Isabel. *The Warmth of Other Suns: The Epic Story of America's Great Migration.* New York: Vintage, 2001.

———. *Caste: The Origins of Our Discontents.* New York: Random House, 2020.

Woodward, C. Vann. *The Strange Career of Jim Crow.* New York: Oxford University Press, 2001.

AFRICAN AMERICANS AND EDUCATION

Christopher Jencks and Meredith Phillips, eds. *The Black-White Test Score Gap*, Washington, DC: Brookings Institution Press.

Connor, David J., Betha A. Ferrie, and Subini A. Annamma, eds. *DisCrit: Disability Studies and Critical Race Theory in Education.* New York: Teachers College Press, 2016.

Dixson, Adrienne D. and Celie K. Rousseau. *Critical Race Theory in Education: All God's Children Got a Song.* New York: Routledge, 2006.

Dixson, Adrienne, ed. *Researching Race in Education: Policy, Practice, and Qualitative Research.* Charlotte, NC: Information Age Publishing, 2014.

Freire, Paulo. *Pedagogy of the Oppressed.* New York: Bloomsbury, 2018.

Kozol, Jonathan. *Savage Inequalities: Children in America's Schools.* New York: Broadway, 1991.

Ladson-Billings, Gloria. *Crossing Over Canaan: The Journey of New Teachers in Diverse Classrooms.* San Francisco, CA: Jossey-Bass, 2001.

———. *The Dreamkeepers: Successful Teachers of African American Children.* San Francisco, CA: Wiley and Sons, 2009.

Ladson-Billings, Gloria and William F. Tate. *Education Research in the Public Interest: Social Justice, Action, and Policy.* New York: Teachers College Press, 2015.

Love, Bettina L. *We Want to do More than Survive: Abolitionist Teaching and the Pursuit of Educational Freedom.* Boston: Beacon Press, 2019.

Lynn, Marvin and Adrienne Dixson, eds. *Handbook of Critical Race Theory in Education.* New York: Routledge, 2013.

Matias, Cheryl E. *Feeling White: Whiteness, Emotionality, and Education (Cultural Pluralism, Democracy, Socio-environmental Justice and Education).* Rotterdam: Sense Publishers, 2016.

Parker, Laurence. *Race Is . . . Race Isn't: Critical Race Theory and Qualitative Studies in Education.* New York: Routledge, 2018.

Patterson, James. *Brown v. Board of Education: A Civil Rights Milestone and Its Troubled Legacy.* New York: Oxford, 2001.

Shange, Savannah. *Progressive Dystopia: Abolition, Antiblackness, and Schooling in San Francisco.* Durham, NC: Duke University Press, 2019.

Singleton, Glenn E. *Courageous Conversations About Race: A Field Guide for Achieving Equity in Schools.* Thousand Oaks, CA: Corwin, 2015.
Taylor, Edward. *Foundations of Critical Race Theory in Education.* New York: Routledge, 2016.
Zamudio, Margaret and Christopher Russell, Francisco Rios, and Jacquelyn L. Bridgeman. *Critical Race Theory Matters: Education and Ideology.* New York: Routledge, 2011.
Zeus, Leonardo and James A. Banks. *Race Frameworks: A Multidimensional Theory of Racism and Education.* New York: Teachers College Press, 2013.

AFRICAN AMERICAN LITERARY AND CULTURAL STUDIES

Angelou, Maya. *I Know Why the Caged Bird Sings.* New York: Random House, 1970.
Baldwin, James. *Notes of a Native Son.* Boston: Beacon Press, 1955.
Baldwin, James. *The Fire Next Time.* New York: Dial Press, 1963.
Coates, Ta-Nehisi. *Between the World and Me.* New York: Random House, 2015.
Collins, Patricia Hill. *Black Sexual Politics: African Americans, Gender, and the New Racism.* New York: Routledge, 2004.
Davis, Angela. *Women, Race, and Class.* New York: Vintage Books, 1983.
Davis, Angela Y, Bryan Stevenson, Marc Mauer, Bruce Western, and Jeremy Travis. *Policing the Black Man: Arrest, Prosecution, and Imprisonment.* New York: Random House, 2018.
Ellison, Ralph. *Invisible Man.* New York: Vintage International, 1995, orig. 1952.
Gates, Henry Louis. *Figures in Black: Words, Signs, and the "Racial" Self.* New York: Oxford University Press, 1987.
———. *The Signifying Monkey: A Theory of African American Literary Criticism.* New York: Oxford University Press, 2014.
hooks, bell. *Black Looks: Race and Representation.* New York: Routledge, 2014.
———. *Talking Back: Thinking Feminist, Thinking Black.* New York: Routledge, 2014.
Lorde, Audre. *Sister Outsider: Essays and Speeches.* New York: Crossing Press, 2007.
Morrison, Toni. *Playing in the Dark: Whiteness and the Literary Imagination.* New York: Vintage, 1993.
———. *The Origin of Others.* Cambridge, MA: Harvard University Press, 2017.
Walker, Alice. *In Search of Our Mothers' Gardens: Womanist Prose.* San Diego, CA: Harcourt Brace Jovanovich, 1983.
Wright, Richard. *Native Son.* New York: Harper & Brothers, 1940.
———. *Black Boy, a Record of Childhood and Youth.* New York: Harper, 1945.

AFRICAN AMERICAN PSYCHOLOGY

DeFreitas, Stacie C. *African American Psychology: A Positive Psychology Perspective*. New York: Springer Publishing Company, 2019.

Fanon, Frantz. *Black Skin, White Masks*. New York: Grove Press, 2008, orig.1952.

———. *The Wretched of the Earth*. New York: Grove Press, 2005, orig. 1963.

Gough, Brendan, ed., *The Palgrave Handbook of Critical Social Psychology*. New York: Palgrave Macmillan, 2017,

Guthrie, Robert V. *Even the Rat was White: A Historical View of Psychology*, 2nd eEdition. New York: Pearson, 2004.

Hill, Robert B. *The Strengths of African American Families: Twenty-Five Years Later*. New York: University Press of America, Inc., 1999.

Neville, Helen A., Brendesha M. Tynes, and Shawn O. Utsey, eds. *Handbook of African American Psychology*. Thousand Oaks, CA: Sage, 2009.

Parham, Thomas, A., Adisa Ajamu, and Joseph L. White. *The Psychology of Blacks: Centering our Perspectives in the African Consciousness*, 4th Edition. New York: Routledge, 2016.

Tatum, Beverly Daniel. *Why Are All the Black Kids Sitting Together in the Cafeteria?" And other Conversations about Race, 20th Anniversary Edition*. New York: Basic Books, 2017.

Turner, Erlanger. *Mental Health among African Americans: Innovations in Research and Practice*. Washington, D.C.:Lexington Books, 2019.

Walker, Rheeda: *The Unapologetic Guide to Black Mental Health: Navigate an Unequal System, Learn Tools for Emotional Wellness, and Get the Help You Deserve*. Oakland, CA: New Harbinger Publications, Inc., 2020.

AFRICAN AMERICAN RELIGION

Anderson, Victor. *Beyond Ontological Blackness*. New York: Continuum, 1995.

Cannon, Katie Geneva. *Katie's Canon: Womanism and the Soul of the Black Community*. New York: Continuum, 1995.

Carter, J. Kameron. *Race: A Theological Account*. New York: Oxford University Press, 2008.

Coleman, Monica, ed. *Ain't I a Womanist Too? Third-Wave Religious Womanist Thought*. Philadelphia: Fortress Press, 2013.

Collier Thomas, Bettye. *Jesus, Justice, and Jobs: African American Women and Religion*. New York: Knopf, 2010.

Cone, James H. *Black Theology and Black Power*. Maryknoll, NY: Orbis Books, 1970.

———. *The Spirituals and the Blues: An Interpretation*. Maryknoll, NY: Orbis Books, 1972.

———. *My Soul Looks Back*. Maryknoll, NY: Orbis Books, 1986.

———. *A Black Theology of Liberation*. Maryknoll, NY: Orbis Books, 1990, orig. 1986.

———. *Martin & Malcolm: A Dream or a Nightmare*. Maryknoll, NY: Orbis Books, 1992.

———. *The Cross and the Lynching Tree*. New York: Orbis Books, 2011.

Copeland, M. Shawn. *Enfleshing Freedom: Body, Race, and Being*. Philadelphia: Fortress Press, 2009.

Curtis, Edward. *Islam in Black America: Identity, Liberation, and Difference in African-American Islamic Thought*. Albany, NY: Suny Press, 2002.

Felder, Cain Hope. *Stony the Road We Trod: African American Biblical Interpretation*. Minneapolis, MN: Augsburg Fortress, 1991.

Glaude, Eddie S. *Exodus! Religion, Race, and Nation in Early Nineteenth Century Black America* Chicago: University of Chicago Press, 2000.

Goetz, Rebecca Anne. *The Baptism of Early Virginia: How Christianity Created Race*. Baltimore, MD: John Hopkins University Press. 2012.

Goldenberg, David. *The Curse of Ham: Race And Slavery In Early Judaism, Christianity, And Islam*. Princeton, NJ: Princeton University Press, 2003.

Higginbotham, Evelyn B. *Righteous Discontent: The Women's Movement in the Black Baptist Church, 1880–1920*. Cambridge, MA: Harvard University Press, 1993.

Hopkins, Dwight N. *Introducing Black Theology of Liberation*. Maryknoll, NY: Orbis Books, 1999.

Jennings, Willie James. *The Christian Imagination: Theology and the Origins of Race*. New Haven, CT: Yale University Press, 2011.

Lincoln, C. Eric and Lawrence Mamiya. *The Black Church in the African American Experience*. Durham, NC: Duke University Press, 1990.

Pinn, Anthony B. *Terror and Triumph: The Nature of Black Religion*. Minneapolis, MN: Augsburg Fortress, 2003.

Raboteau, Albert J. *Slave Religion: The 'Invisible Institution' in the Antebellum South*. New York: Oxford University Press, 2004, orig. 1978.

Smith, Theophus. *Conjuring Culture: Biblical Formations of Black America*. New York: Oxford University Press, 1994.

Turner, Richard Brent. *Islam in the African American Experience*. Bloomington, IN: Indiana University Press, 1997.

Yancy, George and Emily McRae, eds. *Buddhism and Whiteness: Critical Reflections*. New York: Rowman and Littlefield, 2019.

West, Cornel and Eddie S. Glaude Jr., eds. *African-American Religious Thought: An Anthology*. Westminster John Knox Press, 2004.

Wimbush, Vincent. *African Americans and the Bible: Sacred Texts and Social Textures*. New York: Continuum, 2000.

Index

About the Editors and Contributors

ABOUT THE EDITORS

Dr. **Jonathan Chism** is an assistant professor of history at the University of Houston-Downtown and a fellow of the Center for Critical Race Studies. He teaches several courses related to his expertise in religion, civil rights, and African American history. His research explores social and political activism among African American religious groups and seeks to enhance understanding of diverse ways African American religious groups and figures have pursued social justice and transformation in the twentieth century. He is the author of *Saints in the Struggle: Church of God in Christ Activists in the Memphis Civil Rights Movement, 1954–1968.*

Dr. **Stacie Craft DeFreitas** is a licensed psychologist, the Interim Associate Dean of the College of Humanities and Social Sciences, a fellow for the Center for Critical Race Studies, and an associate professor of psychology at the University of Houston- Downtown. She also serves on the Committee for Diversity, Equity, and Inclusion for the Textbook and Academic Authors Association and is the founder of the Sustainability Council at UHD. She received a PhD in clinical psychology from Duke University and is a licensed specialist in school psychology. Currently, her primary research interests are concerning the academic and mental health development of youth, particularly urban, youth of color. She is particularly interested in strengths-based and positive psychology examinations of psychological phenomena and is the author of *African American Psychology: A Positive Psychology Perspective*.

Dr. **Vida Robertson** is an associate professor of English and humanities and serves as the director of the Center for Critical Race Studies at the University of Houston-Downtown. He teaches a wide range of courses that focus on race, identity, and community in African American, Caribbean, LatinX, and Asian American literatures and cultures. His primary research interests are in late nineteenth- and twentieth-century African American literature, cultural studies, minority education, and critical race theory. He has published extensively on the Harlem Renaissance, French Negritude Movement, Chester Himes and minority male student success. In light of his deep appreciation for the persistence and adaptability of systemic oppression, Dr. Robertson co-founded the Men of LEGACI program which strives to help African American and Latino young men navigate and negotiate the challenges of higher education by providing scholarships, institutional support and mentorship.

Dr. **David Ryden** is a professor of history at the University of Houston-Downtown, Interim Dean of the College of Humanities and Social Sciences, and a fellow for the Center for Critical Race Studies. He began teaching at UHD in 2001, after completing a postdoctoral fellowship at Brunel University in London, UK. Dr. Ryden teaches courses on Colonial American History, Slavery, Abolition, British History, and U.S. History. His research focuses on the political economy of British colonial slaveholders, abolition, and manumission.

ABOUT THE CONTRIBUTORS

Dr. **Nina Barbieri** is an assistant professor of Criminal Justice at the University of Houston-Downtown, She teaches and publishes on topics relating to criminological theories of crime and delinquency, bullying, and school-related experiences. She has published in *Aggression and Violent Behavior, Criminal Justice and Behavior, Crime & Delinquency, Deviant Behavior,* and other outlets.

Dr. **Darius M. Benton** is an assistant professor of Communication Studies at the University of Houston-Downtown in the areas of Organizational Communication and Religious Communication. He is a professional educator with various experiences from Pre-K through college, an ordained minister, organizational leader and social scientist. Dr. Benton's research primarily focuses on religious leadership, race, and gender in the workplace, and dynamics of youth serving organizations.

Khyree Davis is a southern poet, home cook, and PhD candidate in African and African Diaspora Studies at the University of Texas at Austin. His research specializations are in Black queer and trans studies, Black geographies/geopolitics, cultural studies, and performance studies. Broadly, his research seeks to understand how and where Black queer and trans communities make alternative use of hostile space to forward practices of resistance, joy, and futurity.

Dr. **Jesús Jesse Esparza** is an assistant professor of history in the College of Liberal Arts and Behavioral Sciences at Texas Southern University, where he has taught since 2009. His area of expertise is on the history of Latinos in the United States, with an emphasis on civil rights activism. Dr. Esparza is currently working on a manuscript entitled *Raza Schools: Latino Educational Autonomy and Activism in Texas, 1920–1980,* which offers a multiracial narrative of a Latino-owned school district in west Texas from the end of the World War I through the postcivil rights era. Dr. Esparza teaches Mexican American, Texas, Civil Rights, and Latin American History. He received his BA and a master's degree in History from Southwest Texas State University and a PhD in History in 2008 from the University of Houston.

Dr. **DoVeanna S. Fulton** is Provost and vice president for Academic Affairs and professor in the Department of History and Interdisciplinary Studies at Norfolk State University. Fulton strives to be a model as a leader-scholar whose principal area of research is the exploration and recovery of African American women's oral culture and discursive practices in written and oral representations in the nineteenth and early twentieth centuries. She is the author and editor or co-editor of four books and published numerous book chapters and articles in distinguished journals and anthologies. Fulton is the immediate past president of the Society for the Study of American Women Writers (SSAWW).

Dr. **Felicia L. Harris** is an assistant professor of communication in media studies and the assistant director for the Center for Critical Race Studies at the University of Houston-Downtown. Prior to joining the faculty at UHD, Harris worked in student affairs for four years while spearheading social media initiatives for University Housing at the University of Georgia, including the award-winning diversity-focused social media campaign, #OneUGA. In her research, Harris explores the intersections of race, gender, power, and privilege within the contexts of mass media, popular culture, and college campuses and classrooms. Harris has contributed articles to the popular press, including *HuffPost*, and is published in academic news outlets and journals, such as *The Chronicle of Higher Education*, *The Black Scholar*, and *FIRE!!! The Multimedia Journal of Black Studies*.

Dr. **Martin J. Hershock** holds a PhD in history from the University of Michigan and is dean of the College of Arts, Sciences, and Letters and professor of history at the University of Michigan-Dearborn. A specialist in nineteenth-century American political and social history, his works include *The Paradox of Progress* and *A New England Prison Diary*. His most recent work focused on the role of African American troops in the Vicksburg Campaign.

Dr. **Darrius D. Hills** is assistant professor of Black Church Studies at Morgan State University in Baltimore, MD. His research addresses various articulations of African American religious thought, theology, womanist religious thought, Black male studies, and religion and culture. Currently, Dr. Hills is working on his first book monograph, tentatively titled: *Black Religious Thought and Black Male Identity*. Hills was recently selected one of ten junior religion scholars nation-wide as part of the 2020–2022 cohort of the prestigious Young Scholars in American Religion program. Hills' research has also been supported by the General Board of Higher Education and Ministry (of the United Methodist Church), The Forum for Theological Exploration (formerly, The Fund for Theological Education), the Louisville Institute for the Study of American Religion, and the Center for the Study of Religion and American Culture.

LeAnna T. Luney is a doctoral candidate in the Comparative Ethnic Studies program at the University of Colorado Boulder. She earned a BA in Psychology and a BA in African & African American Studies at Berea College, and an MA in Pan-African Studies at the University of Louisville. Working from Black feminist and anti-Black settler colonialism frameworks, her current research focuses on the lived experiences and coping strategies of Black womxn and femme undergraduate students at an historically and predominately white university in the American West.

Jenean A. McGee is a PhD candidate in the Comparative Ethnic Studies program at the University of Colorado Boulder. Her research interests center around Black feminism, womanism, critical race theory, and critical social media studies. Currently, she is studying how women of the African diaspora engage with social media platforms such as YouTube and Instagram. She holds a Master of Arts in American Studies from the University of Massachusetts Boston and a Bachelor of Arts in Literary Studies from Southern Oregon University.

Rachael Pasierowska is a dual doctoral degree student at Rice University and the Universidade Estadual de Campinas, São Paulo, where she studies slavery in the Atlantic World. Her dissertation focuses on the relations between slaves and animals in the Atlantic World in the nineteenth century with a comparative focus on the three major slaving societies America,

Brazil, and Cuba. She has published two articles: "'Screech owls allus holler 'round the house before death': Birds and the Souls of Black Folk in the Antebellum South," *Journal of Social History* and "Up from Childhood: When African-American Enslaved Children Learned of their Servile Status," *Slavery and Abolition*.

Dr. **Scott L. Stabler** is a professor of history at Grand Valley State University where he teaches Social Studies Methods and United States History courses. He holds a PhD from Arizona State University. He received a Fulbright Scholarship and has led study abroad trips to Ghana. He has published several articles that include two book chapters on U.S. Colored Troops. He is also working on a biography of General Oliver Otis Howard.

Dr. **Ordner W. Taylor, III** teaches African American Literature and World Literature at Delaware State University in Dover, Delaware. His research interests include African American experiences and the Romantic tradition along with African American experiences within the Spanish historical and literary traditions. His recent publication "Horror, Race and Reality" in the *Palgrave Handbook to Horror Literature* investigates the realities of the cruelties experienced by African Americans during slavery within the context of Gothic and horror literature.

Dr. **Erlanger A. Turner** is a clinical psychologist and assistant professor of psychology at Pepperdine University in Los Angeles, California. Dr. Turner earned his bachelor's degree from Louisiana State University, his PhD in clinical psychology from Texas A&M University, and he completed a clinical postdoctoral fellowship through the Johns Hopkins University School of Medicine. His research and clinical interests include mental health among ethnic and racial communities, access to behavioral health services, and training therapists to work with diverse populations. He has also published his research in numerous book chapters and articles in psychology journals. Dr. Turner is the author of *Mental Health among African American: Innovations in Research in Practice*.

Tinicia C. Turner is currently the director for Career and Leadership Initiatives at Franciscan Missionaries of Our Lady University (FRANU). Prior to joining FRANU, she spent fifteen years gaining valuable experience in education and nonprofit. Tinicia holds a Bachelor's of Science from the University of Louisiana at Lafayette and a Master of Public Administration from the Southern University Nelson Mandela School of Public Policy and Urban Affairs. Tinicia is also an entrepreneur and professional career and college consultant. She recently released the first product from her educational line: the "I Can Achieve" Career Exploration Coloring Activity Book.